The Heinemann
TOEFL®
Preparation Course

M. Kathleen Mahnke and Carolyn B. Duffy

M. Kathleen Mahnke and Carolyn B. Duffy are teacher trainers and professors of ESL at St. Michael's College, Vermont. Each of them has over ten years' experience teaching students in TOEFL classes.

Consultant: Jacqueline Flamm

HEINEMANN

from Heather to Walentyna

Heinemann International
A division of Heinemann Publishers (Oxford), Ltd.
Halley Court, Jordan Hill, Oxford OX2 8EJ, U.K.

OXFORD   LONDON   EDINBURGH
MADRID   ATHENS   BOLOGNA   PARIS
MELBOURNE   SYDNEY   AUCKLAND   SINGAPORE   TOKYO
IBADAN   NAIROBI   HARARE   GABORONE
PORTSMOUTH (NH)

First published 1992

Consultant: Jacqueline Flamm

The publishers would like to thank the following for reading and commenting on the manuscript:
Catherine Georgopoulos, Hellenic American Union, Athens
David Daview, College of Health and Sciences, Bahrain
Susan Gilfert, Trident School of Languages, Nagoya
Marlin Howard, Indiana University, Indiana
Polly Howlett, St. Michael's College, Vermont
Philip Prowse, Bell College, Saffron Walden
Michael Sanetrick, ELS Sundai, Tokyo
Richard Yorkey, St. Michael's College, Vermont

TOEFL test directions and TWE scoring guidelines are reprinted by permission of Educational Testing Service, the copyright owner. However, the test questions and any other testing information are provided in their entirety by Heinemann International. No endorsement of this publication by Educational Testing Service should be inferred.

Production Project Management by Robert Ventre Associates, Newburyport, MA

Interior design by Amick Communications

Printed and bound in the United States

ISBN 0 435 28844 X

92   93   94   95   96   97   10 9 8 7 6 5 4 3 2 1

Preface

The Heinemann TOEFL Preparation Course is designed to help students prepare for the TOEFL (Test of English as a Foreign Language). It is written by teachers with over twenty years of combined experience teaching TOEFL preparation classes to students from a wide variety of language backgrounds. We have learned from our teaching experiences that there are important language skills and test-taking strategies which can be taught and mastered to promote student success on the TOEFL. This book has been written as a step by step guide to developing and practicing these language skills and test-taking strategies.

We also recognize the value of using TOEFL practice tests to practice language skills and test-taking strategies as they are being developed. With this in mind, we conducted extensive research into the TOEFL. We examined TOEFL test items, characterizing them in terms of material tested and difficulty level. Following this analysis, we wrote questions with the same characteristics as those on the TOEFL and incorporated these questions into practice TOEFL tests. We then pilot tested these tests with international students from over twenty different countries. From these pilot tests, we selected only those questions which, when statistically analyzed, worked in the same way that official TOEFL questions do. Using these questions, we created the practice tests that are found in this book and its companion, *The Heinemann TOEFL Practice Tests*. These tests contain all of the question types found on the TOEFL, and they function in the same way that official TOEFL tests do.

By using *The Heinemann TOEFL Preparation Course*, students can develop and practice the language skills and test-taking strategies necessary for TOEFL success. By supplementing this book with *The Heinemann TOEFL Practice Tests*, students can use reliable TOEFL practice tests to gain further practice of what they have learned.

Acknowledgments

We would like to thank our students and our colleagues at Saint Michael's College for their constant support and encouragement throughout the writing of this book. A special thanks to Polly Howlett for her cheerful willingness to pilot test our materials and to give us valuable comments. Thanks as well to the students in our TOEFL classes for working their way through the many drafts of our manuscript. We are also grateful to Renee Bittner, Russell Notestine, Dan Evans, and Michael Provost for their help in making our pilot tapes.

We owe a special debt of gratitude to Cathy Georgopoulos of the Hellenic American Union in Athens, Greece; Marlin Howard of Indiana University; and Richard Yorkey of Saint Michael's College. Their careful and critical reading of our manuscript and their insightful and detailed comments were invaluable in creating our final product. We want to extend a very special thank you to Dick Yorkey for encouraging us as writers and for his constant faith in us.

Our gratitude also goes to the staff at Heinemann. Thanks especially to Michael Boyd, for his insights and for his willingness to listen. It has been a pleasure to work with Heinemann.

To our families we owe the greatest debt of all. Thank you Greg and Len for always being there and for providing us with the time and space we needed to complete this project. Thank you Brennan, Cara, and Daus for your understanding and for being such good sports. We thank you all for your patience, help, and support.

Contents Chart

✔=Checkpoint   G=Grammar   L=Listening Comprehension   R=Reading   V=Vocabulary   W=Writing

Contents Chart (continued)

✔=Checkpoint   G=Grammar   L=Listening Comprehension   R=Reading   V=Vocabulary   W=Writing

✔=Checkpoint   G=Grammar   L=Listening Comprehension   R=Reading   V=Vocabulary   W=Writing

Introduction

About the TOEFL

The TOEFL (Test of English as a Foreign Language) measures the level of English language proficiency of non-native speakers of English. It is written and published by the Educational Testing Service (ETS) of Princeton, New Jersey, U.S.A. The TOEFL is an admissions requirement at over 2,500 colleges and universities in the United States and other parts of the world. In addition, many scholarship and professional certification programs now require their applicants to take the TOEFL. The test currently contains 150 questions and has four sections: Listening Comprehension, Structure and Written Expression, Vocabulary and Reading Comprehension, and the Test of Written English. The first three sections contain multiple choice questions. Each multiple choice question has four answer choices. The fourth section of the test, the Test of Written English, contains one essay question.

Section One: Listening Comprehension
This section of the test is administered by audiocassette and normally takes between 30 and 40 minutes. There are 50 questions in this section, which has three parts.
　　Part A: Restatements (20 questions)—In Part A, you choose the correct written restatement of a spoken sentence.
　　Part B: Mini-Dialogues (15 questions)—In Part B, you choose the correct written answer to a spoken question based on a short spoken dialogue.
　　Part C: Talks and Longer Conversations (15 questions)—In Part C, you choose the correct written answers to a series of questions about a longer spoken dialogue between two speakers or a talk given by one speaker.

Section Two: Structure and Written Expression
You are allowed 25 minutes to complete this section of the test. There are 40 questions in this section, which consists of two subsections.
　　Structure (15 questions)—In this subsection, you choose grammatically *correct* sentence completions for sentences with missing parts.
　　Written Expression (25 questions)—In this subsection, you choose the *incorrect* segments in complete sentences.

Section Three: Vocabulary and Reading Comprehension
You are allowed 45 minutes to complete this section of the test. There are 60 questions in this section, which consists of two subsections.
　　Vocabulary (30 questions)—In this subsection, you choose synonyms for underlined words in sentences.
　　Reading Comprehension (30 questions)—In this subsection, you read passages and answer questions about them.

Section Four: Test of Written English
You are allowed 30 minutes to complete this section of the test. You are given a topic and asked to write an essay about that topic. There are two types of essay questions asked on the Test of Written English: comparison and contrast questions, and questions which ask you to interpret charts and graphs. The Test of Written English is not included in all TOEFLs. It is included during the months of September, October, March, and May.

Questions Commonly Asked About the TOEFL

Students who are going to take the TOEFL often have questions about it. Below are commonly asked questions about the TOEFL followed by answers to these questions.

How do I register for the TOEFL?
You can register to take the TOEFL in the United States or Canada by completing the registration form found in the *Bulletin of Information for TOEFL and TSE.* You can receive this free bulletin by writing to:

> TOEFL Registration Office
> P.O. Box 6151
> Princeton, NJ 08541-6151
> USA

There is a special registration bulletin for TOEFLs that are given outside the United States or Canada. If you plan to take the TOEFL in a country other than the United States or Canada, you should ask for the specially prepared *Bulletin of Information, Overseas Edition* from the above address.

You may also be able to receive the *Bulletin of Information* from a TOEFL representative agency that directly serves the country you are in. For a list of countries that have special TOEFL agencies and for the addresses of these agencies, see the General Appendix, #1, pages 500–501.

Are all TOEFLs the same length?
No. Most TOEFLs contain 150 questions. However, sometimes a longer version of the TOEFL, one containing 200 questions, is given. The extra questions on longer versions are experimental in nature and do not count toward your total TOEFL score. However, these extra questions are all mixed in with the other TOEFL questions. If you are given a longer version of the TOEFL, you should try your best on all of the questions because you will not know for sure which ones are experimental.

How is my TOEFL scored?
Each individual section of the TOEFL (not including Section Four, the Test of Written English) is reported as a converted score based on a scale of from below 30 to a high of 68 points.

Your total TOEFL score is reported on a scale of from below 300 to a high of 677 points. This scale is ten times as large as the scale for the individual sections (from below 30 to 68 points). Very few people ever receive less than 300 points on the TOEFL, because it is possible to answer one-fourth of the questions correctly just by guessing. If you guess at all the questions on the TOEFL, you are likely to get a score of about 330.

You can use Score Conversion Table 1 in the General Appendix, #2, page 505 to estimate your converted score on each of the sections of the Diagnostic, Section, and Complete Practice tests in this book. You can also use Score Conversion Table 2 to estimate your total TOEFL score for these tests.

The Test of Written English is not included in your total TOEFL score. It is scored separately on a scale of 1 to 6. For more information on the scoring of the Test of Written English, see pages 388–398.

What is a passing score on the TOEFL?
There really is no one passing score. Each college and university that requires a TOEFL score has its own minimum acceptable score. Most colleges and universities require a score of between 525 and 550 for both undergraduate and graduate students. However, some undergraduate institutions require a score of less than 525. Some graduate institutions require more than 550 points. To find out for sure what score you need, you should write to the colleges and universities that interest you and ask them what their minimum TOEFL score requirements are.

There is no passing score on the Test of Written English either. However, many colleges and universities like to see a score of 4 or better on this test.

Can I keep my TOEFL test booklet after the test?

Sometimes. You can usually keep your booklet or request that it be sent to you if you take the test in September, October, February, March, or May. However, these dates sometimes change, so you should check the *Bulletin of Information* to verify them.

If you also want copies of the Listening Comprehension Section audiotape, your answer sheet, and the correct answers, you can order these. To do this, you must complete a request form that is in the *Bulletin of Information* and send it, along with eighteen dollars, to the address on page 9.

It is a good idea to take the TOEFL on a day when you can keep the test booklet. It is also a good idea to order the cassette and other test materials. If you do this, you can study the test. Also, if there is an error in the test, you can find it and report it. If you find a question on the test that you think is marked incorrectly or has two correct answers or for any other reason has an error in it, you may write a letter to:

> School and Higher Education Test Development
> Educational Testing Service
> P. O. Box 6656
> Princeton, NJ 08541-6656
> USA

In this letter, you must clearly identify the question and describe what you feel is wrong with it. You should also send a photocopy of the page that contains the question.

Can I complain about a TOEFL test administration?

Yes. If you have a complaint about the way your TOEFL was given, you can write a letter of complaint to:

> TOEFL Program Office
> P. O. 6155
> Princeton, NJ 08541-6155
> USA

You must send this letter within three days after the test date. In your letter, you must include the date and location of the test. Then, you must clearly explain your complaint.

Can I cancel my TOEFL score?

Yes. If you are certain that you did poorly on the TOEFL, you can cancel your test score by completing the Score Cancellation Section of your TOEFL answer sheet immediately after taking the test. You can also cancel your test score by calling:

> 609-951-1100

or by sending a fax to:

> 609-771-7681

or by sending a telegram to:

> EDUCTESTSVC
> Princeton, NJ 08541
> USA

If you call or send a telegram, you must also immediately send a letter with your signature to:

> TOEFL Score Cancellations
> P. O. Box 6151
> Princeton, NJ 08541-6151
> USA

You must cancel your score within seven days of the test. After seven days, you cannot cancel your score.

We do not recommend that you cancel your score unless you feel very certain that you did poorly. Students sometimes cancel good scores because they are nervous about the test.

How do I have my TOEFL scores sent to a college or university?

ETS will send your score to any college or university that you request. On the day you take the test, you can request that three score reports be sent for you. There is a place on your TOEFL answer sheet for making this request. There is no charge for this request.

In addition, you can use the Score Report Request Form published in the *Bulletin of Information*. You must pay eight dollars for each score you request using this form.

Many institutions require that the scores they receive be sent to them directly by ETS. Some institutions, however, will allow you to send them photocopies of score reports. You should check with the institution you are interested in to find out which they want. You should never send a photocopy of your scores without finding out first if it is acceptable. More and more institutions will accept only the official reports sent to them by ETS.

For how long is my test score valid?

Two years. If it has been more than two years since you took the TOEFL, you will have to take it again if you want ETS to send out score reports for you.

How many times can I take the TOEFL?

As many times as you want to. Only your most recent score will be kept and reported by ETS.

What is the best way to prepare for the TOEFL?

The TOEFL is designed to test a wide variety of skills and abilities in English. For this reason, there are two steps that you should follow to prepare for it.

1. The first thing you should do is take part in a regular program of study of English. This is best accomplished by enrolling in a course that aims at teaching general proficiency in English, not just TOEFL preparation. Many colleges and universities in the United States and elsewhere offer intensive English programs for developing general proficiency.

2. The second thing you should do is take part in a regular program of TOEFL preparation study. This study should include taking practice TOEFL tests. However, taking practice tests is not enough. Taking practice tests will not help you if you have not mastered the language being tested on them. Therefore, your TOEFL preparation study should not consist only of taking practice TOEFL tests. It should also include the study and review of specific TOEFL language skills and test-taking strategies. This is best accomplished by using *The Heinemann TOEFL Preparation Course, The Heinemann TOEFL Practice Tests*, and the materials that accompany them. These materials provide the opportunity for in-depth review of all of the language skills that are specifically tested on the TOEFL. In addition, they provide practice using test-taking strategies that are particularly useful for this test.

Students who are the most successful on the TOEFL are those who follow both of the steps listed above.

The general strategies listed on the next page are also helpful and should be followed on the day that you take the TOEFL.

GENERAL TOEFL TEST STRATEGIES

1. Use your time wisely. The TOEFL is a timed test. You must work very quickly and efficiently to finish all of the questions in the time you are allowed. The skill and strategy practice in this book will help you learn to budget your time on each section of the TOEFL. In addition, you should bring a watch to the TOEFL so that you can keep track of your time.

2. Don't read the instructions to each TOEFL section. The test instructions used in this text are exactly the same as the ones used on the TOEFL. You should become familiar with these instructions. If you are familiar with them before you take the TOEFL, you do not have to read them when you begin the test. Instead, you can move immediately to the test questions and begin working.

3. If you don't know the answer to a question, GUESS. This is a very important strategy to use when taking the TOEFL. There is no penalty for guessing. You have a twenty-five percent chance of guessing the correct answer to each question. **Unmarked answers will be counted as wrong and will lower your score.**

4. Mark your answer sheet very carefully. To prevent marking answers in the wrong order, you should follow your place on your answer sheet with one finger. Check to see that the number next to this finger is the same as the number of the question you are looking at in your test booklet. When you choose your answer, fill in the circle completely with a Number 2 pencil. If you need to change an answer, erase it completely, and mark your new answer.

5. Do not write in your test booklet. You are not allowed to make any marks on your TOEFL test book during the test.

6. The night before the TOEFL, relax. Don't try to do any serious studying the night before the test. This will only make you nervous and tired. The night before the TOEFL, it is a good idea to relax and go to bed early. Then, you will be at your best for the test.

7. It is a good idea to eat something substantial before the TOEFL. The TOEFL is a long exam, and having something to eat beforehand can help you to focus and concentrate on the test.

8. Arrive at the test center ahead of time. **If you are late for a TOEFL, you will not be allowed to take it.**

About This Course Book

The Heinemann TOEFL Preparation Course contains a variety of materials to prepare you for success on the TOEFL.

1. The **Diagnostic Test** allows you to evaluate your weak areas in English language proficiency before deciding your course of TOEFL preparation study.

2. **Strategies** are given for taking each section of the TOEFL. These strategies provide you with steps to follow for success on each part of the test.

3. **Checkpoint studies** for each section of the test provide explanations and practice exercises in each of the TOEFL skills. The exercises in these studies are written in a variety of formats. These checkpoints (✔) are identified as follows: L✔ for listening (eg. L✔8), G✔ for grammar, V✔ for vocabulary, R✔ for reading, and W✔ for writing.

4. Whenever possible, **sample questions** illustrating each checkpoint are provided and analyzed in depth. These sample questions make it clear how each checkpoint skill is actually tested on the TOEFL.

5. **Checkpoint tests** are interspersed throughout the checkpoint studies to provide follow-up practice of the strategies and skills you study. All checkpoint tests are written in a TOEFL format.

6. **Section tests** allow you to measure your progress at the end of each chapter of the text. Section tests are written in exactly the same format as the sections of the TOEFL.

7. A **Complete Practice TOEFL Test** at the end of the course book gives you practice in applying all the skills and strategies you learn in the course.

8. A **Score Conversion Table** allows you to estimate your TOEFL score on the Diagnostic, Section, and Complete Practice TOEFL Tests.

9. **The Listening Appendix** provides Word Category Charts and a glossary of idioms commonly tested on the Listening Comprehension Section of the TOEFL.

10. **The Grammar Appendix** gives the extra rules some students find necessary for success on the Structure and Written Expression Section of the TOEFL. In addition, this appendix contains lists of troublesome structures tested on the TOEFL (irregular verbs, verbs followed by gerunds, verbs followed by infinitives, etc.)

11. **The Vocabulary Appendix** provides Word Category Charts for eight topic areas that are commonly used for TOEFL reading passages. A Word Form Chart accompanies each Word Category Chart. The Word Form Charts provide you with valuable practice in working with words from academic topic areas. You are urged to add words to both the Word Category Charts and the Word Form Charts as you complete exercises and reading passages from *The Heinemann TOEFL Preparation Course* and *The Heinemann TOEFL Practice Tests* and from your outside reading.

12. **The Reading Appendix** provides extra practice in active reading of academic passages. Explanations to questions about the reading passages in *The Heinemann TOEFL Preparation Course* are also included. In addition, this appendix contains a list of vocabulary words and structures that express organizational patterns and the author's purpose. This list is also useful for you as you prepare for the Test of Written English.

13. The **Writing Appendix** contains charts for handwriting practice.

14. The **General Appendix** provides the names and addresses of agencies outside the United States that students can write to for TOEFL registration forms. It also includes the Diagnostic Test Scoring Instructions; the Conversion Tables for estimating your TOEFL scores on the Diagnostic Test, the section tests and the Complete Practice TOEFL Test in this book; and the TOEFL Answer Sheets you will need to take these tests. A sample TWE Answer Sheet has been provided for you to photocopy and use when answering the TWE essay questions.

How to Use This Course

The Heinemann TOEFL Preparation Course can be used in a variety of ways:

1. It can be the principal text in a TOEFL preparation course.
2. It can be used as a supplementary text in a more general English language course.
3. It can be used as a self-study text by people who are not enrolled in any formal courses.

In all of these situations, the general procedures recommended for following this course are:

1. Read and understand the introduction to this book.
2. Take the Diagnostic Test which begins on page 19. Record your answers to this test on the Diagnostic Test Answer Sheet found in the General Appendix on page 509. Score your test and follow the instructions on page 502 for using your Diagnostic Test results to determine your weakest areas of TOEFL language proficiency.

Special Note About the Diagnostic Test

Using the Diagnostic Test to determine areas of strength and weakness is very important; weak areas should receive special attention. However, the best preparation for the TOEFL includes review and refinement of stronger areas, as well as strengthening of weak areas. Thus, we do not recommend that only weak areas be covered in a TOEFL preparation course. All areas should be covered.

3. If possible, study the entire text, giving special attention to the areas that the Diagnostic Test indicated were your weakest.

4. If you have only a short time for TOEFL study, move directly to the beginning of the section of the book that corresponds to your weakest area of TOEFL language proficiency. Work on that section first. Then, try to find time to work through the other sections.

5. As you complete sections of the book, take and score the section tests. Estimate your TOEFL scores for these tests by using the Conversion Tables in the General Appendix, #3, page 505.

Special Note About the Meaning of Converted TOEFL Scores

Converted TOEFL scores are only estimates of scores you would actually receive on a TOEFL. If your converted score goes down from one test to the next, it may mean that the second test was slightly more difficult for you than the first or that you were not concentrating quite as well during the second test. Use converted scores only to judge approximately how well you would do on an official TOEFL. Do not be overly concerned about differences in estimated TOEFL scores.

6. As you move through the text, use *The Heinemann TOEFL Practice Tests* described below. You should try to schedule a complete test from this book at regular intervals.

7. Once you have worked through the course, take the Complete Practice TOEFL found at the end of this book. Score this test and estimate your TOEFL score using the Score Conversion Tables in the General Appendix, #3, page 505. If you are still weak in certain areas, review these areas again using the course book.

Accompanying Materials

Additional materials accompany *The Heinemann TOEFL Preparation Course* to complete the Heinemann TOEFL course of study.

The Heinemann TOEFL Preparation Course Tapescripts and Answers provides a script for all listening comprehension exercises and tests. It also contains the answers for all exercises and tests in the book.

A set of cassette tapes contains recordings of the listening comprehension portions of the tests and exercises used in the text.

The Heinemann TOEFL Practice Tests contains five complete practice TOEFLs, Listening Comprehension Section tapescripts, answer keys, scoring information, and study notes. This text is also accompanied by cassette tapes.

NOTES FOR THE TEACHER

Designing your Course

In general, the procedures described above should make it possible for you to design a TOEFL preparation course suited to your students' needs. If you are teaching a class in which most or all of your students have the same native language, the Diagnostic Test will most likely produce similar results for all of your students. You can then rely on it to determine the area or areas you want to give special attention to in your course. No matter the area of special concentration, however, it is important that you try to cover as much of the entire course book as possible. As mentioned above, TOEFL success depends on the review of strong skills and strategies as well as on the strengthening of weak ones.

If your students come from a variety of language backgrounds, the Diagnostic Test may indicate different areas of strength and weakness for different students. When this happens, it may be advisable to cover all skills and strategies equally. To do this, it is possible to start at the beginning of the book and work systematically through each section. Different individual homework assignments can be made in areas of individual weakness. The course book is designed so that students can work on their own on sections that you may not have time to cover in class. You should feel free, for example, to assign extra work from the Vocabulary and Reading Section while you are working on the Structure and Written Expression Section in class.

It is also possible to move back and forth between sections of the book, giving equal treatment to each section. If you choose this method, it is advisable to change sections on a weekly, rather than a daily basis. It is also important to carefully cover the introductory material to each section.

Students should also be encouraged to refer to the appendices for special help in their areas of weakness. In addition to supplementary information in a specific skill area, each appendix contains a list of supplementary textbooks which provide valuable reference material for students who need extra study.

Complete in-depth classroom treatment of all of the material in this text takes approximately seventy-five hours (roughly one hour of class time per day for one semester of fifteen weeks). If regular homework assignments are made, this time frame can be significantly reduced.

Approximate time frames necessary to cover the material in each individual section are as follows:

Introduction and Diagnostic Test.. 3 hours
Section One: Listening Comprehension... 20 hours
Section Two: Structure and Written Expression .... 20 hours
Section Three: Vocabulary and Reading Comprehension.............. 20 hours
Section Four: Test of Written English .... 10 hours
Complete Practice TOEFL Test... 2 hours

It is also advisable to schedule periodic practice tests from *The Heinemann TOEFL Practice Tests*. Each of these tests takes approximately two hours. If the Test of Written English is included, they take approximately two and one-half hours. They can be scheduled after class in two hour blocks of time or used in class, section by section.

Covering the Checkpoints

Each of the checkpoints covered in the course book contains an explanation of the point and, whenever possible, a sample TOEFL question illustrating this point. This material should be covered in class. Once explanations and sample questions have been discussed in class, checkpoint exercises can be assigned as homework.

Checkpoint tests and section tests are all timed to reflect the time constraints of a TOEFL. Because TOEFL checkpoint tests and section tests are timed, it is preferable to do them as class activities. If time does not permit this, they can be assigned as homework.

Using the Tapescripts and Answers

The *Tapescripts and Answers* should be used to check students' answers and to help them understand their mistakes. The tapescript is especially useful as an aid in explaining the answers to the listening comprehension questions in the course book. When students miss listening comprehension questions, they should be referred to the tapescript so that they can check what they think they heard against what was actually said on the tapes.

The *Tapescripts and Answers* contains a great deal of useful explanatory information as well. Explanations accompany the answers to listening and reading checkpoint exercises that deal with long conversations, talks, or reading passages involving difficult skills such as making inferences and determining the main idea, purpose, or attitude of a text. The answers to grammar checkpoint exercises involving the identification of errors include the corrections for these errors. If students can make and understand these error corrections, they will be successful in identifying errors on the TOEFL. Finally, where possible, checkpoint test and section test answer keys refer back to the specific checkpoints on which they are based for further review and study.

Using the Listening Comprehension Section

Everyday vocabulary is stressed throughout this section of the book. For example, all idioms used are specially marked by **bold italics** either in the text or in the tapescript. Students should be encouraged to try to figure out the meaning of each idiom from the context in which it is used. If they cannot determine the meaning of an idiom from context, they can refer to the Glossary of Idioms in the Listening Appendix for a definition.

Lists of words in the most common categories of everyday vocabulary tested on the Listening Comprehension Section of the TOEFL are also included in the Listening Appendix. Students should be encouraged to refer to and add words to these lists.

For students who are especially weak in listening, we recommend supplemental use of the tapescript for this section. Very weak students can read along with the tapescript as they listen to the tapes.

Using the Structure and Written Expression Section

This section of the course book provides a comprehensive review of the grammar tested on the TOEFL. In addition, the Grammar Appendix provides extensive supplementary information for weaker students and for students who are not familiar with grammatical terms and categories. Read through the Grammar Appendix before teaching this section of the book and use this appendix to supplement the Grammar Checkpoint Study.

In order to cover all of the material in this section of the course book, we recommend that you regularly assign exercises as homework. Review of lists of irregular verbs, etc., in the Grammar Appendix can also be assigned as homework.

Using the Vocabulary and Reading Section

Vocabulary development depends on regular study rather than a crash course on learning lists of words. Checkpoints V✔1, Read Widely, and V✔2, Use Special Books, are very general and should be followed up with special assignments which encourage weaker students to work outside of the TOEFL preparation course. V✔9, Word Forms, and V✔10, Word Categories, also lend themselves to application of outside reading and vocabulary assignments. Students should be encouraged to fill out (and hand in, if desired) extensive Word Category Charts and Word Form Charts as they complete outside readings or the reading passages from Section Three of the course book. V✔3, Make and Use Vocabulary Flash Cards, depends in large part on student initiative, but could be encouraged through games and assignments for specific readings which are outside the scope of this book. V✔4, Adverbs, and V✔5, Adjectives, should be supplemented for weaker students with assignments for making sentences using the words and additional work with adjectives from the Vocabulary Appendix, Word Category Chart #8, pages 585–587. Individual study of the extensive word lists provided in V✔6 through V✔8 should be assigned as homework and monitored. Depending on the level of the group or individual student, additional word puzzles and word development exercises should be added.

The reading passages in Section Three will be challenging for the weaker students. Reading Appendix #1, pages 489–495, provides students who have not had much experience reading authentic academic passages with an introduction to "active reading." It is recommended that these students work intensively in class with this section before they begin work on the Checkpoint Study. More advanced students could be assigned Reading Appendix #1 for homework.

The answer key for reading contains extensive explanations for the reading passages in R✔2 through R✔8. You may want to refer to these explanations in class as students check their answers to the checkpoint exercises or refer students to them for out of class work.

Each vocabulary and reading checkpoint should be considered in light of student needs and levels of language proficiency. Lower level students will need to supplement the vocabulary study with exercises from outside vocabulary building textbooks. Stronger students may cover the first eight Vocabulary Checkpoints as a form of review, and should be encouraged to elaborate the Word Category Charts and Word Form Charts. Students who already have knowledge of roots, prefixes and suffixes, or those whom you feel would not profit greatly from direct work on these elements of English vocabulary may use V✔5 through V✔8 as a reference. Outside reading should be encouraged in all topic areas listed in the Word Category Charts.

Using the Writing Section

This section of the course book provides a review of skills and strategies for academic writing. It is meant to provide students with guidelines for essay writing that will satisfy criteria used by readers who score Test of Written English (TWE) essays. In-depth examination of the two TWE question types is followed by sample student writing responses. The Self-scoring Criteria and sample essay evaluations in this section of the book are meant to provide students with enough information to score their own essays somewhat objectively. You should feel free to give additional writing assignments and elaborate on any aspect of the writing task that is difficult for your students.

Using This Course Book for Other Courses

The material covered in this course book has been successfully used to supplement courses that are not designed specifically as TOEFL preparation courses. Each section of this book comprehensively treats language skills that are necessary for all students, not just TOEFL students.

In addition, each section of this book can provide the core material for a course in a particular language skill area. The Structure and Written Expression Section, for example, provides enough material for a review course in grammar. Similarly, the Listening Comprehension Section can constitute a course in conversational and academic listening skills; the Vocabulary and Reading Comprehension Section can be used on its own as the basis for a course in vocabulary development and academic reading skills; the Test of Written English Section can constitute a review course in academic essay writing.

NOTES FOR THE SELF-STUDY STUDENT

Using this course book and the additional materials that accompany it, you can design an individual course of TOEFL study that is just right for your particular needs. Just follow the procedures described above in the section entitled How to Use This Course Book, pages 14–15.

Many of the exercises in the course book are designed to provide time pressures similar to those on the TOEFL. For this reason, when doing the timed exercises, it is important for you to use a clock or a watch and allow yourself only the time listed for each exercise. This is very important for learning how to work quickly and efficiently on all sections of the TOEFL. It is especially important for Section Three, Vocabulary and Reading Comprehension. Students who do not time themselves carefully often do not finish this section of the TOEFL in the time allowed.

When you practice the essay questions for Section Four of the TOEFL, it is important for you to read and score each essay yourself following the instructions given in W✔3, Self-Scoring of a TWE Essay. In addition, it is helpful if you can have your essay read and scored a second time by a native speaker of North American English.

The appendices to this book include extra information and exercises to aid you in your self-study. Try to use these appendices on a regular basis.

Lists of helpful books for extra self-study are also provided in the appendices for this book. These books can help you if you have trouble understanding any of the material covered in this course.

The Heinemann TOEFL Preparation Course Tapescripts and Answers provides a script for all listening comprehension exercises and tests. It also contains the answers for all exercises and tests in the book. You can use the *Tapescripts and Answers* to check your answers and to review what is said on the listening comprehension tapes for the book. The tapescript is especially useful for helping you understand your mistakes in the listening exercises. When you miss listening comprehension questions, you should refer to the tapescript so that you can check what you think you heard against what was actually said on the tapes.

If you are especially weak in listening, you can also read along with the tapescript while you listen to the cassettes for this course book.

Always complete an entire course book exercise before looking at the answer key.

The *Tapescripts and Answers* is full of useful explanatory material. Explanations accompany the answers to listening and reading checkpoint exercises that deal with long conversations, talks, or reading passages involving difficult skills such as making inferences and determining purpose, attitude, or main idea. The answers to grammar checkpoint exercises involving the identification of errors include the corrections for these errors. If you can make and understand these error corrections, you will be successful in identifying errors on the TOEFL. Finally, where possible, checkpoint test and section test answer keys refer back to the specific checkpoints on which they are based for further review and study.

The amount of time that you spend on your TOEFL preparation course will depend on your own pace of study. You should try to develop a program of study that allows you to cover the entire course book, with extra time for study in the areas of weakness determined by the Diagnostic Test.

If possible, you should also schedule practice TOEFLs for yourself using *The Heinemann TOEFL Practice Tests*. You should not do these tests all at once. You should try to do one after you have studied each section of the course book and one at the end of your TOEFL course of study.

Diagnostic Test

On the following pages, you will find the Diagnostic Test for this course book. This test will help you determine your areas of TOEFL strength and weakness for the first three sections of the TOEFL. You should begin your TOEFL study by taking this test.

The Diagnostic Test is the same length and format as an actual TOEFL exam, and it contains all of the item types covered on a TOEFL. It takes approximately two hours to complete this test. If possible, you should take the entire Diagnostic Test at one sitting. If this is not possible, you can take each section separately. If you choose this method, do not look ahead at the sections you have not yet completed. If you look ahead, you will not get good diagnostic results when you actually complete each section as a test.

Steps to follow when taking the Diagnostic Test:

1. Find the Diagnostic Test Answer Sheet in the General Appendix, #4, page 507. Remove it from the appendix and mark your answers on it.

2. Set up a tape player with the audiocassette for the Section One Diagnostic Test.

3. As much as possible, simulate an actual TOEFL test-taking situation. Sit at a comfortable desk in a room that is quiet. Take the test at a time when you will not be interrupted.

4. Take the test according to the time limits set for actual TOEFL tests. Section One will last 30–40 minutes and will be self-timed by the audio cassette that accompanies it. Allow yourself 25 minutes to complete Section Two and 45 minutes to complete Section Three.

5. Score the test, using the Diagnostic Test Scoring Instructions located in the General Appendix, #2, page 502.

6. Use the results of this test to determine your areas of TOEFL strength and weakness. If possible, study the entire text, giving special attention to the areas that the Diagnostic Test indicated were weak areas for you. If you have only a short time for TOEFL study, move directly to the beginning of the section of the book that corresponds to your weakest area of TOEFL language proficiency. Work on that section first. Then, try to find time to work through the other sections.

When you are ready to start the Diagnostic Test, begin the tape. Do not go on to the next page until the tape tells you to do so.

SECTION 1
LISTENING COMPREHENSION

In this section of the test, you will have an opportunity to demonstrate your ability to understand spoken English. There are three parts to this section, with special directions for each part.

Part A

<u>Directions:</u> For each question in Part A, you will hear a short sentence. Each sentence will be spoken just one time. The sentences you hear will not be written out for you. Therefore, you must listen carefully to understand what the speaker says.

After you hear a sentence, read the four choices in your test book, marked (A), (B), (C), and (D), and decide which <u>one</u> is closest in meaning to the sentence you heard. Then, on your answer sheet, find the number of the question and fill in the space that corresponds to the letter of the answer you have chosen. Fill in the space so that the letter inside the oval cannot be seen.

Example I   <u>Sample Answer</u>

You will hear: Ⓐ Ⓑ ● Ⓓ
You will read: (A)   Greg didn't bother to leave a tip.
                 (B)   Greg thought about typing a letter to his brother.
                 (C)   Greg didn't like to type.
                 (D)   My typing bothered Greg.

The speaker said, "Greg thought typing was a bother." Sentence (C), "Greg didn't like to type," is closest in meaning to the sentence you heard. Therefore, you should choose answer (C).

Example II   <u>Sample Answer</u>

You will hear: Ⓐ ● Ⓒ Ⓓ
You will read: (A)   Everyone will be able to take this exam later.
                 (B)   Students should bring a calculator to this exam.
                 (C)   This test will be part of every student's final grade.
                 (D)   No one can calculate the grades for this test.

The speaker said, "Everyone needs a calculator for this test." Sentence (B), "Students should bring a calculator to this exam," is closest in meaning to the sentence you heard. Therefore, you should choose answer (B).

1. (A) Frank's performance was very
       impressive.
   (B) There is nothing impressive about the
       way he does his job.
   (C) Frank expressed disappointment in his
       performance.
   (D) Honestly, I'm not very enthused about
       performing with him.

GO ON TO THE NEXT PAGE

2. (A) If I don't hurry, I won't finish typing.
   (B) I wish I knew how to type.
   (C) I could only find one type.
   (D) This is all that I could get typed.

3. (A) I didn't mind the crossing.
   (B) It didn't bother me.
   (C) That cross is not mine.
   (D) It didn't occur to me.

4. (A) Why isn't George going to have a party?
   (B) I didn't think George would attend the party.
   (C) George didn't think about attending the party.
   (D) George isn't going to have a party, is he?

5. (A) The ground here is hardly dry yet.
   (B) It is hard to find dry soil here.
   (C) This dry soil is hard to remove.
   (D) There is no moisture in the hard ground here.

6. (A) Patricia will take apart her bicycle while she's in Boston.
   (B) Patricia must hurry to Boston to pick up her bicycle.
   (C) Patricia is going to Boston to watch a race.
   (D) Patricia will participate in a competition in Boston.

7. (A) Greg's roommate kept his stereo for him while he was away.
   (B) Greg and his roommate have gone shopping for a stereo.
   (C) Greg's stereo had to be taken back to the store.
   (D) Greg's roommate has had a stereo for a long time.

8. (A) You seem to be very happily married.
   (B) You'll need a new suit for the wedding.
   (C) How soon will you be getting married?
   (D) You look wonderful in your wedding attire.

9. (A) I can't get the lid off of this pan.
   (B) I must buy a new pan.
   (C) I don't want this pan any longer.
   (D) I wish this pan had a lid.

10. (A) I spoke to the group on Friday.
    (B) I asked the group to speak on Friday.
    (C) I am supposed to give a talk next Friday.
    (D) At next Friday's talk, the group will ask questions.

11. (A) Larry plays tennis better than I do.
    (B) Larry and Dennis are waiting on the sidelines.
    (C) Larry's tennis career is on the brink of disaster.
    (D) Larry is coming to play tennis with me later.

12. (A) Professor Bates asked him for his recommendation.
    (B) Professor Bates has agreed to write him a letter of reference.
    (C) I can't believe he wanted to stay at Professor Bates' house.
    (D) Professor Bates would never recommend him.

13. (A) It is hard to get into the calculus and physics classes in this department.
    (B) Both calculus and physics are very hard subjects.
    (C) Everyone who lives in this apartment is studying physics and calculus.
    (D) Calculus is a more difficult subject here than physics.

14. (A) They weren't as organized as they appeared to be at first.
    (B) We will miss them when they leave the organization.
    (C) I don't think they came to the first meeting.
    (D) We must get organized or we will miss their first appearance.

GO ON TO THE NEXT PAGE

15. (A) Karen doesn't dress like you do.
    (B) I think you and Karen have similar dresses.
    (C) Karen seems to like your dress, doesn't she?
    (D) Isn't Karen's address similar to yours?

16. (A) I enjoyed having a free vacation.
    (B) There are no seats free on the plane at this time.
    (C) I am too busy to plan a vacation.
    (D) Because I took the plane, I had more free time on my vacation.

17. (A) Jane piled Bill's dirty clothes on the floor.
    (B) There were clothes and shoes lying on the floor.
    (C) Bill put his tennis racket on the floor next to Jane's shoes.
    (D) Jane's file got dirty from lying on the floor.

18. (A) I feel like learning more about computers.
    (B) People here seem to know more about computers than I do.
    (C) They are just beginning to get computers around here.
    (D) I believe I know more about computers than most beginners.

19. (A) Dennis uses his dictionary less frequently now.
    (B) Dennis no longer has a dictionary.
    (C) I used to let Dennis use my dictionary.
    (D) Dennis didn't use his dictionary very much in the past.

20. (A) Paul's books were so heavy that he didn't remove them from the library all semester.
    (B) Paul only took a few courses, so he didn't study much.
    (C) Paul wants to become a librarian, so he worked in the library all semester.
    (D) Paul worked in the library all semester in an effort to keep up with his schoolwork.

GO ON TO THE NEXT PAGE ➤

Part B

Directions: In Part B you will hear short conversations between two speakers. At the end of each conversation, a third person will ask a question about what was said. You will hear each conversation and question about it just one time. Therefore, you must listen carefully to understand what each speaker says. After you hear a conversation and the question about it, read the four possible answers in your test book and decide which one is the best answer to the question you heard. Then, on your answer sheet, find the number of the question and fill in the space that corresponds to the letter of the answer you have chosen.

Look at the following example.

You will hear:
You will read: (A)   At last winter is almost over.
              (B)   She doesn't like winter weather very much.
              (C)   This winter's weather is similar to last winter's weather.
              (D)   Winter won't last as long this year as it did last year.

From the conversation you learn that the woman thinks the weather this winter is almost the same as the weather last winter. The best answer to the question "What does the woman mean?" is (C), "This winter's weather is similar to last winter's weather." Therefore, you should choose answer (C).

21. (A) She is afraid to ask Pat to work.
    (B) She thinks Pat made the right decision.
    (C) She suspected that Pat would not want to work.
    (D) She thinks that Pat is afraid of working.

22. (A) She understands the chemistry lesson very well.
    (B) She doesn't understand what the man wants.
    (C) She's going to study chemistry today.
    (D) She is having trouble with today's lesson.

23. (A) It's making him sick.
    (B) He doesn't know when to eat it.
    (C) It isn't the right consistency.
    (D) He hasn't had time to try it.

24. (A) She should not try to do too many things today.
    (B) She should try not to sleep today.
    (C) She needs to keep three hours free.
    (D) He can tell her an easy way to get to sleep.

25. (A) The woman should buy a new tire.
    (B) He can help the woman choose a new tire.
    (C) The woman can get her tire repaired at the service station.
    (D) There isn't a service station in the area.

26. (A) He would like the woman's help.
    (B) He doesn't need more light.
    (C) She shouldn't turn right.
    (D) He'd like to pay his fine.

27. (A) He's not sure there are any more math books available.
    (B) He wants to go to the book sale after class.
    (C) He doesn't need a book for that class.
    (D) He'll help the woman find the book she needs.

GO ON TO THE NEXT PAGE ➤

28. (A) He doesn't have time to see Susan.
    (B) Susan has told him a lot about her trip.
    (C) Susan's trip won't be over for a long time.
    (D) He's interested in hearing about Susan's trip.

29. (A) Filing papers.
    (B) Building book shelves.
    (C) Moving into an apartment.
    (D) Working in a library.

30. (A) Mr. Grant doesn't approve of Ben's lifestyle.
    (B) Mr. Grant will never increase Ben's salary.
    (C) Mr. Grant has raised Ben since he was a small child.
    (D) Ben should ask Mr. Grant for more money.

31. (A) She will help the man find what he is looking for.
    (B) The bank is next to the gas station on the corner.
    (C) She will fill the man's tank with gas.
    (D) She doesn't know where the bank is.

32. (A) The man had not ordered any cabinets.
    (B) The man couldn't come and get the cabinets.
    (C) The cabinets could not be installed.
    (D) The cabinets had not arrived yet.

33. (A) She hasn't seen a good movie in years.
    (B) She liked both the acting and the plot.
    (C) The plot of the movie was quite bad.
    (D) The acting in the movie was not good.

34. (A) It has rained too much lately.
    (B) The woman doesn't like Ray.
    (C) Ray is behaving differently than usual.
    (D) The class started late because of the rain.

35. (A) She hasn't seen her grades lately.
    (B) She enjoys studying several hours a day.
    (C) She hasn't been doing very well at school.
    (D) She only has sixteen hours to finish all of her work.

GO ON TO THE NEXT PAGE

Part C

Directions: In this part of the test, you will hear short talks and conversations. After each of them, you will be asked some questions. You will hear the talks and conversations and the questions about them just one time. They will not be written out for you. Therefore, you must listen carefully to understand what each speaker says.

After you hear a question, read the four possible answers in your test book and decide which <u>one</u> is the best answer to the question you heard. Then, on your answer sheet, find the number of the question and fill in the space that corresponds to the letter of the answer you have chosen.

Answer all questions on the basis of what is <u>stated</u> or <u>implied</u> in the talk or conversation.

Listen to this sample talk.
    You will hear:

Now look at the following example.   Sample Answer

You will hear: ● Ⓑ Ⓒ Ⓓ
You will read: (A) Only bumblebees can fertilize red clover plants.
           (B) Bumblebees protect red clover from plant eating insects.
           (C) Bumblebees bring water to red clover plants on their tongues.
           (D) Bumblebees keep mice and other animals away from red clover plants.

The best answer to the question "Why is it impossible to raise red clover where there are no bumblebees?" is (A), "Only bumblebees can fertilize red clover plants." Therefore, you should choose answer (A).

Now look at the next example.   Sample Answer

                                      Ⓐ Ⓑ Ⓒ ●
You will hear:
You will read: (A) They both make honey.
           (B) They both build combs.
           (C) Both of them are found in underground nests.
           (D) They both live through the winter.

The best answer to the question "According to the speaker, in what way are the queen wasp and the queen bee similar?" is (D), "They both live through the winter." Therefore, you should choose answer (D).

36. (A) Find water.
    (B) Get settled in one place.
    (C) Look for food.
    (D) Start walking in a likely direction.

GO ON TO THE NEXT PAGE ➤

37. (A) You will lower your body temperature too much.
    (B) You will become ill.
    (C) It is hard to take in enough snow.
    (D) Snow doesn't really quench your thirst.

38. (A) A month.
    (B) Until you find food.
    (C) One week.
    (D) Until your lips become dry.

39. (A) Keep extremely active.
    (B) Wear a hat.
    (C) Dress warmly.
    (D) Stay dry.

40. (A) They have just heard the talk.
    (B) They have done this many times before.
    (C) They will be well equipped.
    (D) They will be accompanied by a guide.

41. (A) People will tell him after the talk.
    (B) People will raise their hands.
    (C) People will send in a registration.
    (D) People have notified him prior to the talk.

42. (A) In a barber shop.
    (B) In an eye doctor's office.
    (C) In a picture framing shop.
    (D) In a jewelry store.

43. (A) To find a new frame for her picture.
    (B) A replacement for the glass she has broken.
    (C) To have her glasses repaired.
    (D) An eye examination.

44. (A) Ask someone else to help her.
    (B) Choose new frames.
    (C) Take his catalogue.
    (D) Choose a different picture.

45. (A) Wait a few weeks.
    (B) Look in another store.
    (C) Look for a few more hours.
    (D) Order from a catalogue.

46. (A) Mysteries of the Midwater
    (B) Jellyfish and their Relatives
    (C) New Technology in Ocean Exploration
    (D) Bioluminescence in the Midwater

47. (A) In science fiction.
    (B) In every ocean on earth.
    (C) Under the ocean floor.
    (D) In the wilderness.

48. (A) They are the most abundant animals in the midwater.
    (B) They have razor sharp teeth.
    (C) They have no skeleton.
    (D) They can link together to form very long chains.

49. (A) Because people are afraid to go there.
    (B) Because it is so vast.
    (C) Because it is not easy to get there.
    (D) Because no one knows exactly where it is.

50. (A) Their bioluminescence.
    (B) Their huge stomachs.
    (C) Their mating behavior.
    (D) Their ability to find prey.

THIS IS THE END OF THE LISTENING COMPREHENSION SECTION OF THE TEST.

**THE NEXT PART OF THE TEST IS SECTION 2. TURN TO THE DIRECTIONS
FOR SECTION 2 IN YOUR TEST BOOK.
READ THEM AND BEGIN WORK.
DO NOT READ OR WORK ON ANY OTHER SECTION OF THE TEST.**

STOP STOP STOP **STOP** STOP STOP STOP

SECTION 2
STRUCTURE AND WRITTEN EXPRESSION

Time—25 minutes

This section is designed to measure your ability to recognize language that is appropriate for standard written English. There are two types of questions in this section, with special directions for each type.

Directions: Questions 1–15 are incomplete sentences. Beneath each sentence you will see four words or phrases, marked (A), (B), (C), and (D). Choose the one word or phrase that best completes the sentence. Then, on your answer sheet, find the number of the question and fill in the space that corresponds to the letter of the answer you have chosen. Fill in the space so that the letter inside the oval cannot be seen.

Example I   Sample Answer

    Most American families_____ at least one automobile.   ● Ⓑ Ⓒ Ⓓ
    (A) have
    (B) in
    (C) that
    (D) has

The sentence should read, "Most American families have at least one automobile." Therefore, you should choose answer (A).

Example II   Sample Answer

    _____ recent times, the discipline of biology has expanded   Ⓐ Ⓑ Ⓒ ●
    rapidly into a variety of subdisciplines.
    (A) It is since
    (B) When
    (C) Since it is
    (D) In

The sentence should read, "In recent times, the discipline of biology has expanded into a variety of subdisciplines." Therefore, you should choose answer (D).

After you read the directions, begin work on the questions.

1. _____ the Civil War, national trade unions were common in the United States.
   (A) Before they were
   (B) By the time of
   (C) It was
   (D) Because

2. Never before _____ as accelerated as it is now, during the technological age.
   (A) historical change has been
   (B) has been historical change
   (C) has historical change been
   (D) historical has change been

GO ON TO THE NEXT PAGE ➤

3. Inventor and entrepreneur, _____ for radar in 1935.
   (A) was the patent granted to Watson Watt
   (B) Watson Watt was granted a patent
   (C) the patent that Watson Watt was granted
   (D) the patent granted to Watson Watt was

4. The Cheetah, which is _____ land animal, has been hunted almost to extinction.
   (A) fastest in the world
   (B) the world's fastest
   (C) the faster world
   (D) and the world's fastest

5. Although findings are inconclusive, _____ that new solar systems are currently evolving around a number of stars in the universe.
   (A) it is evidence
   (B) the evidence
   (C) there are evidently
   (D) there is evidence

6. It has not yet been determined _____ foster atherosclerosis.
   (A) why may diets low in magnesium
   (B) why low in magnesium may diets
   (C) why diets low in magnesium may
   (D) diets low in magnesium, why may

7. With his first book, *Typee*, which was the story of his captivity by a Polynesian tribe, Herman Melville _____ to establish himself as a popular young nineteenth century author.
   (A) could
   (B) was able
   (C) with ability
   (D) can

8. _____ is depicted in Hawthorne's *The Scarlet Letter*.
   (A) The society corrupted the rapidly decaying Puritan
   (B) Corrupted the rapidly decaying Puritan society
   (C) The Puritan society corrupted rapidly decaying
   (D) The rapidly decaying corrupted Puritan society

9. Research now indicates that lead may have more influence on blood pressure levels than _____.
   (A) dietary salt
   (B) when people eat salt
   (C) to eat salt
   (D) diets have salt

10. _____ in a home where two languages are spoken are often not only bilingual but also bicultural.
    (A) Children raised
    (B) To raise children
    (C) Raising children
    (D) Raising of children

11. Changes in body organs during the first year of life affect a baby's readiness _____ solid foods.
    (A) accepting
    (B) who accept
    (C) accepted
    (D) to accept

12. The home of the kingfisher _____ in the bank of a stream.
    (A) humble, is a hole
    (B) is a humble hole
    (C) a humble hole is
    (D) hole is humble

13. _____ Edgar Allan Poe's works, his own artistic talents would probably have developed quite differently than they did.
    (A) Had not Vladimir Nabokov read
    (B) Had Vladimir Nabokov not read
    (C) Vladimir Nabokov had not read
    (D) Had read Vladimir Nabokov not

GO ON TO THE NEXT PAGE ➡

14. Moderate exercise is not the only behavioral adaptation necessary to promote physical fitness, _____ it is a contributing factor.
(A) however
(B) though
(C) despite
(D) nevertheless

15. After American athletes have participated in Olympic events as amateurs, _____ professional athletes.
(A) and often become
(B) often then become
(C) they often become
(D) often become

Directions: In questions 16–40 each sentence has four underlined words or phrases. The four underlined parts of the sentence are marked (A), (B), (C), and (D). Identify the one underlined word or phrase that must be changed in order for the setence to be correct. Then, on your answer sheet, find the number of the question and fill in the space that corresponds to the letter of the answer you have chosen.

Example I   Sample Answer

The octopus is a unique animal because they has three functioning hearts.   Ⓐ Ⓑ ● Ⓓ
       A   B   C   D

The sentence should read, "The octopus is a unique animal because it has three functioning hearts." Therefore, you should choose answer (C).

Example II   Sample Answer

                                                      Ⓐ Ⓑ Ⓒ ●
The beagle, one of the most ancient breeds of dog known,
                A   B   C

originating in England.
    D

The sentence should read, "The beagle, one of the most ancient breeds of dog known, originated in England." Therefore, you should choose answer (D).

After you read the directions, begin work on the questions.

16. In nature, cats are nocturnal animals; that is, its most active period of the day is at night.
                      A   B C   D

17. Several computer models have been able to succeed predict global climatic changes well
  A   B   C
in advance of their occurrence.
    D

18. Although their larvae can take over a year to mature, some varieties of adult mosquito live
  A   B   C
only a little days.
     D

GO ON TO THE NEXT PAGE

19. Although Jack Kerouac's vision of America was less critical that Allen Ginsberg's, both of
    A   B   C
    these writers encouraged societal change in the 1960s.
                              D

20. The production of computers and their sale overseas has increased dramatically over the past
                   A   B   C   D
    twenty years.

21. In the 1950s, Americans finally recovered a sense of self-confidence that they
                            A   B
    hadn't experiencing since before the stock market crash of 1929.
    C   D

22. In 1640, colonist Roger Williams has applied for a charter for the colony of Rhode Island.
             A   B   C   D

23. Farther evidence is needed to support recent research that suggests that certain chemicals
    A   B
    found in broccoli and other members of the cabbage family may act as cancer preventatives.
                           C   D

24. A major advantage for warm-blooded animals is that are less restricted than cold blooded
      A   B   C
    animals in their geographic distribution and can range over larger expanses of the earth.
                                                                                 D

25. The native animals of grasslands are adapted for running, leaping, or to burrow.
                A   B   C   D

26. As long the United States government supports space exploration, astronauts will have the
    A   B
    opportunity to probe the universe for information about its origins.
                         C   D

27. Many private business firms have been expressed an interest in using mechanical robots
                                 A   B   C
    to carry out their more mechanical tasks.
    D

28. Although a product of the twentieth century, the work of poet Robert Lowell is inspired by
    A   B
    that those of his nineteenth century predecessor, Edgar Allan Poe.
         C   D

29. The triggerfish, equipped with fourteen tooth and tough skin, can assault the sea urchin and
                     A   B   C
    remove its needle sharp spines without serious injury.
                                            D

GO ON TO THE NEXT PAGE

30. Modern Americans <u>are said</u> <u>to prefer</u> the moving image to the <u>printing</u> word or the painting,
                        A   B   C
and motion pictures remain, in the eyes of many, America's <u>most distinguished</u> art form.
                                              D

31. Scientists feel that <u>it</u> is not healthy for people <u>to live</u> in a state in which they <u>chronically</u>
                A   B   C
<u>reactor</u> to excessive stress.
  D

32. Chemical elements <u>with</u> <u>high</u> electronegativity values usually <u>are having</u> negative <u>oxidation</u>
numbers.   A   B   C   D

33. Down syndrome is a <u>genetic</u> disorder <u>that</u> afflicts about one out of every 800 <u>infancies</u> <u>born</u> in
                    A   B   C   D
the United States.

34. In order to avoid <u>flooding</u> the market with excess goods, <u>distributators</u> often store their
                   A   B
<u>surplus</u> goods in private or public <u>warehouses</u>.
  C   D

35. Not only <u>do scientists</u> still know little about variations <u>in</u> the moon's <u>gravitational</u> field
              A   B   C
<u>and they also</u> have limited information about its surface composition.
  D

36. The Chinese <u>has settled</u> <u>along</u> the west coast of North America in large numbers, <u>establishing</u>
               A   B   C
their sizable communities <u>from</u> Vancouver to Los Angeles.
                        D

37. <u>Assimilated</u> the <u>early</u> literature of the United States, one <u>must</u> know <u>its</u> history as well.
     A   B   C   D

38. Before and <u>during</u> the Civil War, abolitionists <u>along</u> the border <u>between</u> North and South <u>hided</u>
             A   B   C   D
fugitive slaves.

39. The wings <u>of many butterflies</u> and moths <u>are marked</u> <u>with</u> colors that form <u>a</u> hourglass pattern.
               A   B   C   D

40. The Arctic stratosphere appears <u>susceptibly</u> to <u>pollutants</u> <u>produced</u> <u>thousands of miles</u> to its south.
                                A   B   C   D

THIS IS THE END OF SECTION 2

**IF YOU FINISH BEFORE TIME IS CALLED, CHECK YOUR WORK ON SECTION 2 ONLY.
DO NOT READ OR WORK ON ANY OTHER SECTION OF THE TEST.
THE SUPERVISOR WILL TELL YOU WHEN TO BEGIN WORK ON SECTION 3.**

STOP   STOP   STOP   **STOP**   STOP   STOP   STOP

SECTION 3
VOCABULARY AND READING COMPREHENSION

Time—45 minutes

This section is designed to measure your comprehension of standard written English. There are two types of questions in this section, with special directions for each type.

Directions: In questions 1–30, each sentence has an underlined word or phrase. Below each sentence are four other words or phrases, marked (A), (B), (C), and (D). You are to choose the one word or phrase that best keeps the meaning of the original sentence if it is substituted for the underlined word or phrase. Then, on your answer sheet, find the number of the question and fill in the space that corresponds to the letter you have chosen. Fill in the space so that the letter inside the oval cannot be seen.

Example

Ladybugs, small brightly colored beetles, feed on plant aphids and have considerable economic value in controlling pest populations.
(A) limiting
(B) finding
(C) increasing
(D) ruling

Sample Answer

● Ⓑ Ⓒ Ⓓ

The best answer is (A) because "Ladybugs, small brightly colored beetles, feed on plant aphids and have considerable economic value in limiting pest populations" is closest in meaning to the original sentence. Therefore, you should choose answer (A).

After you read the directions, begin work on the questions.

1. The effects of the Civil War on the economy of the South lasted long after the war ended.
   (A) continued
   (B) were avoided
   (C) occurred
   (D) developed

2. Examination of artifacts in the cliff dwellings of Mesa Verde has led archaeologists to believe that the inhabitants left hastily and never returned.
   (A) quietly
   (B) methodically
   (C) quickly
   (D) thoroughly

3. The number of high school students who use drugs and alcohol has dropped significantly because of widespread substance abuse programs.
   (A) government funded
   (B) instructional
   (C) extensive
   (D) well attended

4. Despite reports to the contrary, affirmative action hiring practices are often challenged in court.
   (A) In addition to
   (B) In spite of
   (C) Because of
   (D) Including

GO ON TO THE NEXT PAGE

5. Large <u>stores</u> of oil located by offshore drilling offer a possible source of energy for the next decade.
   (A) containers
   (B) maps
   (C) deposits
   (D) sites

6. No news <u>pertaining to</u> the upcoming merger will be released before next week.
   (A) delaying
   (B) derogatory to
   (C) upon
   (D) about

7. The American Philosophical Society, the oldest learned society in the United States, is based in Philadelphia, where it was <u>founded</u> by Benjamin Franklin in 1743.
   (A) discovered
   (B) overseen
   (C) established
   (D) supported

8. In some cultures direct eye contact with those in authority is considered rude and <u>defiant</u> behavior.
   (A) unacceptable
   (B) challenging
   (C) submissive
   (D) unlucky

9. White is the <u>conventional</u> color of a wedding gown in the United States.
   (A) traditional
   (B) required
   (C) distinctive
   (D) serviceable

10. Plans for the new model were not <u>sufficiently</u> developed to justify the proposed marketing strategy this year.
    (A) efficiently
    (B) adequately
    (C) positively
    (D) graphically

11. Eye surgeons need to work with <u>precision</u> to remove cataracts from the eye.
    (A) speed
    (B) exactness
    (C) difficulty
    (D) understanding

12. This area of the city has recently been <u>zoned</u> for industrial use.
    (A) mentioned
    (B) suggested
    (C) designated
    (D) prepared

13. Most doctors recommend bed rest for <u>relief</u> of back pain.
    (A) treatment
    (B) medication
    (C) diagnosis
    (D) alleviation

14. Most banks will not allow you to <u>withdraw</u> money for ten days after opening a new account.
    (A) accrue
    (B) transfer
    (C) remove
    (D) initiate

15. <u>Harsh</u> winters in the northern regions of the United States convince many older people to retire in the South.
    (A) Long
    (B) Unpredictable
    (C) Severe
    (D) Monotonous

16. According to the map the two roads <u>intersect</u> five miles south of the town.
    (A) end
    (B) cross
    (C) join
    (D) change

GO ON TO THE NEXT PAGE

17. The judge was known for his impartial and just decisions.
    (A) fair
    (B) thoughtful
    (C) quick
    (D) beneficial

18. John Paul Getty made his fortune in the oil industry during the 1890s.
    (A) reputation
    (B) living
    (C) money
    (D) investment

19. The volume of air traffic at Chicago's O'Hare airport has caused inconvenience for many travelers.
    (A) loudness
    (B) amount
    (C) decrease
    (D) congestion

20. Her quick acquiescence to our demands made us suspicious of her motives.
    (A) acknowledgment of
    (B) agreement to
    (C) dispute with
    (D) rejection of

21. The morbid nature of Edgar Allan Poe's short stories often leaves the reader with a sense of foreboding.
    (A) apprehension
    (B) sadness
    (C) realism
    (D) fancifulness

22. Noise is a feature of city life that some people find distasteful.
    (A) a disadvantage
    (B) a characteristic
    (C) a notion
    (D) an attribute

23. The fashion industry depends on trends and the media to promote sales of new lines of clothing.
    (A) fads
    (B) research
    (C) seasons
    (D) prosperity

24. Industrialization and its impact on the lives of the working class is a social theme in the works of American novelists of the late 19th century.
    (A) collision with
    (B) effect on
    (C) improvement of
    (D) attitude toward

25. Members of the committee were instructed to show temperance in their spending for the holiday party.
    (A) restraint
    (B) accuracy
    (C) ingenuity
    (D) taste

26. The delay in the performance was due to a technical problem with the sound equipment.
    (A) a result of
    (B) a cause of
    (C) incited by
    (D) introduced by

27. The man was a popular guest at parties because of his jovial manner.
    (A) jolly
    (B) courteous
    (C) appreciative
    (D) proper

28. The stormy sea engulfed the small boat and its crew.
    (A) frightened
    (B) threatened
    (C) flooded
    (D) challenged

29. The oncoming recession has made investors wary of any new ventures in the near future.
    (A) sales
    (B) undertakings
    (C) buildings
    (D) inquiries

GO ON TO THE NEXT PAGE

30. Fish are coated with a thin film of mucus
which makes them <u>slippery</u> and difficult
to hold.
(A) slick
(B) unmanageable
(C) rough
(D) fast

<u>Directions:</u> In the rest of this section you will read several passages. Each one is followed by several questions about it. For questions 31–60, you are to choose the <u>one</u> best answer, (A), (B), (C), or (D), to each question. Then, on your answer sheet, find the number of the question and fill in the space that corresponds to the letter of the answer you have chosen.

Answer all questions following a passage on the basis of what is <u>stated</u> or <u>implied</u> in that passage.

Read the following passage:

The flamingo is a beautiful water bird with long legs and a curving neck like a swan's. Most flamingos have deep red or flame-colored feathers with black quills. Some have pink or white feathers. The long legs and webbed feet are well suited for wading. The flamingo
line eats in a peculiar manner. It plunges its head underwater and sifts the mud with a fine
(5) hairlike "comb" along the edge of its bent bill. In this way, it strains out small shellfish and other animals. The bird nests on a mound of mud with a hollow on top to hold its single egg. Flamingos are timid and often live together in large colonies. The birds once lived in the southern United States, but plume hunters killed them faster than they could breed, and the flamingo no longer lives wild in the United States.

Example I   <u>Sample Answer</u>

The flamingo can eat shellfish and other animals because of its   Ⓐ ● Ⓒ Ⓓ
(A) curved neck
(B) specially formed bill
(C) long legs
(D) brightly colored feathers

According to the passage, the flamingo sifts mud for food with "a fine hairlike 'comb' along the edge of its bent bill." Therefore, you should choose answer (B).

Example II   <u>Sample Answer</u>

How many young would you expect the flamingo to raise at one time?   Ⓐ Ⓑ ● Ⓓ
(A) several
(B) two
(C) one
(D) four

The passage states that the flamingo nests on a mound of mud with a "single egg." Therefore, you should choose answer (C).

After you read the directions, begin work on the questions.

GO ON TO THE NEXT PAGE ➡

Questions 31–35

       In recent years evidence has accumulated that polyunsaturated fatty acids function in protecting humans and some laboratory animals from diseases of the arteries and heart such as atherosclerosis. In this disease, small patches of fatty material, composed mostly of
line cholesterol, form on the inside lining of the arteries. As the deposits increase in thickness,
  (5) they may cut down on the blood flow to the organs supplied by the arteries until the structures are severely damaged. If this occurs in a branch of the coronary artery supplying the heart muscle, that portion of the muscle dies and the person experiences a painful and sometimes fatal heart attack. Another danger of atherosclerosis is that pieces of the fatty deposits may break free and travel in the bloodstream until they lodge in small vessels and
(10) block the flow of blood. This blockage may also cause heart damage, or if it occurs in the brain, may damage brain cells and lead to a stroke.

31. What does this passage mainly discuss?
    (A) Atherosclerosis
    (B) Fats
    (C) Cholesterol
    (D) Heart damage

32. The author of the passage describes atherosclerosis as
    (A) a cause of fatty material or cholesterol buildup
    (B) a disease causing heart damage
    (C) a restriction of the flow of blood
    (D) a heart attack

33. According to the passage, the parts of the body most directly affected by cholesterol buildup are
    (A) the brain cells
    (B) the major organs
    (C) the arteries
    (D) the muscles

34. According to the passage, atherosclerosis may cause all of the following EXCEPT
    (A) a stroke
    (B) a heart attack
    (C) blockage of the arteries
    (D) cholesterol breakdown

35. The pronoun 'it' in line 10 refers to
    (A) heart damage
    (B) the flow of blood
    (C) a blockage
    (D) a stroke

GO ON TO THE NEXT PAGE

Questions 36–40

Although most grain crops have light dry pollen and are wind-pollinated, the pollen of other plants including legumes, fruits, and many flowers and vegetables is moist and sticky. It cannot travel on air currents and must be transferred from anther to stigma by external
line agents. This process is known as cross-pollination. Cross-pollination allows plants to evolve
(5) and to adapt to changing environments.

Cross-pollination is accomplished mainly by insects and among pollinators, the honeybee reigns supreme. Bees collect nectar and pollen from flowers to use as food and unwittingly transfer pollen from flower to flower as they go about their work.

A bee's body is ideally adapted to carry pollen. Its body and legs are covered with stiff,
(10) branched hairs, which catch and hold pollen grains. The hind legs are equipped with pollen baskets that are concave areas of the hind leg edged with long curving hairs. In these baskets, the worker bee deposits pollen and carries it back to the hive where it serves as a major food source for the young brood.

As bees are busy gathering pollen, their bodies become almost entirely covered with
(15) sticky pollen grains. Field bees inadvertently transfer pollen from one flower to another as they make their rounds.

36. What is the topic of this passage?
    (A) A description of bees
    (B) Types of pollen
    (C) Cross-pollination by bees
    (D) Sources of pollen

37. According to the passage, cross-pollination may occur in all of the following plants EXCEPT
    (A) legumes
    (B) grain crops
    (C) fruits
    (D) flowers

38. According to the passage, why do bees collect pollen?
    (A) For use as food
    (B) As a complement to nectar
    (C) To help plants evolve and change
    (D) To cover their bodies

39. We can infer from the passage that bees are well suited to collecting pollen because of
    (A) their attraction to flowers
    (B) their ability to fly
    (C) the structure of their bodies
    (D) their ability to work hard

40. The word "It" in line 3 refers to
    (A) light, dry pollen
    (B) a kind of flower
    (C) moist, sticky pollen
    (D) an external agent

GO ON TO THE NEXT PAGE

Questions 41–45

Modern science is an ongoing process. Our body of scientific knowledge is constantly
being revised and updated. The hypotheses being proposed and tested this year will be
line substantiated or disproven over time. New questions are constantly being asked and new
(5) techniques are being developed to answer those questions. Just as the concept of vitalism
(once held as truth by some of the most respected scientists of the time) gave way in the face
of overwhelming evidence to the contrary, so will some of today's ideas fall by the wayside

in the future.

41. What is the author's main purpose in this
passage?
(A) To discuss the inexactness of science
(B) To show that scientific concepts are apt to
change over time
(C) To describe how scientific knowledge
originates
(D) To predict scientific concepts of the future

42. We can infer from the passage that all of the
following are true about vitalism EXCEPT
(A) It is no longer a valid scientific concept
(B) It was highly regarded by scientists at one
time
(C) It was challenged by more convincing
scientific evidence
(D) It was the result of poor scientific research

43. As used in line 3, the word "substantiated"
could best be replaced by
(A) validated
(B) developed
(C) questioned
(D) reviewed

44. As used in line 6, the phrase "fall by the
wayside" could best be replaced by
(A) get lost
(B) be replaced
(C) be misunderstood
(D) be admired

45. Which of the following best describes the
organization the author uses in lines 4–7?
(A) a description
(B) a definition
(C) a comparison
(D) a process

GO ON TO THE NEXT PAGE

Questions 46–52

The trail West was long indeed. From the Missouri River to the West Coast, it ran 2,000-odd zigzag miles, with constant detours for pasture or water. But the distance in miles
line mattered less than the distance in time. It usually took about four and a half months to reach
(5) the Far West, and the trip became a race against the seasons, in which sure timing made the difference between success and failure.

Late April or early May was the best time to get rolling, though the departure date had to be calculated with care. If a wagon train started too early in the spring, there would not be enough grass on the prairie to graze the livestock. Then animals would start to sicken,
(10) slowing up the train and causing alterations of schedule that might bring trouble later. On the other hand, a train that pushed off after other trains were already on the trail found campsites marked by trampled grass and fouled water holes. Worse still, an emigrant company that dallied too long could get trapped at the far end of the journey by early winter blizzards in the coastal mountains. Obviously it was important to get to the departure point on the Missouri at the right moment, and keep pretty close to schedule.

46. What is the main point the author makes in the passage?
   (A) The trail West was very long.
   (B) The spring was the best time to leave for the West.
   (C) Early winter blizzards caused travelers problems.
   (D) The timing of the departure was extremely important for the trip West.

47. We can infer all of the following from the passage about the route to the West EXCEPT that
   (A) it was not direct
   (B) it included many stops
   (C) it required careful planning
   (D) it was a short, easy trip

48. According to the passage all of the following were possible problems for those who departed late EXCEPT
   (A) winter snowstorms in the mountains
   (B) spoiled campsites
   (C) unusable water holes
   (D) losing the way

49. According to the passage, schedules of those who departed early might need to be changed because of
   (A) bad weather
   (B) poor campsites
   (C) lack of pasture for the animals
   (D) broken wagons

50. We can infer from the passage that travelers wanted to reach their destinations
   (A) by fall
   (B) by midsummer
   (C) by late spring
   (D) during the winter

51. According to the passage, the wagon trains departed from
   (A) the West coast
   (B) somewhere along the Missouri River
   (C) the coastal mountains
   (D) the prairie trail

52. As used in line 12, the word "dallied" could best be replaced by
   (A) traveled
   (B) stocked up
   (C) delayed
   (D) grazed

GO ON TO THE NEXT PAGE

Questions 53–60

Beginning about 1670, on the stormy, windswept peninsula of Cape Cod, a local dwelling type developed that became a continuing feature of the landscape into the nineteenth *line* century and beyond. Inhabitants of small fishing villages transformed the one-room-and-loft (5) house of the Pilgrims into snug, ship-shape cottages. Generally facing south to catch the winter sun, and nestled against a hill for protection against the hostile elements, the structures rested on wooded sills without foundations in order to ride the shifting sands the same way that schooners rode the waves. If a site happened to blow away, the sturdy house could be trundled across the dunes, or even floated to a new location. A recognizable type (10) by the late 1700s, the Cape Cod cottage persisted with minor variations through the first half of the 1800s. Newlyweds commonly erected a three-quarter house, intending to enlarge it with the arrival of children. Thrifty families occasionally built double houses in order to share an end wall. Some cottages sported bowed or gambrel roofs, and details that reflected the influences of the Federal and Greek Revival styles. The era of the authentic Cape Cod (15) cottage ended around 1850 when the advent of the stove eliminated the massive chimney block that had previously anchored the house to its site. At that time, homebuilders also had to import precut lumber from Maine. Thoreau explained the reason, "The old houses...are built of the timber of the Cape, but instead of the forest in the midst of which they originally stood, barren heaths...now stretch away on every side."

53. The best title for this passage is
(A) The Cape Cod House: A Type of Early American Dwelling
(B) The Importance of Location to Early Builders
(C) The Usefulness of the Cape Cod House
(D) The Ingenuity of American Builders

54. According to the passage, when did the Cape Cod house first appear?
(A) In the late 1600s
(B) In the 1700s
(C) In the 1800s
(D) In 1850

55. The author of the passage states that the early Cape Cod house was built without foundations in order to
(A) keep the cost of building low
(B) increase the mobility of the house
(C) replicate a sailing ship

(D) better withstand the winter cold

56. It can be inferred from the passage that a precursor of the Cape Cod cottage was
(A) Federal Style houses
(B) Greek Revival houses
(C) loft houses of the Pilgrims
(D) schooners of the North Atlantic

57. As used in line 8 the word "trundled" can best be replaced by
(A) rebuilt
(B) moved
(C) redesigned
(D) enlarged

58. According to the passage, what was the effect of the appearance of stoves in Cape Cod cottages?
(A) Heating was more expensive
(B) The large chimney block was no longer needed
(C) New roofs were designed
(D) Houses were more sturdily built

GO ON TO THE NEXT PAGE

59. Thoreau's quotation in lines 16–18 commented on
    (A) the depletion of natural resources
    (B) the excellence of the original construction material
    (C) the need for more open land
    (D) the growing economy of Maine

60. The author indicates that the era of the authentic Cape Cod house ended in part due to which of the following reasons
    (A) Windstorms on the sandy house sites
    (B) Lack of local building material
    (C) Larger families in need of larger houses
    (D) The growing influence of newer architectural styles

THIS IS THE END OF SECTION 3

**IF YOU FINISH BEFORE TIME IS CALLED
CHECK YOUR WORK ON SECTION 3 ONLY.
DO NOT READ OR WORK ON ANY OTHER SECTION OF THE TEST.**

STOP   STOP   STOP   STOP   STOP   STOP   STOP

LISTENING COMPREHENSION

The purpose of Section One of the TOEFL is to test your understanding of spoken North American English. Vocabulary, spoken structures, and English sounds and intonation are tested. For the most part, topics used in this section are informal and conversational. Some general academic topics are used in the short lecture segments of this section. Even in these topics, however, the language is not as formal as that used in written English.

GENERAL STRATEGIES FOR SECTION ONE

1. Be familiar with Section One instructions before you take the official TOEFL. Then, during the test, you do not have to listen to all of the instructions. Listen only long enough to familiarize yourself with the voices on the tape. Be sure you can hear the tape loudly and clearly. Look ahead at answers that appear on the page. Think about what each question may be about. **DO NOT turn the page to look ahead while the instructions for Section One are being read.**

2. Listen carefully for meaning in statements, dialogues, and talks. Concentrate on trying to understand the overall meaning.

3. Use your time wisely. You have only 12 seconds to answer each question in Section One of the test.

Listening Comprehension: Question Types

Section One contains 50 questions. The questions and the information you need to answer them are played for you on a tape. Only the answer choices for the questions are printed in the TOEFL test booklet. All Section One questions are spoken just one time. You are allowed 12 seconds to answer each question. It takes approximately 40 minutes to complete this section of the test.

There are three parts in Section One of the TOEFL.

Part A: **Restatements** (20 questions)
You choose the correct printed restatement of a spoken sentence.

Part B: **Mini-Dialogues** (15 questions)
You choose the correct printed answer to a spoken question based on a very short spoken dialogue.

Part C: **Talks and Longer Conversations** (15 questions)
You choose the correct printed answers to a series of questions about a longer spoken dialogue between two speakers or a talk given by one speaker.

Each part of Section One is treated separately in the listening checkpoint studies beginning on page 45. A Listening Comprehension Section Test follows these checkpoint studies. This test should be taken after you have studied the listening checkpoints.

Listening Comprehension: Vocabulary

Everyday vocabulary is tested in all three parts of Section One of the TOEFL. This vocabulary includes words in two major categories: (1) school and college life, and (2) daily life.

Vocabulary in these categories can be found in the Listening Appendix #1, page 428. These are words that you are likely to hear on the TOEFL. You should familiarize yourself with these words. If you do not know the definition of a word, you should look it up in a dictionary. The Listening Appendix contains a list of recommended dictionaries.

The Listening Appendix also provides blank spaces to write new words as you hear or read them.

Another type of vocabulary tested in Section One of the TOEFL is idioms. An idiom is a word or an expression which has a special meaning. The meaning is often difficult to predict by looking at only the word or words in the idiom. All the idioms tested in Section One of the TOEFL are conversational idioms—common idioms you hear in informal spoken English.

I've been *knocking myself out* on this paper.

In this sentence, the idiom *to knock oneself out* means *to work very hard at something*. You cannot understand the meaning of this idiom by only knowing the literal meaning of *knock* (to hit or tap) or *knock out* (to render unconscious by hitting). The total meaning of this expression must be memorized or learned by listening to English, NOT by defining the individual words of the idiom.

Spoken idioms are tested extensively in Part A and Part B of Section One of the TOEFL. There are thousands of idioms in English. To help you learn some of them, each spoken idiom used in the listening comprehension checkpoint studies, as well as in the diagnostic and practice section tests, is printed in bold italics (e.g., *knocking myself out*) the first time it is used. The idiom will also be listed in the Glossary of Idioms in the Listening Appendix, #2, page 432. You can refer to this appendix if you do not understand the idioms used in the listening comprehension checkpoint studies.

Learning the idioms used in the listening comprehension checkpoint studies will greatly improve your chances for success on the TOEFL. However, it is important to learn other idioms as well. One way to do this is to listen to native speakers of North American English as much as possible. They will often use idioms in their spoken English.

If you are unable to listen to native speakers of North American English, you can still learn idioms. There are several excellent books available to help you with this. See the Listening Appendix for a list of recommended books on idioms.

The systematic study of common vocabulary and idioms will develop your overall mastery of spoken English. The listening comprehension checkpoint studies will help you master the specific listening skills tested on the TOEFL. These two types of study combined will greatly increase your chances for TOEFL success.

Listening Comprehension
Part A: Restatements

The Part A questions in Section One of the TOEFL measure your ability to understand spoken English sentences. For each question in Part A, you hear a sentence. After you hear the sentence, read the four answer choices in the test book and choose the one that is closest in meaning to the sentence you heard.

The test uses three types of sentences: declaratives, exclamations, and questions. When written, each type of sentence uses different punctuation. A written declarative sentence is a statement followed by a period (.). A written exclamation is an emotional statement followed by an exclamation point (!). A written question is followed by a question mark (?). Most of the sentences you hear in this part are declarative sentences.

There are 20 restatement questions in Part A of the TOEFL. You hear each sentence one time. You have 12 seconds to read four answer choices and choose the one that best restates the meaning of the sentence you heard. The best restatement is the answer choice that is closest in meaning to the sentence that you heard.

MODEL

You will hear:
   Larry doesn't *get along with* Dave.

You will read:
   (A)   Larry and Dave aren't going.
   (B)   The days are getting long.
   (C)   Larry and Dave are good friends.
   (D)   Larry disagrees with Dave.

Answer:

▼ Explanation ▲

In this question, you hear a statement containing the idiom, *to get along with*. This idiom means *to agree with* or *to cooperate with*. This question also contains the negative contraction, *doesn't*, which gives the statement a negative meaning.

The incorrect answer choices for this question contain sounds, vocabulary, and/or spoken structures which can be confusing.

Answer (A) contains the phrase *aren't going*, which seems close in meaning to *doesn't get along with*. You might choose this answer if you do not know the meaning of the idiom *get along with*. Answer (B) contains the phrase *getting long*, which sounds very much like *get along*, and the word *days*, which sounds very much like *Dave*. You might choose this answer if you did not correctly hear and understand the sounds in the spoken sentence. Answer (C) has the opposite meaning of the spoken sentence. You might choose this answer if you did not hear and understand the negative spoken structure in the spoken sentence. Answer (D) is the correct answer to the question even though it is different in vocabulary, sound, and structure. It is the only answer choice which restates the meaning of the spoken sentence.

RESTATEMENT STRATEGIES

1. QUICKLY look ahead at the restatement answer choices while the instructions are read. Look for key words in the answers that help you to understand the overall meaning of each answer choice. This will help you match the meaning of the spoken sentences with the meaning of the restatements. **DO NOT turn the page.**

2. Be careful of vocabulary. Words with more than one meaning will be tested in Section One of the TOEFL. Listen for idioms. See checkpoints L✔1 through L✔3 for practice.

3. Be careful of sounds. Look for sound-alikes in the restatement answer choices. Do not be tricked by words and expressions which sound like those in the spoken sentences but which are different in meaning. See L✔4 for practice.

4. Listen carefully to the intonation and stress of each spoken sentence. Intonation and stress have meaning in English. They can be used to show strong emotion or even to change a statement into a question. See L✔5 and L✔6 for practice.

5. Be careful of spoken structures. Listen carefully for tricky spoken structures such as contractions, negatives, causative verbs, conditions, tag questions, modals, passives, and relationship signals. See L✔7 through L✔10 for practice.

6. Guess if you don't know the answer to a question. Choose the answer that sounds LEAST like the spoken sentence. This answer is often the correct answer.

7. Use the extra time between questions to look ahead at the answer choices. Look for key words and key word synonyms in the answer choices. Try to understand the overall meaning of the answer choices. This will help you to match the meaning of the sentence you hear with the correct written restatement.

✔ RESTATEMENT CHECKPOINTS

Below is a list of the Restatement Checkpoints covered in the Restatement Checkpoint Study. Page numbers are provided for your reference. If the Diagnostic Test on pages 19–41 indicated that Listening Comprehension was your weak area, you should begin your TOEFL study with these checkpoints.

While you should give special attention to the Restatement Checkpoints if Part A was your weak listening area, we recommend that you review all of the listening checkpoints in this book.

This study ends with a Restatement Checkpoint Test.

✔ RESTATEMENT CHECKPOINT STUDY

L✔1   Check Key Words and Key Word Synonyms

The English sentences you hear in Part A of Section One of the TOEFL all contain key words. Key words are important words in the sentence that give you an overall understanding of the statement. Listen carefully for key words in the spoken sentences.

In addition, look for repeated words and their synonyms in the printed answer choices for Part A questions. These words are also key words because they usually relate to the key meaning in the spoken sentences. Listening for key words in spoken sentences helps you match spoken sentences with their restatements. Looking ahead for repeated key words and their synonyms in answer choices helps you to predict the general meaning of each sentence you hear.

MODEL

You will hear:
   Peter wrote this composition for his history class.

You will read:
   (A) This class was for Peter.
   (B) Peter composed this essay for a course.
   (C) Peter's taking this composition to class.
   (D) Peter is not interested in his composition course.

Answer:

▼ Explanation ▲

In this question, the key words *Peter, wrote, composition,* and *class* give you important information about the overall meaning of the sentence. All four answer choices for this question contain the key word *Peter*. However, only answer (B) contains key word synonyms for *wrote, composition,* and *class*. These words are *composed, essay,* and *course*. Answer (B) is the correct answer.

☞ ON THE TOEFL TEST

- Listen for the key words in the spoken sentences in TOEFL questions.
- Check ahead for repeated words and their synonyms in answer choices so that you can predict spoken sentences before you hear them.

EXERCISE 1A: Practice with Key Words and Key Word Synonyms

In each of the sentences below, two key words are underlined. Write a restatement for each sentence. Use key word synonyms for the underlined key words.

1. I will <u>make</u> a cake for <u>supper</u>.

    I will bake a cake for dinner.

2. The laboratory is <u>closed</u> this <u>evening</u>.

3. Students always <u>enjoy</u> this <u>course</u>.

4. I <u>misplaced</u> the <u>snapshots</u> of Denmark.

5. We <u>mailed</u> the <u>box</u> to Laurie.

6. Harvey was <u>hurt</u> in the <u>crash</u>.

7. The <u>carpet</u> in this room is <u>dirty</u>.

8. Gary <u>completed</u> his <u>test</u> early.

9. I didn't really <u>understand</u> the <u>lecture</u>.

10. The <u>teacher</u> of this course <u>requires</u> a lot of work.

11. Rick has been <u>sick</u> a lot <u>lately</u>.

EXERCISE 1B: **Practice Predicting Key Meanings**

Each of the four answer choices contains key words. *Quickly* underline the repeated words and synonyms that appear in the four answer choices. Then use these key words to predict the topic. Write your prediction on the line beneath each set of answer choices.

1. (A) Jane is at the library studying for the test.
   (B) Jane thinks the library is a good place to study.
   (C) Jane took the exam in the library.
   (D) We should go to the library to find Jane.

   Probable topic: _____ *Jane studying at the library* _____

2. (A) I didn't have time to eat.
   (B) I needed some dinner.
   (C) I couldn't eat all of my dinner.
   (D) Please let me eat the rest of my dinner.

   Probable topic: _____

3. (A) We attempted the ascent.
   (B) We tried to solve the crime.
   (C) The climb was easy for us.
   (D) We tried to climb over the wall.

   Probable topic: _____

4. (A) Clarence just got some gifts that are cheap.
   (B) Clarence gave Judy a costly present.
   (C) Judy's gift for Clarence was expensive.
   (D) Judy doesn't like expensive presents.

   Probable topic: _____

5. (A) Jim knows a talented painter.
   (B) Jim gave his painting to the gallery.
   (C) Jim is a gifted artist.
   (D) Jim has many paintings.

   Probable topic: _____

6. (A) She moved her purse.
   (B) She needed some change.
   (C) I paid her for the purse.
   (D) The money is in her bag.

   Probable topic: _____

EXERCISE 1C: **Tape Practice Predicting Key Meanings**

Using the tape, now listen to the spoken sentences for Exercise 1B. Keep in mind the written predictions you made about these sentences. Circle the letter of the answer choice that is closest in meaning to the sentence you heard.

L✔2   Check Idioms

Idioms are tested extensively in Section One of the TOEFL. (See page 49.) In Part A questions, idioms are often included in the sentences you hear. When you hear an idiom used in a sentence, you must look for the best restatement of the meaning in the printed answer choices. Incorrect answer choices often contain the literal or non-idiomatic meaning of idioms.

MODEL

You will hear:
    Jane *had a hand in* this mess.

You will read:
    (A)   Jane's job is messy.
    (B)   Jane is partly responsible for this situation.
    (C)   Jane put her hand in the dirt.
    (D)   Jane applauded.

Answer:

▼ Explanation ▲

In this question, the meaning of the idiom *to have a hand in* is being tested. Answer (A) contains a form of the key word *messy*, but it does not contain a restatement of the idiom. Answer (C) contains a literal (non-idiomatic) restatement of the meaning of the individual parts of the idiom. However, the meaning of an idiom cannot be understood by understanding its parts. Answer (D) restates the meaning of a different idiom, *to give a hand*, which sometimes means *to applaud*. Answer (B) is the correct answer to the question. It is the only answer that contains an accurate restatement of the meaning of the idiom *to have a hand in*. This idiom means *to be partly responsible for*.

☛ ON THE TOEFL TEST

- Listen for idioms in TOEFL questions.
- Beware of restatements which contain the literal meaning of idiom parts.

See the Listening Appendix #2, page 432 for a glossary of the idioms used in this chapter.
See the Grammar Appendix #24, page 451 for a list of verb and preposition combinations which often have idiomatic meaning.

EXERCISE 2A: Understanding Idiomatic Expressions

A literal definition and an idiomatic meaning are given for each expression. Read the expression. Circle the letter of the phrase listed below that is the idiomatic meaning of the expression.

1. *to hit the nail on the head*
   (A) to pound the nail on its top
   (B) to be right about something

2. *to look on the bright side*
   (A) to see the side that is bright or lit by the sun
   (B) to be optimistic

3. *on the side*
   (A) in addition to a main thing
   (B) beside or next to

4. *on the whole*
   (A) on top of the entire thing
   (B) in most ways

5. *can of worms*
   (A) container full of bugs
   (B) complex problem

6. *to get off the ground*
   (A) to make a successful beginning
   (B) to leave the earth

7. *ball of fire*
   (A) person with great energy
   (B) globe of flames

8. *to be short*
   (A) not to have enough
   (B) not to be tall

9. *to be tied up*
   (A) to be busy
   (B) to be secured with a rope

10. *to blow the whistle*
    (A) to breathe heavily into a whistle until it makes a loud sound
    (B) to tell secret information about

11. *to pull someone's leg*
    (A) to grab someone's leg
    (B) to tease someone

EXERCISE 2B: Idiomatic and Literal Expressions

Put an **I** on the line in front of each sentence which uses an expression as an idiom. Put an **L** on the line in front of each sentence which uses an expression literally.

_____ 1. The president *hit the nail on the head* with his analysis of our budget problems.

_____ 2. Jane always seems happy. She really knows how to *look on the bright side* of things.

_____ 3. There was a big scratch *on the side* of his new car.

_____ 4. *On the whole*, Clark has done well in school.

_____ 5. The young boy gathered up his fishing pole and his *can of worms* and headed off to the lake.

_____ 6. The airplane couldn't *get off the ground* because of the bad weather.

_____ 7. Peter is a real *ball of fire*.

_____ 8. The police officer *blew the whistle* to stop the cars.

_____ 9. Grace *is short* three cups of sugar, so she can't bake the cake.

_____ 10. The horse *was tied up* at the corral so he wouldn't run away.

_____ 11. I thought Jake was serious, but he was only *pulling my leg*.

EXERCISE 2C: 🎞 Tape Practice with Idioms

Circle the letter of the sentence that is closest in meaning to the sentence you hear on the tape.

1. (A) I am having trouble holding on to Janet.
   (B) Janet is holding a meeting this week.
   (C) I have been unable to contact Janet.
   (D) Janet is getting four weeks vacation.

2. (A) John stopped to buy this in the afternoon.
   (B) I think John will visit me today.
   (C) I will stop waiting for John.
   (D) John is hoping to stop before the end of the day.

3. (A) They can't make anything to take to the dinner.
   (B) They are afraid of going to the dinner.
   (C) They might not be able to go to the dinner tonight.
   (D) They fear they will be late to tonight's dinner.

4. (A) We were unable to do what we had planned because it started raining.
   (B) We slipped and fell through the ice when it started to melt in the rain.
   (C) We planned to take our ski trip in spite of the rain.
   (D) We weren't through skiing when it started to rain.

5. (A) I scratched my eye on the necklace.
   (B) It hurt my eyes to look at the diamond necklace.
   (C) I didn't like looking at the diamond necklace.
   (D) That diamond necklace really attracted my attention.

6. (A) I don't take care of my new bike.
   (B) It doesn't bother me if you borrow my new bike.
   (C) I don't really like my new bike very much.
   (D) My new bike doesn't need much maintenance.

7. (A) You should write this information down.
   (B) Don't forget this information.
   (C) Please don't give anyone else this information.
   (D) You can have this information yourself.

8. (A) The house needs to be put in order.
   (B) We need to straighten the structure of the house.
   (C) The house really stands straight up.
   (D) Let's move out of the house.

9. (A) We never look at each other.
   (B) We never agree with one another.
   (C) Neither one of us sees very well.
   (D) We haven't been together for a long time.

10. (A) Roger came for me at my house and took me to the hospital.
    (B) Roger carried me from my house to the hospital.
    (C) Roger drove to the hospital in his truck.
    (D) Roger chose me to work with him at the hospital.

11. (A) Marsha is learning how to make ropes where she works.
    (B) Marsha is learning what to do at her new job.
    (C) Marsha feels uncomfortable where she works.
    (D) All of Marsha's work is tied up.

L✔3   Check Words with Many Meanings

Some English words have only one meaning and one function. Many, however, have several functions and many meanings. Look at the following examples:

I would like to buy a new winter *coat*.
This wall needs a second *coat* of paint.
She *coated* her ice cream with chocolate syrup.

In the first sentence above, *coat* is a noun meaning *a heavy jacket worn over other clothing*.
In the second sentence above, *coat* is a noun meaning *layer*.
In the third sentence above, *coat* is a verb meaning *to cover* or *to layer*.

In Part A of Section One of the TOEFL, words with many meanings are used. In a spoken sentence, you will often hear a key word having one meaning. Then, in the written answer choices, you may see the same word used again, but it will have a different meaning. Answer choices containing words with many meanings are usually not the correct answers. You should be careful not to be tricked by words with many meanings.

MODEL

You will hear:
    Jack runs his father's office for him.

You will read:
    (A)   Jack runs to his father's office.
    (B)   Jack's father is running for a public office.
    (C)   Jack manages his father's office.
    (D)   Jack is running away from his father's office.

Answer:

▼ Explanation ▲

In this question, the many meanings of *run* and *office* are being tested. In the sentence you hear, *runs* means *manages,* and *office* means *place of work*. In answer (A), *runs* means *goes faster than a walk*. In answer (B), *is running* means *is trying to win a political race*, and *office* means *political position*. In answer (D), *running* is combined with *away* to mean *leaving without permission*. Answer (C) is the correct answer to this question. It replaces *runs* with *manages*, and *office* has the same meaning as it does in the statement you hear.

☛ ON THE TOEFL TEST

• Check for words with many meanings in TOEFL questions.

EXERCISE 3A: Words with Many Meanings

On the lines provided write at least two different meanings for each word listed below. Use your dictionary if necessary.

2. light ___*month, day, year*___   ___*go out with*___

2. light _____   _____

3. just _____   _____

4. box _____   _____

5. mean _____   _____

6. finish _____   _____

EXERCISE 3B: **Tape Practice with Words with Many Meanings**

Listen to the sentences containing the key words given. Then circle the letter of the word or phrase that has the same meaning as the key word you heard in the sentence.

1. **clear**
   (A) cloudless
   (B) obvious
   (C) approve
   (D) intelligible

2. **band**
   (A) stripe
   (B) orchestra
   (C) gather
   (D) assembly

3. **park**
   (A) garden
   (B) playground
   (C) leave in a place
   (D) boulevard

4. **following**
   (A) audience
   (B) according to
   (C) after
   (D) admirers

5. **major**
   (A) field of study
   (B) important
   (C) officer
   (D) urgent

6. **copy**
   (A) imitate
   (B) replica
   (C) forge
   (D) manuscript

7. **class**
   (A) category
   (B) course
   (C) elegance
   (D) school group

8. **see**
   (A) meet
   (B) understand
   (C) perceive
   (D) inspect

9. **course**
   (A) route
   (B) sequence
   (C) flow
   (D) class

10. **plain**
    (A) modest
    (B) obvious
    (C) prairie
    (D) unattractive

11. **trip**
    (A) expedition
    (B) stumble
    (C) activate
    (D) blunder

12. **show**
    (A) exhibition
    (B) performance
    (C) reveal to
    (D) explain to

EXERCISE 3C: More Tape Practice with Words with Many Meanings

Read the four answer choices in each question set. Listen to each sentence on the tape. Circle the letter of the sentence that is closest in meaning to the sentence you hear on the tape.

1. (A) Please check this for me.
   (B) May I please have money in exchange for this check.
   (C) I will put a check next to each incorrect answer.
   (D) I will not be able to pay with cash.

2. (A) He found a lovely source of water at the bottom of the hill.
   (B) He hurt his foot this spring while running down the hill.
   (C) It has been a beautiful spring for him.
   (D) He accidentally uncovered a beautiful spring with his foot.

3. (A) Clara wears as much makeup as possible to work every day.
   (B) It will not be possible for Clara to come to work today.
   (C) Clara will make it upstairs to work as soon as she can.
   (D) Clara wants to do the work she missed right away.

4. (A) Andrew wasn't sure what to call you.
   (B) You didn't answer when Andrew telephoned last night.
   (C) Andrew visited you last night but you weren't home.
   (D) The man you met last night is called Andrew.

5. (A) This restaurant is for people with money.
   (B) This restaurant is beautifully decorated.
   (C) They serve very rich food at this restaurant.
   (D) The owners of this restaurant are rich.

6. (A) John is associated with me on this project.
   (B) It is difficult for me to associate with John.
   (C) My colleague has been working with John.
   (D) John's project is related to mine.

L✔4   Check Sound-Alikes

There are many words in English that sound almost the same. These sound-alikes include minimal pairs, numbers, and longer sound-alikes.

Some sound-alikes are separated by only one difference in sound. Words which differ by only one sound are called minimal pairs.

*t*all	*b*all
b*i*t	b*ea*t
pi*ck*	pi*t*

The different sound in a minimal pair can occur at the beginning of a word (as in *tall/ball*). It can also occur in the middle of a word (as in *bit/beat*) or at the end of a word (as in *pick/pit*). Although minimal pairs differ by only one sound, they usually differ a great deal in meaning. If you cannot hear minimal pair sound differences, you will be confused about the meanings of English sentences.

Many English numbers are also sound-alikes.

four   forty   fourteen

Four has one syllable. *Forty* and *fourteen* have two syllables. *Forty* receives stress on its first syllable. *Fourteen* receives stress on its second syllable. If you cannot hear these syllable and stress differences, you can be confused about the meanings of English sentences.

first   fourth   fifth

These three numbers all begin with the same sound. If you cannot hear the difference in their endings, you might be confused about the meanings of English sentences.

Longer English phrases also can be sound-alikes.

reception   exception
make a mistake   bake a cake
clearing out the store   cleaning up the floor

The first set of longer sound-alikes above consists of two long words. The second two sets consist of phrases including minimal pairs (*bake/make*) as well as other similar sounding words and phrases (*clearing/cleaning*, *a cake/mistake* and *the floor/the store*). If you cannot hear the differences in these longer sound-alikes, you might be confused about the meanings of English sentences.

The TOEFL tests your ability to distinguish between sound-alikes. Often the answer that sounds the LEAST like the spoken sentence is the correct answer in TOEFL questions.

MODEL

You will hear:
    Their thirty-year-old son is living with his father.

You will read:
    (A)   Their son, who is thirteen years old, is leaving his father's.
    (B)   The child who is thirty years old stays with his dad.
    (C)   Their thirty-year-old son will go a little farther.
    (D)   The third son lives with his father.

Answer:

▼ **Explanation** ▲

In this question, several sound-alikes are used. Answer (A) contains the number *thirteen*, which sounds like *thirty*. It also contains *leaving his father's*, which sounds like *living with his father*. Answer (C) contains *farther*, which sounds like *father*. Answer (D) contains *third*, which sounds like *thirty*. Answer (B) is the correct answer to the question even though it sounds the least like the spoken sentence.

☞ **ON THE TOEFL TEST**

• Check for sound-alikes in TOEFL questions.

EXERCISE 4A: 🎞️ Tape Practice with Minimal Pairs

Listen to the sentences on the tape. For each sentence, circle the word you hear.

1. (pest)   past

2. gold   cold

3. watched   washed

4. yam   jam

5. breed   bred

6. far   fair

7. whale   hail

8. west   vest

9. fan   van

10. folding   holding

11. tense   tenth

EXERCISE 4B: 🎞️ Tape Practice with Sound-Alike Numbers

Listen to the sentence. Write the number you hear on the blank line provided.

1. Last week I saw her for the ____4th____ time this year.

2. I wish they'd spend their _____ anniversary here with us.

3. It took _____ days to drive to Los Angeles.

4. This is the _____ year of professional basketball.

5. _____ children came running around the corner.

6. I can't help wondering who won _____ place.

7. The _____ members of the executive board made this decision.

8. There were _____ new students at the meeting.

9. Her new address is _____ Maple Street.

10. The _____ person to call this number will win a prize.

11. I have _____ friends in Chicago.

EXERCISE 4C: Tape Practice with Longer Sound-Alikes

Listen to each pair of sentences. As you listen, underline the parts of the sentences that sound alike but are different in meaning.

1. (A) I like your new coat.
   (B) My bike's down the road.

2. (A) The music in this country is expressive.
   (B) On the contrary, this is excessive.

3. (A) I use it to cream the butter.
   (B) I used to clean for my mother.

4. (A) The corporation chief disapproved of the explanation.
   (B) The cooperation of the chef fulfilled our expectations.

5. (A) Today I had to work for awhile after school.
   (B) Every day I walk a mile by the pool.

6. (A) Grandmother made a big steak last night.
   (B) Our mother made a mistake yesterday.

7. (A) The sensitive child gave his mother a rose.
   (B) The sensible man covers his nose in the cold.

8. (A) The light of the candle was behind you.
   (B) The bright sun at an angle can blind you.

9. (A) My sunny room faces west.
   (B) My son's new room is the best.

10. (A) He was last seen eating pie and apples at the lake.
    (B) We make a fast and easy pineapple cake.

11. (A) The young man returned later on.
    (B) John can turn the light on.

EXERCISE 4D: Tape Practice with Sound-Alikes

Circle the letter of the sentence that is closest in meaning to the sentence you hear on the tape.

1. (A) We *took a seat* by the door.
   (B) We looked for it on the floor.
   (C) We have seen that before.
   (D) We sat down on the floor.

2. (A) They tried very hard to leave that place.
   (B) They hid the rest in another place.
   (C) They tried very hard to win the competition.
   (D) They did the rest before the race.

3. (A) The crew had its own barber.
   (B) The boat left the harbor.
   (C) The barber sailed out on the cruise.
   (D) They took their sheep to the harbor.

4. (A) The preacher was shocked when he opened the door.
   (B) The teacher found chalk when she opened the drawer.
   (C) Each of her talks was behind closed doors.
   (D) The teacher was shocked when she opened the drawer.

5. (A) You can borrow my book, but I must have it back.
   (B) You can borrow his story, but you can't keep it.
   (C) I'll send you his story about the thirsty man.
   (D) You can borrow my book on Thursday.

6. (A) I have an elderly cousin who gets up precisely at 6:15 A.M.
   (B) My young cousin gets up each day at exactly 6:50 A.M.
   (C) My eighteen-year-old cousin nicely gets up each day at 6:15 A.M.
   (D) My eighty-year-old cousin gets up every day at 6:50 A.M.

7. (A) Tomorrow Anne is going to the neighbor's to bake.
   (B) Anne is with her neighbor at the lake.
   (C) Anne has gone to the neighbor's to borrow a garden tool.
   (D) Anne is going to her neighbor's lake tomorrow.

8. (A) On Sundays, I see him walking in the garden.
   (B) On Sundays, he works in the garden.
   (C) He works for the Gardiners some days.
   (D) Some days I see him walking in the garden.

9. (A) I troubled my aunt for tea a lot before I returned.
   (B) I had a lot of trouble with my aunt when I was fourteen.
   (C) I traveled a lot with my aunt before I was fourteen.
   (D) My aunt and I took a lot of trips together before I was forty.

10. (A) She wants advancement.
    (B) She lives by the ocean near here.
    (C) She doesn't like the motion here.
    (D) She'll soon hear about her promotion.

11. (A) Bill gets by at the store.
    (B) Bill got a good buy at the store.
    (C) We filled the safe by the door.
    (D) Bill bid us farewell at the entrance.

L✔5   Check Exclamations

One sentence type that is commonly used in spoken English is the exclamation. Exclamations are sentences which express strong emotion, such as pleasure, disbelief, excitement, anticipation, enthusiasm, and displeasure.

An exclamation can occur in the following forms.

1. What (+ adjective) + noun (+ subject + verb)!
   What   a beautiful   day   it   is!
        (It is a very beautiful day.)

   What   a day!

2. How + adjective/ + adverb (+ subject + verb)!
   How   beautiful   it   is!
        (It is really beautiful.)

   How beautiful!

Exclamations occurring in these two forms are accompanied by strong stresses.

Another type of exclamation can occur when a regular statement or question is given special stress and intonation.

    Is   this   good?

    Is | this | good!

Both sentences have the same form as a question. However, the second sentence in this pair does not function as a true question. It functions as an exclamation which expresses a strong emotion—pleasure.

    I'm *looking forward* to seeing him.

    I'm looking | forward | to | seeing \ him!

Both sentences have the same form as a statement. However, the second sentence in this pair does not function as only a single statement of fact. It functions as an exclamation which expresses strong emotions—excitement and anticipation.

The TOEFL tests your ability to recognize exclamations.

MODEL

You will hear:
   How could you do that!

You will read:
   (A)   How were you able to do that?
   (B)   How often did you do that?
   (C)   You do that very well.
   (D)   That wasn't a wise thing to do.

Answer:

▼ Explanation ▲

In the spoken sentence, a question form is being used as an exclamation. Answer (A) contains a restatement of the question form, but not of its exclamatory meaning. Answer (B) asks *how often* rather than *how.* Answer (C) contains parts of the spoken statement, but it also contains *very well,* which is not part of the meaning of the spoken sentence. Answer (D) is the correct answer to the question because it is the only answer which restates the exclamatory meaning of the spoken sentence.

```
┌─────────────────────────────────────────────────────────────┐
│                    ☛ ON THE TOEFL TEST                        │
├─────────────────────────────────────────────────────────────┤
│  • Listen carefully for exclamations in TOEFL questions.      │
└─────────────────────────────────────────────────────────────┘
```

EXERCISE 5A: Tape Practice with Exclamations

Listen to each exclamation. Write it on the first blank line. Then write a restatement for each exclamation on the second blank line. Stop the tape after each question to allow yourself extra time to write.

1. _How lovely she looks in that dress!_

She looks very lovely in that dress.

2. _____

_____

3. _____

_____

4. _____

_____

5. _____

_____

6. _____

_____

EXERCISE 5B: Tape Practice with Questions, Declarative Statements, and Exclamations

Listen to the sentence pairs. At the end of each sentence, write a period (.) if it makes a statement, a question mark (?) if it asks a question, and an exclamation point (!) if it is an exclamation.

1. (A) What do you mean ___?___
   (B) What do you mean ___!___

2. (A) Has this been difficult _____
   (B) Has this been difficult _____

3. (A) I can't believe he's a thief _____
   (B) I can't believe he's a thief _____

4. (A) What are you doing that for _____
   (B) What are you doing that for _____

5. (A) I'm tired _____
   (B) I'm tired _____

6. (A) Doesn't this poetry inspire you _____
   (B) Doesn't this poetry inspire you _____

EXERCISE 5C: More Tape Practice with Questions, Declarative Statements, and Exclamations

Listen to each sentence. At the end of each sentence, write a period (.) if it makes a statement, a question mark (?) if it asks a question, and an exclamation point (!) if it is an exclamation.

1. We need a new tire __!___

2. Have you ever seen this many people before _____

3. Rita could be in France by now _____

4. Hasn't the seminar been good _____

5. What could he want _____

6. She likes raw fish _____

EXERCISE 5D: Tape Practice with Exclamations

Circle the letter of the sentence that is closest in meaning to the sentence you hear on the tape.

1. (A) She looks very tired.
   (B) She needs to change the tire.
   (C) She's looking for a tire.
   (D) How can she be tired?

2. (A) What day is this?
   (B) This has been quite a day.
   (C) What do you want to do today?
   (D) How are you today?

3. (A) I'd like to take a vacation.
   (B) Have you had a good vacation?
   (C) This has been a wonderful vacation.
   (D) When shall we take our vacation?

4. (A) You'll have to wait to see me.
   (B) I won't be able to wait until you arrive.
   (C) I'm very excited about seeing you.
   (D) Shall I wait for you?

5. (A) He certainly is tall.
   (B) Did he call?
   (C) How tall is he?
   (D) He finally called.

6. (A) Did you build this house?
   (B) Is this house well-built?
   (C) When was this house built?
   (D) This house certainly is well-constructed.

L✔6   Check Question Intonation

Questions in English are normally asked using question forms, in which the subject and the verb of the sentence change places (V+S). Sometimes, however, questions are asked using regular declarative statement forms, in which the subject comes before the verb in the sentence (S+V). When questions are asked using declarative forms, these forms end with a rising, question intonation. This question intonation tells you that what you hear is a question and not a statement.

He wants to go.   (a statement telling what he wants to do)

He wants to go?   (a question asking what he wants to do)

Another type of question used in English is the tag question. Tag questions are questions added on to statements. Speakers use tag questions to find out information or to seek agreement. Tag questions normally take one of the following two forms.

Affirmative sentence   +   negative tag
Tom is here,   *isn't he?*

Negative sentence   +   affirmative tag
Tom isn't here,   *is he?*

Tag questions may be spoken with two different intonation patterns.

Jane   lives   near   here,   doesn't   she?

It's   a   beautiful   day   today,   isn't   it.

In the first sentence above, a rising question intonation is used because the speaker is questioning whether her/his information or idea is correct.

In the second sentence above, a falling intonation is used because the speaker is expressing an idea with which s/he is almost certain the listener will agree.

The TOEFL tests your ability to hear question intonation.

MODEL

You will hear:

> You called Martha?   (rising question intonation)

You will read:
- (A)   You telephoned Martha.
- (B)   You should call Martha.
- (C)   Did you call Martha?
- (D)   When did Martha call you?

Answer:

▼ Explanation ▲

In the spoken sentence, a statement form is being used to ask a question. Answer (A) and answer (B) contain statements, not questions. Answer (D) contains a question, but this question is not a restatement of the question in the spoken sentence. Answer (C) is the correct answer to this question because it contains a question which is a restatement of the spoken question.

```
┌─────────────────────────────────────────────────────────────────┐
│                            MODEL                                  │
│                                                                   │
│   You will hear:                                                  │
│                                                                   │
│       Ann has a brother, doesn't she?   (rising question          │
│                                          intonation)              │
│   You will read:                                                  │
│       (A) I don't think Anne has a brother.                       │
│       (B) Does Anne have a brother?                               │
│       (C) I am quite sure that Anne has a brother.                │
│       (D) What do you think of Anne's brother?                    │
│                                                                   │
│   Answer:                                                         │
└─────────────────────────────────────────────────────────────────┘
```

▼ Explanation ▲

In this question, the rising question intonation of a tag is being tested. The rising question intonation of the spoken sentence indicates that the speaker is really asking if Anne has a brother. Answer (A) is a negative statement. Answer (C) contains a restatement of a falling intonation tag. Answer (D) asks a question, but it is not the question asked in the spoken sentence. Answer (B), which asks if Anne has a brother, is the correct answer to this question.

```
┌─────────────────────────────────────────────────────────────────┐
│                    ☞ ON THE TOEFL TEST                           │
├─────────────────────────────────────────────────────────────────┤
│                                                                   │
│   •  Listen carefully for question intonation in TOEFL questions. │
│                                                                   │
└─────────────────────────────────────────────────────────────────┘
```

EXERCISE 6A: Tape Practice with Question Intonation in Statement Form

Listen to each spoken sentence. Write a *Q* on the line for each sentence that asks a question. Write an *S* on the line for each sentence that makes a statement.

1. _Q_   4. _____

2. _____   5. _____

3. _____   6. _____

EXERCISE 6B: Tape Practice with Question Intonation in Tag Questions

Listen to each spoken sentence. Write the letter of the correct restatement for each sentence that you hear.

_A_ 1. (A) Is the dog sleeping next to the fire?
        (B) I think the dog is sleeping next to the fire.

____ 2. (A) Was the accident a terrible tragedy?
        (B) The accident was a terrible tragedy.

____ 3. (A) Is Greg's boss a compassionate man?
        (B) I believe that Greg's boss is a compassionate man.

_____ 4. (A) Is Nancy a teacher like her mother?
      (B) I think Nancy is a teacher like her mother.

_____ 5. (A) Is this the best season of the year?
      (B) I think this is the best season of the year.

_____ 6. (A) Is Mary coming at around 8:00?
      (B) I'm quite sure Mary is coming at around 8:00.

_____ 7. (A) Are you the man I saw at the bus station?
      (B) I think you are the man I saw at the bus station.

_____ 8. (A) Is he the one who showed us the factory?
      (B) I believe he is the one who showed us the factory.

_____ 9. (A) Does your typewriter need a new ribbon?
      (B) I think your typewriter needs a new ribbon.

_____ 10. (A) Are you going to finish this project on time?
       (B) I believe you are going to finish this project on time.

_____ 11. (A) Does Willie live with his mother?
       (B) I am quite sure that Willie lives with his mother.

EXERCISE 6C: More Tape Practice with Question Intonation

Circle the letter of the sentence that is closest in meaning to the sentence you hear on the tape.

1. (A) Someone else delivered the package.
   (B) I think you brought the package.
   (C) Did you receive the package?
   (D) Would you mind delivering the package?

2. (A) Did she borrow your books?
   (B) She lent you her books.
   (C) Did she lend you her books?
   (D) Are you going to borrow her books?

3. (A) Peter doesn't like classical music.
   (B) Peter is enjoying his music class.
   (C) Doesn't Peter like classical music?
   (D) Isn't Peter studying music?

4. (A) Boston is three hours away by car.
   (B) How long does it take to drive to Boston?
   (C) Does it only take three hours to get to Boston from here?
   (D) The three of us will drive from here to Boston.

5. (A) Won't you be starting your new job next week?
   (B) You're going to look for a job again, aren't you?
   (C) What are you going to do at your new job?
   (D) How long have you been working at your new job?

6. (A) What did the doctor say about the child?
   (B) Someone took the child to the doctor.
   (C) The doctor is talking to the child.
   (D) Did someone take the child to the doctor?

L✔7   Check Negatives

Negative meaning is common in English sentences. There are several negative structures.

1. *Not* (which is often shortened to ——*n't*) and other negative words, such as *never, nobody, no, none, no one, nothing,* and *nowhere*:

   John is *not* here today.

   John is*n't* here today.

   Kelly has *never* been here before.

   Nobody/No one lives in this house.

   None of that soup has been eaten.

   There is *no* reason to be worried.

   Nothing bothers her.

   Michael was *nowhere* to be found.

2. Negative prefixes such as *de——, dis——, il——, im——, in——, ir——, non——,* and *un——.* These prefixes can be added to the beginning of some words to change them to their opposite meanings:

   *de*emphasize
   (not emphasize)

   *in*considerate
   (not considerate)

   *dis*interested
   (not interested)

   *ir*replaceable
   (not replaceable)

   *il*logical
   (not logical)

   *non*payment
   (lack of payment)

   *im*possible
   (not possible)

   *un*attractive
   (not attractive)

3. Almost negative expressions such as *barely, hardly,* and *scarcely* (which describe how much), and *rarely* and *seldom,* (which describe how often):

   We   *barely*   had enough money to pay for the concert.
        scarcely
        hardly

   We   *rarely*   go to concerts.
        seldom

It is common for one negative structure to occur in an English sentence. In addition, two or more negatives can be used in one sentence. When this happens, the total meaning of the sentence is sometimes difficult to understand. Compare the two sentences below.

   John was *not* impressed.
   John was *not un*impressed. (John was impressed.)

The second sentence contains two negatives. The two sentences are opposite in meaning. When two negatives are used, the meaning is affirmative.

The TOEFL tests your ability to understand negatives. Restatements of negative sentences can often be made without using negative words or structures. Thus, the correct restatement of negative TOEFL questions often does not contain a negative.

MODEL

You will hear:
  John didn't disobey his father.

You will read:
    (A)   John didn't do what his father wanted.
    (B)   John did what his father wanted him to do.
    (C)   John's father was not happy with him.
    (D)   This wasn't approved by John's father.

Answer:

▼ Explanation ▲

There are two negatives in the spoken sentence, ——n't (not) and dis—— (disobey). These two negatives give the sentence an affirmative meaning. Answers (A), (C), and (D) all have negative meanings. Answer (B) is the correct answer to this question because even though it contains no negative structures, it accurately restates the meaning of the spoken sentence.

MODEL

You will hear:
  Peter can't deny that he is very clever.

You will read:
    (A)   Peter must admit that he is clever.
    (B)   No one can deny that Peter is clever.
    (C)   Peter is not very clever.
    (D)   Peter pays careful attention to details.

Answer:

▼ Explanation ▲

In the spoken sentence, the negative ——n't (not) is used to change the meaning of deny from not admit to admit. Answer (A) is the correct answer to this question even though it does not contain a negative.

☛ ON THE TOEFL TEST

• Check the negatives in TOEFL questions.

EXERCISE 7A: ◻◻◻ Tape Practice with Negative Words

Listen to each spoken sentence. Write a restatement for each sentence you hear. In some of your restatements, you will need to use negatives. In others you will not need to use negatives. Stop the tape after each question to allow yourself time to write.

1. _I didn't get any calls about my ad./There weren't any responses to my ad._

2. _____

3. _____

4. _____

5. _____

6. _____

7. _____

8. _____

9. _____

10. _____

11. _____

EXERCISE 7B: Negative Prefixes

Change the following words to negatives by writing the appropriate negative prefix.

1. _il___ legal
2. _____ like
3. _____ value
4. _____ loyal
5. _____ pure
6. _____ frequent
7. _____ honest
8. _____ reverent
9. _____ legitimate
10. _____ perfect
11. _____ observant
12. _____ motivated
13. _____ contaminate
14. _____ tolerant
15. _____ decided
16. _____ obey
17. _____ realistic
18. _____ human
19. _____ patient
20. _____ judge
21. _____ sense

EXERCISE 7C: Tape Practice with Almost Negative Expressions

Listen to each spoken sentence. Write a restatement for each sentence you hear. In some of your restatements, you will need to use negatives. In others you will not need to use negatives. Stop the tape after each question to allow yourself time to write.

1. _I have the minimum amount of gas I need to get to school./_
   I almost do not have enough gas to get to school.

2. _____

3. _____

4. _____

5. _____

6. _____

7. _____

8. _____

9. _____

10. _____

11. _____

EXERCISE 7D: Tape Practice with Sentences Containing More than One Negative

Listen to each spoken sentence. Write a restatement for each sentence you hear. In some of your restatements, you will need to use negatives. In others you will not need to use negatives. Stop the tape after each question to allow yourself time to write.

1. _Reading Shakespeare's plays is something I don't mind_
   doing./It doesn't bother me to read Shakespeare's plays.

2. _____

3. _____

4. _____

5. _____

6. _____

EXERCISE 7E: 🔲 **More Tape Practice with Negatives**

Circle the letter of the sentence that is closest in meaning to the sentence you hear on the tape.

1. (A) Carl said he would improve his grade.
   (B) Carl had a great job.
   (C) Carl's grade wasn't very good.
   (D) Carl wasn't unhappy about his grade.

2. (A) Visits from his parents are rare.
   (B) He visits his parents often.
   (C) His parents live near here.
   (D) He doesn't see his parents very often.

3. (A) Nothing was surprising.
   (B) This news was surprising.
   (C) I was surprised by these views.
   (D) Why was the news so surprising?

4. (A) We don't really like losing the game.
   (B) We aren't likely to win the game.
   (C) We will probably win the game.
   (D) This is a game that we don't like.

5. (A) I didn't think he was feeling well.
   (B) He isn't very well thought of.
   (C) Why wasn't he feeling well?
   (D) I thought he was feeling much better.

6. (A) The results of the experiment were incorrectly analyzed.
   (B) The scientist accurately interpreted the results of his experiment.
   (C) The scientist hasn't had time to analyze the results of his experiment.
   (D) The scientist needs to re-analyze the results of his experiment.

L✔8   Check Time

Each English sentence contains a reference to time. Time is expressed using different verb tenses and different time marker words, such as *after, before*, and *while*. Some tense and time marker differences are especially important to keep in mind when you listen for the time in restatement questions in Section One of the TOEFL.

1. The present tense usually means that the time of the action in a sentence is habitual or repeated.

   > He *eats* breakfast at 7:30.

   This sentence expresses the idea that he habitually (every day) eats breakfast at the same time.

2. The present continuous tense (present tense of BE + present participle) usually means that the time of the action in a sentence is: (A) happening right now, or (B) going to happen in the future.

   > He *is eating*.

   > He *is eating* at the country club tomorrow night.

   The first sentence expresses the idea that he is eating right now. The second sentence expresses the idea that he will eat tomorrow.

3. The simple past tense usually means that the time of the action in a sentence began and ended in the past.

   > He *ate* breakfast at 7:30.

   This sentence expresses the idea that he started and finished his breakfast in the past.

4. The present perfect tense (*have/has* + past participle) usually means that the time of the action in a sentence began in the past and is still continuing or is still important in the present.

   > He *has eaten* breakfast at 7:30 for several years.

This sentence expresses the idea that he ate breakfast at 7:30 in the past and that he continues to eat breakfast at 7:30 in the present.

5. The past perfect tense (*had* + past participle) is usually used in a sentence which also contains the past tense. These two tenses are used together to mean that one action occurred before another action in a sentence.

> He *had* already *eaten* breakfast by the time we arrived.

This sentence expresses the idea that he ate before we arrived.

6. The verb *used to* usually means that the action of the sentence occurred in the past and no longer occurs in the present.

> He *used to* eat breakfast at 8:00.

This sentence expresses the idea that he ate breakfast at 8:00 in the past, but now he eats breakfast at a different time.

7. Many time markers, including *after, as soon as, before, once*, and *until* are used to show that one action happens before another in a sentence.

> *After* he eats breakfast, he goes to work.
>
> *As soon as* he finishes his breakfast, he will go to work.
>
> *Before* he goes to work, he eats breakfast.
>
> *Once* he finishes his breakfast, he will go to work.
>
> He won't go to work *until* he finishes breakfast.

All five of these sentences express the idea that he eats first and then goes to work.

8. Other time markers, including *as* and *while*, are used to show that two actions in a sentence happen at the same time.

> *As* he was eating his breakfast, the phone rang.
>
> *While* he was eating his breakfast, the phone rang.

Both of these sentences express the idea that the phone rang at the same time that he was eating.

9. Sometimes the conjunction *and* is used as a time marker to show that one action occurs before another in a sentence.

> He ate breakfast *and* went to work.

This sentence expresses the idea that he ate first and then went to work.

The TOEFL tests your ability to understand the time expressed in English sentences. The tense and time marker information discussed above is frequently tested.

MODEL

You will hear:
Andrew bought a new car last week.

You will read:
(A)   Andrew is buying a new car this week.
(B)   Andrew's new car lasted only a week.
(C)   Andrew has borrowed my new car for the week.
(D)   Andrew purchased a new car a week ago.

Answer:

▼ Explanation ▲

The time of the spoken sentence is in the past. Andrew began and finished buying a car in the past. Only answer (B) and answer (D) contain verbs in the past. Answer (B), however, has a completely different meaning from the spoken sentence. Answer (D) is the correct answer to this question because it restates the general meaning and the correct time of the spoken sentence.

MODEL

You will hear:
Once the doctor gives you permission, you can leave the hospital.

You will read:
(A)   You may leave the hospital at once.
(B)   Get the doctor's approval before you leave the hospital.
(C)   After you leave the hospital, talk to the doctor.
(D)   You may leave the hospital before you talk to the doctor.

Answer:

▼ Explanation ▲

In this question, the time marker *once* is used in the spoken sentence to show that the time sequence of the actions is: (1) doctor gives permission, and then (2) you leave. In answer (A), only one action, *leave the hospital*, takes place. No mention of the doctor or his approval is made in this answer. In answer (C) and answer (D), the time sequence of the actions is reversed so that *leaving the hospital* takes place before *talking to the doctor*. Answer (B) is the correct answer to this question because the time sequence of the actions is the same as in the spoken sentence.

☛ ON THE TOEFL TEST

- Listen carefully for the time in TOEFL questions.
- Check tenses and time markers for help in understanding time and time sequences.

See G✔8, pages 157–160 if you need more information on verb tense meanings and time markers.
See the Grammar Appendix #15, page 445 if you need more information on verb tense forms.

EXERCISE 8A: Tape Practice with Time Sequences

Listen to each sentence. In the space provided, write the letter of the action which occurs/occurred first or is most likely to occur first. If both actions are likely to happen at the same time, write an *S* in the blank.

_B_ 1. (A) buying the dog
    (B) buying the cat
    (S) both happen at the same time

____ 2. (A) talking
    (B) writing on the blackboard
    (S) both happen at the same time

____ 3. (A) eating lunch
    (B) calling mother
    (S) both happen at the same time

____ 4. (A) Anne arriving
    (B) beginning the meeting
    (S) both happen at the same time

____ 5. (A) watching other people dance
    (B) dancing
    (S) both happen at the same time

____ 6. (A) finding a job
    (B) moving
    (S) both happen at the same time

____ 7. (A) moving to New Jersey
    (B) the semester ending
    (S) both happen at the same time

____ 8. (A) phoning
    (B) receiving my message
    (S) both happen at the same time

____ 9. (A) her writing to him
    (B) his writing to her
    (S) both happen at the same time

____ 10. (A) the lights going out
    (B) watching a movie
    (S) both happen at the same time

____ 11. (A) moving to New York
    (B) making several good friends
    (S) both happen at the same time

____ 12. (A) giving the letter to John
    (B) reading the letter
    (S) both happen at the same time

____ 13. (A) drinking tea
    (B) drinking coffee
    (S) both happen at the same time

____ 14. (A) our moving in
    (B) their moving out
    (S) both happen at the same time

____ 15. (A) our calling
    (B) their taking her to the hospital
    (S) both happen at the same time

____ 16. (A) listening to music
    (B) working
    (S) both happen at the same time

EXERCISE 8B: More Tape Practice with Time

Circle the letter of the sentence that is closest in meaning to the sentence you hear on the tape.

1. (A) Most of us are waiting in the bus.
   (B) The bus will be here in an hour.
   (C) We are still waiting for the bus.
   (D) The bus was an hour late.

2. (A) I think we should go to a movie after you finish writing.
   (B) After the movie, you can start doing your paper.
   (C) I didn't see any good movies advertised in the paper.
   (D) Before you finish your paper, let's go out to a movie.

3. (A) Nancy will get married after she finds a job.
   (B) Now that Nancy is married, she no longer works.
   (C) Nancy plans to quit working once she is married.
   (D) Nancy used to work with Mary.

4. (A) Last week we took a lot of pictures.
   (B) We are supposed to bring our photos with us to the party.
   (C) We asked them to take our pictures at the party.
   (D) We took our pictures to last week's party.

5. (A) Marsha recently received her schedule of courses.
   (B) Marsha will get her class schedule in a few days.
   (C) Marsha doesn't know which classes she wants to take.
   (D) Marsha only has a few classes left to schedule.

6. (A) He always does his homework after he eats.
   (B) He often eats while he's studying.
   (C) When his homework is done, he can eat.
   (D) He doesn't eat much while he's studying.

7. (A) I'm not used to seeing movies.
   (B) They used someone I know in that movie.
   (C) I've never seen that movie.
   (D) I don't remember everything about that movie anymore.

8. (A) They responded promptly to my request.
   (B) I mailed them the information as soon as they asked for it.
   (C) It took them a long time to answer my inquiry.
   (D) They asked for the information after I sent it.

9. (A) She will move at the beginning of the month.
   (B) She moved into the dormitory on the fourth.
   (C) She has lived in the dormitory since the first of the month.
   (D) She's making her first move into a dormitory.

10. (A) Joan does her laundry every weekend.
    (B) She goes to Joan's once a week to wash clothes.
    (C) She and Joan are looking for a place to do their laundry.
    (D) She is at Joan's doing her laundry right now.

11. (A) Irene is still a professor, but she also sells real estate.
    (B) Irene has changed professions.
    (C) Irene inherited the professor's estate.
    (D) Irene teaches courses on real estate sales.

L✔9   Check Conditions, Wishes, and Causes and Results

It is common in spoken English sentences to express conditions and wishes. It is also common to describe the causes and results of ideas and actions.

Sentences which express conditions are called conditional sentences. Four main types of conditional sentence forms are tested in Section One of the TOEFL.

1. Factual conditionals with *If* + present tense in the *if* clause—present tense in the main clause. Factual conditionals express facts which are true when certain conditions are met.

    > *If* you *eat* spinach, you *get* iron in your diet.
    > IF + present   present

    According to this sentence, it is a fact that people get iron in their diet when they eat spinach.

2. Future conditionals with *If* + present tense in the *if* clause—future tense in the main clause. Future conditionals express facts which may be true in the future.

    > *If* they *eat* their spinach, they *will get* iron in their diet.
    > IF + present   future

    According to this sentence, getting lots of iron is a fact that will become true if they eat their spinach.

3. Hypothetical conditionals with *If* + past tense in the *if* clause—*would* + the simple form of the verb in the main clause. Hypothetical conditionals express facts which are not likely to be true, but which are possible.

    > *If* they *ate* their spinach, they *would get* iron in their diet.
    > IF + past   would + simple form

    According to this sentence, it is not likely that they will eat their spinach; however, it is possible. If they eat their spinach, they will get iron in their diet.

4. (A) Counterfactual conditionals I with *If* + *were* (or sometimes other verbs in past tense) in the *if* clause—would + the simple form of the verb in the main clause. Counterfactual conditional I sentences express facts which are untrue in the present.

    > *If* he *were* here, he *would eat* this spinach.
    > IF + were   would + simple form

    According to this sentence, he is not here (if he were here = he is not here). Therefore, he will not eat the spinach.

    (B) Counterfactual conditionals II with *If* + past perfect in the *if* clause—would have + past participle in main clause. Counterfactual conditional II sentences express facts which are untrue in the past.

    > *If* they *had eaten* their spinach, they *would have gotten* iron in their diet.
    > IF   past perfect   would have + past participle

    According to this sentence, they did not eat their spinach (if they had eaten their spinach = they did not eat their spinach), so they did not get iron in their diet.

The truth value of these conditional sentence types can be summarized as follows:

TRUE—Factual conditionals
POSSIBLY TRUE IN THE FUTURE—Future conditionals
LESS POSSIBLY TRUE IN THE FUTURE—Hypothetical conditionals
UNTRUE—Counterfactual conditionals

NOTE: There are other forms possible for factual, future, hypothetical, and counterfactual conditionals. However, they are not tested in Section One of the TOEFL. Only those forms discussed above are important for Section One of the TOEFL.

Wish sentences are used when a speaker wants reality to be different than it is. The verb forms used to express wishes are similar to those used in conditional sentences.

Wish: I *wish* that you were a rock star.
Reality: You are not a rock star.

Causes and results can be expressed in several ways in English sentences. Many verbs express cause or result.

| Injury (cause) | causes leads to creates results in produces contributes to is responsible for gives rise to | pain. (result) |

| Pain (result) | results from is caused by is due to stems from | injury. (cause) |

In addition to verbs, there are many other words that can be used to express cause and result.

| John is very tired; (cause) | therefore, consequently, for this reason, because of this, as a result, | he is going to bed. (result) |

Two common words used to express cause and result are *because* and *so*. *Because* is always followed by the cause. *So* is always followed by the result.

Because he is very tired, John is going to bed.
BECAUSE + cause   result

He is very tired, so he is going to bed.
        Cause   SO + result

The TOEFL tests your ability to hear and understand conditions, wishes, and causes and results.

MODEL

You will hear:

> If I had known you were coming, I would have baked a cake.

You will read:

    (A)   I will bake a cake for you as soon as possible.
    (B)   I knew you were coming, so I baked a cake.
    (C)   I didn't know you were coming, so I didn't bake a cake.
    (D)   Let's bake a cake when you come.

Answer:

▼ Explanation ▲

In this question, a counterfactual conditional sentence is being used; that is, a fact (baking a cake) which was not true in the past is being expressed. Answer (A) states that a cake will be baked in the future. Answer (B) has just the opposite meaning of the spoken sentence because it states that a cake was baked in the past. Answer (D) makes a suggestion to bake a cake in the future. Answer (C) is the correct answer to this question because it states that a cake was not baked in the past. It is the best restatement of the spoken sentence.

MODEL

You will hear:

> Her low grade is due to her inability to write well.

You will read:

    (A)   She will not be able to finish her writing assignment when it is due.
    (B)   She will learn to write better to improve her grade.
    (C)   Her poor writing did not affect her grade.
    (D)   She received a low mark because of her poor writing ability.

Answer:

▼ Explanation ▲

In this question, a cause and a result are expressed in the spoken statement, using the verb phrase *is due to*. Answer (A) and answer (B) have very different meanings from this spoken sentence. Answer (C) has the opposite meaning of the spoken sentence. Answer (D) is the correct answer to this question because it expresses a cause and a result using the word *because*. This cause and result are the same as those expressed in the spoken statement.

☛ ON THE TOEFL TEST

- Listen carefully for conditions and wishes in TOEFL questions.
- Listen carefully for cause and result.

See the Grammar Appendix #34, page 461 if you need more information on conditional sentences.

EXERCISE 9A: Tape Practice with Conditions and Wishes

Listen to each spoken sentence. Read the printed sentence for each answer. Decide whether the printed sentence is true or false, according to the information given in the spoken sentence. If the printed sentence is true, write a *T* in the answer space. If the printed sentence is false, write an *F* in the answer space.

_F_ 1. I had a week's vacation.

____ 2. It might be possible to have peace.

____ 3. You own this car.

____ 4. You are talking loudly.

____ 5. I can buy you that ring.

____ 6. I have as much experience as you do.

____ 7. You asked Greg to help you.

____ 8. We are with our families.

____ 9. He is not a child.

____ 10. I was not worried about you.

____ 11. You can make gray paint.

____ 12. Jane can call me at my office.

____ 13. It is not summer now.

____ 14. We were very careful.

____ 15. Your housework is finished.

____ 16. Beatrice is relieved.

____ 17. They have stopped working.

____ 18. I don't have any money.

____ 19. I am very scared.

____ 20. Mark didn't go out with us.

____ 21. She isn't lazy.

____ 22. We will certainly finish this soon.

EXERCISE 9B: Tape Practice with Cause and Result

Listen to each spoken sentence. Write a *C* on the line next to each word or phrase that is a cause in the spoken statement. Write an *R* on the line next to each word or phrase that is the result in the spoken statement.

_R_ 1. this mess

____ 2. Claire was angry

____ 3. his efforts

____ 4. unfortunate circumstance

____ 5. malicious rumors

____ 6. static electricity

____ 7. I left

____ 8. disorganization

____ 9. her insecurity

____ 10. I don't have to work anymore

____ 11. heavy traffic to the lake

____ 12. everyone works until 5:00

____ 13. unemployment

____ 14. overuse of computers

____ 15. don't try to sell me a car

____ 16. my family lives in Montana

EXERCISE 9C: **Tape Practice with Conditions, Wishes, and Causes and Results**

Circle the letter of the sentence that is closest in meaning to the sentence you hear on the tape.

1. (A) I didn't find my watch.
   (B) My watch is worn out.
   (C) I wore my watch today.
   (D) I didn't want to wear my watch.

2. (A) John didn't like the party.
   (B) John has come with us to the party.
   (C) I'm sorry that John didn't come to the party.
   (D) John must leave the party soon.

3. (A) I will not be home today.
   (B) I have called everyone at home.
   (C) I can be reached at home.
   (D) I do not have a phone.

4. (A) Jane's heart problem makes her very anxious.
   (B) Jane thinks stress is the cause of her ill health.
   (C) For her part, Jane is not distressed.
   (D) Jane probably feels she is not working hard enough.

5. (A) We should leave in about an hour.
   (B) We were lost for an hour.
   (C) We arrived an hour ago.
   (D) Let's try to find our way out of here.

6. (A) I wish it weren't so cold.
   (B) I'm sorry I sold it.
   (C) I can't seem to get rid of this cold.
   (D) I wish I were younger.

L✔10   Check Who Does What

It is sometimes difficult to understand who does what in English sentences. This can be true whenever there is more than one person being talked about. It is especially difficult to understand who does what in passive sentences and in causative constructions using *have, let, make,* and *get.*

> **Peter gave Mary a ring.**
> Who gave the ring?   Peter
>
> **This ring was given to Mary by Peter.** (Passive sentence)
> Who gave the ring?   Peter
>
> **Peter got Joe to give Mary a ring.** (Causative construction)
> Who gave the ring?   Joe

The TOEFL tests your ability to understand who does what in spoken sentences.

```
┌─────────────────────────────────────────────────────────────────────┐
│                              MODEL                                    │
│                                                                       │
│   You will hear:                                                      │
│       I'll have Janice clean the porch.                               │
│                                                                       │
│   You will read:                                                      │
│       (A)   Janice will clean the porch for me.                       │
│       (B)   Janice is out on the porch.                               │
│       (C)   I will clean the porch for Janice.                        │
│       (D)   Janice cleaned for me.                                    │
│                                                                       │
│   Answer:                                                             │
└─────────────────────────────────────────────────────────────────────┘
```

▼ Explanation ▲

In this question it is important to understand that Janice is the one who will do the cleaning. Answer (B) mentions Janice, but does not talk about cleaning. Answer (C) has the opposite meaning of the spoken sentence. Answer (D) takes place in the past tense, while the spoken sentence takes place in the future. Answer (A) is the correct answer because it restates the meaning of the spoken sentence.

```
┌─────────────────────────────────────────────────────────────────────┐
│                     ☛ ON THE TOEFL TEST                               │
├─────────────────────────────────────────────────────────────────────┤
│                                                                       │
│   • Listen carefully for who does what in TOEFL questions.            │
│                                                                       │
└─────────────────────────────────────────────────────────────────────┘
```

See the Grammar Appendix, #21, page 449 for more information on passive sentences.

EXERCISE 10A: 📼 Tape Practice with Who Does What

Listen to each spoken sentence. Write who does what.

1. Who was in the play? _____Sally_____

2. Who cuts hair? _____

3. Who made progress? _____

4. Who did the nominating? _____

5. Who cleaned? _____

6. Who received the letter? _____

7. Who respects? _____

8. Who saw? _____

9. Who brings? _____

10. Who was on vacation? _____

11. Who owns the car? _____

EXERCISE 10B: More Tape Practice with Who Does What

Circle the letter of the sentence that is closest in meaning to the sentence you hear on the tape.

1. (A) Greg got a cake for Nancy.
   (B) Greg and Nancy took the truck to the lake.
   (C) Nancy went and got the cake.
   (D) Greg will take the truck later.

2. (A) Harry delivered the car on Tuesday.
   (B) Harry wanted to see his new car today.
   (C) Harry arranged for the delivery of his car on Tuesday.
   (D) Harry asked about the condition of his new car.

3. (A) Karen told her to start her new job next week.
   (B) Karen has several forms to fill out before she begins work next week.
   (C) Karen said that she started feeling weak at work.
   (D) Karen will begin her new job next week.

4. (A) I'll have someone repair my car as soon as I can afford it.
   (B) I'm in a terrible fix for money.
   (C) I'm going to work on my car as soon as I can.
   (D) I have to find a new car as quickly as possible.

5. (A) The hiker helped the park employees.
   (B) Many park employees helped the hiker.
   (C) The employees parked the hiker's car.
   (D) The hiker dedicated the park to the employees.

6. (A) Her saw works well for chopping wood.
   (B) She saw me chopping wood.
   (C) She was chopping wood when I saw her.
   (D) I saw her when I was shopping.

Restatement Checkpoint Test for L✔1 through L✔10

On the TOEFL, several restatement checkpoints are often tested in one question. The following checkpoint test will give you combined practice of all the restatement checkpoints. You will only be allowed 12 seconds to answer each question. This is the amount of time allowed on the TOEFL.

Directions: For each question, you will hear a short sentence. Each sentence will be spoken just one time. The sentences you hear will not be written out for you. Therefore, you must listen carefully to understand what the speaker says.

After you hear a sentence, read the four choices marked (A), (B), (C), and (D), and decide which *one* is closest in meaning to the sentence you heard. Then, circle the letter that corresponds to the answer you have chosen.

1. (A) How are you today?
   (B) Four days is too long.
   (C) Today is so long.
   (D) Good-bye.

2. (A) Peter put the signs in the mail.
   (B) The post office accepted Peter's signature.
   (C) Peter resigned from his job at the post office.
   (D) After signing the papers, Peter mailed them.

3. (A) I'm going to take a great vacation.
   (B) Did you receive your grades during vacation?
   (C) I've really enjoyed this vacation.
   (D) Haven't you had a vacation lately?

4. (A) Half of the people in Spanish 304 missed class the first few days.
   (B) For a while, Spanish class must be held in the conference room.
   (C) We have met 3 or 4 Spanish people at the conference.
   (D) The Spanish conference will last three or four days.

5. (A) We know the main problem.
   (B) His job is still difficult.
   (C) His remark deserves a comment.
   (D) It isn't possible to find a calendar of Maine.

6. (A) Dan thinks this stereo is *a very good buy* for you.
   (B) I think you're the person who's buying this stereo.
   (C) Someone else is buying this stereo.
   (D) Aren't you the person who's buying these curios?

7. (A) He's left to buy gasoline.
   (B) Philip will go with him to get the car.
   (C) He's gone to pick up Philip.
   (D) The car was full, so he's going *on foot*.

8. (A) Larry had the doctor check his injury.
   (B) The doctor had a sore muscle.
   (C) Larry put the saw on the dock.
   (D) Larry's musical was put on by the doctors.

9. (A) The store was open.
   (B) She didn't shop for new clothes.
   (C) The shop wasn't close enough.
   (D) She didn't think the store sold clothes.

10. (A) I've only been studying Finnish for half a semester.
    (B) I finished my paper half an hour ago.
    (C) I still have half of my paper left to finish.
    (D) I only have to write my Finnish paper.

11. (A) She isn't a good worker.
    (B) She no longer works there.
    (C) She never stops working.
    (D) She needs to do more work there.

12. (A) Kevin couldn't strain enough juice from the fruit.
    (B) Kevin liked his new job very much.
    (C) Kevin was unable to cope with the stress of his new position.
    (D) Kevin hurt himself while working.

13. (A) When we got there, they were ready to start the movie.
    (B) The movie started as we were leaving.
    (C) The movie started before we got there.
    (D) After we got there, we waited for the movie to begin.

14. (A) She was happy to see us.
    (B) She received our invitation.
    (C) She took us by the arm.
    (D) She opened the gift we gave her.

15. (A) I don't think Mary wants to go with us.
    (B) Does Mary want to join us?
    (C) Mary wants to join us.
    (D) Mary went with us.

16. (A) Are you ready to go home?
    (B) Your house certainly is lovely.
    (C) What does your house look like?
    (D) What shall we do in this beautiful room?

17. (A) Hank succeeded in making a will.
    (B) Hank will succeed if he tries.
    (C) Hank feels stronger after this success.
    (D) Hank achieved his goals through great determination.

18. (A) Clarence finally did well in spite of the problems he had.
    (B) After falling several times, Clarence could still stand up.
    (C) Although the race had to be started several times, Clarence was finally able to finish it.
    (D) Clarence doesn't run very fast because he has large feet.

19. (A) We found a way to get from the mountains to the city.
    (B) In the summer we vacation in the mountains, where it is cool.
    (C) In the summer, we often get away from the city and go eat in the mountains.
    (D) We escaped from the police by going up into the mountains.

20. (A) Susan waited until the end of the semester to take her test.
    (B) Susan did poorly on her oral exam.
    (C) Susan had better wait until the end of the semester to take her oral exam.
    (D) Susan needs to take her test before the end of the semester.

Listening Comprehension
Part B: Mini-Dialogues

The Part B questions in Section One of the TOEFL measure your ability to understand mini-dialogues between two people, as well as to understand and respond to spoken questions about each dialogue. Each short dialogue in this section is two lines long and involves a woman and a man. A third person asks a question about what was said. You hear each dialogue and the question about it just one time.

    After you hear the question, you have 12 seconds to read the four answer choices and decide which one is the best answer to the question you heard. There are 15 mini-dialogues and 15 questions in Part B.

MODEL

You will hear:
    (Man)   M: This view is really *something else!*
    (Woman)   W: I'll say!
    (Question) Q: What does the woman mean?

You will read:
    (A)   She has something to say.
    (B)   She agrees with the man.
    (C)   She wants to see something else.
    (D)   She thinks it's time to review something else.

Answer:

▼ **Explanation** ▲

In this mini-dialogue and question, several things are being tested. The man uses the idiom *something else* to express his enthusiasm for the view. *I'll say*, the response of the woman, functions to show her agreement with the man about his opinion. Answer (A) contains a different meaning of *say*, and does not describe what the woman means. Answer (C) contains *see*, which sounds like *say*. It also contains *something else* used to mean *another thing*. This is not the idiomatic meaning of *something else*. Answer (D) contains *review*, which sounds like *view*, and again uses *something else* in its literal (non-idiomatic) meaning. Answer (B) is the correct answer to this question because it restates the function of the woman's response even though it sounds the least like the mini-dialogue.

Mini-Dialogue: Spoken Questions

All questions you hear in this part of the TOEFL begin with question words. These words include: *who, what, when, where, which, why,* and *how.*

There are two basic question types in Part B that use these words: **fact** questions and **inference** questions. Fact questions ask about specific information that has been mentioned in the dialogue. Inference questions ask about information that has NOT been mentioned specifically in the dialogues. The information has only been implied or suggested by the speakers, but not stated directly.

The most common types of fact and inference questions used in Part B are listed below in two groups. Group 1 questions can be either fact or inference questions. Group 2 questions can only be inference questions because they contain words like *probably, assume, imply,* and *infer.*

Group 1
> What does the woman/man mean?*
> What is the woman/man doing?
> What does the woman/man want to know?
> What is the woman/man asking?
> What does the woman/man say about X?
> What does the woman/man think about X?
> What is the woman's/man's opinion about X?
> What does the woman/man suggest?
> How does the woman/man feel?
> What are the man and woman going to do?
> What do we learn from this conversation?
> What does the man think the woman should do?
> What does the woman think the man should do?

Group 2
> Where does this conversation probably take place?
> What will the woman/man probably do next?
> What can we assume about the woman/man?
> What had the woman/man assumed?
> What does the woman/man imply?**
> What can we infer from the woman's/man's response?**
> What job/profession does the woman/man probably have?

* NOTE: The most common question asked on this part of the TOEFL is: What does the woman/man mean?

** NOTE: *Imply* and *infer* are related terms with slightly different meanings. *Imply* is what the speaker does when s/he indirectly expresses an idea. *Infer* is what the listener does when s/he figures out what the indirectly expressed idea is.

SPECIAL NOTE: The spoken questions in Part B are almost always asked about what the second speaker says. Only once in a while do they ask about what the first speaker says or about the situation of the dialogue.

MINI-DIALOGUE STRATEGIES

1. QUICKLY look ahead at the answer choices on the page while the instructions are read. Try to predict questions that might be asked as you look at the answers choices. **DO NOT turn the page.** See checkpoint L✔14 for practice.

2. Be careful of vocabulary, sounds, spoken structures, and intonation and stress in dialogues and questions. See Restatement Strategies page 45 for more information.

3. Listen carefully to the second speaker. The second speaker always gives important information. The correct answer to Part B questions is often contained in the second speaker's sentence.

4. Determine the situation in the dialogue. Try to determine *who* is speaking and *where* the speakers are having their conversation. See L✔11 for practice.

5. Determine the topic of the dialogue. Try to determine *what* the speakers are talking about. See L✔12 for practice.

6. Determine the language functions in the dialogue. Try to determine the function of the language being used by the speakers. See L✔13 for practice.

7. Guess if you don't know the answer to a question: choose the answer that sounds LEAST like the dialogue. This answer is often the correct answer.

8. Use extra time between questions to look ahead at the answer choices. Try to predict what the question types might be for each dialogue.

✔ MINI-DIALOGUE CHECKPOINTS

To improve your score on Section One Part B, you should first study the Restatement Checkpoints covered on pages 45–46. These checkpoints are also tested in Part B.

While you should give special attention to L✔11 through L✔14 if Part B was your weak listening area, we recommend that you review all of the listening checkpoints in this book.

Below is a list of the Mini-Dialogue Checkpoints covered in the Mini-Dialogue Checkpoint Study. This Checkpoint Study ends with a Mini-Dialogue Checkpoint Test that includes L✔1 through L✔14. This test should be taken after you have studied all the checkpoints listed below, as well as the Restatement Checkpoints, L✔1 through L✔10.

✔ MINI-DIALOGUE CHECKPOINT STUDY

L✔11   Check the Situation

Understanding the situation in which a dialogue takes place is an important part of understanding the meaning of a dialogue. It is important to understand *who* is speaking and *where* or in *what* circumstance they are talking.

Understanding the situation for each mini-dialogue in Part B helps you to answer fact and inference questions. Some dialogue questions specifically ask about the situation. These include questions such as:

Who is the woman/man? What job does the woman/man probably have? Where does this conversation probably take place?

MODEL

You will hear:
    W: I should be able to perform your surgery tomorrow morning.
    M: I'll be glad when it's over.
    Q: What job does the woman probably have?

You will read:
    (A)   Doctor
    (B)   Performer
    (C)   Lawyer
    (D)   Plumber

Answer:

▼ Explanation ▲

This question specifically asks about the situation. You need to be able to infer that the woman in the dialogue is a doctor. The key word *surgery* makes it possible for you to do this. Answer (A) is the correct answer to this question because it identifies *who* the woman is in the situation.

> **NOTE:**   In the question above, you may have been surprised to hear a woman in the role of the doctor. All roles in Part B can be played by either women or men. For example, you may hear a man discussing housework and cooking. You may hear a woman discussing how to make automobile repairs. Do not be surprised by these situations. They are increasingly common in the United States. If you are surprised by them, you will lose your concentration, and you will not do as well on this part of the test.

```
┌─────────────────────────────────────────────────────────────────┐
│                            MODEL                                  │
│                                                                   │
│  You will hear:                                                   │
│          M:   Would you please bring me a larger size?            │
│          W:   Right away!                                         │
│          Q:   What does the woman mean?                           │
│                                                                   │
│  You will read:                                                   │
│          (A)  She thinks the prize is all right.                  │
│          (B)  She'll bring another size immediately.              │
│          (C)  She needs to write down the man's request.          │
│          (D)  She'll send away for a nice prize immediately.      │
│                                                                   │
│  Answer:                                                          │
└─────────────────────────────────────────────────────────────────┘
```

▼ Explanation ▲

This question does not specifically ask about the situation. It is primarily testing the meaning of the idiom *right away*. However, it is important to understand the situation in order to correctly answer this question. The man in this dialogue is a client and the woman is a salesperson. The conversation probably takes place in a clothing store or a shoe store. If you do not understand this situation, you might choose answer (A) or answer (D), which contain *prize*, a sound-alike for *size*, and in which the situation is completely different from that in the dialogue. In answer (C), the situation could be the same as that of the dialogue. However, *write* is used instead of *right* to change the meaning of the idiom completely. Answer (B) is the correct answer to the question because it restates the meaning of the idiom in the correct situation.

```
┌─────────────────────────────────────────────────────────────────┐
│                    ☛ ON THE TOEFL TEST                            │
│                                                                   │
│  •  Listen carefully to determine the situation (who and where)   │
│     of each mini-dialogue.                                        │
└─────────────────────────────────────────────────────────────────┘
```

EXERCISE 11A: 📼 Tape Practice Understanding Where a Dialogue Takes Place

Listen to each dialogue. On the first line, identify *where* the dialogue probably takes place. Use the places listed below:

airplane	dentist's office
apartment	doctor's office
business office	library
classroom	on the telephone
clothing store	restaurant

It may be necessary to use some locations more than once.

On the second line, write the *key words* that helped you identify *where* the dialogue takes place. Stop the tape after each question to allow yourself time to write.

1. Where: _____ *apartment* _____

    Key Words: _____ *stay home* _____

2. Where: _____

   Key Words: _____

3. Where: _____

   Key Words: _____

4. Where: _____

   Key Words: _____

5. Where: _____

   Key Words: _____

6. Where: _____

   Key Words: _____

7. Where: _____

   Key Words: _____

8. Where: _____

   Key Words: _____

9. Where: _____

   Key Words: _____

10. Where: _____

    Key Words: _____

11. Where: _____

    Key Words: _____

EXERCISE 11B: Tape Practice Identifying Who Speakers Are in a Conversation

On your tape, listen again to the short dialogues in exercise 11A. This time, identify *who* each speaker is in the dialogues. Use the names listed below:

airline hostess/host	library user
client	patient
co-worker	professor
dentist	salesperson
doctor	student
friend	waitress/waiter
librarian	

It may be necessary to use some names more than once. Stop the tape after each question to allow yourself time to write.

1. First Speaker: ___friend___   7. First Speaker: _____

   Second Speaker: ___friend___   Second Speaker: _____

2. First Speaker: _____   8. First Speaker: _____

   Second Speaker: _____   Second Speaker: _____

3. First Speaker: _____   9. First Speaker: _____

   Second Speaker: _____   Second Speaker: _____

4. First Speaker: _____   10. First Speaker: _____

   Second Speaker: _____   Second Speaker: _____

5. First Speaker: _____   11. First Speaker: _____

   Second Speaker: _____   Second Speaker: _____

6. First Speaker: _____

   Second Speaker: _____

EXERCISE 11C: 🎞️ More Tape Practice Identifying Where a Dialogue Takes Place

Listen to the sentence. On the first line, identify *where* the sentence probably takes place. Use the places listed below:

airport	apartment
bank	classroom
gas station	grocery store
hospital	post office
restaurant	

It may be necessary to use some of the locations more than once.

On the second line, write the *key words* that help you understand *where* the sentence takes place. Stop the tape after each question to allow yourself time to write.

1. Where: ___airport___   5. Where: _____

   Key Words: ___aircraft, boarding___   Key Words: _____

2. Where: _____   6. Where: _____

   Key Words: _____   Key Words: _____

3. Where: _____   7. Where: _____

   Key Words: _____   Key Words: _____

4. Where: _____   8. Where: _____

   Key Words: _____   Key Words: _____

9. Where: _____

   Key Words: _____

10. Where: _____

   Key Words: _____

11. Where: _____

   Key Words: _____

EXERCISE 11D: Tape Practice with Situations

Listen carefully to each dialogue and the corresponding question. Circle the letter that best answers the question you hear.

1. (A) Dentist.
   (B) Nurse.
   (C) Weather reporter.
   (D) Teacher.

2. (A) In a library.
   (B) In a classroom.
   (C) In a bookstore.
   (D) In a lawyer's office.

3. (A) She thinks the man's luggage will arrive soon.
   (B) She wants to turn at the next street.
   (C) She is too short to see what's in the bag.
   (D) She will pick up the man's groceries for him.

4. (A) A librarian.
   (B) A teacher.
   (C) A student.
   (D) The woman's best friend.

5. (A) In a movie theater.
   (B) In an airport.
   (C) In a car.
   (D) In Chicago.

6. (A) She would like to have her coat back.
   (B) Her house doesn't need another coat of paint.
   (C) She wants the man to pay her now.
   (D) She would like to buy the coat she has.

L✔12   Check the Topic

Once you understand the situation in which a dialogue takes place, it is important to understand the topic of the dialogue, or *what* the speakers are talking about.

Understanding the topic for each mini-dialogue in Part B helps you answer all fact and inference questions.

MODEL

You will hear:
    M: Today is my birthday.
    W: Really? How old are you?
    Q: What does the woman want to know about the man?

You will read:
    (A)   What he does for a living.
    (B)   How many days he will be staying in town.
    (C)   His age.
    (D)   His name.

Answer:

▼ Explanation ▲

To correctly answer this question, you must understand the key word, *birthday*, to know what the speakers are talking about. The topic of the dialogue is the man's birthday. If you know this, you can correctly answer the spoken question. Answers (A), (B), and (D) do not contain any reference to the man's birthday. Answer (C) is the correct answer to this question.

☛ ON THE TOEFL TEST

• Listen carefully for the topic of each TOEFL dialogue.

EXERCISE 12A: Practice Associating Topics with Situations

For each situation given, write down two possible topics that might be discussed in a mini-dialogue.

1. Situation
    Who: a salesperson and a client
    Where: in a shoe store

    Possible topics   *the price of shoes*

    trying on a pair of shoes

2. Situation
   Who: two friends
   Where: at a football game

   Possible topics _____

   _____

3. Situation
   Who: two students
   Where: a chemistry laboratory

   Possible topics _____

   _____

4. Situation
   Who: a student and a professor
   Where: the professor's office

   Possible topics _____

   _____

5. Situation
   Who: two friends
   Where: at the beach

   Possible topics _____

   _____

6. Situation
   Who: a telephone operator and a client
   Where: *on the phone*

   Possible topics _____

   _____

7. Situation
   Who: a police officer and a person driving a car
   Where: on the freeway

   Possible topics _____

   _____

8. Situation
   Who: a nurse and a patient
   Where: a hospital

   Possible topics _____

   _____

9. Situation
   Who: two friends
   Where: a movie theater

   Possible topics _____

   _____

10. Situation
    Who: a librarian and a library user
    Where: a college library

    Possible topics _____

    _____

11. Situation
    Who: two friends
    Where: the kitchen

    Possible topics _____

    _____

EXERCISE 12B: 🎞 Tape Practice with Topics

Listen to each mini-dialogue. Identify the topic.

1. Topic: _going to a movie or staying at home_____

2. Topic: _____

3. Topic: _____

4. Topic: _____

5. Topic: _____

6. Topic: _____

7. Topic: _____

8. Topic: _____

9. Topic: _____

10. Topic: _____

11. Topic: _____

L✔13   Check Language Functions

In English conversation, one sentence can have several different functions, depending upon the context in which it is used. These functions include expressing agreement or disagreement; complaining; showing excitement, confusion or surprise; making and refusing requests; stressing the importance of an idea; and making suggestions and giving advice.

> M: I didn't care very much for John's painting. Did you?
> W: I thought it was very nice.

> M: I liked John's painting very much. How about you?
> W: I thought it was very nice.

In the first dialogue, the man's statement about John's painting is negative. In this context, the woman's positive statement, *I thought it was very nice*, functions to express disagreement with the man. In the second dialogue, the same sentence has a different function. In this dialogue, the woman agrees with the man.

Sometimes stress and/or intonation determine the function of a sentence.

> W: Did you find Michael?
> M: He is waiting in the other room.

> W: Did you find Michael?
> M: He *is* waiting in the other room!

In the first dialogue, the man's sentence functions simply to answer the woman's question. In the second, with heavy stress on *is*, the same sentence has a different function. It is used to answer the woman's question and simultaneously express surprise. The man had assumed that Michael was not in the other room. To his surprise, Michael was there after all.

Stress and/or intonation can also have the function of emphasizing or exaggerating the importance or difficulty of something. Certain expressions also function to exaggerate meaning.

> I've worked *30 hours* today!!
> I've seen that movie *a hundred times*!
> You *really* overdid it this time!

In the first two sentences above, *30 hours* and *a hundred times* intensify or stress the importance of the sentences through exaggeration. There are only 24 hours in a day, and it is highly unlikely that anyone would actually see a movie one hundred times.

In the third sentence, the heavy stress on *really* functions to intensify the meaning of the sentence.

Certain special expressions also have important language functions in English. There are hundreds of these expressions. Listed below are some of these expressions that frequently appear on the TOEFL. Each is used in a sentence to help you understand its function.

LANGUAGE FUNCTION	SOME EXPRESSIONS USED
Requesting permission	*Do you mind* if I use your pen? *Would it be OK (with you)* if I came, too? *I wonder if I could* borrow your pencil.
Requesting information	*Do you know* where the library is? *Can you tell me* how to get to Church Street? *Is there* a library around here?
Requesting that someone do something	*Would you mind* opening the window? *Would you please* take out the trash? *Could you please* get me that book? *How about* sharing that dessert with me?
Requesting advice or an opinion	*What do you think* of this dress? *Do you think* Larry will come? *Would it be better for me to* call or write? *How does this* look to you? *Should I* ask for a raise? *Do you like* this book?
Giving advice or an opinion	*Shouldn't you* eat before you go out? *Why not* do your homework now? *Try* calling him in the afternoon. *You really should* be careful on the highway.
Suggesting speaker and listener do something together	*Why don't we* go to the concert tonight? *Let's* see that movie we were talking about. *What would you say to* a vacation? *How about* going to dinner on Tuesday? *How would you feel about* going to a concert?
Offering to do something	*Shall I* do that for you now? *May I* take your hat? *Can I* take your coat? *Would you like* another cup of tea? *Would you like me to* get you some more tea?
Agreeing with suggestions, advice, etc.	*Sure.* *I'll say!* *No problem.* *Great idea.* *Sure, why not.* *Good idea.* *Sounds good to me.* *No kidding.* *So do I.* *Neither do I.* *Isn't/Won't/Doesn't it, though.*

LANGUAGE FUNCTION	SOME EXPRESSIONS USED (CONTINUED)
Disagreeing with suggestions, advice, opinions, etc.	*No, thanks.* I really shouldn't. *Thanks, anyway, but* I can't. *Sorry, but* I don't really agree with you.
Refusing offers and requests	*That's out of the question.* *Not likely!* *You must be kidding!*

Understanding the language functions expressed in each mini-dialogue in Part B helps you answer all fact and inference questions.

MODEL

You will hear:
   M: Do you mind if I turn down the stereo?
   W: The volume is already quite low.
   Q: What can be inferred from the woman's response?

You will read:
   (A)   She is feeling low.
   (B)   The man should not turn down the music.
   (C)   The stereo is broken.
   (D)   The man should listen to the stereo with her.

Answer:

▼ Explanation ▲

This question tests your understanding of language function. With *do you mind if*, the man requests permission to lower the volume of the stereo. In this context, the woman's response functions to deny the man's request. If you did not understand this, you might choose answer (A), (C), or (D). Answer (B) is the correct answer because it implies what the woman means.

MODEL

You will hear:
   M: Do you know who has a dictionary I could borrow?
   W: Why not buy your own? You seem to need one all the time!
   Q: What does the woman mean?

You will read:
   (A)   The man should borrow a dictionary.
   (B)   The man should try to get along without a dictionary.
   (C)   She doesn't know where the man can borrow a dictionary.
   (D)   She thinks the man should buy his own dictionary.

Answer:

▼ Explanation ▲

This question tests language function. The man's question asks for information. The woman's response does not simply give information. Instead, it functions to give the man advice. If you didn't understand these language functions, you might choose answer (A), (B), or (C). Answer (D) is the correct answer because it implies what the woman means.

```
☞ ON THE TOEFL TEST

• Listen carefully for the language function of each spoken sentence in
  TOEFL questions.
• Pay careful attention to the language functions of certain special
  expressions.
```

EXERCISE 13A: Tape Practice with Language Functions of Special Expressions

Listen to each sentence. On the line, write the letter that corresponds to the language function of each sentence you hear. The language functions are listed below:

(A) giving advice or an opinion
(B) offering to do something
(C) requesting advice or an opinion
(D) requesting information
(E) requesting permission
(F) requesting that someone do something
(G) suggesting speaker and listener do something together

Stop the tape after each question to allow yourself time to choose your answer.

1. ___D___   9. _____

2. _____   10. _____

3. _____   11. _____

4. _____   12. _____

5. _____   13. _____

6. _____   14. _____

7. _____   15. _____

8. _____   16. _____

EXERCISE 13B: 📼 **Tape Practice with Language Functions**

Listen to each dialogue. Circle the letter of the correct answer to the written question.

1. Who is disagreeing?
   (A) the woman
   (B) the man

2. Who is requesting that someone
   do something?
   (A) the woman
   (B) the man

3. Who is giving a compliment?
   (A) the woman
   (B) the man

4. Who is giving advice?
   (A) the woman
   (B) the man

5. Who is exaggerating?
   (A) the woman
   (B) the man

6. Who is showing concern or worry?
   (A) the woman
   (B) the man

7. Who is surprised?
   (A) the woman
   (B) the man

8. Who is rejecting a suggestion?
   (A) the woman
   (B) the man

9. Who is complaining?
   (A) the woman
   (B) the man

10. Who is surprised?
    (A) the woman
    (B) the man

11. Who is accepting a suggestion?
    (A) the woman
    (B) the man

12. Who is emphasizing?
    (A) the woman
    (B) the man

13. Who is requesting an opinion?
    (A) the woman
    (B) the man

14. Who is agreeing?
    (A) the woman
    (B) the man

15. Who is exaggerating?
    (A) the woman
    (B) the man

16. Who is requesting permission?
    (A) the woman
    (B) the man

EXERCISE 13C: 📼 **More Tape Practice with Language Functions**

Listen carefully to each dialogue and the corresponding question. Circle the letter of the sentence that best answers the question you hear.

1. (A) He will get the woman a bowl of soup.
   (B) He thinks the woman is very smart.
   (C) He'd like to play chess.
   (D) He has a great deal of pain in his chest.

2. (A) Come over for lunch.
   (B) Read his book at lunch time.
   (C) Take only an hour for his lunch break.
   (D) Buy the novel during his lunch hour.

3. (A) He disagrees with the woman.
   (B) He didn't like the television program.
   (C) He hasn't thought about watching television.
   (D) He would like to see the TV show.

4. (A) The stereo was not for sale.
   (B) He would have to buy the stereo.
   (C) He could not pay for the stereo with a check.
   (D) The stereo was not being sold at a discount.

5. (A) She eats at work every day.
   (B) She enjoys her job very much.
   (C) She does nothing but work all week.
   (D) She has been working at her new job for eight days.

6. (A) The woman should put on a coat before going outside.
   (B) The woman should leave the window closed.
   (C) The view through the window is beautiful.
   (D) He has caught a cold because of the open window.

L✔14   Check Ahead to Predict Questions

As suggested in Mini-Dialogue Strategies #1 and #8, page 85, it is a good idea to look ahead at the answer choices in Part B questions when you have extra time. You can do this when the instructions for this part of the test are being read. You can also read ahead between questions if you finish early. Look for key words to predict what information may be important in the spoken questions.

MODEL

You will read:
   (A)   In a barber shop.
   (B)   At a bank.
   (C)   In a restaurant.
   (D)   On the bus.

What is a possible question for these answer choices?

▼ Explanation ▲

Although you have not heard the mini-dialogue or the spoken question about it, these answer choices tell you that the question will be about *where*. The most common *where* question on the TOEFL is one which asks about *where* the mini-dialogue takes place: in this case, *where does this conversation probably take place?*

☞ **ON THE TOEFL TEST**

• Whenever possible, look ahead at answer choices to predict Part B TOEFL questions.

EXERCISE 14A: Practice Predicting Questions

Read the four answer choices. On Line 1 write a possible spoken question for these answer choices. If you need suggestions, refer to the lists of questions on page 84.

NOTE: Line 2 in this exercise will be used in the following exercise, 14B.

1. (A) Artist.
   (B) Writer.
   (C) Lawyer.
   (D) Teacher.

   Line 1 _____What is probably the woman's/man's profession?_____

   Line 2 _____

2. (A) Have dinner after they take a walk.
   (B) Take a walk later.
   (C) Talk about repairing their walk.
   (D) Learn to tie knots.

   Line 1 _____

   Line 2 _____

3. (A) Excited.
   (B) Angry.
   (C) Tired.
   (D) Frustrated.

   Line 1 _____

   Line 2 _____

4. (A) Carpenter.
   (B) Housekeeper.
   (C) Mover.
   (D) Truck driver.

   Line 1 _____

   Line 2 _____

5. (A) The plot of the book is quite good.
   (B) The plot of the book is quite bad.
   (C) The pictures in the book are quite good.
   (D) The book is very poetic.

   Line 1 _____

   Line 2 _____

6. (A) He would like her to give him her pin.
   (B) He thinks she should stop spinning around.
   (C) He wants her to take him with her when she goes.
   (D) He thinks she should try driving the car.

   Line 1 _____

   Line 2 _____

7. (A) Eating.
   (B) Writing.
   (C) Reading.
   (D) Walking away from the man.

   Line 1 _____

   Line 2 _____

8. (A) Ask someone to finish writing her paper for her.
   (B) Give her paper to the librarian.
   (C) Stop working on her paper.
   (D) Try to finish her paper as soon as possible.

   Line 1 _____

   Line 2 _____

9. (A) In a department store.
   (B) At the beach.
   (C) In a beauty salon.
   (D) In a restaurant.

   Line 1 _____

   Line 2 _____

10. (A) The food doesn't have enough seasoning in it.
    (B) She doesn't like the main course.
    (C) She likes the food.
    (D) The food is too spicy.

    Line 1 _____

    Line 2 _____

11. (A) Lend the woman his math book.
    (B) Take off his mask.
    (C) Help the woman with her studies.
    (D) Go talk to the math teacher.

    Line 1 _____

    Line 2 _____

EXERCISE 14B: 📼 Tape Practice Checking Your Predictions

Listen to each dialogue for the answer choices in Exercise 14A. Circle the correct answer to each spoken question. On Line 2 write down each spoken question that you hear. Check to see if your predicted question corresponds in meaning to the one spoken on the tape. Stop the tape between questions to allow yourself time to write.

Mini-Dialogue Checkpoint Test for L✔1 through L✔14

The following checkpoint test gives you combined practice of all of the listening checkpoints covered thus far. You will only be allowed 12 seconds to answer each question. This is the amount of time allowed on the TOEFL.

📼 Directions: In this checkpoint test, you will hear short conversations between two speakers. At the end of each conversation, a third person will ask a question about what was said. You will hear each conversation and question about it just one time. Therefore, you must listen carefully to understand what each speakers says. After you hear a conversation and the question about it, read the four possible answers in your book and decide which one is the best answer to the question you heard. Then, circle the letter that corresponds to the answer you have chosen.

1. (A) Receptionist.
   (B) Teacher.
   (C) Doctor.
   (D) Librarian.

2. (A) She doesn't know the house.
   (B) She agrees with the man.
   (C) She likes the house very much.
   (D) She doesn't know what to say.

3. (A) Larry didn't want to borrow the book.
   (B) Larry hadn't read the book yet.
   (C) Larry had lost the book.
   (D) Larry found the book he had lost.

4. (A) She didn't want to see Peter.
   (B) She saw Peter after she left.
   (C) She arrived after Peter left.
   (D) She will miss Peter.

5. (A) It is very frank.
   (B) Frank typed it.
   (C) It is the wrong type.
   (D) He got it from Frank.

6. (A) She has never had such a delicious dessert before.
   (B) She loves living in the desert.
   (C) She is quite sure there are better desserts available.
   (D) She can't understand why the man likes the desert so much.

7. (A) In a bank.
   (B) In an attorney's office.
   (C) In a math class.
   (D) In an art class.

8. (A) Bob and Judy shouldn't go away for so long.
   (B) Bob is feeling too weak to go anywhere.
   (C) They should also tell Bob about their plans.
   (D) He doesn't want Bob to know about their plans.

9. (A) She will try to help the man find a good job.
   (B) The descent is too steep for her bike.
   (C) She will be able to ride her bike to work.
   (D) She can't purchase a bike until she earns some money.

10. (A) Anxiety about exams is keeping the man awake.
    (B) Final exams are nothing to worry about.
    (C) She's finally going to take her exam next week.
    (D) The man must be careful not to fall asleep during exams.

11. (A) The man thinks buying a used car is a bad idea.
    (B) The man wants to borrow Jane's car.
    (C) The man thinks Jane should buy a car.
    (D) Jane will find the man a used car after all.

12. (A) He doesn't want to proofread the woman's paper
    (B) He doesn't see very well.
    (C) He will be back in two days.
    (D) He isn't there.

13. (A) It is violent.
    (B) The volume is too high.
    (C) He wants to think about it.
    (D) It helps him think.

14. (A) A coach.
    (B) An athlete.
    (C) A close friend of the woman's.
    (D) A teacher.

15. (A) Has everyone been invited to the wedding?
    (B) Should she invite her family?
    (C) Did the man take her family to the wedding?
    (D) Is her family included in the people counted?

Listening Comprehension Part C: Talks and Longer Conversations

The Part C questions in Section One of the TOEFL measure your ability to understand longer passages of spoken English. There are two types of passages in Part C. One type is a longer dialogue between a man and a woman. The other type is a lecture or talk given by one person, either a man or a woman. Part C of the TOEFL contains three passages, which always include at least one of the two types described above. The third passage may be of either type.

The topics in Part C passages are often about college life. The longer conversations often involve two students talking about a class, a professor, or some aspect of college life. The talks frequently discuss classroom procedures and assignments or are short lectures in a general academic area, such as science, history, psychology, or anthropology. No previous knowledge of any of the topics is necessary to answer the questions on this part of the TOEFL.

Although most of the topics for Part C are college related, some are daily life topics. These include such things as conversations in grocery stores or apartments, and talks by tour guides and sports coaches.

Each passage in Part C is between 100 and 300 words long and lasts an average of one to two minutes. You are not allowed to take notes while listening to the spoken passages. Each passage and the questions about it are spoken only one time.

> **SPECIAL NOTE:** Each passage in Part C begins with a short spoken introduction. You will hear a sentence, such as, "Questions 36 to 40 refer to the following conversation." These introductions give you valuable information about the passage you are going to hear. Notice that in this short statement you find out (1) whether the selection will be a talk or a conversation; and (2) how many questions will be asked about it. Sometimes even more information is provided in the introductory statement, as in "Questions 36 to 40 refer to the following talk given by a tennis coach at a college." Notice that in this short statement you find out (1) that the selection will be a talk, not a conversation; (2) that there will be five questions about the talk; (3) who will give the talk; and (4) where the talk will take place. Because you can learn so much valuable information from the short introductory statements, it is extremely important that you listen to them carefully.

After each passage, you will hear several spoken questions about it. After each question, you will have 12 seconds to read four answer choices and choose the one that answers the spoken question. There are 15 questions in Part C.

Talks and Longer Conversations: Spoken Questions

As in Part B, there are two basic question types asked in Part C of Section One of the TOEFL: fact questions and inference questions. Fact questions ask about specific information that has been mentioned in the passages. Inference questions ask about information that has *not* been specifically mentioned in the passages. This information has only been implied or suggested by the speakers. All question types begin with the question words *who, what, when, where, which, why,* and *how*.

A larger variety of questions using these words is possible in Part C than in Part B because topics are discussed in greater detail in this part of Section One of the TOEFL. (See the model below.)

One question that is frequently asked, however, is a main idea or topic question. The following are examples of this kind of question:

What is the main idea of this talk?
What is the main topic of the conversation?
What is the purpose of the talk?
What would be the best title for this talk?

NOTE: The major words in the answer choices for questions which ask about the title of a talk all begin with capital letters.

MODEL

You will hear:
   Questions 1 to 6 are based on the following talk:

Last week we talked about the Declaration of Independence. Today I'd like to discuss the United States Constitution. The Constitution is the basic instrument of American government and the supreme law of the land. It was completed in September of 1787, and was officially adopted by the American people in 1789. For over two centuries, it has guided our government and provided the basis for political stability, economic growth, and social progress. It is the oldest written constitution currently being used in any nation of the world. The Constitution owes its long life and its lasting influence to its magnificent simplicity and flexibility. Originally designed to provide a framework for governing thirteen very different former colonies, its basic elements were so carefully conceived that it still serves well the needs of all Americans.

You will hear:
   1. What would be a good title for this talk?

You will read:
   1. (A) The Founding of the Thirteen Colonies.
      (B) The Declaration of Independence.
      (C) The United States Constitution.
      (D) Economic Growth.

You will hear:
   2. Where does this talk most likely take place?

Continued

You will read:
2. (A) In a United States history class.
   (B) In a science class.
   (C) In a library.
   (D) In the school cafeteria.

You will hear:
3. According to the speaker, what is the supreme law of the land?

You will read:
3. (A) The American people.
   (B) The Constitution.
   (C) The government.
   (D) The Declaration of Independence.

You will hear:
4. When was the Constitution officially adopted?

You will read:
4. (A) In 1787.
   (B) In 1887.
   (C) In 1789.
   (D) In 1813.

You will hear:
5. According to the speaker, why has the United States Constitution lasted so long?

You will read:
5. (A) Because it was designed for the thirteen colonies.
   (B) Because it is simple and flexible.
   (C) Because it is the basic instrument of the American government.
   (D) Because it is being used in many nations.

You will hear:
6. How does the speaker probably feel about the Constitution?

You will read:
6. (A) He would like to have a copy of the Constitution.
   (B) He is afraid that the Constitution will not last much longer.
   (C) He is critical of the Constitution.
   (D) He admires the Constitution.

Answers:

▼ Explanation ▲

The introductory statement for this passage tells you that it will be a talk, not a conversation. In addition, it tells you that you will answer six questions about this talk.

Question 1 is a main idea question. The answer to this question is given at the beginning of the talk, in the second sentence. Answer (C) is the correct answer to this question because it restates the main idea of the talk in a title. **The answers to main idea questions are often given at the beginning of the passages in Part C of the Listening Section of the TOEFL.**

Question 2 is an inference question about the situation in which the talk takes place. Although the location of the talk is not directly mentioned, it is an academic talk about an aspect of United

States history. Therefore, we can assume that it would take place in an American history class. Answer (A) is the correct answer to this question because it implies *where* the talk will take place.

Question 3 is a fact question which asks about a direct statement made by the speaker. Answer (B) is the correct answer to this question.

Question 4 is another fact question which asks for a detail given by the speaker after the information mentioned in Question 3. Fact questions are always asked in the order that the information is given in the passage. To answer this question, you need to remember an important date mentioned in the passage. Answer (C) is the correct answer to this question.

Question 5 is a third fact question. It asks about a direct statement made by the speaker after the information asked for in Question 4. Answer (B) is the correct answer to this question.

Question 6 is an inference question. It asks about the feelings or the attitude of the speaker. The speaker does not tell us directly how he feels about the Constitution. However, there are clues to his feelings in the passage. *Magnificent simplicity and flexibility* and *serves well* are positive expressions which tell us that the speaker probably admires the Constitution. Answer (D) is the correct answer to this question because it implies the speaker's attitude about the topic.

STRATEGIES FOR TALKS AND LONGER CONVERSATIONS

1. QUICKLY look ahead at the answer choices while the instructions are read. Try to predict the topics and questions you will hear. **DO NOT turn the page**. See L✔15 below for practice.

2. Listen carefully to the short introductory statement given before each passage. You can learn from this statement whether the passage will be a talk or a conversation. You can also learn how many questions you will answer about the passage. The introductory statement can also give you information about the situation and topic of the passage—who, where, and what.

3. Quickly determine the situation and the topic of the passage. This information is often at the beginning of a passage. You should listen carefully to the beginning of each passage. See L✔16 for practice.

4. Listen carefully for facts and details. Details such as places, dates, names, and times are tested in Part C of the TOEFL. See L✔17 for practice.

5. Questions about facts and details occur in the same order that you hear them in the passage. Many TOEFL test-takers find it helpful to read along with the answer choices while listening to the passage. You can practice this strategy while doing the exercises and practice tests in this book. Only use this strategy if it works for you. If it distracts you from understanding a passage, DO NOT use this strategy.

6. Guess if you don't know the answer to a question. Choose the answer that sounds the MOST like the passage. In this part of the TOEFL, this is often the correct answer to the question.

   NOTE: This strategy is different from the guessing strategy for Parts A and B. You will need to change your guessing approach for Part C.

7. Use extra time between questions to look ahead at the answer choices. Try to predict questions.

✔ CHECKPOINTS FOR TALKS AND LONGER CONVERSATIONS

To improve your score on Part C of Section One, you should first study the Mini-Dialogue Checkpoints covered on page 85. Except for length, the longer conversations in Part C are similar to the mini-dialogues in Part B. Studying checkpoints L✔11 through L✔14 can help you a great deal with Part C.

While you should give special attention to L✔11 through L✔17 if Part C was your weak listening area, we recommend that you review all of the listening checkpoints in this book.

Below is a list of the Talks and Longer Conversations Checkpoints. This study ends with a Talks and Longer Conversations Checkpoint Test that includes L✔11 through L✔17.

A Listening Comprehension Section Test follows this checkpoint study.

✔ TALKS AND LONGER CONVERSATIONS CHECKPOINT STUDY

L✔15   Check Ahead to Predict Topics and Questions

As discussed in previous checkpoints, (See L✔1 and L✔14), it is helpful to look ahead at answer choices in Section One of the TOEFL. This can help you predict possible questions or at least parts of questions. In Part C, this strategy is also useful for predicting topics. It is very helpful if you know what topics to expect in Part C of the TOEFL.

The instructions for this part of the TOEFL are very long. If you have studied this text and used the practice tests in the *Heinemann Practice Tests*, you do not need to listen to these instructions. Instead, you can look ahead at answer choices while these instructions are being read.

The following is a set of answer choices for a longer conversation. While you read through the answer choices, try to predict the topic of the conversation and some of the questions that might be asked about it.

MODEL

You will read:

1. (A) Buy a car.
   (B) Have her car repaired.
   (C) Borrow her friend's car.
   (D) Walk to the gas station.

2. (A) At a car dealership.
   (B) In the man's apartment.
   (C) On the freeway.
   (D) In the woman's new car.

3. (A) She doesn't know yet.
   (B) The black one.
   (C) The red one.
   (D) The white one.

4. (A) The woman should make her decision right away.
   (B) The woman should get a loan from the bank.
   (C) The woman should wait until the prices are reduced.
   (D) The car is too expensive for the woman.

Possible Topic and Possible Questions:

▼ Explanation ▲

Without hearing the passage, you can predict the topic and some of the questions that will be asked about it simply by thinking about the answer choices. Related key words can be found in all four sets of answer choices. These key words include *buy, car, car dealership, get a loan from the bank,* and *prices.* With these key words in mind, you might predict that the topic of this passage will be *buying a car.*

You can also predict the questions or at least parts of the questions in this set of answer choices:

Topic: buying a car
Questions:
1. What does the woman want to do?
2. Where does this conversation take place?
3. Which car does the woman want?
4. What does the man advise the woman to do?

By doing this, you can gain valuable information about the topics and the questions in Part C.

☞ ON THE TOEFL TEST

- Look ahead at answer choices to predict topics and questions in Part C of TOEFL Section One.

EXERCISE 15A: Practice Predicting Topics and Questions

The answer choices given below are all related to the same conversation. Circle the number of the possible question that is *most* likely to be asked about each set of answer choices.

At the end of the exercise, answer the question: What is a possible topic that might go along with these questions and answers?

1. (A) A teacher.
    (B) Reviewing chemistry concepts.
    (C) Finding a textbook.
    (D) Relaxing at the student center.

    Possible question 1:   What is the topic of this passage?
    Possible question 2:   Who is this passage about?

2. (A) They are in a class together.
    (B) They both know a lot about chemistry.
    (C) They are both teachers.
    (D) They have both been to the bookstore today.

    Possible question 1:   What are these two people doing?
    Possible question 2:   What do these two people have in common?

3. (A) She doesn't have time to study right now.
    (B) She can't understand her chemistry assignment.
    (C) She doesn't know how to read very well.
    (D) The textbook she needs is not available in the bookstore.

    Possible question 1:   Why is the woman worried?
    Possible question 2:   Why is the woman in a hurry?

4. (A) That he's a fair teacher.
    (B) That he will want to review the chapters at the next class meeting.
    (C) That he will find them some books to use.
    (D) That they can find him at the student center.

    Possible question 1:   What does the woman/man think of the teacher?
    Possible question 2:   What does the teacher think of the woman/man?

5. (A) He knows very little about chemistry.
    (B) He doesn't like Professor Jenkins.
    (C) He doesn't get worried easily.
    (D) He wants to go back to the bookstore again.

    Possible question 1:   What do we learn about the man?
    Possible question 2:   Why is the professor pleased?

6. (A) Review her assignment.
    (B) Watch television and relax.
    (C) Help the man review the chemistry lesson.
    (D) Go back to the bookstore.

    Possible question 1:   What is the woman doing?
    Possible question 2:   What will the woman probably do next?

7. What is a possible topic that might go along with these questions and answers?

_____ *A chemistry book/A chemistry class* _____

EXERCISE 15B: More Practice Predicting Topics and Questions

The answer choices given below are all related to the same talk. Choose one of the possible questions listed below for each set of answer choices. Write the question on the line provided.

> How tall is an elephant?
> Where does this talk take place?
> What will the speaker probably do next?
> What is the speaker's job?
> Who is the speaker talking to?
> What is the main topic of this talk?
> According to the speaker, what does the term X mean?
> How much does an elephant weigh?

At the end of this exercise, answer the question: What is a possible topic that might go along with these questions and answers?

1. (A) Impressive zoo exhibits.
    (B) Facts about elephants.
    (C) Two kinds of elephants.
    (D) The size of elephants.

    Possible question: _____*What is the main topic of this talk?*_____

2. (A) Circus performer.
    (B) Elephant trainer.
    (C) Tour guide.
    (D) Ticket vendor.

    Possible question: _____

3. (A) Having a highly arched back.
    (B) Moving rhythmically back and forth.
    (C) Having a back which curves down in the middle.
    (D) Having a very flexible back.

    Possible question: _____

4. (A) 11,000 pounds.
    (B) 22,000 pounds.
    (C) 200 pounds.
    (D) 15,000 pounds.

    Possible question: _____

5. (A) Look for a baby elephant.
    (B) Wait for a little while.
    (C) Enter the zoo.
    (D) Leave the lion's den.

    Possible question: _____

6. What is a possible topic that might go along with these questions and answers?

    _____

EXERCISE 15C: More Practice Predicting Topics and Questions

The answer choices given below are all related to the same talk. Choose one of the possible questions listed below for each set of answer choices. Write the question on the line provided.

Who is the speaker?
Where does this talk probably take place?
Why was this colony a failure?
What is the name of the settlement being discussed?
What will the next lecture probably be about?
What happened to the settlers?
Why was this colony a success?
What would be a good title for this talk?
In what course was this talk most probably given?

At the end of this exercise, answer the question: What is a possible topic that might go along with these questions and answers?

1. (A) The Lost Colony
   (B) The Colonists at Jamestown
   (C) The Voyages of John White
   (D) Croatoan Island

   Possible question: _____

2. (A) Environmental studies.
   (B) History.
   (C) Geography.
   (D) Political science.

   Possible question: _____

3. (A) Plymouth Rock.
   (B) Jamestown.
   (C) Chesapeake Bay.
   (D) Roanoke.

   Possible question: _____

4. (A) They moved farther north.
   (B) The left for Croatoan.
   (C) They were never found.
   (D) They returned to England.

   Possible question: _____

5. (A) Because the Indians learned from it.
   (B) Because the colonists arrived in England safely.
   (C) Because the colonists were able to settle in Roanoke.
   (D) Because future colonists learned from it.

   Possible question: _____

6. (A) Other mysteries.
   (B) Marine life in the Chesapeake Bay area.
   (C) The settlement of Jamestown.
   (D) John White's family.

7. What is a possible topic that might go along with these questions and answers?

_____

EXERCISE 15D: More Practice Predicting Topics and Questions

The answer choices given below are all related to the same longer conversation. On the line provided, write a possible question or part of a question for each set of answers. In some cases, you may only be able to predict the first word or two of this question.

At the end of this exercise, answer the question: What is a possible topic that might go along with these questions and answers?

1. (A) Things to do and see in Idaho.
   (B) Places to go on vacation.
   (C) Fishing.
   (D) Features of the moon.

   Possible question: _____ *What is the main topic of this conversation?* _____

2. (A) Because she doesn't think he has time for a vacation now.
   (B) She knows he doesn't like to fish.
   (C) She didn't think he was leaving.
   (D) He's going so far away.

   Possible question: _____

3. (A) To look for a new job.
   (B) To spend time fishing and sightseeing.
   (C) To get as far away as possible.
   (D) To find out about a new heating method for his home.

   Possible question: _____

4. (A) An exhibit of rocks brought back from the moon.
   (B) The site of a dead volcano.
   (C) Caves with ice that never melts.
   (D) Homes heated with water from caves.

   Possible question: _____

5. (A) Go fishing.
   (B) Go home and pack.
   (C) Ask the woman if she'd like to join him.
   (D) Turn up the heat.

   Possible question: _____

6. What is a possible topic that might go along with these questions and answers?

_____

L✔16   Check the First Lines of Each Passage

The first few lines of any talk or conversation contain information that is essential for understanding overall meaning. These lines give information about the situation (*who* and *where*) of the passage, as well as about the topic (*what*) of the passage.

Understanding *who*, *where*, and *what* about each passage is important to understanding overall meaning. Some Part C questions specifically ask for this information. These questions include: *What is the topic of this conversation? Where does this conversation take place? Who is the speaker? What is the woman's/ man's job?* Often this information is not stated directly in the passage, but can be inferred from the first few lines. Other times this information will be stated directly in the beginning of the passage.

MODEL

You will hear:
    M: May I help you?
    W: Well, I hope so. I'm thinking about buying a new car, and I saw one
         that I liked in your showroom.

▼ Explanation ▲

These are the first two lines from a longer conversation. Just from these two lines, you learn that the speakers are a car salesman and a woman shopping for a car. You also learn that the conversation probably takes place in a place where cars are sold—a car dealership. The key expression, *May I help you?*, which is used by salespeople, and the key words *buying, car,* and *showroom* help you infer this information.

At least part of this information will be asked about in the spoken questions for this conversation. This information is also important for understanding the rest of the conversation.

☞ ON THE TOEFL TEST

• Listen carefully to the first few lines of Part C passages to determine *who*, *where*, and *what*.

EXERCISE 16: **Tape Practice with Who, Where, and What**

Listen to the first few lines of each passage. Predict *who* the speaker(s) will be, *where* the passage will take place, and *what* the passage will be about.

If you are unable to make a prediction from the information given, place a question mark (?) on the line. Stop the tape after each passage to allow yourself extra time to write.

1. Who: *two students*

   Where: *on a college campus*

   What: *a textbook that they need for chemistry class*

---

2. Who: _____

   Where: _____

   What: _____

3. Who: _____

   Where: _____

   What: _____

4. Who: _____

   Where: _____

   What: _____

5. Who: _____

   Where: _____

   What: _____

6. Who: _____

   Where: _____

   What: _____

7. Who: _____

   Where: _____

   What: _____

8. Who: _____

   Where: _____

   What: _____

9. Who: _____

   Where: _____

   What: _____

10. Who: _____

    Where: _____

    What: _____

11. Who: _____

    Where: _____

    What: _____

12. Who: _____

    Where: _____

    What: _____

13. Who: _____

    Where: _____

    What: _____

14. Who: _____

    Where: _____

    What: _____

15. Who: _____

    Where: _____

    What: _____

16. Who: _____

    Where: _____

    What: _____

17. Who: _____

    Where: _____

    What: _____

18. Who: _____

    Where: _____

    What: _____

19. Who: _____

    Where: _____

    What: _____

20. Who: _____

    Where: _____

    What: _____

21. Who: _____

    Where: _____

    What: _____

L✔17   Check to Answer Fact and Inference Questions

Although the first few lines of passages in Part C are important for answering fact and inference questions, it is also important to listen carefully to the rest of the passage. You should concentrate on the overall meaning of the passage. From this information, you will be asked to make further inferences. Typical inference questions on Part C of the TOEFL include:

What can we assume about the speaker?
What can be inferred about X?
What does the speaker imply about X?
What will the speaker probably do next?

When you listen to the rest of the passage, you should also listen for facts. These facts may include general information about what the speakers say. They may also include detailed information such as numbers, dates, amounts, and names. Many fact questions are possible. The following are examples:

What does the speaker say about his job?
How long has the speaker been living in the dorm?
Which book does the professor recommend?
How much time will it take to finish the paper?
How many years has the speaker been doing X?
When will the students have their exam?

MODEL

You will hear:
    M: May I help you?
    W: Well, I hope so. I'm thinking about buying a new car and I saw one
           that I liked in your showroom.
    M: Which one was that?
    W: The red one with the black interior. Sitting next to the big white one.
    M: Oh, that little beauty. Well, you're in luck. That one's *on sale*—
           today only. The sale ends at 6:00 this evening.

  3. Which car does the woman want?

Continued

You will read:
3. (A) She doesn't know yet.
   (B) The black one.
   (C) The red one.
   (D) The white one.

You will hear:
4. What does the man imply?

You will read:
4. (A) The woman should make her decision right away.
   (B) The woman should get a loan from the bank.
   (C) The woman should wait until the prices are reduced.
   (D) The car is too expensive for the woman.

Answers:

▼ Explanation ▲

These two questions ask about information that comes in the middle and at the end of the passage.

Question 3 is a fact question. To answer this question correctly, you need to listen carefully for the details in the passage. Answer (C) is the correct answer to this question.

Question 4 is an inference question. The man does not directly say that the woman should buy the car right away; however, he does mention that the car will be on sale for only one day. From this information, we can infer that he thinks the woman should hurry and buy the car. Answer (A) is the correct answer to this question.

☞ ON THE TOEFL TEST

- Listen carefully to the rest of the passage so that you can answer fact and inference questions.

EXERCISE 17A: Tape Practice Listening for Facts

Listen to each short passage and the question about it. Circle the correct answer to each spoken question.

1. (A) 1814.
   (B) 1804.

2. (A) In four days.
   (B) On Thursday.

3. (A) Seventeen.
   (B) Seventy.

4. (A) If she wants to go camping.
   (B) What she wants to do.

5. (A) Watching a film.
   (B) Reading a novel.

6. (A) She doesn't have enough money.
   (B) She is not feeling well.

7. (A) They hate them.
   (B) They find them pleasant.

8. (A) In a practice room.
   (B) At the concert.

9. (A) The teacher.
   (B) The secretary.

10. (A) In the 1770s.
    (B) In the 1870s.

11. (A) Go to the admissions office.
    (B) Make a phone call.

EXERCISE 17B: 📼 **Tape Practice Making Inferences**

In this exercise, you will hear the same short passages that you heard in Exercise 17A. This time, however, you will be asked inference questions about these passages. On your tape, listen again to the short passages in Exercise 17A. Listen to each short passage and the question about it. Circle the correct answer to each spoken question.

1. (A) He was not a very wise president.
   (B) He was very old when he became president.

2. (A) Skiing.
   (B) Studying.

3. (A) That they carry germs.
   (B) That he hides his food from them.

4. (A) She likes to be outdoors.
   (B) She has some new camping equipment.

5. (A) She was a happy person.
   (B) She was a writer.

6. (A) They will be costly.
   (B) They will be postponed.

7. (A) That they are helpful.
   (B) That life would be easier without them.

8. (A) Watching a concert.
   (B) Playing in a concert.

9. (A) Collect the papers.
   (B) Go to her office.

10. (A) She is no longer alive.
    (B) She was a pony express rider.

11. (A) Wait a while before making his phone call.
    (B) Forget about making his phone call.

EXERCISE 17C: 📼 **Tape Practice with Overall Meaning in a Passage**

Listen to each passage and the questions which follow it. Remember to listen to the short introductory sentences that precede each passage. Circle the correct answer to each spoken question.

1. (A) A teacher.
   (B) Reviewing chemistry concepts.
   (C) A textbook.
   (D) Relaxing at the student center.

2. (A) They are in a class together.
   (B) They both know a lot about chemistry.
   (C) They are both teachers.
   (D) They have both been to the bookstore today.

3. (A) She doesn't have time to study right now.
   (B) She can't understand her chemistry assignment.
   (C) She doesn't know how to read very well.
   (D) The textbook she needs is not available in the bookstore.

4. (A) That he's a fair teacher.
   (B) That he will want to review the chapters in the next class.
   (C) That he will find them some books to use.
   (D) That they can find him at the student center.

5. (A) He knows very little about chemistry.
   (B) He doesn't like Professor Jenkins.
   (C) He doesn't get worried easily.
   (D) He wants to go back to the bookstore again.

6. (A) Review her assignment.
   (B) Watch television and relax.
   (C) Help the man review the chemistry lesson.
   (D) Go back to the bookstore.

7. (A) Impressive zoo exhibits.
   (B) Facts about elephants.
   (C) Two kinds of elephants.
   (D) The size of elephants.

8. (A) Circus performer.
   (B) Elephant trainer.
   (C) Tour guide.
   (D) Ticket vendor.

9. (A) Having a highly arched back.
   (B) Moving rhythmically back and forth.
   (C) Having a back which curves down in the middle.
   (D) Having a very flexible back.

10. (A) 11,000 pounds.
    (B) 22,000 pounds.
    (C) 200 pounds.
    (D) 15,000 pounds.

11. (A) Look for a baby elephant.
    (B) Wait for a little while.
    (C) Enter the zoo.
    (D) Leave the lion's den.

12. (A) The Lost Colony
    (B) The Colonists at Jamestown
    (C) The Voyages of John White
    (D) Croatoan Island

13. (A) Environmental studies.
    (B) History.
    (C) Geography.
    (D) Political science.

14. (A) Plymouth Rock.
    (B) Jamestown.
    (C) Chesapeake Bay.
    (D) Roanoke.

15. (A) They moved farther north.
    (B) The left for Croatoan.
    (C) They were never found.
    (D) They returned to England.

16. (A) Because the Indians learned from it.
    (B) Because the colonists arrived in England safely.
    (C) Because the colonists were able to settle in Roanoke.
    (D) Because future colonists learned from it.

17. (A) Other mysteries.
    (B) Marine life in the Chesapeake Bay area.
    (C) The settlement of Jamestown.
    (D) John White's family.

18. (A) Things to do and see in Idaho.
    (B) Places to go on vacation.
    (C) Fishing.
    (D) Features of the moon.

19. (A) She doesn't think he has time for a vacation now.
    (B) She knows he doesn't like to fish.
    (C) She didn't think he was leaving.
    (D) He's going so far away.

20. (A) To look for a new job.
    (B) To spend time fishing and sightseeing.
    (C) To get as far away as possible.
    (D) To find out about a new heating method for his home.

21. (A) An exhibit of rocks brought back from the moon.
    (B) The site of a dead volcano.
    (C) Caves with ice that never melts.
    (D) Homes heated with water from caves.

22. (A) Go fishing.
    (B) Go home and pack.
    (C) Ask the woman if she'd like to join him.
    (D) Turn up the heat.

Talks and Longer Conversations Checkpoint Test for L✔11 through L✔17

The following checkpoint test will give you combined practice in checkpoints L✔11 through L✔17. You will only be allowed 12 seconds to answer each question. This is the amount of time allowed on the TOEFL exam.

Directions: In this part of the test, you will hear short talks and conversations. After each of them, you will be asked some questions. You will hear the talks and conversations and the questions about them just one time. They will not be written out for you. Therefore, you must listen carefully to understand what each speaker says.

After you hear a question, read the four possible answers in your book and decide which _one_ is the best answer to the question you heard. Then, circle the letter that corresponds to the answer you have chosen.

Answer all questions on the basis of what is <u>stated</u> or <u>implied</u> in the talk or conversation.

1. (A) The man's trip.
   (B) Buying luggage.
   (C) How to file a baggage claim.
   (D) Travel by train.

2. (A) He walked.
   (B) He took a taxi.
   (C) He drove.
   (D) Someone picked him up.

3. (A) Her baggage has been lost.
   (B) She has been delayed.
   (C) She has taken a taxi.
   (D) She has taken the man to the airport.

4. (A) He forgot.
   (B) He didn't think it would help.
   (C) He was too tired.
   (D) He found his baggage.

5. (A) Buy a ticket.
   (B) Go to the airport.
   (C) Get some rest.
   (D) Look for the man's ticket.

6. (A) Preventing Forest Fires
   (B) Factors Affecting a Tree's Resistance to Fire
   (C) The Redwood's Ability to Withstand Fire
   (D) Ground Fires and Crown Fires

7. (A) 100 degrees centigrade.
   (B) 20 degrees centigrade.
   (C) 40 degrees centigrade.
   (D) 120 degrees centigrade.

8. (A) They have deep roots.
   (B) They have few leaves.
   (C) They have thick bark.
   (D) They grow close together.

9. (A) They are more likely to have large leaves.
   (B) They are susceptible to ground fires.
   (C) They have a high resistance to all types of fire.
   (D) They usually fall down during a fire.

10. (A) The top of a tree.
    (B) A very hot fire.
    (C) Tree roots that grow close to the surface.
    (D) The highest flame in a fire.

11. (A) He needs some experience acting.
    (B) The drama club needs some male actors.
    (C) She thinks he's the best actor on campus.
    (D) She wants him to meet the playwright.

12. (A) He doesn't enjoy acting.
    (B) He doesn't like comedies.
    (C) He wants to be free on Friday nights.
    (D) He doesn't think he'll have enough time.

13. (A) A student.
    (B) The woman.
    (C) A professor.
    (D) A famous playwright.

14. (A) One or two times a week.
    (B) On Friday nights.
    (C) Every day.
    (D) Whenever they have time.

15. (A) Write a play as soon as possible.
    (B) Meet the woman at 6:30.
    (C) Find a part that is perfect for him.
    (D) Wait a week and then decide what to do.

Listening Comprehension Section Test

On the following pages you will find a practice section test for Section One of the TOEFL.

Use the first part of the SECTION TESTS ANSWER SHEET from the General Appendix, #4, page 509 to record your answers for this test.

When answering each question, use the strategies and skills you have reviewed in the Listening Comprehension Section.

Score your test using *The Heinemann TOEFL Course Tapescripts and Answers*. When you finish scoring your test, determine which parts of Section One, if any, you need to study again.

Estimate your TOEFL score for this section test using Score Conversion Table 1 in the General Appendix, #3, page 505.

 When you are ready, begin the tape at the Listening Comprehension Section Test. Do not go on to the next page until the tape tells you to do so.

SECTION 1

LISTENING COMPREHENSION

In this section of the test, you will have an opportunity to demonstrate your ability to understand spoken English. There are three parts to this section, with special directions for each part.

Part A

Directions: For each question in Part A, you will hear a short sentence. Each sentence will be spoken just one time. The sentences you hear will not be written out for you. Therefore, you must listen carefully to understand what the speaker says.

After you hear a sentence, read the four choices in your test book, marked (A), (B), (C), and (D), and decide which <u>one</u> is closest in meaning to the sentence you heard. Then, on your answer sheet, find the number of the question and fill in the space that corresponds to the letter of the answer you have chosen. Fill in the space so that the letter inside the oval cannot be seen.

Example I   <u>Sample Answer</u>

You will hear: Ⓐ Ⓑ ● Ⓓ
You will read: (A)   Greg didn't bother to leave a tip.
                 (B)   Greg thought about typing a letter to his brother.
                 (C)   Greg didn't like to type.
                 (D)   My typing bothered Greg.

The speaker said, "Greg thought typing was a bother." Sentence (C), "Greg didn't like to type," is closest in meaning to what the speaker said. Therefore, the correct choice is answer (C).

Example   <u>Sample Answer</u>

You will hear: Ⓐ ● Ⓒ Ⓓ
You will read: (A)   Everyone will be able to take this exam later.
                 (B)   Students should bring a calculator to this exam.
                 (C)   This test will be part of every student's final grade.
                 (D)   No one can calculate the grades for this test.

The speaker said, "Everyone needs a calculator for this test." Sentence (B), "Students should bring a calculator to this exam," is closest in meaning to the sentence you heard. Therefore, you should choose answer (B).

1. (A) Jack tried to buy the shoes.
   (B) Jack tied the shoes after he put them on.
   (C) After trying the shoes on, Jack purchased them.
   (D) Jack found it difficult to choose a new tie.

2. (A) We will look at it.
   (B) We'll take responsibility for it.
   (C) We have done it before.
   (D) We don't understand it.

GO ON TO THE NEXT PAGE ➤

3. (A) I don't receive the newspaper any more.
   (B) I'd like to use your paper.
   (C) The local news isn't too good.
   (D) Please call me if you get any news.

4. (A) Those are realistic goals.
   (B) We can work on those goals all together.
   (C) You can't possibly achieve those goals.
   (D) We must all agree on the purpose of our project.

5. (A) Someone else wants to drop this class.
   (B) Drop by my office and talk about this after class.
   (C) I believe you said you don't want to take this class.
   (D) I believe you want to take this class, don't you?

6. (A) We will have to send these papers back.
   (B) These deals are not at all acceptable to us.
   (C) These postponements have hurt us a great deal.
   (D) We won't get back from the lake until quite late.

7. (A) Jane did not meet with me.
   (B) Jane got to the apartment before I did.
   (C) I missed my appointment with Jane.
   (D) Jane was appointed my assistant.

8. (A) The museum will lend her the pictures.
   (B) She is portrayed in one of the pictures at the museum.
   (C) The museum used her donation to buy these portraits.
   (D) She gave the museum these portraits.

9. (A) So long for today.
   (B) What day is it?
   (C) This has certainly been a long day.
   (D) Have you been here for long?

10. (A) He pulled it out.
    (B) He didn't complete it.
    (C) He knew where to put it.
    (D) He felt it was unfair.

11. (A) I read 44 pages in 30 minutes.
    (B) I spent half of my time doing the reading for tomorrow.
    (C) It took me 30 minutes to do my reading assignment.
    (D) I won't be able to do this reading before tomorrow.

12. (A) Did you let him borrow your notes?
    (B) You should borrow his notes.
    (C) Did you give him the note?
    (D) Do you have any notes?

13. (A) No one can contradict Jan.
    (B) The facts about Jan are being denounced.
    (C) Jan certainly knows a lot about computers.
    (D) Jan denies that she is a computer expert.

14. (A) Why can't we get to the other side of the lake?
    (B) We don't have time to send it to the other side of the lake.
    (C) How often do you spend time at the lake?
    (D) Let's go to the lake together sometime.

15. (A) I thought you were coming.
    (B) I didn't know you were waiting.
    (C) I knew you weren't coming.
    (D) You came too late.

16. (A) Typing paper is being sold outside of the bookstore.
    (B) I wrote a check at the bookstore the last time I bought typing paper.
    (C) The last time I looked for typing paper at the bookstore, there wasn't any.
    (D) I was told last night to buy typing paper at the bookstore.

17. (A) Jane didn't have time to eat.
    (B) When I called, Jane was ready to eat.
    (C) After Jane ate, she called me.
    (D) Jane ate before I called.

GO ON TO THE NEXT PAGE ➤

18. (A) We should give Professor Hillman a hand.
    (B) Professor Hillman is out of town, so she can't help us.
    (C) Professor Hillman will help us after she takes off her gloves.
    (D) There is nothing Professor Hillman can do to assist us.

19. (A) John took movies at the dedication of his new business.
    (B) John is doing well because he works hard.
    (C) John is going to do another film about business.
    (D) John's next movie is due to come out soon.

20. (A) Move in to your apartment at once.
    (B) The landlady will get your deposit after you move in to your apartment.
    (C) The landlady will be relieved when you move in to your apartment.
    (D) Give the landlady your deposit before you move into your apartment.

Part B

Directions: In Part B you will hear short conversations between two speakers. At the end of each conversation, a third person will ask a question about what was said. You will hear each conversation and question about it just one time. After you hear a conversation and the question about it, read the four possible answers in your test book and decide which one is the best answer to the question you heard. Then, on your answer sheet, find the number of the question and fill in the space that corresponds to the letter of the answer you have chosen.

Look at the following example.   Sample Answer

You will hear: Ⓐ Ⓑ ● Ⓓ
You will read: (A)   At last winter is almost over.
                  (B)   She doesn't like winter weather very much.
                  (C)   This winter's weather is similar to last winter's weather.
                  (D)   Winter won't last as long this year as it did last year.

From the conversation you learn that the woman thinks the weather this winter is almost the same as the weather last winter. The best answer to the question "What does the woman mean?" is (C), "This winter's weather is similar to last winter's weather." Therefore, you should choose answer (C).

21. (A) He isn't too fond of reading.
    (B) He would like to read the articles, too.
    (C) He read two articles.
    (D) He agrees with the woman.

22. (A) He hasn't spoken to her for a while.
    (B) She doesn't hear well.
    (C) She has been going to work late.
    (D) She enjoys her new job.

GO ON TO THE NEXT PAGE ➤

23. (A) In a laundromat.
    (B) On a farm.
    (C) In a grocery store.
    (D) At a restaurant.

24. (A) She's going to bed.
    (B) She's feeling much better.
    (C) She is feeling worse all the time.
    (D) She's going to see a doctor.

25. (A) She doesn't like the painting.
    (B) She thinks the man is joking.
    (C) There are no children in the painting.
    (D) She agrees with the man.

26. (A) The woman shouldn't study too hard.
    (B) He doesn't want to study for any more tests.
    (C) The woman should study for both tests.
    (D) There are too many tests this term.

27. (A) Happy.
    (B) Lonely.
    (C) Excited.
    (D) Frustrated.

28. (A) He has to check on a few things first.
    (B) He has never heard of such a thing.
    (C) The woman may take the test early.
    (D) He isn't sure it will be possible.

29. (A) Janice called someone for him.
    (B) He didn't actually make it home.
    (C) Janice called him.
    (D) He took Janice home.

30. (A) She has finished her writing.
    (B) He doesn't know where she put her things.
    (C) She is postponing her work.
    (D) He doesn't know when she will do the dishes.

31. (A) That the man had fallen in the snow.
    (B) That the man didn't like to ski.
    (C) That there wouldn't be any snow.
    (D) That the weather would be too bad for travelling.

32. (A) She is hungry.
    (B) She will show the man where to go.
    (C) The cafeteria is too far away to walk to.
    (D) She has never been to the cafeteria before.

33. (A) Jane owns the dictionary the woman wants to borrow.
    (B) He doesn't want the woman to use his dictionary.
    (C) His dictionary is not available right now.
    (D) Jane has the right information.

34. (A) He doesn't want to go out in this traffic.
    (B) It's too noisy to hear the birds now.
    (C) The birds are terrific.
    (D) He can hear the birds over the noise of the cars.

35. (A) He knows a tour guide in the park.
    (B) He knows the park very well.
    (C) He has a good guide book the woman can use.
    (D) He isn't used to taking tours.

GO ON TO THE NEXT PAGE

Part C

<u>Directions:</u> In this part of the test, you will hear several short talks and conversations. After each of them, you will be asked some questions. You will hear the talks and conversations and the questions about them just one time. They will not be written out for you.

After you hear a question, read the four possible answers in your test book and decide which <u>one</u> is the best answer to the question you heard. Then, on your answer sheet, find the number of the question and fill in the space that corresponds to the letter of the answer you have chosen.

Answer questions on the basis of what is <u>stated</u> or <u>implied</u> in the talk or conversation.

Listen to this sample talk.
    You will hear:

Now look at the following example.

<u>Sample Answer</u>

● Ⓑ Ⓒ Ⓓ

You will hear:
You will read: (A)   Only bumblebees can fertilize red
                            clover plants.
                  (B)   Bumblebees protect red clover from
                            plant eating insects.
                  (C)   Bumblebees bring water to red clover
                            plants on their tongues.
                  (D)   Bumblebees keep mice and other animals
                            away from red clover plants.

The best answer to the question "Why is it impossible to raise red clover where there are no bumblebees?" is (A), "Only bumblebees can fertilize red clover plants." Therefore, you should choose answer (A).

Now look at the next example.

<u>Sample Answer</u>

Ⓐ Ⓑ Ⓒ ●

You will hear:
You will read: (A)   They both make honey.
                  (B)   They both build combs.
                  (C)   Both of them are found in underground nests.
                  (D)   They both live through the winter.

The best answer to the question "According to the speaker, in what way are the queen wasp and the queen bee similar?" is (D), "They both live through the winter." Therefore, you should choose answer (D).

36. (A) A student.
    (B) A guidance counselor.
    (C) A professor.
    (D) An organizer.

37. (A) A branch of biology.
    (B) A group of people working together.
    (C) A club.
    (D) A living thing.

GO ON TO THE NEXT PAGE

38. (A) Categorize major groups of organisms.
    (B) Write a comprehensive definition of the word *life*.
    (C) Study all of the organisms that exist today.
    (D) Study similarities in the activities and functions of organisms.

39. (A) Because there are too many of them.
    (B) Because they are too complex to understand.
    (C) Because they are not easy to find.
    (D) Because no one knows everything about them.

40. (A) Their appearance.
    (B) Their activities and functions.
    (C) The means by which they make food.
    (D) Their methods of communication.

41. (A) Washing clothes.
    (B) The effects of hard water.
    (C) How to buy a water softener.
    (D) How to keep your pipes from freezing.

42. (A) Containing minerals.
    (B) Frozen.
    (C) Difficult.
    (D) Soapy.

43. (A) He doesn't wash them often enough.
    (B) He wonders where they are.
    (C) He uses the wrong kind of soap to wash them.
    (D) They are discolored.

44. (A) Moving to a new apartment.
    (B) Buying a machine.
    (C) Using a powder.
    (D) Heating his home better.

45. (A) Wash some clothes.
    (B) Buy some water-softening powder.
    (C) Clean his house.
    (D) Call the man who tested his water.

46. (A) To explain the rewards of long distance running.
    (B) To raise some funds for a sports event.
    (C) To describe the sacrifices necessary to be on the running team.
    (D) To discuss the first day of team practice.

47. (A) The parents of students on the cross-country running team.
    (B) Swimming coaches.
    (C) Potential members of the running team.
    (D) Professional runners.

48. (A) Rest all day.
    (B) Work out on their own.
    (C) Meet with their coach.
    (D) Participate in a race.

49. (A) Team members will enjoy a busy social life on weekends.
    (B) Team members won't have much time for social activities on weekends.
    (C) Friday nights will be free for social activities.
    (D) Team members will be too tired to do much on the weekend.

50. (A) Practice will begin.
    (B) The speaker will talk about the advantages of sports.
    (C) The speaker will collect the money.
    (D) Parents will go home.

THIS IS THE END OF THE LISTENING COMPREHENSION SECTION OF THE TEST

THE NEXT PART OF THE TEST IS SECTION 2.
TURN TO THE DIRECTIONS FOR SECTION 2 IN YOUR TEST BOOK. READ THEM,
AND BEGIN WORK. DO NOT READ OR WORK ON ANY OTHER SECTION OF THE TEST.
FOR MORE PRACTICE, TAKE A COMPLETE TEST FROM *THE HEINEMANN TOEFL PRACTICE TESTS.*

STOP   STOP   STOP   **STOP**   STOP   STOP   STOP

STRUCTURE AND WRITTEN EXPRESSION

The purpose of Section Two of the TOEFL is to test your knowledge of the structure of standard written English. The language tested in this section is mostly formal, not conversational. Many of the sentence topics used in this section are of a general academic nature. The vocabulary used in Section Two questions is similar to the vocabulary used in TOEFL Section Three, Vocabulary and Reading Comprehension.

GENERAL STRATEGIES FOR SECTION TWO

1. Be familiar with Section Two instructions before you take the actual TOEFL. Then, during the test, you do not need to read the instructions. Move immediately to the first question and begin working.

2. Use your time wisely. You have only about 35 seconds to complete each question in this section.

3. Try to identify the grammar point being tested in each question you read. You can often discover the correct answer right away if you do this. See the Grammar Checkpoint exercises beginning on page 133 for practice.

Structure and Written Expression: Question Types

Section Two contains 40 questions. You have 25 minutes to answer all the questions. There are two parts in this section of the TOEFL. Each part has a different type of question.

Structure (15 questions)
You choose the *correct* sentence completions.

Written Expression (25 questions)
You choose the *incorrect* sentence segments.

Structure Questions

The Structure questions in Section Two of the TOEFL measure your understanding of basic grammar. There are 15 incomplete sentences in this part of the test. Four possible completions are provided in the answer choices for each of the sentences. You must choose the *one correct* answer that completes the sentence.

MODEL

_____ Americans like movies is a well-known fact.

- (A) Most
- (B) That most
- (C) Some
- (D) Because

What is needed in this sentence?
Answer: The subject

▲ Explanation ▼

In this sample question, the subject is being tested. The verb is complete. However, the subject of this sentence, which is a noun clause, is incomplete. You should look for a word to complete this subject. Answer (B) is the correct answer to the question because it completes the subject.

STRUCTURE QUESTION STRATEGIES

1. Read the whole sentence before you choose your answer. In the model above, answer choices (A) and (C) sound correct if you only read the first part of the sentence. You must consider the entire sentence before choosing your answer.

2. Ask yourself, "What is needed in this sentence?" Then, look for the answer choice that completes the sentence. If you cannot immediately identify what is needed, follow the steps in strategy 3.

3. A. Locate the *subject* and the *verb* of the main clause. If the *subject* or *verb* is missing or incomplete, look for it in the answer choices. If the two sentence parts are not missing or incomplete, proceed to Step B.

   B. Look for the *object* or the *complement* of the sentence. If the *object* or *complement* is needed but is missing or incomplete, look for it in the answer choices. If one of these parts is not needed or is not missing, proceed to Step C.

   C. Look for a *subordinate clause*. If the *subordinate clause* is needed and if it is missing a *subject*, a *verb*, or a *clause marker*, look for the missing part in the answer choices. If none of these sentence parts is missing, proceed to Step D.

   D. Look for a *phrase*. If there is a modifying phrase, and if any part of the phrase is missing, look for it in the answer choices.

4. Do not look for ungrammatical segments in the answer choices. Most of the answer choices are grammatically correct by themselves. They only become incorrect when they are put into the sentence.

Written Expression Questions

The Written Expression questions in Section Two of the TOEFL measure your understanding of the grammar of written English. There are 25 sentences in this part of the test. Each sentence has four underlined segments. You must choose the *one incorrect* segment.

MODEL

Mining <u>is</u> the most <u>importantest</u> industry <u>in</u> <u>this</u> state.
      A   B   C D

What is wrong with this sentence?
Answer: The form of the adjective

▲ Explanation ▼

In this question, the correct formation of superlative adjectives is being tested. *Importantest* is not a word in English. Answer (B) is the correct answer to the question because *importantest* is incorrect.
Correction: *important*

MODEL

Tomorrow we <u>went</u> to <u>the store</u> to buy <u>some</u> new <u>furniture</u>.
            A   B   C   D
What is wrong with this sentence?
Answer: The verb tense

▲ Explanation ▼

In this sentence, the tense of the verb is being tested. The past tense *went* does not agree with the time marker *tomorrow*. Answer (A) is the correct answer to the question because *went* is incorrect.
Correction: *are going/ will go/are going to*

WRITTEN EXPRESSION QUESTION STRATEGIES

1. Ask yourself, "What is wrong with this sentence?" In this part of the test, you are looking for the *incorrect* part of a sentence. This is a very different task from the task in the Structure questions. You must remember to quickly change your approach when you begin the Written Expression part of the test.

2. QUICKLY scan the four underlined segments to find what is wrong. One of these segments may be incorrect on its own, as in the first model above. If none of the choices is incorrect on its own, proceed to strategy 3.

3. Read the entire sentence. Compare the underlined segments to other parts of the sentence. Most of the incorrect segments in this section are wrong because of their relationship to other parts of the sentence, as in the second model above.

4. Do not waste time looking for errors that are not underlined. All errors occur in the underlined segments of the sentences.

5. Do not waste time thinking about how to correct the incorrect segment of the sentence. Once you locate the incorrect segment, mark it on your answer sheet and move on.

NOTE: Strategy 5 is very important to follow when you take the TOEFL. Many students, however, feel that correcting errors while studying for the TOEFL is helpful. By correcting errors in practice questions, students learn to more efficiently identify errors on the actual TOEFL. For this reason, many exercises in the Grammar Checkpoint Study provide practice in error correction. The Section Two Checkpoint Test and comprehensive Section Test will not provide this practice. Remember that on the actual TOEFL, there is *no time* and *no need* for error correction.

Careful review of grammar and practice with Structure and Written Expression questions in the Grammar Checkpoint Study will help you prepare for Section Two of the TOEFL. This type of review, however, is not meant to replace a regular plan of study of all aspects of English. A regular plan of study is best accomplished in daily English language classes where you practice not only grammar, but also reading, vocabulary, writing, listening, and speaking in English. Studying all aspects of English is the best way to improve your overall mastery of English grammar. As you read and hear English inside and outside the classroom, you should work to develop an awareness of the function of words, phrases, and clauses in both spoken and written sentences and longer conversations. Punctuation of written sentences is also an important part of mastering English grammar.

General language study inside and outside the classroom will develop your overall mastery of English grammar. The Grammar Checkpoint Study will help you master the specific points of grammar tested on the TOEFL. These combined types of study will greatly increase your chances to succeed on the TOEFL.

✔ GRAMMAR CHECKPOINTS

Below is a list of the Grammar Checkpoints covered in the Grammar Checkpoint Study. Checkpoint Tests are included in this list. Page numbers are provided for easy reference.

   The Diagnostic Test on pages 19–41 has been cross-referenced to this list of Grammar Checkpoints. Use the answer key for this test to refer you to the checkpoints you need to concentrate on in the Grammar Checkpoint Study. While you should concentrate on the checkpoints that you missed on the Diagnostic Test, we recommend that you review all of the Grammar Checkpoints.

   A Structure and Written Expression Section Test follows the Grammar Checkpoint Study. This test should be taken after you have studied all the checkpoints listed below.

These Grammar Checkpoints cover the structures that are tested in Section Two of the TOEFL. Most of this grammar is tested in both the Structure questions and the Written Expression questions. Some grammar points, however, are only tested in one type of question or the other. This is noted for you under each checkpoint heading. The Grammar Checkpoint Test questions have the same formats as those on the TOEFL.

> **NOTE:** The Grammar Checkpoint explanations and exercises utilize and review fundamental grammar terms and concepts. For extra help, refer to the Grammar Appendix on page 435. You should refer to the Grammar Appendix for the following reasons:
>
> 1. If the Diagnostic Test indicated that grammar was your weak area;
>
> 2. If you had trouble understanding the grammar terms used in the Structure Question Strategies (e.g., *object*, *complement*, *clause marker*); or,
>
> 3. If you feel you need to review some of the basic grammatical terms and concepts of English.

✔ GRAMMAR CHECKPOINT STUDY

G✔1   Check Subjects, Objects, and Noun Complements

All of the English sentences tested in Section Two of the TOEFL contain subjects. In addition, many of them contain objects (direct, indirect, or objects of prepositions) and noun complements.

Subject (S): Doer of the action in a sentence

    <u>Peter</u> eats at 5:00.
     S

Object (O):
1. Direct receiver of the action of a sentence *(DO)*
2. Indirect receiver of the action of a sentence *(IO)*
3. Object of a preposition *(O of Prep)*

    I gave <u>Jane</u> a <u>book</u> for her <u>birthday</u>.
         IO   DO   O of Prep

Noun Complement (C):
1. Subject identifier—after the verb BE *(SC)*
2. Object identifier—after the direct object of a sentence *(OC)*

    Jack is a <u>doctor</u>.
         SC
    They elected him <u>president</u>.
             OC

The subjects, objects, and noun complements of English sentences normally occur as one of the five noun structure forms given below.

Noun (phrase):   <u>Roses</u> are <u>beautiful plants</u>.
                        S   *C*

Pronoun: <u>You</u> like roses.
                        S

                        <u>You</u> gave <u>him</u> the roses.
                        S   *IO*

Gerund (phrase):   <u>Growing roses</u> is your favorite hobby.
                        S

                        You relax by <u>growing roses</u>.
                                  O of Prep

Infinitive (phrase): You like <u>to grow roses</u>.
                            DO

Noun clause: Everyone says <u>that you grow beautiful roses</u>.
                              DO

The TOEFL tests your understanding of noun structures used as subjects, objects, and complements by:
1. using incorrect word order in these noun structures;
2. repeating subjects, objects, and complements unnecessarily;
3. leaving out necessary parts of subject, object, and complement noun structures; or,
4. using other structures where noun structure subjects, objects, or complements are needed (e.g., using a prepositional phrase instead of a noun clause).

MODEL
They didn't know _____.
 (A)   what to do (B)   do (C)   to do what (D)   they should do **What is needed in this sentence?** **Answer:** The direct object

▼ Explanation ▲

In this question, the direct object is being tested. Answer (B) is a verb. It cannot be a direct object. In answer (C), the word order of the direct object is incorrect. In answer (D) the direct object is incomplete. Answer (A) is the correct answer to the question because it contains all the parts of a direct object in the correct order.

+---+
| ☛ **ON THE TOEFL TEST** |
+---+
| • Check to see that the subjects, objects, and complements in TOEFL |
| questions are correctly formed. |
+---+

See the Grammar Appendix #1, #2, and #3, pages 435–436 if you need more information on subjects, objects, and complements.

See the Grammar Appendix #32, #33, and #28, pages 455–459 if you need more information on gerunds, infinitives, and noun clauses.

EXERCISE 1A: Practice with Noun Structures: Subjects, Objects, and Noun Complements

In each of the sentences, underline the noun structures. Then, beneath each of these structures, identify it as one of the following:

Noun (phrase)
Pronoun
Gerund (phrase)
Infinitive (phrase)
Noun clause

1. <u>The girls</u> like <u>to shop</u>.
    Noun phrase   Infinitive

2. We haven't completed our assignment yet.

3. What I want is to be happy.

4. Patricia put the plate on the table.

5. Clark enjoys singing.

6. What Susan wants most is to succeed.

EXERCISE 1B: Practice with the Functions of Noun Structures

In each of the sentences below, underline the noun structures. Then, beneath each structure, identify its function as one of the following:

S   (subject)
DO (direct object)
IO   (indirect object)
O   of Prep (object of the preposition)
C   (complement)

1. <u>Whatever he does</u> will be the <u>right thing</u>.
          S   C

2. Carol makes very good meals for us.

3. Swimming is not permitted at this beach.

4. Jerome loves to laugh.

5. I thought that he would be here by now.

6. The receptionist handed the doctor a note.

EXERCISE 1C: More Practice with Subjects, Objects, and Noun Complements

Circle the correct answer. Then, on the line provided, use the choices provided to answer the question: *What is needed in this sentence?* Choices:
   A subject
   A direct object
   An indirect object
   The object of a preposition
   A complement

1. _____ didn't deliver the mail today.
   (A) For the postman
   (B) Because of the snow
   (C) The postman
   (D) Although the postman

   What is needed in this sentence? _____A subject_____

2. Andrew likes _____ .
   (A) fast cars
   (B) in a fast car
   (C) he will buy a fast car
   (D) that a fast car

   What is needed in this sentence? _____

3. My older brother is _____ .
   (A) he's a doctor
   (B) a doctor
   (C) for a doctor
   (D) when he's a doctor

   What is needed in this sentence? _____

4. _____ in the dorm is not always easy.
   (A) Living
   (B) While living
   (C) I live
   (D) When I live

   What is needed in this sentence? _____

5. We gave _____ a new bicycle.
   (A) he's our son
   (B) it to our son
   (C) that's our son
   (D) our son

   What is needed in this sentence?_____

6. The problem is _____ .
   (A) haven't arrived the textbooks
   (B) that the textbooks haven't arrived yet
   (C) haven't the textbooks arrived yet
   (D) that the textbooks that haven't arrived yet

   What is needed in this sentence?_____

7. _____ is not running well today.
   (A) That Jane's car
   (B) Jane has a car
   (C) In Jane's car
   (D) Jane's car

   What is needed in this sentence?_____

8. Clarence won't be able to go with _____ .
   (A) us
   (B) where we go
   (C) he will stay home
   (D) to the game

   What is needed in this sentence?_____

9. He always enjoys _____ .
   (A) he does whatever
   (B) he does
   (C) whatever he does
   (D) of his doing

   What is needed in this sentence?_____

10. I don't want _____
    (A) when shopping
    (B) shopped
    (C) I shop
    (D) to shop

    What is needed in this sentence?_____

11. _____ is my favorite hobby.

    (A) While reading
    (B) Reading
    (C) If I read
    (D) When I read

    What is needed in this sentence?_____

G✔2   Check Subjects and Verbs

Each sentence and subordinate clause tested in Section Two of the TOEFL must have a subject and a finite verb (a verb which can show past and present tense and to which the third person singular -s can be attached.)

Peter <u>wants</u>   to go with us tomorrow.
S   *Finite V*

Peter <u>has</u>   been wanting to go with us for a long time.
S   *Finite V*

▼▼▼

The TOEFL tests your knowledge of subjects and verbs by:
1. leaving out subjects or finite verbs when they are needed;
2. adding extra subjects or finite verbs to sentences or subordinate clauses; or,
3. introducing clause markers (e.g., *which, how, because*) in front of the finite verbs of main clauses.

MODEL

Because he didn't feel well, _____ to stay home from school.
   (A)   the boy he wanted
   (B)   the boy
   (C)   the boy wanted
   (D)   what the boy wanted

What is needed in this sentence?
Answer: The subject and the verb of the main clause

▼ **Explanation** ▲

In this question, the subject and verb are being tested. All four of the answers contain the subject, *boy*. However, answer (A) contains two subjects. Answer (B) contains a subject only. Answer (D) contains a noun clause subject. Answer (C) is the correct answer to the question because it contains the missing subject and finite verb.

MODEL

<u>Until have</u> matured, <u>most children</u> live with <u>their</u> parents.
     A   B   C   D
     Sub. clause   Main clause

What is wrong with this sentence?
(Remember you are looking for the error in the sentence.)
Answer: The subject of the subordinate clause is missing.

▼ Explanation ▲

In this question, there are two clauses—a main clause and a subordinate clause. The main clause has a subject, *most children*, and a verb, *live*. The subordinate clause, however, has only a verb, *have matured*. In this clause, the subject is missing. Answer (A) is the correct answer to the question because *until have* is incorrect.

Correction: *Until they have matured*

MODEL

This exam _____ everything in chapter five.
  (A) which covers
  (B) it covers
  (C) covers it
  (D) covers

What is needed in this sentence?
Answer: The verb

▼ Explanation ▲

In this question, the finite verb is missing. Answer (A) contains both a clause marker and a verb. Answer (B) contains both a subject and a verb. Answer (C) contains both a verb and an object. Answer (D) is the correct answer to the question because it contains only the finite verb.

☞ ON THE TOEFL TEST

• Check to see that the subjects and verbs in TOEFL questions are correct.

See the Grammar Appendix, #14–#22, pages 442–450 if you need more information on finite verbs.
See the Grammar Appendix, #26–#30, pages 454–457 if you need more information on clause markers and clauses.

EXERCISE 2A: Practice with Subject and Verb Errors

Each of the sentences below contains one main clause. Some also contain a subordinate clause. Circle each subject and underline each verb in the sentences. Then, on the line provided, put an *I* if the sentence is incorrect and a *C* if the sentence is correct. Correct all errors. More than one correction in a sentence is possible.

_I_ 1. Last year <u>he bought</u> a new computer.

_C_ 2. When (he) was sick, (I) took him some chicken soup.

____ 3. These curtains they need to be pressed.

____ 4. Clearing away the dead leaves to plant a garden.

____ 5. My brother's best friend staying with us this weekend.

---

140   Structure and Written Expression

_____ 6. Last weekend we played basketball together at the new gym.

_____ 7. This can is contains more coffee than the other one does.

_____ 8. The party last night which was a lot of fun.

_____ 9. We enjoyed our vacation even though it was very short.

_____ 10. I hope that I will do well on my next Spanish exam.

_____ 11. When graduates, my roommate will give me his stereo.

_____ 12. The airplane that he flies it is a small one.

EXERCISE 2B: More Practice with Subjects and Verbs

Circle the correct answer. Then, use the choices provided to answer the question: *What is needed in this sentence?* Choices:
    The verb
    The subject and the verb

1. Although he was tired, William _____ working on his paper.
    (A) who continued
    (B) continued
    (C) he continued
    (D) continuing

What is needed in this sentence? _____ *The verb* _____

2. _____ on me to lend him my history notes.
    (A) Andrew counted
    (B) Andrew counting
    (C) That Andrew counted
    (D) Since Andrew counted

What is needed in this sentence? _____

3. According to recent studies, winter _____ the season when the most traffic accidents occur.
    (A) being
    (B) in
    (C) when
    (D) is

What is needed in this sentence? _____

4. In the 1970s students in American colleges and universities _____ many protests and demonstrations.
    (A) they staged
    (B) staged
    (C) staging
    (D) to stage

What is needed in this sentence? _____

5. _____ more susceptible to certain diseases than adults are.
    (A) Children
    (B) Children who are
    (C) Children are
    (D) Children being

What is needed in this sentence? _____

6. Although they had no money, _____ content.
    (A) being that they
    (B) and they
    (C) they were
    (D) for they were

What is needed in this sentence? _____

EXERCISE 2C: More Practice with Subjects and Verbs

Choose the letter of the underlined word or group of words that is incorrect. Then, use the choices provided to answer the question: *What is wrong with this sentence?* Choices:
        Missing subject or verb
        Repeated subject or verb
        Unnecessary clause marker
    Correct each error.

        was
_A_ 1. I not happy about going home so early last night.
        A   B   C D

What is wrong with this sentence? ___*Missing verb*_____

_____ 2. Many people enjoy tennis, which find relaxing.
             A   B   C   D

What is wrong with this sentence? _____

_____ 3. My cousin, Angelica, she lives in California, and she likes it there very much.
           A   B   C D

What is wrong with this sentence? _____

_____ 4. The snow is makes winter driving a hazard, especially in areas where no one plows the
                A   B   C   D
    roads.

What is wrong with this sentence? _____

_____ 5. Fireflies which are insects that glow in the dark and are often captured by children and
                 A   B   C
    kept in jars.
    D

What is wrong with this sentence? _____

_____ 6. Last week Marietta <u>sad</u> <u>because</u> she lost the cat that she <u>loved</u> so much and that
            A   B   C

her son gave her.
       D

What is wrong with this sentence? _____

G✔3   Check Expressions of Quantity

Some English expressions of quantity are used only with countable nouns (nouns which can be made plural, e.g., *boy – boys*). Other expressions of quantity are used only with uncountable nouns (nouns that normally cannot be made plural, e.g., *happiness*). Still other expressions of quantity are used with both countable and uncountable nouns.

USED WITH COUNTABLE NOUNS	USED WITH UNCOUNTABLE NOUNS
many	much
number of	amount of
few	little
a few	a little
fewer	less
none	none
some	some
any	any
a lot of	a lot of
one, two, three…	
several	

▼▼▼

The TOEFL tests your understanding of expressions of quantity by using them incorrectly with countable and uncountable nouns.

MODEL

The professor <u>will require</u> <u>us</u> to conduct research, <u>many</u> of which can be done
                A   B   C

in <u>our own library</u>.
      D

What is wrong with this sentence?
Answer: *Many* and *research* are not in agreement.

▼ **Explanation** ▲

In this question, *research* is an uncountable noun. The expression of quantity, *many*, refers back to *research*, but *many* cannot be used with uncountable nouns. Answer (C) is the correct answer to the question because *many* is incorrect.
Correction: *much*

☞ ON THE TOEFL TEST

- Check to see that the expressions of quantity used in TOEFL questions agree with the nouns they refer to.

See the Grammar Appendix, #4, page 436 if you need more information about countable and uncountable nouns.

EXERCISE 3A: Agreement Practice for Expressions of Quantity and Nouns

Draw a line through the phrases that cannot be used to complete the sentences.

1. Elizabeth has _____ .
   ~~too much cars~~
   several cars
   a few cars
   a little cars
   some cars
   less cars than Joe does

2. Mothers sometimes give _____ .
   too much advice to their children
   several advice to their children
   a few advice to their children
   a little advice to their children
   some advice to their children
   less advice to their children than fathers do

EXERCISE 3B: More Practice with Expressions of Quantity

In each sentence, there are two expressions of quantity. One of them is incorrect. Choose the letter of the incorrect expression of quantity, and then correct the error.

                                                   many
_B_ 1. <u>Many</u> people feel that there are too <u>~~much~~</u> rules in this organization.
        A   B

____ 2. <u>Several</u> chemicals, a <u>little of</u> which can be dangerous, exist in water.
          A   B

____ 3. They had <u>some</u> trouble last night with <u>an amount of</u> the lights in the theater.
                    A   B

____ 4. Vincent has <u>fewer</u> fruit and <u>less</u> cereal in his bowl than I do.
                       A   B

____ 5. Harry has <u>much</u> worries this semester, but Rick has <u>none</u>.
                     A   B

____ 6. We have <u>a lot of</u> housework to do, <u>many</u> of which should have been done yesterday.
                   A   B

G✔4   Check Articles

The English articles are *a/an* and *the*. The article *a/an* is used with singular, countable indefinite nouns (nouns referring to things that are new to either the speaker or the listener). The spelling of this article changes from *a* to *an* when the word it precedes begins with a vowel sound.

> I need to buy *a* book.
> I need to buy *an* English book.

The article *the* is used with singular and plural nouns as well as uncountable nouns. However, the article *the* only occurs with definite nouns (nouns referring to things the speaker and listener already know about or which are made specific by their use in a sentence).

> *The* book I want is *The Heinemann TOEFL Preparation Course.*

The TOEFL tests your knowledge of articles by:
1. using articles incorrectly with definite and indefinite countable and uncountable nouns;
2. leaving out articles when they are needed;
3. adding articles when they are not needed; or,
4. spelling *a/an* incorrectly.

MODEL

Patricia <u>is taking</u> a very <u>difficult</u> <u>classes</u> <u>this</u> semester.
       A   B   C D

What is wrong with this sentence?
Answer: The article and the noun it refers to do not agree.

▼ Explanation ▲

In this question, a singular article is being used with a plural noun. The article *a* should only be used with singular, indefinite, countable nouns. In this sentence, *a* is used with the noun *classes*, which is plural. Answer (C) is the correct answer because *classes* is the incorrect form of the noun.
Correction: *class*

MODEL

<u>The mongoose</u> <u>is very clever</u> creature <u>that</u> catches <u>snakes</u>.
       A   B   C   D

What is wrong with this sentence?
Answer: An article is missing.

▼ Explanation ▲

In this question, the singular indefinite noun *creature* needs an article. Answer (B) is the correct answer to the question because *is very clever* is incorrect.
Correction: *is a very clever*

MODEL

A sun was shining brightly when we arrived at the lake.
A   B   C   D

What is wrong with this sentence?
Answer: An incorrect article has been used.

▼ Explanation ▲

In this question, the wrong article has been chosen. *Sun* is a definite noun. There is only one sun above the earth; it is definite to everyone. Definite nouns do not take the article *a*. Answer (A) is the correct answer to this question because *a sun* is incorrect.
Correction: *The sun*

MODEL

Peter is looking for an university where he can play basketball.
A   B   C   D

What is wrong with this sentence?
Answer: The incorrect article has been used.

▼ Explanation ▲

In this question, the article is spelled incorrectly. The indefinite article has two spellings. Before a consonant sound or a *y* or *w* sound, it is spelled *a*. However, before a vowel sound, it is spelled *an*. In this sentence, *university* begins with a vowel symbol. However it begins with a *y* sound. Answer (C) is the correct answer to this question because *an university* is incorrect.
Correction: *a university*

☞ ON THE TOEFL TEST

- Check to see that *a/an* is spelled correctly.
- Check to see that articles are used only when they are needed.
- Check to see that the correct articles are used with the nouns they refer to.

See the Grammar Appendix, #4, page 436 if you need more information on definite and indefinite countable and uncountable nouns.

See the chart in the Grammar Appendix, #6, page 438 if you need more information on articles.

EXERCISE 4A: Practice Identifying Problems with Articles

In each sentence below underline the articles. Then, on the line provided, put an *I* if the sentence is incorrect and a *C* if the sentence is correct. Correct the errors.

            an
I   1. After a hour of waiting patiently, Larry left the doctor's office without seeing the doctor.

C   2. They don't have much money, so they can't buy a house.

___ 3. The lion is generally considered to be the ferocious animal.

___ 4. Many dogs are bred for a specific purposes.

___ 5. He tried to tell truth about the accident, but he was too upset to remember all of the details.

___ 6. The man in the corner, who is the new director of the library, is her husband.

___ 7. Karen's portfolio provided me with a clear indications of her qualifications.

___ 8. Marilyn is very talented artist whose works are being displayed in an art gallery on First Avenue.

___ 9. The post office is a very busy place during the holiday season when well-wishers send cards and packages to their families and friends.

___ 10. A honest person always returns borrowed things.

___ 11. Craig bought his new camera at discount store.

___ 12. Charles has the oldest car in the parking lot.

EXERCISE 4B: More Practice with Articles

Choose the letter of the underlined word or group of words that is incorrect. Then, correct each error.

          the
A   1. Under table were some boots, a scarf, and three books.
         A   B   C   D

___ 2. The happiness is a quality that comes from within a person.
         A   B   C   D

___ 3. My uncle used to be a umpire at the local baseball games.
         A   B   C   D

___ 4. Before leaving the office, please turn off computer and lock the filing cabinets.
                A   B   C   D

___ 5. In the United States, cattle rustling is still a serious crimes.
     A   B   C   D

_____ 6. <u>The</u> reason that I do not want to buy <u>a</u> new car is that I don't have <u>a</u> money necessary for
     A   B   C

     such <u>an</u> extravagant expense.
           D

G✔5   Check Personal, Possessive, and Reflexive Pronouns

In English, pronouns are used to replace or refer to nouns, gerunds, infinitives, and sometimes entire clauses. Pronouns change form depending on their functions in sentences.

PRONOUNS				
Personal		**Possessive**		**Reflexive**
Subject	**Object**	**Adjective**	**Pronoun**	
I	me	my	mine	myself
you	you	your	yours	yourself
he	him	his	his	himself
she	her	her	hers	herself
it	it	its	——	itself
we	us	our	ours	ourselves
they	them	their	theirs	themselves
one	one	one's	——	oneself

The TOEFL tests your understanding of pronouns by:
1. using the wrong pronoun types (subject, object, possessive, or reflexive);
2. using pronouns that do not agree in number with the nouns they refer to or replace;
3. using pronouns that do not agree in gender with the nouns they refer to or replace; or,
4. forming reflexive pronouns incorrectly.

MODEL
Although Alexander liked <u>him</u> new apartment very <u>much</u>, <u>he</u> found <u>it</u>   A   B C   D somewhat noisy. **What is wrong with this sentence?** **Answer:** The possessive adjective form

▼ Explanation ▲

In this question, the pronoun *him* is in object form. It should be in possessive adjective form. Answer (A) is the correct answer to this question because *him* is incorrect.
Correction: *his*

☛ ON THE TOEFL TEST

- Check to see that the pronouns used in TOEFL questions agree in type (subject, object, possessive, or reflexive), number (singular or plural), and gender (masculine or feminine) with the nouns they replace or refer to.
- Check to see that reflexive pronouns are correctly formed.

See the Grammar Appendix, #8, page 440, if you need more information on pronoun forms and functions.

EXERCISE 5A: Practice with Pronouns

Circle the correct pronoun in each pair.

1. They took (their/theirs) children to the amusement park.

2. Everybody except (he/him) came to the rehearsal last night.

3. Bryan finished the project by (himself/hisself).

4. Delilah will show this work to a colleague of (her/hers).

5. Mobile homes are relatively inexpensive, so many people own (it/them).

6. Cats bathe (theirselves/themselves) several times a day.

7. Playing a musical instrument is the best way to understand (its/their) capabilities.

8. Only (he/him) was injured in the accident.

9. It was (they/them) who sent us the information about colleges.

10. (Him/His) writing is more polished than (mine/my).

11. Because Margaret and Sue were late, we had to start the meeting without (they/them).

12. The apartment manager gave (we/us) back our deposit.

13. I'm sorry that you have to clean your room by (you/yourself).

14. I didn't expect Anne to be at home this evening, but it was (her/she) who came to the door when I arrived.

15. I must keep (myself/me) busy, or I will get bored.

EXERCISE 5B: Practice Identifying Incorrect Pronouns

In each sentence, choose the letter of the underlined pronoun that is incorrect. Then, correct the error.

its

__B__ 1. This library was founded by <u>our</u> college in 1865 and took <s>it</s> name from a secret
             A   B
benefactor who donated <u>his</u> fortune for <u>its</u> development.
                       C   D

____ 2. <u>He</u> who hesitates can lose <u>him</u> place in the race and do damage to <u>himself</u> and to <u>his</u>
          A   B   C   D
chances for success.

____ 3. <u>They</u> gave <u>us</u> <u>his</u> undivided attention but still couldn't understand what <u>we</u> were
          A   B   C   D
saying.

____ 4. <u>We</u> cannot finish <u>it</u> without <u>you</u> and <u>they</u>.
          A   B   C   D

____ 5. Only <u>her</u> had the courage to try <u>our</u> challenge by <u>herself</u>, and <u>she</u> succeeded.
               A   B   C   D

____ 6. While <u>they</u> were helping <u>theirselves</u> to the sandwiches, <u>I</u> was treating <u>myself</u> to the
                A   B   C   D
salad.

G✔6   Check Adjectives and Nouns

English nouns are often modified by adjectives. Adjectives usually come before the nouns they modify. Adjectives cannot be made plural. Nouns must be made plural when they are countable and plural in meaning.

▼▼▼

The TOEFL tests your understanding of adjectives and nouns by:
1. using incorrect singular or plural noun and adjective forms; or,
2. using incorrect adjective-noun word order

MODEL
<u>A</u> <u>bolt</u> of lightning travels <u>twenty thousands</u> <u>miles</u> in one <u>second</u>. A   B   C   D **What is wrong with this sentence?** **Answer:** The form of an adjective

▼ Explanation ▲

In this question, *twenty thousands* is a compound adjective modifying *miles*. As discussed above, adjectives cannot be made plural in English. Answer (B) is the correct answer to this question because *twenty thousands* is incorrect.

Correction: *twenty thousand*

MODEL

Some trees grow to be over three hundred foot high.
  A   B   C   D

What is wrong with this sentence?
Answer: The form of a noun

▼ Explanation ▲

In this question, *three hundred* is a compound adjective. It is plural in meaning and the noun it modifies should be plural. *Foot* is not in its plural form in this sentence. Answer (D) is the correct answer to this question because *foot* is incorrect.

Correction: *feet*

MODEL

The paint bright yellow that she chose for her bedroom creates a cheery
            A   B   C   D
atmosphere.

What is wrong with this sentence?
Answer: The order of adjectives

▼ Explanation ▲

In this question, the adjectives *bright* and *yellow* come after the noun *paint*, which they modify. They should come before this noun. Answer (A) is the correct answer to this question because *paint bright yellow* is incorrect.

Correction: *bright yellow paint*

☛ ON THE TOEFL TEST

- Check to see that all of the adjectives and nouns in TOEFL questions are in the correct order.
- Check to see that all of the adjectives and nouns are in the correct form.

See the Grammar Appendix, #4, page 436 if you need more information on nouns.
See the Grammar Appendix, #12, page 442 if you need more information on adjectives.

EXERCISE 6:   Practice with Adjectives and Nouns

In each sentence, choose the letter of the underlined word or group of words that is incorrect. Then, correct the error.

_D_ 1. The average American college costs more than eight thousand dollar per year.
                   A   B   C   D

_____ 2. Alice always wore magnificents costumes to the Halloween parties she attended at the
                 A   B   C
country club.
D

_____ 3. Winters in the northern Rocky Mountains last up to nine month; spring, summer, and
                     A   B   C
fall last only about one month each.
                               D

_____ 4. Sophisticated cameras of today require only two or three second to make automatic
      A   B   C
focusing adjustments.
          D

_____ 5. Hundreds of thousand of tourists visit Washington D.C. every spring to see the beautiful
      A   B   C
cherry blossoms there.
         D

_____ 6. The woodchuck is a creature territorial that does not allow other woodchucks
                       A   B
within fifty feet of its burrow.
     C D

_____ 7. Computers of the past were cumbersome and complicated, but a six-years-old child can
                           A   B
easily use today's computers.
   C   D

_____ 8. The five-men team ran fifty miles in less than three hours
         A   B   C   D

_____ 9. A bicycle popular is the mountain bike, which people of all ages are enjoying.
       A   B   C D

_____ 10. During the winter months, clears skies are usually accompanied by low temperatures.
           A   B   C   D

_____ 11. After her long day, Angela took a bath hot and relaxed on her comfortable sofa with a
              A   B   C
good book.
D

Grammar Checkpoint Test One for G✔1 through G✔6

Allow yourself 5 minutes to complete this checkpoint test. There are 11 questions on the test. Check your answers in the answer key. Next to each answer is the number of the checkpoint that is being tested in each of these questions. Use these numbers to determine which checkpoints, if any, you need to study again.

Questions 1 through 7

Circle the letter of the underlined part of the sentence that is incorrect.

1. Although he <u>has written</u> several plays and poems, John Ashbery <u>is best known</u> for <u>him</u> work in
           A   B   C
   the <u>area of</u> art criticism.
       D

2. In the late spring, <u>the honeysuckle</u>, with <u>its</u> delicate yellow blossoms, <u>fills</u> the air with <u>a aroma</u>
                     A   B   C   D
   resembling that of honey.

3. <u>Kites</u> vary in size, shape, and <u>weight</u>, according to <u>the</u> fancy of <u>its</u> creators.
    A   B   C   D

4. <u>The most</u> visible <u>changes physical</u> of aging <u>take place</u> in <u>the skin</u>.
     A   B   C   D

5. The Richter scale provides a <u>fairly accurate</u> <u>measurements</u> of seismic <u>disturbances</u>.
    A   B   C   D

6. Analysis of the <u>small number</u> of known native language families in eastern North America
              A
   <u>demonstrates</u> that <u>they</u> are no more than five <u>thousands</u> years old.
     B   C   D

7. There is <u>fewer</u> oxygen available in <u>the</u> atmosphere of Jupiter than <u>there is</u> on <u>earth</u>.
        A   B   C   D

Questions 8 through 11

Circle the letter of the one word or phrase that best completes each sentence.

8. _____ can result from damage to DNA molecules.
   (A) cells mutate
   (B) Cell mutation
   (C) While cells mutate
   (D) During cell mutation

9. New York ironweed, with its small, dark purple thistle flowers, sometimes _____ to a height of eight feet.
   (A) grows
   (B) growing
   (C) it grows
   (D) up

10. _____ is susceptible to subtle political changes is well-known.
(A) That the stock market
(B) What the stock market
(C) Because the stock market
(D) The stock market

11. Phillis Wheatley, whose first book of poems was published when she was only nineteen years old, _____ the object of public attention because she was a black slave.
(A) who was
(B) being
(C) as
(D) was

G✔7   Check Verb Tense Forms

The English verb has five principle parts. These principle parts are used in forming English verb tenses. The principle parts of some English verbs are given in the chart below.

PRINCIPLE PARTS OF SOME ENGLISH VERBS				
Base Form	Present	Present Participle	Past	Past Participle
start	start(s)	starting	started	started
hope	hope(s)	hoping	hoped	hoped
study	study(ies)	studying	studied	studied
eat	eat(s)	eating	ate	eaten
give	give(s)	giving	gave	given
have	have (has)	having	had	had
be	am/is/are	being	was/were	been

When parts of the verb BE (*am, is, are, was, were, be, been, being*) are used to form active verb tenses, they are followed by a *present participle* as, for example, in the continuous tenses. (Sometimes the verb BE *is* used to form passive sentences. When this happens, it is followed by a past participle. See G✔9, below, for study of this use of BE.)

I <u>am</u> <u>living</u> here now.
  BE + Present participle

I have <u>been</u> <u>living</u> here for a long time.
    BE + Present participle

When parts of the verb HAVE (*have, has, had, having*) are used to form verb tenses, they are followed by a *past participle* as, for example, in the perfect tenses.

I <u>have</u> <u>lived</u> here for a long time.
  HAVE + Past participle

I <u>have been</u> living here for a long time.
  HAVE + Past participle

The —*ing* form of the verb can NEVER function as the finite verb of a clause.

Incorrect:	George <u>having</u> <u>had</u> his paper finished for a few days.
Correction:	George <u>has</u> <u>had</u> his paper finished for a few days.
Incorrect:	Bill feels that we <u>making</u> too much noise.
Correction:	Bill feels that we <u>are</u> <u>making</u> too much noise.

▼▼▼

The TOEFL tests your understanding of the use of verb parts to form English verb tenses by:

1. leaving out verb parts or adding extra verb parts to tense forms;
2. combining verb parts incorrectly;
3. using the ——ING form of verbs when finite verb forms are needed; or,
4. forming irregular verbs incorrectly.

MODEL

David <u>has eating</u> <u>in</u> <u>this</u> restaurant <u>several</u> times.
      A   B   C   D

What is wrong with this sentence?
Answer: The verb form following *has*

▼ Explanation ▲

In this question, the verb *has* is followed by the present participle form of *eat*. This results in the incorrect formation of the present perfect tense. As mentioned above, when *has* is used, it should be followed by a past participle. Answer (A) is the correct answer to this question because *has eating* is incorrect.

Correction: *has eaten*

MODEL

The professor <u>writed</u> the answers on <u>the blackboard</u> <u>so</u> everyone <u>could see</u>
            A   B   C   D

them.

What is wrong with this sentence?
Answer: The past form of an irregular verb

▼ Explanation ▲

Write is an irregular verb. It does not make its past form by adding ——*ed* the way regular verbs do. Answer (A) is the correct answer to this question because *writed* is incorrect.

Correction: *wrote*

☞ ON THE TOEFL TEST

- Check to see that verb tenses in TOEFL questions are formed correctly.
- Check to see that irregular verb forms are correct as well.

See the Grammar Appendix, #14, page 442 for a list of irregular verbs.
See the Grammar Appendix, #15, page 445 if you need more information on verb tense formation.

EXERCISE 7A: Practice with Verb Tense Formation

Change the following verbs to the past tenses indicated.

	Simple Past	Past Continuous	Past Perfect
1. sit	sat	was/were sitting	had sat
2. come			
3. walk			
4. play			
5. have			
6. make			
7. forget			
8. open			
9. look			
10. think			
11. show			

EXERCISE 7B: Practice Identifying Incorrect Verb Forms

Choose the letter of the incorrect verb form in each sentence.

__A__ 1. Television <u>has became</u> a popular form of entertainment for people who <u>prefer</u> not to go
            A   B
         out in the evening.

_____ 2. John <u>tried</u> to stay awake while the professor <u>was spoke</u>.
              A   B

_____ 3. Amelia Earhart <u>disappeared</u> at sea while she <u>flying</u> her airplane.
                            A   B

_____ 4. Physical exercise <u>has help</u> many people because it <u>relieves</u> stress.
                               A   B

_____ 5. Richard <u>had been live</u> in Chicago for five years when his company <u>transferred</u> him to
                     A   B
         New York.

_____ 6. Edward <u>has been playing</u> a lot of golf since he <u>gotted</u> his new golf clubs.
                    A   B

_____ 7. For the past few years, scientists <u>have studying</u> the effects that pollution <u>has</u> on the
                                          A   B

ozone layer.

_____ 8. Rain <u>maked</u> it impossible for us to play football, so we all <u>went</u> to the movies instead.
              A   B

_____ 9. People who <u>want</u> to improve their carpentry skills sometimes go to special schools
                    A

where they <u>learning</u> to build houses.
            B

_____ 10. Paula <u>buyed</u> her car in the fall when prices <u>had been reduced</u>.
                A   B

_____ 11. I <u>like</u> the work he <u>has doing</u> for the committee.
            A   B

G✔8   Check Verb Tense Meanings

Each different tense form in English has a different meaning. The chart below summarizes these verb tense meanings.

TENSE FORM	TENSE MEANING
Simple present:	Expresses an event or situation that exists now or that *usually*, *always*, or *often* exists. He always eats supper at 7:30. Water boils at 100 degrees centigrade.
Simple past:	Expresses an event or situation that began and ended in the past. He ate supper last night at 7:30.
Simple future:	Expresses an event or situation that will happen at one particular time in the future. He will eat dinner tomorrow night at 7:30.
The continuous tenses:	Give the idea that an event or situation is in progress during a particular time. While he was eating, the doorbell rang.
The perfect tenses:	Give the idea that one event happens or happened before another time or event. He had eaten before she arrived.

The meaning of a tense used in an English sentence must agree with the time meaning of the rest of the sentence. The time meaning of a sentence is often determined by words or expressions that act as *time markers*. Some of the most common English time markers are listed on page 158.

SOME COMMON TIME MARKERS USED ON THE TOEFL	
Since	Often used with the perfect tenses—to indicate a particular time
For	Often used with the perfect tenses or the simple tenses—to indicate a duration of time
Yet	Often used with the perfect tenses—in negative meaning and in questions
Already	Often used with the perfect tenses—in affirmative meanings
Yesterday	Often used with the past tenses
Today	Often used with the present tenses
Tomorrow	Often used with the future tenses or with the present continuous tense when it refers to the future
During	Often used with the simple and continuous tenses to show a duration of time. Not usually used with the perfect tenses
Over the past few	Often used with the present perfect to indicate time starting in the past and continuing to the present
Usually	Often used with the simple tenses to indicate habitual actions
Now	Often used with the present continuous

There are other uses for some of the time markers listed above, but the uses given are very common and are often tested on the TOEFL. In addition, there are many other time markers in English. You should look for these time markers and use them to help you understand the time meaning of the sentences used in TOEFL questions. Then, check to see that the tense meaning of the verb agrees with the time meaning of the rest of the sentence.

The TOEFL tests your understanding of the meaning of verb tenses by using tenses that do not agree in meaning with the time meaning of the rest of a sentence.

MODEL

In 1988, George Bush <u>has become</u> president of <u>the</u> United States, <u>beating</u> his
                              A   B   C
opponent by <u>a</u> wide margin.
            D
 	
What is wrong with this sentence?
Answer: There is no agreement in meaning between the time marker and the verb.

▼ Explanation ▲

In this sentence, the verb *has become* does not agree in meaning with the rest of the sentence. The time marker *in 1988* indicates that the action in this sentence took place in the past only. *Has become* indicates an action that began in the past and has continued to the present. Answer (A) is the correct answer to the question because *has become* is incorrect.
Correction: *became*

MODEL

Since the 1960s, rock and roll music <u>became</u> <u>more popular</u> with <u>young</u> people
                                      A   B   C

than any other music <u>form</u>.
                    D

What is wrong with this sentence?
Answer: There is no agreement between the time marker and the verb.

▼ Explanation ▲

In this question, *Since* is the time marker. *Since* is usually used with the perfect tenses. This sentence uses the simple past tense. Answer (A) is the correct answer to the question because *became* is incorrect.
Correction: *has become*

☛ ON THE TOEFL TEST

- Check to see that the verb tense meaning in each TOEFL question is correct.

EXERCISE 8A: Practice with Time Markers and Verb Tenses

In each sentence, circle the verb(s) and underline the time marker(s). Then, on the line provided, put an *I* if the sentence is incorrect and a *C* if the sentence is correct. Correct each error.

_C_ 1. Carla (had not seen) snow <u>before</u> coming to New York.

_I_ 2. They (live) *have lived* here <u>since</u> 1942.

____ 3. Yesterday we are going shopping for a new motorcycle.

____ 4. The children of today had used computers to bring them the information they want.

____ 5. In the early part of last week, Americans everywhere are going to the polls to vote.

____ 6. Recently, the weather has been very unpredictable.

____ 7. We thought that our original plan was a good one, but we modify it a great deal over the past few weeks.

____ 8. I have just arrived when he called.

____ 9. I have just received his message; I will call him in a few minutes.

_____ 10. Although we sometimes go to a restaurant, we usually are eating at home.

_____ 11. We celebrate Halloween every year on October 31.

_____ 12. We have been worried about our project during several months.

EXERCISE 8B: Practice Identifying Incorrect Verb Tenses

Choose the letter of the incorrect verb in each sentence. Correct each error.

                                                                    is
__B__ 1. My brother, who <u>was</u> a biology student, <s>was</s> now <u>studying</u> to be a doctor.
                         A   B

_____ 2. Americans <u>found</u> themselves with less free time over the past few decades even though
                   A

        they <u>are</u> earning more money.
             B

_____ 3. Since it <u>was</u> first invented in 1879, the light bulb <u>became</u> indispensable in American
                  A   B

        households.

_____ 4. At this time, more and more women who work <u>felt</u> it <u>is</u> difficult to manage their careers
                                                    A   B

        and their private lives.

_____ 5. James <u>had started</u> his career as a pianist before he <u>is</u> thirteen years old.
                A   B

_____ 6. We always <u>are going</u> for a walk after we <u>eat</u> dinner.
                   A   B

G✔9   Check Passive and Active Sentences

Sentences in English can be either active or passive.

    Active: <u>Clifford</u> <u>ate</u> the whole <u>pie</u>.
                 S   V   DO

    Passive 1:   The whole <u>pie</u> <u>was eaten</u> by <u>Clifford</u>.
                         S   V   O of Prep

    Passive 2:   The whole <u>pie</u> <u>was eaten</u>.
                         S   V

Passive sentences are formed in the following ways:
  1. changing the direct object of an active sentence into the subject of the passive sentence;
  2. changing the verb to include a form of BE and the past participle of the active verb; or,
  3. deleting the active sentence subject or placing it after the preposition *by*.

▼▼▼

The TOEFL tests your understanding of the form and meaning of active and
passive sentences by:
1. forming passive sentences incorrectly; or,
2. using active verb forms where passive forms are needed and vice versa.

MODEL

The answer was knew by most of the class.
    A   B   C   D

What is wrong with this sentence?
Answer: The formation of the passive

▼ Explanation ▲

In this question, the passive is incorrectly formed. The past form of *know* has been used when the
past participle is needed. Answer (B) is the correct answer to the question because *was knew* is
incorrect.
Correction: *was known*

MODEL

The authors of this book have been expressed great concern
  A   B   C

about the environment.
        D

What is wrong with this sentence?
Answer: The passive has been used when the active is needed.

▼ Explanation ▲

In this question, the passive form of the verb is used. However, the sentence contains a direct
object, *great concern*. Direct objects come after active verbs, not passive verbs. Answer (C) is the
correct answer to this question because *have been expressed* is incorrect.
Correction: *have expressed*

MODEL

The piano _____ to the museum.
    (A)   being donated
    (B)   that was donated
    (C)   donated
    (D)   was donated

What is needed in this sentence?
Answer: The passive

▼ Explanation ▲

In this question, the passive form of the verb is needed. Answer (A) does not contain a finite verb. Answer (B) contains more than a finite verb. Answer (C) looks like an active finite verb. However, *piano* cannot be the subject of *donate*. A piano cannot donate things. Only humans can donate. Answer (D), which contains a correctly formed passive verb, indicates that someone donated the piano. Using this passive verb form, the piano becomes the receiver, not the doer, of the action. Answer (D) is the correct answer to this question.

☞ ON THE TOEFL TEST

- Check to see that passive verbs are formed correctly in TOEFL questions.
- Check to see that active verbs are not used where passive verbs are needed and that passive verbs are not used where active verbs are needed.

See the Grammar Appendix, #21, page 449 if you need more information about active and passive verb forms and meanings.

EXERCISE 9A: Practice with Passives

Complete the following sentences with a passive form of the verb given in parentheses. More than one passive form is possible.

1. The pants that he wanted (sell) *have been sold/were sold* .

2. After the car (repair) _____ they took it out for a long drive.

3. The winner of the contest (determine) _____ last night by a unanimous vote.

4. American Beauty roses (grow) _____ for fun and profit.

5. Sometimes teachers (call on) _____ to help their students with personal problems.

6. Some people (think) _____ to have allergies to cats.

7. The only product that (produce) _____ in this area last year was wood furniture.

8. Although the black horse (favor) _____ in the race, the brown horse won.

9. Larry's proposal (withdraw) _____ when it was discovered that he had not written it himself.

10. The window (break) _____ yesterday by the wind.

11. The old clothes (give) _____ to the Salvation Army.

EXERCISE 9B: More Practice with Active and Passive Verbs

Circle the correct answer. Then, on the line provided, use the choices given to answer the question:
What is needed in this sentence? Choices:
- The passive form of the verb
- The active form of the verb

1. This can _____ enough soup for three people.
   (A) containing
   (B) to contain
   (C) contains
   (D) is contained

   What is needed in this sentence? *The active form of the verb*

2. This watch _____ to me by a friend.
   (A) gave
   (B) is giving
   (C) was given
   (D) to give

   What is needed in this sentence?_____

3. Bryan's house _____ into several times.
   (A) had been broken
   (B) was broke
   (C) broken
   (D) had broken

   What is needed in this sentence?_____

4. Olivia _____ when her attorney arrived.
   (A) questioning
   (B) questions
   (C) being questioned
   (D) was being questioned

   What is needed in this sentence?_____

5. The message _____ on an envelope.
   (A) writing
   (B) had written
   (C) wrote
   (D) was written

   What is needed in this sentence?_____

6. These parrots _____ several words.
   (A) to say
   (B) can say
   (C) can be said
   (D) saying

   What is needed in this sentence?_____

G✔10 Check Modals and Modal-Like Verbs

Many English sentences contain modals and modal-like verbs. Modal-like verbs have similar meanings to modals, but they have different forms.

MODALS	MODAL-LIKE VERBS
may	
might	
can	be able to
could	be able to
shall	
should	be to/ought to/had better/be supposed to
would	used to
must	have to/have got to
will	be going to
	would like to
	would rather

In English sentences, modals and modal-like verbs are followed by the base form of the main verb.

Harry <u>must go</u> to Chicago this week.

Harry <u>has to go</u> to Chicago this week.

The modal *would* is often combined with *like to* or *rather to* form a modal-like verb. The modal-like verb *would like to* means *want to*. The modal-like verb *would rather* means *prefer to*.

I <u>would like to go</u> to the dance tonight.

I <u>would rather go</u> to the dance tonight than go to a movie.

Modals and modal-like verbs used in passive sentences are followed by BE and the past participle of the main verb. These forms are called modal passives.

The man <u>could be identified</u> with his passport.

The man <u>was able to be identified</u> with his passport.

The TOEFL tests your understanding of modals and modal-like verbs by:
1. following modals and modal-like verbs with something other than the base form of the main verb or BE;
2. leaving out or mixing up parts of modals and modal-like verbs; or,
3. using other verb forms where modals or modal-like verbs are needed.

MODEL

<u>According to</u> Joe, his puppy <u>can recognizing</u> <u>its</u> own <u>name</u>.
    A   B   C   D

What is wrong with this sentence?
Answer: The verb form that follows a modal

▼ Explanation ▲

In this sentence, the verb following *can* is in its present participle form. It should be in its base form. Answer (B) is the correct answer to the question because *can recognizing* is incorrect.
Correction: *can recognize*

MODEL

That book _____ in the library.
    (A)   can be finding
    (B)   found
    (C)   to be found
    (D)   can be found

What is needed in this sentence?
Answer: A modal passive

▼ Explanation ▲

In this question, a modal passive is needed. Answer (A) contains a present participle where a past participle is needed. Answers (B) and (C) do not contain modals. Answer (D) is the correct answer to the question because it contains the correct forms for this sentence.

☞ ON THE TOEFL TEST

- Check to see that all modals and modal-like verbs are followed by the base form of the main verb or BE.
- Check to see that modal-like verbs are correctly formed.

See the Grammar Appendix, #22, page 450 if you need more information about modals and modal-like verbs.

EXERCISE 10A: Practice with Modals and Modal-Like Verbs

Circle the correct answer. On the line provided, use the following choices to answer the question, *What is needed in this sentence?* Choices:

        A modal
        A modal passive
        A modal-like verb

1. You _____ to attend the meeting on Thursday.
    (A) must
    (B) have
    (C) required
    (D) be

    What is needed in this sentence?_____*A modal-like verb*_____

2. Karen's stereo _____ before she uses it again.
    (A) should repair
    (B) repaired
    (C) repair
    (D) should be repaired

    What is needed in this sentence?_____

3. Marie _____ bake a cake for tonight's party.
    (A) is able
    (B) can
    (C) has
    (D) is

    What is needed in this sentence?_____

4. In most cases, the current balance available in a checking or savings account _____.
    (A) can be verified by telephone
    (B) on the telephone can verify
    (C) in verification by telephone
    (D) being verified by telephone

    What is needed in this sentence?_____

5. New England winters _____ among the coldest in the United States.
    (A) may be considering
    (B) in consideration
    (C) may be considered
    (D) being considered

    What is needed in this sentence?_____

6. Mrs. Jones _____ arrive at 6:00.
    (A) supposed to
    (B) to be supposed
    (C) is supposed to
    (D) is supposed

    What is needed in this sentence?_____

EXERCISE 10B: More Practice with Modals and Modal-like Verbs

In each sentence, there are two modals or modal-like verbs. One of them is incorrect. Choose the letter of the incorrect modal or modal-like verb, and correct the error.

_B_ 1. Many people <u>can't understand</u> how bees <u>can ~~to~~ fly</u>.
                          A   B

____ 2. Michael <u>can't stop thinking</u> that there <u>going to be</u> a problem with this project.
                          A   B

____ 3. Rodney has always <u>to been able</u> swim faster than <u>I can</u>.
                                  A   B

____ 4. Our class <u>supposed to</u> finish this book before we <u>can move</u> on to the next one.
                          A   B

____ 5. All of the books that you <u>will</u> need for this report <u>can found</u> in the library.
                                      A   B

____ 6. John can <u>giving</u> you the information you <u>are going to need</u> for your report tomorrow.
                      A   B

G✔11   Check Subject–Verb Agreement

English subjects and finite verbs agree in number.

> The <u>boy lives</u> here.   **NOTE:** Verb + ——s/~~——es~~ = singular
>   *sing sing*
>
> The <u>boys live</u> here.   **NOTE:** Noun + ——s/——es = plural
>   *plural plural*

There are really only two situations in English when the finite verb needs a special form or the ——s/——es ending to show subject-verb agreement:

1. when the verb BE is the main verb or the main helping verb of a sentence. In this situation, the verb BE has its own special forms (*am, is, are, was, were*) in both the singular and the plural to show subject-verb agreement.

    She <u>is</u> working at the bank.

    She <u>is</u> a bank executive.

    They <u>are</u> working at the bank.

    They <u>are</u> bank executives.

2. when another verb is the main verb of a sentence and
    a. this verb is in one of the present tenses (e.g., present, present perfect, present continuous, present perfect continuous) and
    b. the subject of the sentence is third person singular (e.g., *he, she, it, boy, John*). In this situation, the ending ——s or ——es is added to the verb.

    She <u>works</u> at the bank.

    She <u>goes</u> to work every day.

In all other situations in English sentences, only the base form of the verb is needed in the present tenses. Only the past form is needed in the past tenses.

They <u>work</u> at the bank.

They <u>worked</u> at the bank.

The TOEFL tests your knowledge of subject-verb agreement by:
1. using third person singular verbs (with ——s/——es) with plural subjects or vice versa;
2. separating subjects from verbs with phrases and clauses, which sometimes makes subject-verb agreement unclear;
3. using unusual subjects that are difficult to classify as either singular or plural; or,
4. using subjects that have special subject-verb agreement rules.

MODEL

<u>My brother</u> and my mother <u>is coming</u> <u>to see</u> me <u>graduate</u>.
    A   B   C   D

What is wrong with this sentence?
Answer: Subject-verb agreement

▼ Explanation ▲

In this question, the subject has two parts, *my brother* and *my mother*. These two together make a plural subject. The helping verb in this sentence is BE. As discussed above, BE has special forms to show singular and plural subject-verb agreement. The form *is* is used in the present tense for singular subjects. Answer (B) is the correct answer to the question because *is coming* is incorrect.
Correction: *are coming*

MODEL

Mathematics <u>have been</u> my <u>most difficult</u> subject <u>so far</u> this <u>year</u>.
             A   B   C   D

What is wrong with this sentence?
Answer: Subject-verb agreement

▼ Explanation ▲

In this question, *mathematics* looks like a plural noun. However, it is singular. In addition, the present perfect tense is being used. As discussed above, when one of the present tenses is used, and when the subject is third person singular, the ——s/——es ending is needed to show subject-verb agreement. The verb *have been* does not have this ending. Answer (A) is the correct answer to this sentence because *have been* is incorrect.
Correction: *has been*

MODEL

The house cat, one of people's <u>favorite pets</u>, <u>enjoy</u> human attention <u>and</u>
                             A   B   C

<u>company</u>.
 D

What is wrong with this sentence?
Answer: Subject-verb agreement

▼ Explanation ▲

In this question, the subject, *house cat*, and the verb, *enjoy*, are separated by the phrase *one of man's favorite pets*. This makes it difficult to determine subject-verb agreement. However, *house cat* is third person singular and *enjoy* is in the present tense. As discussed above, when this situation exists, the ——*s*/——*es* ending is necessary to show subject-verb agreement. Answer (B) is the correct answer to this question because *enjoy* is incorrect.

Correction: *enjoys*

☛ ON THE TOEFL TEST

- Check to see that subject-verb agreement is correct in sentences used in TOEFL questions.

See the Grammar Appendix, #20, page 447 if you need more information about subject-verb agreement and for a list of special subject-verb agreement rules.
See the Grammar Appendix, #14, page 442 if you need more information about finite verbs and #15, page 445 if you need more information about verb tenses.

EXERCISE 11: Practice with Subject-Verb Agreement

Circle the correct verb form in each sentence.

1. Both the book and the notebook on the table (is/are) mine.

2. The fly is an insect that (lives/live) in people's homes.

3. The sugar maple tree, from which maple sugar (is/are) made, (grows/grow) in New England.

4. Either her uncle or her cousins (is/are) coming to pick her up.

5. Linguistics, sociology, and anthropology (is/are) social sciences concerned with the study of humankind.

6. A number of students (wants/want) to go to Boston this weekend.

7. The motorcycle, like other two-wheeled vehicles, (is/are) more dangerous than vehicles having four wheels.

8. My brother believes that cabbage and broccoli (is/are) bad for your health.

9. This library, with over 700 million volumes, (offers/offer) students a wide variety of reference materials.

10. Poetry (is/are) recognized as one of the most complex means of artistic expression.

11. Anybody who (wants/want) to join us at the dance should let us know.

12. It (was/were) Peter's friends who called last night.

13. Twenty gallons of water (is/are) a lot to carry.

14. There (is/are) species of fish that never (comes/come) to the surface of the ocean.

15. A pair of gloves (was/were) found at the scene of the crime.

16. The oranges in the bowl on the counter (is/are) from California.

Grammar Checkpoint Test Two for G✔7 through G✔11

Allow yourself 5 minutes to complete this checkpoint test. There are 11 questions on the test. Check your answers in the answer key. Next to each answer is the number of the checkpoint that is being tested in each of these questions. Use these numbers to determine which checkpoints, if any, you need to study again.

Questions 1 through 7

Circle the letter of the underlined part of the sentence that is incorrect.

1. Nutritionists currently believe that vitamin A and beta-carotene aids in preventing some kinds
                       A   B   C   D
   of cancer.

2. The Swedish settlers who builded the first log cabins in the state of Delaware brought their logs
                       A   B   C
   with them from their homeland.
   D

3. During the early 1970s, the American public collectively has become health conscious, turning
                                          A   B   C
   away from the highly processed foods that had been so popular in the past.
                                              D

4. In 1968, John Steinbeck was gave the Nobel Prize for literature for his acclaimed novel, The
   A   B   C   D
   Grapes of Wrath.

5. It has always been thought that cell mutation is a random event; however, geneticists find
           A   B   C   D
   evidence to the contrary over the past few years.

6. Important news are now conveyed electronically from one side of the globe to the other
                 A   B   C
   in a matter of seconds.
   D

7. Democrats had dominate the White House for five terms when Republican Dwight D.
                 A   B   C
   Eisenhower was elected in 1952.
              D

Questions 8 through 11

Circle the letter of the one word or phrase that best completes the sentence.

8. Unlike the young of most animal species, human children _____ to depend on adult care for many years.
   (A) must
   (B) needing
   (C) have
   (D) has

9. One variety of wild rose, the sweetbrier, _____ to the United States by the Pilgrims.
   (A) bringing
   (B) was brought
   (C) brought
   (D) that was brought

10. Glaciers covering the west coast of Greenland _____ about 7,500 icebergs a year into the North Atlantic.
    (A) are dropped
    (B) drops
    (C) dropping
    (D) drop

11. Newly installed gypsum board walls _____ before they are painted.
    (A) with a sealant coated
    (B) should coat with a sealant
    (C) should be coated with a sealant
    (D) coating with a sealant

G✔12   Check Prepositions and Prepositional Phrases

Many English sentences contain prepositional phrases. A prepositional phrase consists of a preposition and an object. The object in a prepositional phrase can be one of the following noun structures.

Noun (phrase):   I sat by <u>my mother</u>.

Pronoun: I sat by <u>her</u>.

Gerund (phrase):   She entertains herself by <u>reading</u>.

Noun clause: I could tell from <u>what you said</u> that you are not interested in this book.

NOTE: Infinitives cannot function as objects of prepositions.

Some prepositions contain more than one word and are called compound prepositions.

<u>According to</u> Max, Dolores will be late.
Compound Prep

Certain verb + preposition combinations having special meanings are very common. (Many of these combinations are often referred to as *two-word verbs*.)

Jerry <u>looked up</u> the word in the dictionary.
V + Prep

Some adjective + preposition combinations are very common.
She is <u>capable of</u> almost anything.
Adj + Prep

▼▼▼

The TOEFL tests your understanding of prepositions and prepositional phrases by:

1. leaving out necessary prepositions or parts of compound prepositions;
2. using incorrect prepositions, especially after certain verbs or certain adjectives; or,
3. adding extra words to prepositional phrases.

MODEL

In yesterday's class, Professor Cummings talked _____ the discovery of gold in California in the 1800s.
    (A)   for
    (B)   in
    (C)   at
    (D)   about

What is needed in this sentence?
Answer: A preposition

▼ Explanation ▲

In this question, a verb + preposition combination is being tested. The verb *talk* is often followed by the preposition *about*. Answer (D) is the correct answer to the question.

MODEL

Angela <u>relaxes</u> <u>by she swimming</u> in the lake <u>every</u> afternoon <u>after</u> class.
        A   B   C   D

What is wrong with this sentence?
Answer: Extra parts have been added to a prepositional phrase.

▼ Explanation ▲

A prepositional phrase consists of a preposition and an object. *By she swimming* contains a preposition, a subject, and an object. Answer (B) is the correct answer to this question because *by she swimming* is incorrect.
Correction: *by swimming*

☞ ON THE TOEFL TEST

• Check to see that the compound prepositions and prepositional phrases in TOEFL questions are formed correctly.
• Check to see that the correct prepositions are used and that prepositions have not been omitted when they are needed.

See the Grammar Appendix, #24 and #25, pages 451–454 if you need more information on prepositions and prepositional phrases as well as for lists of prepositions, compound prepositions, verb + preposition combinations, and adjective + preposition combinations.

EXERCISE 12A: Practice Identifying Preposition Errors

On the line provided, put an *I* if the sentence is incorrect and a *C* if the sentence is correct. Then, correct each error.

I 1. Please look after my things while I am ~~to~~ *in* the doctor's examining room.

____ 2. We must think about our arguments before we take up our concerns with the president.

____ 3. Prior yesterday, I thought we had a good working atmosphere in this office.

____ 4. I think Carla's answer is different to yours.

____ 5. Marion was pleased with the work the children had done on their own.

____ 6. In spite of recent setbacks, employees of this company shouldn't have to give up any benefits.

____ 7. The color yellow, in contrast to the color blue, is associated warmth and sunshine.

____ 8. The students enjoy going to downtown on Saturday afternoons.

____ 9. Regardless of how you feel today, you should have your sore shoulder looked by a doctor.

____ 10. While we were on our way at my mother's house, she was preparing for our arrival.

____ 11. The dog sat under the table during the dinner.

EXERCISE 12B: More Practice with Prepositional Phrases

Choose the letter of the underlined preposition or prepositional phrase that is incorrect, and correct the error.

B 1. <u>During summer vacation</u>, they recovered ~~over~~ *from* the long semester <u>behind</u> them by
        A   B   C
   spending time <u>at the beach</u>.
                    D

____ 2. The flowers <u>in</u> this valley are <u>similar to those that</u> <u>on the other side</u> <u>of</u> the hill.
            A   B   C   D

____ 3. <u>According my science professor</u>, the atmosphere <u>of the earth</u> is being polluted <u>by</u>
                 A   B   C
   humans <u>at</u> an ever-increasing rate.
          D

____ 4. His parents, <u>together his teachers</u>, objected <u>to his behavior</u> both <u>in school</u> and <u>at home</u>.
              A   B   C   D

____ 5. Students <u>from all over the world</u> took part <u>in</u> the ceremony <u>in</u> the school auditorium
            A   B   C
   <u>in Friday afternoon</u>.
      D

_____ 6. <u>While listening</u> to the Latin American music, I dreamed <u>about</u> <u>being a warm country</u>
        A   B   C

<u>without any snow</u>.
   D

G✔13   Check Main and Subordinate Clause Markers

All English sentences contain at least one main clause. A main clause contains a subject and a verb and can stand alone as a sentence.

> <u>Karina</u> <u>has</u> a new coat.
>   S   V
>
> *Main clause*

Many English sentences also contain subordinate clauses. Like a main clause, a subordinate clause contains a subject and a verb. However, a subordinate clause cannot stand alone as a sentence.

> Although <u>Karina</u> <u>has</u> a new coat
>   S   V
>
> *Subordinate clause*

There are three types of subordinate clauses in English: noun clauses, adjective clauses, and adverb clauses.

A noun clause functions as a subject, object, or complement in a sentence.

> I like <u>what you said</u>.
>   *Noun clause direct object*

An adjective clause functions as an adjective in a sentence.

> I like the book <u>that you gave me</u>.
>   *Adjective clause describing* book.

An adverb clause functions as an adverb in a sentence.

> Jack will call you <u>as soon as he gets home</u>.
>   *Adverb clause telling* when *Jack will call.*

Clause markers *(CM)* are used to connect clauses in English. Each English clause type has its own special clause markers.

Main clauses can be connected with main clause markers called coordinating conjunctions. These include *and, but, or, so, for,* and *yet.* A comma is usually placed just before these conjunctions.

> <u>Karina has a new coat</u>, <u>and</u> <u>Carolyn has new boots</u>.
>   *Main clause*   *CM*   *Main clause*

Main clauses can also be connected with clause markers such as *however, nevertheless, in addition, as a result, on the other hand, furthermore,* and *moreover.* When these clause markers are used on the TOEFL, they are preceded by a semicolon (;). (They could also be preceded by periods (.). However, on the TOEFL, this is never the case. Only semicolons are used.)

> <u>Carolyn has new boots</u>; <u>in addition</u>, <u>she has new gloves</u>.
>   *Main clause*   *CM*   *Main clause*

The clause markers for noun clauses are *that, how, how many, how much, what, when, where, why, who, whom, whose,* and *which.*

<u>I am not sure</u> <u>that</u> we will be able to take a vacation.
   Main clause CM
          _____*Subordinate noun clause*_____/

The clause markers for adjective clauses are *who, whom, whose, which, that,* (relative pronouns) and, sometimes, *when, where,* and *why.*

<u>I like the cat</u>   <u>that</u>   has yellow stripes.
Main clause   *CM*
        *Subordinate adjective clause*/

There are many clause markers for adverb clauses. Some of these include *after, as long as, because, as, if, unless, although, while, when,* and *since.*

<u>We will take a walk</u> <u>after</u> we finish studying.
   Main clause   *CM*
          *Subordinate adjective clause*/

When an adverb clause comes at the beginning of a sentence, it is followed by a comma.

<u>After</u>   we finish studying,   <u>we will take a walk</u>.
 CM   *Main clause*
*Subordinate adjective clause*/

▼▼▼

The TOEFL tests your understanding of the clause markers used in main clauses and subordinate clauses by:
1. leaving out parts of compound clause markers;
2. adding unnecessary parts to clause markers; or,
3. using the incorrect forms of relative pronouns (clause markers used in adjective clauses).

MODEL

Larry <u>will drive</u> his car <u>to</u> New York <u>even although</u> he <u>would rather</u> fly.
      A   B   C   D

What is wrong with this sentence?
Answer: The clause marker has extra parts.

▼ Explanation ▲

In this question, the clause marker is incorrectly formed. *Even although* is a combination of parts of two different English clause markers. Answer (C) is the correct answer to the question because *even although* is incorrect.
Correction: *even though/although*

▼ Explanation ▲

In this question, the adjective clause *which is sitting next to her* modifies a person noun, *woman*. *Which* cannot be used to refer to people. Answer (A) is the correct answer to the question because *woman which* is incorrect.
Correction: *woman who*

☞ ON THE TOEFL TEST

- Check to see that the clause markers used in TOEFL questions are formed correctly.
- Check to see that the correct relative pronouns are used.

See the Grammar Appendix, #26–#30, page 454–457 if you need more information on clauses and for more comprehensive lists of clause markers.

EXERCISE 13A: Practice with Main Clause Markers

In the sentences below, underline and label the subject *S* and the verb *V* of each main clause. Then, circle the clause marker that correctly separates the main clauses.

    Remember: *and, but, or, so, for, nor* and *yet* are preceded by commas (,). Other main clause markers on the TOEFL are preceded by semicolons (;).

1. <u>Lawrence</u> <u>likes</u> pumpkin pie; (ⓗowever,/but) <u>I</u> <u>prefer</u> mince pie.
    S   V   S V

2. They may want to go to New York this weekend; (on the other hand/on other hand), they may prefer to stay home.

3. Flower gardens are beautiful, (however/but) they are a lot of work.

4. We would like to give you this card, (in addition/and) we all want to congratulate you on your great success.

5. During the storm, the lights went out; (moreover,/and) the telephone lines were damaged.

6. Maria didn't receive her check; (as result,/as a result,) she has no money for the weekend.

EXERCISE 13B: Practice with Clauses and Subordinate Clause Markers

Each sentence below contains one main clause and one subordinate clause. Fill in the blank with a clause marker that can begin the subordinate clause. More than one clause marker may be possible. Underline the subject and the verb of the main clause. Then, circle the subject and the verb of the subordinate clause.

Adjective clauses

1. The <u>man</u> _____*that*_____ I spoke to <u>was</u> in a hurry.
   who/whom (written above "that"; "that" is circled; "spoke" is circled)

2. The person to _____ this gift will be given is my mother.

3. The police officer _____ stopped me gave me a ticket for speeding.

4. I don't understand the assignment _____ the professor gave us for next Monday.

5. Crystal, _____ is used in making fine glassware, contains lead.

6. My sister, _____ lives in Cincinnati, is coming to my house next week.

Noun clauses

7. I would like to know _____ you are thinking about.

8. I would also like to know _____ this costs.

9. From _____ I understand, the meeting has been cancelled.

10. His idea is _____ we should all go to the movie together.

11. _____ they want to leave work early doesn't surprise me.

Adverb clauses

12. Jack chews gum _____ it helps him concentrate.

13. Although he was very sad, Bill acted _____ nothing had happened.

14. _____ Frank had not helped me study, I would never have passed my exam.

15. I won't come _____ you want me to.

16. _____ I don't really want to babysit tonight, I will do it anyway.

EXERCISE 13C: Practice Identifying Clause Marker Errors

For each sentence choose the letter of the incorrect clause marker, and correct the error.

B 1. <u>After</u> she took the exam, <u>the which</u> lasted three hours, Cecilia was exhausted.
     A   B

____ 2. <u>About what</u> he wanted to know was <u>what</u> your name is.
       A   B

____ 3. Adrian will bring the dessert <u>that</u> you like so much, <u>in addition</u> Joyce will bring your
                                       A   B

    favorite salad.

_____ 4. The girl <u>who</u> is sitting in the red chair is the person <u>to who</u> you must give this envelope.
        A   B

_____ 5. <u>Even</u> Leroy had said he was going to quit school, I was surprised <u>when</u> he actually did.
        A   B

_____ 6. <u>Unless</u> he asks me to, I will not correct the papers <u>who</u> he gave me.
        A   B

_____ 7. I don't like the shoes he has on; <u>addition</u>, I don't care for the tie <u>that</u> he is wearing.
                                A   B

_____ 8. <u>In spite fact that</u> he had good intentions, Fred was not able to give us the help <u>that</u> we
            A   B
needed.

_____ 9. The doctor <u>which</u> gave me this medicine told me <u>that</u> I need to stay in bed for three
                      A   B
days.

_____ 10. I haven't seen Joseph today; <u>as result</u>, I'm worried <u>that</u> he might be sick.
                                      A   B

_____ 11. The teacher <u>whom</u> book I have said <u>that</u> I could keep it.
                      A   B

G✔14   Check Prepositional Phrases and Subordinate Clauses

English prepositional phrases and subordinate clauses are easily confused. Confusion often happens because, although they are formed differently, prepositional phrases and subordinate clauses can function in similar ways in English.

> <u>Because of her financial difficulties</u>, Anne could not go.
>   *Prepositional phrase*

> <u>Because she had financial difficulties</u>, Anne could not go.
>   *Subordinate clause*

In this pair of sentences, the prepositional phrase and the subordinate clause both function as adverbs telling why Anne could not go.

> The book <u>on the table</u> is mine.
>   *Prep phrase*

> The book <u>that is on the table</u> is mine.
>   *Subordinate clause*

In this pair of sentences, the prepositional phrase and the subordinate clause both function as adjectives telling which book.

Because prepositional phrases and subordinate clauses function similarly, it is important to remember the differences in their forms when taking the TOEFL.

1. A prepositional phrase contains a preposition followed by a noun structure object.

   Despite his problems, John was able to finish.
     Prep   Noun phrase
     ____*Prep phrase*____/

2. A subordinate clause contains a subordinate clause marker followed by a clause (including a subject and a verb).

     Although John had some problems, he was able to finish.
   Clause marker   Clause
   _____*Subordinate clause*_____/

▼▼▼

The TOEFL tests your understanding of clauses and prepositional phrases by:
1. using subordinate clauses where prepositional phrases are needed or vice versa;
2. using clause markers where prepositions are needed or vice versa;
3. using one type of subordinate clause or clause marker where another is needed; or,
4. using main clauses where prepositional phrases or subordinate clauses are needed.

REMEMBER: Certain of the clause markers used to join main clauses must be preceded in TOEFL questions by a semicolon (;). Some of the more common of these are *in addition, for example, however,* and *nevertheless.* A more complete list is contained in the Grammar Appendix, #27, page 455. See the first model below for an example of how this punctuation fact can help you on TOEFL questions.

MODEL

Samuel wasn't tired, _____ he hadn't slept for a very long time.
    (A)   however
    (B)   though
    (C)   despite
    (D)   nevertheless
 	
What is needed in this sentence?
Answer: An adverb clause marker

▼ Explanation ▲

In this question, there are two clauses, *Samuel wasn't tired* and *he hadn't slept for a very long time.* A clause marker is needed to join these two clauses. Answers (A) and (D) contain clause markers. However, these clause markers are main clause markers and would need to be preceded by a semicolon (;). A comma separates the two clauses in this question, so answers (A) and (D) cannot be correct. Answer (C) contains a preposition, not a clause marker, so it cannot be correct. Answer (B) is the correct answer to the question. It contains a clause marker that can join these two clauses, making the second clause into an adverb clause.

MODEL

_____ Laurie has no formal training in computer science, she knows a great deal about computers.
- (A) Despite
- (B) In spite of
- (C) Although
- (D) That

What is needed in this sentence?
Answer: An adverb clause marker

▼ **Explanation** ▲

In this question, there are two clauses, _Laurie has no formal training in computer science_ and _she knows a great deal about computers_. A clause marker is needed at the beginning of the first clause. Answers (A) and (B) do not contain clause markers. Instead, they contain prepositions. Answer (D) contains a clause marker. However, this clause marker would create a noun clause or an adjective clause. The clause in this sentence is an adverb clause. Answer (C) is the correct answer to this question because it contains a clause marker that can begin an adverb clause.

MODEL

_____, Jane enjoys gardening.
- (A) She is like her mother
- (B) Like her mother
- (C) That she is like her mother
- (D) Because her mother

What is needed in this sentence?
Answer: A prepositional phrase

▼ **Explanation** ▲

In this question, a prepositional phrase or an adverb clause is needed at the beginning of the sentence. Answer (A) is a main clause. Answer (C) is a noun clause. Answer (D) is part of an adverb clause, but it is missing a verb. Answer (B) is the correct answer to this sentence because it contains a prepositional phrase that can be used to complete the sentence.

MODEL

My father, _____ an immigrant, came to the United States in 1925.
- (A) who he was
- (B) he was
- (C) that he was
- (D) who was

What is needed in this sentence?
Answer: The first part of an adjective clause

▼ Explanation ▲

An incomplete adjective clause follows the noun, *father*, in this sentence. The beginning of this adjective clause is missing. Answers (A) and (C) contain noun clauses. Answer (B) contains a main clause. Answer (D) is the correct answer to this sentence because it contains the necessary first part of an adjective clause.

☛ ON THE TOEFL TEST

- Check to see that prepositional phrases and subordinate clauses are used correctly in TOEFL questions.
- Especially check the clause markers and prepositions.

See the Grammar Appendix, #27–#30, pages 455–457 if you need more information on clauses and clause markers.
See the Grammar Appendix, #25, page 454 if you need more information on prepositional phrases.

EXERCISE 14A: Practice Identifying Main Clauses, Subordinate Clauses, and Prepositional Phrases

Use the choices provided to identify the underlined clause or phrase in each sentence. Choices:
   MC (main clause)
   ADJ C (an adjective clause)
   NC (a noun clause)
   ADV C (an adverb clause)
   PREP P (a prepositional phrase)

ADJ C 1. Nancy, <u>who wants to go to Spain</u>, has been studying Spanish for five years.

_____ 2. Wilbur has been living here <u>since last summer</u>.

_____ 3. Lola will not be able to get <u>what she wants</u> this time.

_____ 4. Yesterday, Carlotta looked <u>like a movie star</u>.

_____ 5. When scientists perform experiments, <u>they learn about the world around us</u>.

_____ 6. <u>Because of his academic achievements</u>, Ralph was given a scholarship.

_____ 7. He might want to join us tonight; <u>on the other hand, he might want to stay home</u>.

_____ 8. The large number of students <u>who want to take this course</u> is encouraging.

_____ 9. <u>As I told you earlier</u>, I am not interested in buying a new car.

_____ 10. Mabel wants to see you <u>before you leave</u>.

_____ 11. Nobody wants to watch the movie <u>that is on television tonight</u>.

EXERCISE 14B: Practice Identifying Errors in Prepositional Phrases and Subordinate Clauses

On the line provided, put an *I* if the sentence is incorrect and a *C* if the sentence is correct. Then, correct each error.

during
__I__ 1. Student life ~~while~~ the 1960s was chaotic.

_____ 2. What worries me the most is your health.

_____ 3. That he said in his letter, he will be home next week.

_____ 4. The three people who they were here early were Joyce, Lee, and Tom.

_____ 5. Marcia cannot come with us because of she has a play rehearsal tonight.

_____ 6. I cannot tell you how you should budget your time.

EXERCISE 14C: More Practice with Phrases and Clauses

Circle the correct answer.

1. Writing a research paper takes a lot of time _____ it requires library work.
    (A) because of
    (B) how
    (C) as
    (D) due to

2. _____ his youth, Professor Hanagan was a boy scout.
    (A) While
    (B) During
    (C) When
    (D) That

3. Skiing is a popular American sport, _____ quite expensive.
    (A) however it is
    (B) even though it is
    (C) despite its
    (D) it is

4. William is a hardworking person; _____.
    (A) while he likes to have a good time
    (B) nevertheless, he likes to have a good time
    (C) that he also likes to have a good time
    (D) but also likes to have a good time

5. _____ day were just a little bit longer, I would have time to finish my work.
    (A) Each
    (B) Since each
    (C) If each
    (D) Were each

6. Maple syrup _____ is light in color and free of impurities is the most expensive kind.
    (A) and
    (B) which
    (C) it
    (D) about which

7. Bread is one type of food _____.
    (A) all cultures seem to have it
    (B) that all cultures seem to have
    (C) by all cultures
    (D) that all cultures seem to have it

8. _____ is cooking, we can eat our salad.
    (A) While the steak
    (B) During the steak
    (C) The steak
    (D) Because of the steak

9. _____ a dentist, Mike is very concerned about having healthy teeth.
   (A) Because
   (B) He is
   (C) As
   (D) That he is

10. She had many unfortunate experiences _____ her childhood.
    (A) it was
    (B) while
    (C) in addition
    (D) during

11. We will not go swimming today _____.
    (A) because the bad weather
    (B) the weather is bad
    (C) because the weather is bad
    (D) because the bad weather is

G✔15 Check Appositives and the Noun Structures They Rename

An appositive is a noun structure which comes just after or just before another noun structure. The appositive renames or has the same meaning as the noun structure it accompanies. Appositives are often set off by commas. Appositives come from adjective clauses.

> Carol, <u>who is my colleague</u>, studies psycholinguistics.
>   *Adjective clause*

> Carol, <u>my colleague</u>, studies psycholinguistics.
>   *Appositive*

Notice the following pair of sentences:

> Gary, <u>who is the boy</u>   <u>who will be staying with us</u>, is from Connecticut.
>   *Adjective clause I*   *Adjective clause II*

> Gary, <u>the boy</u> <u>who will be staying with us</u>, is from Connecticut.
>   *Adjective clause II*
>   _____Appositive_____/

In this sentence pair, the first adjective clause is reduced to form the appositive. The second adjective clause does not change. Appositives can be modified by adjective clauses.

▼▼▼

The TOEFL tests your understanding of appositives and the noun structures they rename by using other structures—especially finite verb phrases, main clauses, prepositional phrases, and possessive constructions—where noun structures or their appositives are needed.

NOTE: The commas used in many appositives are very important. See the next model for an example of how this punctuation fact can help you in TOEFL questions.

MODEL

Minnesota, _____, actually has 12,034 lakes.
    (A)   the Land of 10,000 Lakes
    (B)   it is the Land of 10,000 Lakes
    (C)   its Land of 10,000 Lakes
    (D)   to a Land of 10,000 Lakes

What is needed in this sentence?
Answer: An appositive to rename Minnesota

▼ Explanation ▲

In this question, the subject, *Minnesota*, and the verb, *has*, are complete. The commas around the missing segment show that something is needed to modify or rename the subject. Answer (B) contains a main clause; answer (C) contains a noun phrase subject; and, answer (D) is a prepositional phrase which shows motion. None of these could act to rename the subject. An adjective clause could be used in this sentence. However, there are no adjective clauses in the answer choices. Answer (A) is the correct answer to this question. It is an appositive which renames the subject.

MODEL

_____, Maria, is joining me for the holidays.

    (A)   She is my roommate
    (B)   For my roommate
    (C)   Next week
    (D)   My roommate

What is needed in this sentence?
Answer: A subject

▼ Explanation ▲

In this question, the subject of the sentence is missing. *Maria* cannot be the subject because *Maria* is followed by a comma. Subjects that stand right next to their verbs are never followed by commas. *Maria* is an appositive. Answer (A) contains more than a subject. It contains an entire sentence. Answer (B) contains a prepositional phrase. Answer (C) contains a time marker. Answer (D) is the correct answer to this question because it contains a noun phrase which can act as the subject of this sentence.

☞ ON THE TOEFL TEST

- Check to see that the appositives and the noun structures they rename are formed correctly in TOEFL questions.

See the Grammar Appendix, #5, page 438 if you need more information on noun structures.

EXERCISE 15A: Practice Recognizing Appositive Errors

Some of the sentences below contain appositives. Some do not. Circle each appositive you find. Then, underline and label each subject *S* and each finite verb *V*. On the line provide, put an *I* if the sentence is incorrect and a *C* if the sentence is correct. Correct each error.

                                 S   V

<u>I</u> 1. Last week, <u>an old friend, came</u> to see me.

____ 2. Lobster, my favorite food, is served fresh at this restaurant.

____ 3. Ethan Allen, he was a famous American revolutionist, lived in Vermont.

____ 4. Born on June 22, 1973, my son he is Charles will be eighteen years old on his next birthday.

____ 5. Old Maid, a favorite children's game, is played with cards.

____ 6. For Christmas, Charles, wants a new stereo.

____ 7. *Huckleberry Finn*, a book which is often read to children, remains popular with adults as well.

____ 8. My father, of a man who loved to read, gave books to his children every Christmas.

____ 9. Broccoli, it is a vegetable which can be prepared in many ways, contains many essential vitamins and minerals.

____ 10. Montana, it is the fourth largest state in the United States, only has a population of about 200,000.

____ 11. On the table, Harold, found the pen he thought he had lost.

EXERCISE 15B: More Practice with Appositives

Circle the correct answer.

1. The town of Cody, Wyoming, is named after Buffalo Bill Cody, _____.
   (A) he was a wild West cowboy and entertainer
   (B) a wild West cowboy and entertainer
   (C) to be a wild West cowboy and entertainer
   (D) was a wild West cowboy and entertainer

2. Liz Moses, _____, grows beautiful vegetables in her garden.
   (A) is my next-door neighbor
   (B) of my next-door neighbor
   (C) whom my next-door neighbor
   (D) my next-door neighbor

3. Marie Curie, _____, eventually died from the side effects of her work.
   (A) was the scientist who discovered radium
   (B) whose scientific discovery of radium
   (C) the scientist discovered radium
   (D) the scientist who discovered radium

4. _____, *to look up*, means to search for something in a book or a dictionary.
   (A) This phrase
   (B) For this phrase
   (C) It is this phrase
   (D) Phrased

5. My cousin, _____ when I need her, knows me very well.
   (A) always available is a friend
   (B) she is a friend who is always available
   (C) a friend who is always available
   (D) her friend is always available

6. _____, tender little plants which are good to eat, can be found in the forests.
   (A) They are fiddleheads
   (B) In the early spring
   (C) Fiddleheads
   (D) Sometimes

Grammar Checkpoint Test Three for G✔12 through G✔15

Allow yourself 5 minutes to complete this checkpoint test. There are 11 questions on the test. Check your answers in the answer key. Next to each answer is the number of the checkpoint that is being tested in each of these questions. Use these numbers to determine which checkpoints, if any, you need to study again.

<u>Questions 1 through 7</u>
Circle the letter of the one word or phrase that best completes the sentence.

1. Since 1905, _____ of Albert Einstein's first important scientific publication, the real world has become the world of the mathematician.
   (A) the year
   (B) his year
   (C) years
   (D) a year

2. _____ in his autobiography,Benjamin Franklin was born in Boston and was apprenticed to his brother James to learn the printer's trade.
   (A) That he states
   (B) As he states
   (C) He states
   (D) States

3. _____ colonial statesman William Bradford attended no formal school, he was a well- educated man.
   (A) Despite
   (B) In spite of
   (C) Although
   (D) Even

4. The pony express, _____ between Saint Joseph, Missouri, and Sacramento, California, was put out of business with the invention of the electric telegraph.
   (A) was a ten-day mail service
   (B) its ten-day mail service
   (C) a ten-day mail service
   (D) of a ten-day mail service

5. Scientists still know little about variations _____ the moon's gravitational field or about its surface composition.
   (A) into
   (B) in
   (C) at
   (D) during

6. The four U.S. presidents in _____ log cabins were Lincoln, Fillmore, Buchanan, and Garfield.
   (A) were born
   (B) they were born
   (C) who were born
   (D) who they were

7. In linguistics, _____ morphology refers to the study of the formation of words and smaller units of meaning.
   (A) is termed
   (B) to term
   (C) be termed
   (D) the term

Questions 8 through 11

Circle the letter of the underlined part of the sentence that is incorrect.

8. Even <u>when</u> the warmest part of the day in the hottest season of the <u>year</u>, desert sand dunes
      A   B

   teem with *Bembex*, <u>more</u> commonly <u>known as</u> sand wasps.
                        C   D

9. The 1960 presidential campaign was marked by an innovation <u>into</u> American politics — a
                                                                   A

   series <u>of television debates</u> <u>in</u> which the two candidates <u>responded to</u> questions put by
          B   C   D

   newspaper reporters.

10. In 1914, Congress <u>established</u> the Federal Trade Commission, <u>who</u> steadily increased the
                        A   B

    extent and <u>nature</u> of its regulation of the <u>advertising</u> industry.
               C   D

11. Even <u>although</u> the negative <u>and</u> positive charges <u>of isotopes</u> are identical, <u>their</u> masses are
         A   B   C   D
    not.

G✔16   Check One-Word ——ING and ——ED Adjectives

The present participle ——*ing* and the past participle ——*ed* forms of verbs can function as adjectives in English sentences.

> The <u>printing</u> press was invented long ago.
>   *Adj*

> <u>Printed</u> books are now widely available.
> *Adj*

> <u>Sponsoring</u> agencies give scholarships to worthy students.
>   *Adj*

> <u>Sponsored</u> students do not have to pay college tuition.
>   *Adj*

> **NOTE:** For irregular verbs, the ——*ed* may be an ——*en* or some other irregular ending.

The major difference between ——*ing* and ——*ed* adjectives is an active-passive difference.

In the first sentence of each pair above, the ——*ing* adjective tells us that the noun it modifies is doing the action. Any ——*ing* adjectives and the nouns they modify can be rewritten as subjects and verbs of active sentences: *presses print* and *agencies sponsor*.

In the second sentence of each pair above, the ——*ed* participle tells us that the noun it modifies is receiving the action from the verb. Any ——*ed* adjectives and the nouns they modify can be rewritten as subjects and verbs of passive sentences: *books are printed* and *students are sponsored*.

▼▼▼

The TOEFL tests your understanding of ——*ing* and ——*ed* adjectives by using ——*ing* adjectives in place of ——*ed* adjectives or vice versa.

MODEL

Even though the <u>parking</u> car was locked, someone <u>was able to</u> steal the tape
   A   B   C

player <u>from</u> inside.
    D

What is wrong with this sentence?
Answer: The wrong participle form has been used as an adjective.

▼ Explanation ▲

In this question, the car receives the action of *park*. The adjective-noun combination could be rewritten *the car was parked*. Therefore, the past participle of *park* should be used as an adjective to describe the car. Answer (B) is the correct answer to this question because *parking* is incorrect.
Correction: *parked*

☞ ON THE TOEFL TEST

• Check to see that ——*ing* and ——*ed* adjectives are used correctly in TOEFL questions.

See the Grammar Appendix, #14, page 442 if you need more information about -ing and -ed participle forms and for a chart of irregular verbs.

EXERCISE 16: Practice with ——ING and ——ED Adjectives

Circle the correct adjective given in each pair.

1. Last night I read a very (exciting/excited) short story.

2. Priscilla listened to a (boring/bored) newscast on the radio.

3. (Tiring/Tired), Marsha went to bed early.

4. The dog's habit of barking was extremely (annoying/annoyed).

5. The (burning/burned) sun beat down on the desert floor.

6. The man (involving/involved) refused to respond to my questions.

7. (Working/Worked) women find it difficult to spend time with their families.

8. Lisa put the (polishing/polished) teapot on the shelf.

9. The man was (startling/startled) by the noise in the bushes.

10. The woman was (embarrassing/embarrassed) by the behavior of her child.

11. The (visiting/visited) professor taught a special class.

G✔17   Check ——ING and ——ED Modifying Phrases

In English, ——*ing* and ——*ed* participles are used in phrases which modify noun structures. These phrases modify the noun structures which are closest to them in sentences.

> <u>Though tired</u>, <u>Hank</u> continued working.
> ——*ed phrase Noun modified*
>
> <u>Remembering her promise</u>, <u>Margy</u> bought her daughter a new toy.
> ——*ing phrase   Noun modified*

NOTE: For irregular verbs, the ——*ed* may be an ——*en* or some other irregular ending.

▼▼▼

> The TOEFL tests your understanding of the form and meaning of ——*ing* and ——*ed* modifying phrases by:
> 1. using other structures in their place—especially finite verbs, gerunds, and infinitives;
> 2. placing them so that they modify the wrong noun structures—sometimes called the *dangling modifier* problem;
> 3. using incorrect word order in these phrases; or,
> 4. using an ——*ing* phrase (active) where an ——*ed* phrase (passive) is needed or vice versa.

MODEL
This college, _____ in 1800, is the oldest in this part of the United States.
(A)   it was established
(B)   has been established
(C)   having established
(D)   established
What is needed in this sentence?
Answer: An ——*ed* (passive) participle to complete the modifying phrase

▼ Explanation ▲

In this question, there is an incomplete modifying phrase. A participle is needed to complete this phrase. Answer (A) contains a complete main clause. Answer (B) contains a finite verb phrase. Answer (C) begins with a participle, but it has an active meaning (the college established something). This is not the meaning of the sentence. Answer (D) is the correct answer to the question because it contains an ——*ed* participle which carries the passive meaning needed in this sentence.

MODEL

Not thinking clearly,_____.

    (A)   Jane's purse was left in the car
    (B)   in the car was Jane's purse
    (C)   Jane left her purse in the car
    (D)   the car had Jane's purse in it

What is needed in this sentence?
Answer: A main clause with a subject that can be modified by the ——*ing*
phrase

▼ Explanation ▲

In this question, the main clause is missing. In answers (A) and (B), *purse* is the subject. *Purse* cannot be modified by *not thinking clearly*, because purses do not think. In answer (D), *the car* is the subject. Cars cannot think, either. Answer (C) is the correct answer to the question because it contains the subject *Jane*, which can be modified by the ——*ing* phrase, *not thinking clearly*.

☞ ON THE TOEFL TEST

- Check to see that ——*ing* and ——*ed* modifying phrases in TOEFL questions are formed correctly and used where they are needed.
- Check to see that ——*ing* and ——*ed* phrases modify the nouns they should modify.

See G✔16, above, if you need more information on the active/passive difference between
——ing and ——ed participles.
See the Grammar Appendix, #31, page 458 if you need more information on -ing and -ed
modifying phrases.

EXERCISE 17A: Practice with ——ING and ——ED Phrases and Modified Nouns

Underline each ——*ing* and——*ed* modifying phrase and circle the noun structure it modifies. Then, on the line provided, put an *I* if the sentence is incorrect and a *C* if the sentence is correct. Correct each error. You may need to change several sentence parts to make your corrections. More than one correction may be possible.

_I_ 1. While reading, *I was* ~~the lights~~ went out.

____ 2. Anyone wanting tickets should get in line.

____ 3. There are eight children in the family lived on B Street.

____ 4. Hoping to see her father, the factory was visited by the little girl.

____ 5. We were frightened by the man standing in the corner.

____ 6. Since moving to Miami, the weather has been beautiful.

_____ 7. When buying a car, you must shop carefully.

_____ 8. I didn't understand the instructions giving by the teaching assistant.

_____ 9. Hoping to get business, a sale was sponsored by local merchants.

_____ 10. How many of the papers given to you yesterday have you corrected?

_____ 11. After losing his wallet three times, Mark's keychain was lost, too.

EXERCISE 17B: More Practice with ——ING and ——ED Modifying Phrases

Circle the correct answer.

1. Temperatures _____ above 110 degrees Fahrenheit are common in the American Southwest.
   (A) they climb
   (B) climb
   (C) that they climb
   (D) climbing

2. _____ his hat on the table, Edward entered the room.
   (A) Placed
   (B) He placed
   (C) Placing
   (D) To place

3. _____ by all, Professor Jones will be missed when he retires.
   (A) Loved
   (B) He is loved
   (C) Loving
   (D) To love

4. Interested in the plot, _____.
   (A) John to stay awake to see the end of the movie
   (B) John staying awake to see the end of the movie
   (C) the end of the movie John stayed awake to see
   (D) John stayed awake to see the end of the movie

5. The squirrel, _____, hid its nuts in a variety of places.
   (A) tried to prepare for winter
   (B) trying to prepare for winter
   (C) to prepare for winter tried
   (D) for winter trying to prepare

6. With its antlers _____ the feet of a duck, the North American moose is easy to identify.
   (A) web-like
   (B) webbed like
   (C) like a web
   (D) the webs like

G✔18   Check Gerunds and Infinitives

Gerunds and infinitives occur in many English sentences. Infinitives can function as nouns, adverbs, and adjectives. Gerunds function only as nouns.

<u>Smiling</u> is good for you.
Gerund (noun)

You like <u>to smile</u>.
Infinitive (noun)

The man <u>to see</u> is Mr. Jones.
Infinitive (adjective)

He ran <u>to meet</u> her.
Infinitive (adverb)

Although both gerunds and infinitives can function as subjects, objects, and complements in English sentences, infinitives cannot function as objects of prepositions. Only gerunds can function as objects of prepositions.

Correct: Today's weather is perfect for <u>swimming</u>.

Incorrect: Today's weather is perfect for <u>to swim</u>.

While some verbs can be followed by either gerunds or infinitives, others cannot be followed by both forms.

Correct: I enjoy <u>eating</u>.

Incorrect: I enjoy <u>to eat</u>.

Gerunds and infinitives that come from transitive verbs (verbs that have objects) can be followed by objects; nouns cannot.

Correct: <u>Contemplating</u> <u>life</u> is a favorite human pastime.
            Gerund   *Noun object*

Incorrect: The <u>contemplation</u> <u>life</u> is a favorite human pastime.
            Noun   *Noun object*

Some adjectives can be followed by infinitives. These adjectives usually describe a person, not a thing, and often express feelings or attitudes. These adjectives are not normally followed by gerunds.

Correct: I was sad <u>to learn</u> that he had gone.

Incorrect: I was sad <u>learning</u> that he had gone.

▼▼▼

The TOEFL tests your knowledge of gerunds and infinitives by:
1. using gerunds where infinitives should be used and vice versa;
2. using other structures—especially finite verbs and clauses—where gerunds or infinitives should be used; or,
3. forming gerund and infinitive phrases incorrectly.

▼ Explanation ▲

In this question an object is needed for the preposition *for*. Answer (A) contains an infinitive, which cannot be the object of a preposition. Answer (B) contains a gerund with an added, unnecessary pronoun in front of it. Answer (D) contains a noun, which cannot occur before the object *strong teeth and bones*. Answer (C) is the correct answer to the question. It contains a gerund, which can function as the object of the preposition *for*, and which can be followed by the object, *strong teeth and bones*.

▼ Explanation ▲

In this question the infinitive *to write* occurs twice. The verb *start* can be followed either by a gerund or an infinitive, so the first instance of *to write* is correct. However, the verb *finish* should be followed by a gerund. Answer (C) is the correct answer to the question because the second instance of *to write* is incorrect.
Correction: *writing*

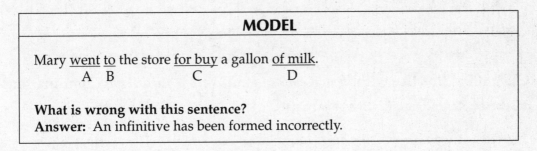

▼ Explanation ▲

In this question, the infinitive is formed with *for* instead of with *to*. Answer (C) is the correct answer to the question because *for buy* is incorrect.
Correction: *to buy*

- Check to see that gerund and infinitive phrases are formed correctly in TOEFL questions.
- Check to see that gerunds are not used when infinitives are needed and vice versa.
- Check to see that other structures are not used when gerunds or infinitives are needed.

See the Grammar Appendix, #32 and #33, pages 458–459 if you need more information on gerunds and infinitives, as well as for a list of verbs followed by gerunds, a list of verbs followed by infinitives, and a list of adjectives followed by infinitives.

EXERCISE 18A: Practice Distinguishing Gerunds and Infinitives from Other Verb Forms

In each sentence, circle the gerunds and infinitives. Then, underline and label the subjects *S* and finite verbs *V*.

1. The two brothers were eating when the sheriff came to see them.
   S   V   S   V

2. Her reading is improving a little bit every day.

3. Voting is becoming less and less popular with the American public.

4. Hearing her sing made me want to dance.

5. We don't mind waiting for you to finish your housework.

6. They are discussing going out for dinner.

7. I was advised to see Doctor Smith about having my eyes checked.

8. The man is considering giving his wife a new toaster for their anniversary.

9. The guests were thinking about leaving when the phone started ringing.

10. I hate waiting for the mail.

11. You should try to walk to school every day.

EXERCISE 18B: Practice with *Verb + Gerund* and *Verb + Infinitive* Combinations

Circle the correct gerund or infinitive in each pair.

1. He regretted (giving/to give) her his favorite shirt.

2. George needs Margaret (helping/to help) him walk.

3. If you care (seeing/to see) the apartment again, please give me a call.

4. Nancy suggested (going/to go) to the lake this weekend.

5. We should urge them (visiting/to visit) us more often.

6. If you don't hand your assignment in on time, you risk (receiving/to receive) a lower grade.

7. I cannot allow you (going/to go) out driving in this weather.

8. Elizabeth claims (knowing/to know) the president of the company.

9. We finished (eating/to eat) at about 7:30.

10. The doctor recommended (walking/to walk) every day for extra exercise.

11. Please don't hesitate (calling/to call) me at home.

EXERCISE 18C: Practice with Gerunds and Infinitives That Take Objects

Circle the form that correctly completes each of the sentences.

1. (Creating/The creation) of new jobs in this community has greatly helped the economy.

2. (To explain/The explanation) my position would take a great deal of time.

3. (Eliminating/The elimination) toxic wastes from the environment is crucial to the future health of our children.

4. (To consume/The consumption) electrical energy without replenishing it is dangerous.

5. (To generate/The generation) of some new ideas by new people will greatly enhance our marketing strategy.

6. Your teacher's (recommendation/recommending) was mailed to the college yesterday.

EXERCISE 18D: Practice Identifying Problems with Gerunds and Infinitives

For each sentence choose the letter of the underlined gerund (phrase) or infinitive (phrase) that is incorrect. Then, correct the error.

_A_ 1. *To* ~~For~~ solve this math problem, I will need <u>to use</u> my calculator.
         A   B

____ 2. His behavior leads me <u>believe</u> that he doesn't enjoy <u>studying</u>.
                      A   B

____ 3. She was hesitant <u>making</u> a commitment <u>to work</u> on our project at this time.
                     A   B

____ 4. When trying <u>to understand</u> the assignment, don't forget <u>read</u> your notes.
                  A   B

____ 5. Larry wants <u>to postpone</u> <u>to leave</u> until tomorrow.
                A   B

_____ 6. The children are anxious <u>going</u> to the party, but the parents would be content <u>to stay</u> at
                                          A   B

home.

_____ 7. Max used his wrench <u>removing</u> the tire from his car before <u>taking</u> it to the garage.
                                       A   B

_____ 8. Several of the necessary ingredients for <u>bake</u> my cake are nowhere <u>to be</u> found.
                                                   A   B

_____ 9. I want you <u>be</u> comfortable while you are trying <u>to work</u>.
                        A   B

____10. The type of paint needed <u>to completion</u> this picture is difficult <u>to find</u>.
                                        A   B

____11. Although I wanted <u>to go</u> to the concert tonight, I decided <u>staying</u> home.
                                A   B

EXERCISE 18E: More Practice with Gerunds and Infinitives

Circle the correct answer.

1. _____ has improved over the past
   few weeks.
   (A) Jane drives
   (B) Jane drove
   (C) To drive Jane
   (D) Jane's driving

2. A clever game for _____ is
   tic-tac-toe.
   (A) keeping children occupied
   (B) children keep occupied
   (C) to keep children occupied
   (D) it keeps children occupied

3. Freezing, drying, and canning have long
   been used _____ nutrients and
   freshness in foods.
   (A) for preservation
   (B) to preserve
   (C) preserved
   (D) preserve

4. Valerie decided _____ a
   garden this year.
   (A) for growing
   (B) to grow
   (C) grow
   (D) grown

5. This hot weather has affected my ability
   _____
   (A) concentrating
   (B) concentrated
   (C) to concentrate
   (D) for me concentrating

6. The fastest way _____ to my house is to
   take the freeway.
   (A) gotten
   (B) to get
   (C) getting
   (D) you get

G✔19 Check IT and THERE Sentences

The standard word order of subjects and verbs in English sentences is *Subject + Verb*. However, sometimes the real subject occurs at the end of a sentence, and *It* or *There* is used at the beginning of the sentence to take its place.

Use of IT

When the subject of a sentence is a noun clause beginning with *that* or when the subject is an infinitive, it can be moved to the end of the sentence and *It* can take its place at the beginning of the sentence.

<u>That he loves me</u> is nice.
Noun clause subject

<u>It</u> is nice that he loves me.
IT subject

<u>To hear him sing</u> is exciting.
Infinitive subject

<u>It</u> is exciting to hear him sing.
IT subject

<u>To get to Chicago</u> takes 5 hours.
Infinitive subject

<u>It</u> takes 5 hours to get to Chicago.
IT subject

Use of THERE

When the subject of a sentence is indefinite and the verb BE occurs as the main verb, the subject can be moved to the end of the sentence, and *There* can take its place at the beginning of the sentence.

<u>Some books</u> are on the table.
Indefinite subject

<u>There</u> are some books on the table.
THERE subject

The TOEFL tests your understanding of *It* and *There* sentences by:
1. using *It* when *There* is needed or vice versa;
2. using other structures when *It* or *There* structures are needed;
3. using incorrect word order in *It* and *There* constructions; or,
4. incorrectly forming other parts of *It* and *There* sentences.

```
┌─────────────────────────────────────────────────────────────┐
│                          MODEL                                │
├─────────────────────────────────────────────────────────────┤
│  _____ important to work hard at school.            │
│        (A)   There is                                         │
│        (B)   It is                                            │
│        (C)   That it is                                       │
│        (D)   Because it is                                    │
│                                                               │
│  What is needed in this sentence?                             │
│  Answer:  An It subject and a verb                            │
└─────────────────────────────────────────────────────────────┘
```

▼ Explanation ▲

In this question, the subject and verb are missing. Answers (C) and (D) contain parts of clauses; these clause parts cannot act as subjects and verbs. Answer (A) contains *there is* which can act as a subject and a verb. However, this sentence contains the infinitive *to work* as the true subject at the end of the sentence. Answer (B) is the correct answer to the question because in this sentence type, *It* is needed.

```
┌─────────────────────────────────────────────────────────────┐
│                          MODEL                                │
├─────────────────────────────────────────────────────────────┤
│  It has long been believed as smoking causes heart disease.  │
│           A              B         C        D                 │
│                                                               │
│  What is wrong with this sentence?                            │
│  Answer:  The noun clause following It is incorrectly formed. │
└─────────────────────────────────────────────────────────────┘
```

▼ Explanation ▲

In this question, the noun clause which has been moved to the end of the *It* sentence begins with *as*, which is not a noun clause marker. Answer (B) is the correct answer to the question because *as* is incorrect.

Correction: *that*

```
┌─────────────────────────────────────────────────────────────┐
│                 ☛ ON THE TOEFL TEST                           │
├─────────────────────────────────────────────────────────────┤
│  • Check to see that It and There sentences are correctly     │
│    formed in TOEFL questions.                                 │
└─────────────────────────────────────────────────────────────┘
```

See the Grammar Appendix, #4, page 436 if you need more information on definite and indefinite nouns.

EXERCISE 19A: Practice with *It* and *There*

Complete the following sentences with *It is*, *There is*, or *There are*.

1. ___*It is*___ unusual to see Mark and Mike together.

2. _____ only a few apples in this bowl.

3. _____ obvious that Loretta isn't coming.

4. _____ amazing that there have not been more accidents on these bad roads.

5. _____ someone waiting to see you.

6. _____ some people who feel that these meetings are unnecessary.

7. _____ crazy for him to worry like that.

8. _____ my belief that time is more valuable than money.

9. _____ a new student in our class.

10. _____ a good idea to eat before you take an exam.

11. _____ too late to start over now.

EXERCISE 19B: More Practice with *It* and *There*

Circle the correct answer.

1. Lately, _____ nobody using the library.
   (A) there has been
   (B) it has been
   (C) has been
   (D) been

2. By the time we left the dance, _____ that she was not feeling well.
   (A) there was obvious
   (B) an obvious
   (C) it was obvious
   (D) to be obvious

3. I would like to see you tomorrow because _____ several things we need to discuss.
   (A) there have
   (B) they are
   (C) it is
   (D) there are

4. _____ colds are caused by viruses.
   (A) That the knowledge
   (B) It is known that
   (C) To know that
   (D) The knowledge that

5. I was pleased to see that _____ several easy recipes for cake in this cookbook.
   (A) there are
   (B) it is
   (C) to be
   (D) are there

6. _____ one hour for me to get ready for work in the morning.
   (A) Usually taking
   (B) To take it usually
   (C) It usually takes
   (D) Usually takes it

Grammar Checkpoint Test Four for G✔16 through G✔19

Allow yourself 5 minutes to complete this checkpoint test. There are 11 questions on the test. Check your answers in the answer key. Next to each answer is the number of the checkpoint that is being tested in each of these questions. Use these numbers to determine which checkpoints, if any, you need to study again.

<u>Questions 1 through 7</u>

Circle the letter of the one word or phrase that best completes the sentence.

1. _____ Depression years, American painters seemed to turn away from Europe as a source of inspiration.
   (A) It was
   (B) While
   (C) There were
   (D) During

2. _____, Dwight Eisenhower resigned his post as commander of NATO in 1951.
   (A) He was seeking the Republican presidential nomination
   (B) The Republican presidential nomination seeking
   (C) Seeking the Republican presidential nomination
   (D) The Republican presidential nomination was sought

3. _____ Native American myths and poems, American anthropologists have preserved much that is beautiful in a threatened culture.
   (A) By recording
   (B) Recorded
   (C) Record
   (D) To be recorded

4. _____ several weeks for a person to starve to death, but without sleep the human body dies in about 10 days.
   (A) Usually taking it
   (B) Usually takes it
   (C) It usually takes
   (D) To take it usually

5. _____ its rigid home on its back, the land tortoise is well protected from predators.
   (A) Carried
   (B) It carries
   (C) Carrying
   (D) To carry

6. Descendant of a long line of New Englanders, Robert Lowell chose, in his early poems,_____ against his background of Bostonian eminence and public service.
   (A) for reacting
   (B) to react
   (C) reacted
   (D) to the reaction

7. Today Edward Taylor is generally regarded as the finest poet _____ in America before the nineteenth century.
   (A) he wrote
   (B) written
   (C) wrote
   (D) writing

Questions 8 through 11

Circle the letter of the underlined part of the sentence that is incorrect.

8. <u>In</u> the spring of 1932 some 15,000 <u>unemploying</u> American war veterans converged on
   A   B
   Washington and <u>established</u> the <u>shanty</u> community of Anacostia Flats.
                      C   D

9. Special tools have been <u>designed</u> <u>opening</u> coconuts <u>without</u> <u>throwing</u> them against hard
                              A   B   C   D
   surfaces.

10. <u>It</u> is wise <u>avoiding</u> overconsumption of alcohol <u>because of</u> its detrimental effects on <u>the</u> heart,
    A   B   C   D
    liver and central nervous system.

11. *Ms.* magazine, <u>which</u> began in 1972, <u>has long been</u> considered one of the <u>led</u> publications of the
                      A   B   C
    <u>feminist</u> movement.
       D

G✔20   Check Word Form and Function

The form of an English word must agree with its function in a sentence. For many English words, several forms are possible. Different word forms are created by adding endings, called suffixes, to the original form of a word.

Below are some of the common suffixes used to create different word forms.

To form a *noun* from a *verb*:

SUFFIX	EXAMPLE	
——*al*	remove	removal
——*tion*	inform	information
——*ion*	impress	impression
——*ment*	move	movement
——*ant*	consult	consultant
——*er*	teach	teacher
——*or*	act	actor
——*ure*	please	pleasure
——*ence*	depend	dependence
——*ance*	accept	acceptance

To form an *adjective* from a *noun* or a *verb*:

SUFFIX	EXAMPLE	
——*ish*	fool	foolish
——*ive*	act	active
——*ic*	hero	heroic
——*ent*	differ	different
——*al*	tradition	traditional
——*able*	comfort	comfortable
——*less*	care	careless
——*ful*	care	careful
——*ly*	year	yearly
——*ous*	fame	famous
——*y*	ease	easy
——*en*	wood	wooden
——*some*	trouble	troublesome
——*ary*	compliment	complimentary

To form an *adverb* from an *adjective*:

SUFFIX	EXAMPLE	
——*ly*	faint	faintly

To form a *verb* from an *adjective* or a *noun*:

SUFFIX	EXAMPLE	
——*fy*	clear	clarify
——*ize*	moisture	moisturize

NOTE: The suffix ——*ly* can be used to form both adjectives and adverbs. Some nouns take ——*ly* to become adjectives (*king* + ——*ly* = *kingly*). Many adjectives take ——*ly* to become adverbs (*evident* + ——*ly* = *evidently*).

A noun functions to name a person, place, thing, or idea.

An <u>analysis</u> of the problem was impossible.
    Noun

A verb functions to express action or state of being.

They <u>analyze</u> problems like this one every day.
    Verb

An adjective functions to modify a noun or noun structure.

Their <u>analytical</u> approach to problems is impressive.
    Adjective

An adverb functions to modify a verb, an adjective, or another adverb.

They approached the problem <u>analytically</u>.
                  Adverb

The TOEFL tests your understanding of word form and function by using word forms that do not agree with their functions in English sentences.

MODEL

<u>She</u> told the <u>truthful</u> when we asked her <u>about</u> her <u>past</u>.
A   B   C   D

What is wrong with this question?
Answer: An adjective form has been used where a noun form is needed.

▼ **Explanation** ▲

In this question, a noun is needed after the article *the*. *Truthful* is not a noun; it is an adjective. Answer (B) is the correct answer to this question because *truthful* is incorrect.
Correction: *truth*

MODEL

The <u>happily</u> man spoke <u>cheerfully</u> <u>about</u> his family <u>and</u> friends.
      A   B   C   D

What is wrong with this sentence?
Answer: An adverb form has been used where an adjective form is needed.

▼ **Explanation** ▲

In this question, an adjective form is needed to describe *man*. *Happily* is an adverb formed from the adjective *happy*. Answer (A) is the correct answer to this question because *happily* is incorrect.
Correction: *happy*

See the Grammar Appendix, #4, #12, #13 and #14, pages 436–442 if you need more information on nouns, verbs, adjectives, and adverbs.
See the Vocabulary Appendix, #2, page 470 if you need more information on word forms.

EXERCISE 20A: Practice with Word Forms

Using the suffixes given above and a dictionary if you need one, fill in the chart with the appropriate word forms. There may be more than one possibility for some forms.

NOUN	VERB	ADJECTIVE	ADVERB
category	categorize	categorical	categorically
success			
		rational	
			imaginatively
	confuse		
	confide		
			excessively
excellence			
	satisfy		
		persuasive	
decision			

EXERCISE 20B: Practice with Word Forms and their Functions

Identify each word as one of the following:
  N (noun)
  V (verb)
  Adj (adjective)
  Adv (adverb)

_V_ 1. glorify

_____ 2. delivery

_____ 3. quickly

_____ 4. convenient

_____ 5. sensitize

_____ 6. creation

_____ 7. terrify

_____ 8. recovery

_____ 9. useful

_____ 10. independence   _____ 16. baker

_____ 11. curiously   _____ 17. sensation

_____ 12. liberation   _____ 18. repeat

_____ 13. easy   _____ 19. worldly

_____ 14. seriously   _____ 20. enjoyment

_____ 15. recent   _____ 21. revolutionize

EXERCISE 20C: Practice with Adjective and Adverb Forms

On the first line, identify each underlined word as an *Adj (adjective)* or an *Adv (adverb)*. On the second line, write the word that the underlined word modifies.

1. I can see his point <u>clearly</u>.

   _____Adv_____   _____see_____

2. The <u>stately</u> redwood tree was over 200 feet tall.

   _____   _____

3. I have met many <u>friendly</u> people here.

   _____   _____

4. She has a low <u>yearly</u> income.

   _____   _____

5. The young boy watched <u>passively</u> as his mother opened her gift.

   _____   _____

6. She was <u>pleasantly</u> surprised by the weather.

   _____   _____

EXERCISE 20D: Practice Identifying Word Form Errors

In each of the following sentences, choose the letter of the underlined word that is incorrectly formed. Then, correct the error.

_D_ 1. <u>Careful</u> <u>consideration</u> of the <u>alternatives</u> led us to a <s>practice</s> solution.
     A   B   C   D

practical

_____ 2. Her <u>creative</u> <u>talent</u> is not <u>easy</u> captured in <u>simple</u> words.
       A   B   C   D

_____ 3. Unfortunately, the vigorously daily exercise he has been engaging in has not helped his
            A   B   C

health.
D

_____ 4. The plaintive cry of the lonely lamb failure to reach its mother last night.
            A   B   C   D

_____ 5. Water, an important natural resourceful, is being polluted by acid and other harmful
                    A   B   C

industrial wastes.
D

_____ 6. The loosely woven rug on our kitchen floor is made of a rarely grass found in marshy
            A   B   C   D

areas.

_____ 7. To have a business that is a successful, a person must work diligently and efficiently.
                    A   B   C   D

_____ 8. They careful planned their vacation to include a quick trip to the secluded tropical island
              A   B   C   D

where they first met.

_____ 9. Last week, Lana and Lance developers a truly unique method for finding plumbing
                                    A   B   C

leaks.
D

_____ 10. In desert areas, long periods of drought often alternate with long periods of excessive
             A   B   C

rainy and flooding.
D

_____ 11. Plants often responsive to pressure cues such as wind and human touch.
                       A   B   C   D

G✔21   Check Word Form After Verbs

An adverb often follows a verb in English. This adverb modifies the verb it follows.

>   Jane ran quickly down the street.
>   *Adverb*

However, after a linking verb such as *appear, be, become* (and *get, turn,* and *grow* when they mean *become*), *feel, look, remain, seem, smell,* and *taste,* an adjective is used. This adjective describes the subject of the sentence.

>   Jane is quick.
>   *Adjective*

The TOEFL tests your understanding of the word forms necessary after verbs by using adverbs where adjectives should be used and vice versa.

MODEL

Jim seemed quite <u>happily</u> <u>this</u> evening <u>at</u> the <u>party</u>.
           A   B   C   D

What is wrong with this sentence?
Answer: An adverb has been used after a linking verb.

▼ Explanation ▲

In this question, the linking verb *seemed* has been used. Linking verbs should be followed by adjectives. *Happily* is an adverb. Answer (A) is the correct answer to the question because *happily* is incorrect.
Correction: *happy*

☞ ON THE TOEFL TEST

- Check to see that the correct word forms are used after verbs.

See the Grammar Appendix, #16, page 446 if you need more information on linking verbs.

EXERCISE 21:   Practice with Word Forms After Verbs

Circle the correct word in each pair.

1. Edward felt (sleepy/sleepily) after the big meal.

2. Jack looked up (sleepy/sleepily) from the book he was reading.

3. The theater got (quiet/quietly) when the movie began.

4. Leroy smiled (cheerful/cheerfully) when the teacher gave him his grade.

5. That car looks quite (comfortable/comfortably).

6. She tasted the spaghetti sauce (careful/carefully) because it was very hot.

7. He grew more and more (angry/angrily) as she told him the story.

8. Marsha sighed (heavy/heavily) at the thought of all the work she had to do.

9. A trip to the country sounds (wonderful/wonderfully).

10. They sounded the alarm (loud/loudly) when they smelled the smoke of the fire.

11. The sun was shining (bright/brightly) when we arrived at the beach.

G✔22   Check Word Form: Person Nouns and Activity Nouns

Some English nouns refer to people and some refer to related things or activities. Below are a few examples of *person* noun and *activity* noun pairs.

PERSON	ACTIVITY
gardener	gardening
biologist	biology
innovator	innovation

▼▼▼

The TOEFL tests your understanding of *person* nouns and *activity* nouns by using one where the other is needed.

MODEL

Richard Burton <u>is</u> a very well-known British <u>acting</u> who married Elizabeth
             A   B

Taylor, an <u>equally</u> famous American film <u>star</u>.
        C   D

What is wrong with this sentence?
Answer: An *activity* noun is being used where a *person* noun is needed.

▼ Explanation ▲

In this question, a *person* noun is needed after the verb *is* to rename *Richard Burton*. Instead, an *activity* noun, *acting*, has been used. Answer (B) is the correct answer to this question because *acting* is incorrect.
Correction: *actor*

☞ ON THE TOEFL TEST

- Check to see that *person* nouns and *activity* nouns are used correctly in TOEFL questions.

EXERCISE 22:   Practice with *Person* and *Activity* Nouns

On the line provided, put an *I* if the sentence is incorrect and a *C* if the sentence is correct. Then, correct each error.

<u>I</u> 1. The ~~direction~~ *director* of the play said that he would like us to arrive one hour early for rehearsal tonight.

____ 2. Twelve employees were hurt in the accident at the factory.

____ 3. The chemist who won the Nobel Prize last week was very happy.

____ 4. My son wants to study engineer.

____ 5. The carpentry will finish building our cabinets next week.

____ 6. No one is sure who the creation of this beautiful sculpture is.

____ 7. Manhattan city plans have worked very hard to regulate the flow of downtown traffic.

____ 8. We buy fresh bread every day from a bakery on the corner of Fifth Avenue and Pine Street.

____ 9. The scientist department at this school is not very strong.

____ 10. The company is very happy with the architecture who designed this building.

____ 11. Although she is a famous actress, Diana still likes her privacy.

G✔23   Check Word Form: Words that Don't Exist in English

Occasionally, a word that does not exist in English is used on the TOEFL. This form is always closely related to a real English word form. Below are a few examples of words that don't exist and their corresponding real English word forms.

DOESN'T EXIST	ENGLISH WORD
adaptator	adaptor
estable	stable
explorator	explorer
plastical	plastic

▼▼▼

The TOEFL tests your ability to recognize words that don't exist in English by using them in the place of real English words.

MODEL
Christopher Columbus <u>may not</u> have been the <u>first</u> <u>explorator</u> to <u>discover</u> 　　　　　　　　　　　　　　A　　　　　　　　　　B　　C　　　　　D America. **What is wrong with this sentence?** **Answer:** A word has been used that does not exist in English.

▼ Explanation ▲

In this question, the word *explorator* is a word that does not exist in English. Answer (C) is the correct answer to this question because *explorator* is incorrect.
Correction: *explorer*

• Check TOEFL questions for word forms that do not exist in English.

EXERCISE 23:   Practice with Words that Do Not Exist in English

In each sentence, choose the letter of the underlined word that is incorrect. Then, correct the error.

_B_ 1. The <u>beautiful</u> woman was standing alone in front of the ~~estation~~. *station*
         A   B

____ 2. The <u>defectator</u> sought refuge at the home of the <u>ambassador</u>.
         A   B

____ 3. The <u>economic</u> situation in our country is not very <u>estable</u> at this time.
         A   B

____ 4. As far as I am concerned, the son of that <u>politator</u> should not take up his father's
                                                    A

      <u>profession</u>.
         B

____ 5. Kim's <u>success</u> on the exam made today <u>an especial</u> day for her.
               A   B

____ 6. While most of the books in this pile have been <u>classificated</u>, some are still in need of
                                                         A

      <u>categorization</u>.
         B

G✔24   Check Equative, Comparative, and Superlative Degree

Three degrees of comparison are possible in English. Special forms or words are added to adjectives and adverbs to form these degrees.

   To make the equative, comparative, and superlative degree of adjectives and adverbs, the following forms are used:

	One syllable Adj or Adv	Two syllable Adj or Adv ending in ——y	Two or more syllable Adj or Adv
Equative	as…as *as tall as*	as…as *as happy as*	as…as *as beautiful as*
Comparative	——er than *taller than*	…——er than *happier than*	more/less…than *more beautiful than*
Superlative	the…——est *the tallest*	the…——est *the happiest*	the most/least… *the most beautiful*

NOTE: Some words have irregular degree forms. The most common of these are:

ADJECTIVES			ADVERBS		
good	better	best	well	better	best
bad	worse	worst	badly	worse	worst
much/many	more	most	much	more	most
little	less	least	little	less	least
far	farther	farthest	far	farther	farthest
——	further	furthest	——	further	furthest

The equative degree is used to show equality.

Annie is <u>as tall as</u> Jacob.

This sentence tells us that Annie and Jacob are the same height.

The comparative degree is used to compare two things that are not equal.

Annie is <u>taller than</u> Jacob.

This sentence tells us that Annie's height and Jacob's height are not the same. In addition, it tells us that Annie's height is greater than Jacob's.

The superlative degree is used to compare three or more things that are not equal.

Annie is <u>the tallest</u> student in the class.

This sentence tells us that there are more than two students in the class and that Annie's height is the greatest of all the students.

▼▼▼

The TOEFL tests your understanding of equative, comparative, and superlative degree by:
1. forming degree structures incorrectly;
2. using incorrect word order in long degree constructions; or,
3. using one degree structure where another is needed.

MODEL

<u>Although</u> Tom's paper was <u>longer than</u> Alice's, Alice's paper <u>was</u>
  A   B   C
<u>more insightful that</u> Tom's.
          D

What is wrong with this sentence?
Answer: The comparative degree has been incorrectly formed.

▼ Explanation ▲

In this question, there are two comparative structures. The first, *longer than*, is correctly formed. However, the second, *more insightful that*, is incorrectly formed. *That* is not used in forming the comparative degree. Answer (D) is the correct answer to this question because *more insightful that* is incorrect.
Correction: *more insightful than.*

```
┌─────────────────────────────────────────────────────────────┐
│                          MODEL                                │
│                                                               │
│   Professor Clark's chemistry class is _____ Professor Smith's. │
│        (A)   more than difficult                              │
│        (B)   to the difficult                                 │
│        (C)   as difficult as                                  │
│        (D)   the most difficult                               │
│                                                               │
│   What is needed in this sentence?                            │
│   Answer: The equative degree                                 │
└─────────────────────────────────────────────────────────────┘
```

▼ Explanation ▲

In this question, two classes are being compared. Therefore, either the comparative or the equative degree is needed. Answer (A) contains an incorrectly formed comparative degree. Answer (B) contains a prepositional phrase. Answer (D) contains the superlative degree. Answer (C) is the correct answer to this question because it contains a correctly formed equative degree.

```
┌─────────────────────────────────────────────────────────────┐
│                   ☛ ON THE TOEFL TEST                         │
│                                                               │
│   • Check to see that equative, comparative, and superlative degree structures │
│     are formed correctly in TOEFL questions.                  │
│   • Check to see that the correct degree structure is used where needed. │
└─────────────────────────────────────────────────────────────┘
```

EXERCISE 24A: Practice with Equative, Comparative, and Superlative Structures

In each of the following sentences, choose the letter of the equative, comparative, or superlative that is incorrect. Then, correct the error.

_B_ 1. Rice is <u>more important than</u> meat in many of the countries with <u>highest</u> *the* populations in
            A   B
the world.

____ 2. Cats are <u>more independent as</u> dogs, but they are not <u>as loyal as</u> dogs are.
                        A   B

____ 3. My car is <u>as fast</u> yours, but yours is <u>more beautiful than</u> mine.
                      A   B

____ 4. Winter is colder in Montana <u>that</u> it is in Vermont; winter in Alaska is <u>the coldest</u> in the
                                       A   B
United States.

____ 5. The <u>most difficult</u> part of the exam was given at the end when everyone was the
                 A
<u>most exhaustedest</u>.
         B

____ 6. The <u>more easily understood</u> alphabet in the world is also one of <u>the oldest</u>.
                 A   B

EXERCISE 24B: **More Practice with Equative, Comparative, and Superlative Degree**

On the line provided, put an *I* if the sentence is incorrect and a *C* if the sentence is correct. Then, correct each error.

_I_ 1. This cake is the ~~sweeter~~ _sweetest_ I have ever eaten.

____ 2. The books that I am reading for history class are the most interesting by far than the ones I'm reading for science.

____ 3. We bought the heavier coats that we could find.

____ 4. I would like to read as short as article of them all.

____ 5. Mabel wanted to buy Victor the better new watch she could find.

____ 6. This record album is not as interesting as the one you gave me to listen to last week.

____ 7. My brother is the taller person in our family.

____ 8. Greg's understanding of computers is better than mine.

____ 9. The color that absorbs sunlight the more easily of all is black.

____ 10. This stereo is the most expensive of the two that we have looked at today.

____ 11. Tonight's concert was much more enjoyable than last night's play.

EXERCISE 24C: **More Practice with Equative, Comparative, and Superlative Degree**

Circle the correct answer. Then, use the choices provided to answer the question: *What is needed in this sentence?* Choices:

      Equative degree
      Comparative degree
      Superlative degree

1. Texas is larger _____, but it has fewer people than California does.
    (A) of California
    (B) that California
    (C) California
    (D) than California

    What is needed in this sentence?_____

2. Antarctica is the site of _____ elevations on earth.
    (A) the highest
    (B) the highest are
    (C) and the highest
    (D) higher

    What is needed in this sentence?_____

3. Lately, Joyce has been _____ her health.
   (A) more than worried about her job
   (B) worried more than about her job
   (C) more worried about her job than
   (D) worried about more than her job

   What is needed in this sentence?_____

4. A warm-blooded animal requires _____ than does a cold-blooded creature of the same size.
   (A) most food
   (B) the most food
   (C) more food
   (D) the more food

   What is needed in this sentence?_____

5. The instructions for this model are _____ as possible, so it will not be difficult to put together.
   (A) clearly more defined
   (B) as clearly defined
   (C) as defined clearly
   (D) more clearly defined

   What is needed in this sentence?_____

6. Small cars are _____ large ones, which generally use much more gasoline.
   (A) as popular today as
   (B) of as much popularity as today
   (C) as the popularity is the same today as
   (D) as today's popularity is the same as

   What is needed in this sentence?_____

Grammar Checkpoint Test Five for G✔20 through G✔24

Allow yourself 5 minutes to complete this checkpoint test. There are 11 questions on the test. Check your answers in the answer key. Next to each answer is the number of the checkpoint that is being tested in each of these questions. Use these numbers to determine which checkpoints, if any, you need to study again.

Questions 1 through 11

Circle the letter of the underlined part of the sentence that is incorrect.

1. Thomas Bangs Thorpe, American author <u>and</u> artist of the nineteenth century, <u>produced</u> short
    A   B
    stories and sketches <u>which</u> are appreciated for their <u>humorous</u>.
    C   D

2. An <u>amazing</u> variety of animals, <u>by means of</u> elaborate <u>adaptators</u>, <u>are able to</u> thrive in
    A   B   C   D
    conditions of extreme heat and dryness.

3. At the time of <u>their first</u> contact with Europeans, the Native Americans of the Great Plains were
    A
    <u>considerable more</u> spread out <u>than</u> they <u>are now</u>.
    B   C   D

4. The processes <u>involved in</u> the creation <u>of the universe</u> remain <u>mysteriously</u> to <u>astronomers</u>.
    A   B   C   D

5. <u>Most</u> Americans' blood cholesterol <u>levels</u> rise <u>as</u> they <u>grow more</u> older.
    A   B   C   D

6. <u>Musical</u> celebrities <u>from all over</u> the world appear <u>regular</u> in the <u>exclusive</u> nightclubs and
    A   B   C   D
    casinos of Las Vegas.

7. Many <u>successful</u> American film <u>directions</u> are <u>former</u> actors with a desire <u>to expand</u> their
    A   B   C   D
    experience in the film industry.

8. Homing pigeons are <u>especial</u> good <u>at finding</u> their way home over <u>hundreds of miles</u> of
    A   B   C
    <u>unfamiliar</u> terrain.
    D

9. Humans have a <u>very large</u> and <u>densely</u> brain <u>in proportion to</u> <u>their</u> body size.
    A   B   C   D

10. The <u>worse</u> winter of all for the settlers <u>at</u> Jamestown was <u>that</u> of 1607, <u>when</u> several in their
    A   B   C   D
    party died.

11. <u>In the</u> nineteenth century, new nails, screws, and <u>cutting</u> tools <u>revolutionized</u> the <u>constructed</u>
    A   B   C   D
    of houses.

G✔25　Check Standard Word Order

The standard word order of the principle parts of English sentences is:

SUBJECT + VERB (+ OBJECT AND/OR + COMPLEMENT)

The subject comes before the verb. The verb comes before its objects and/or before the complement of the sentence.

Kathy is eating.
　S　　V

Kathy is happy.
　S　V　Comp

Kathy is eating chocolate.
　S　　V　　　DO

The TOEFL tests your understanding of standard word order by mixing up the order of the principle parts of English sentences.

NOTE: The testing of standard word order is often combined with the testing of many of the other checkpoints covered on the TOEFL.

MODEL

Karen's home _____ on a busy downtown street.
- (A)　small, is an apartment
- (B)　a small apartment is
- (C)　an apartment is small
- (D)　is a small apartment

What is needed in this sentence?
Answer: A verb and a complement

▼ Explanation ▲

In this question, the verb is missing. The verb BE is contained in all of the answer choices. A complement, *a small apartment* is also contained in all of the sentences. However, the word order is incorrect in all of the answer choices except for answer (D). Answer (D) is the correct answer to this question.

☞ ON THE TOEFL TEST

- Check to see that the standard word order in TOEFL questions is correct.

EXERCISE 25A: Practice with Standard Word Order

In each of the sentences, the standard word order is incorrect. Unscramble each sentence to correct the word order.

1. A book Carol gave to Robin for his birthday.

   Carol gave a book to Robin for his birthday.

2. Many animals hurt by cars are each year.

   _____

3. Is finishing his math homework Bob.

   _____

4. Although Nancy a good friend is, she sometimes makes me angry.

   _____

5. Over the past few weeks, Mark has a new opinion developed of biology.

   _____

6. Of the six days of vacation that we had for Thanksgiving, only remain three days.

   _____

EXERCISE 25B: More Practice with Standard Word Order

Circle the correct answer.

1. In consideration of her feelings, _____.
   (A) we should not tell her the bad news yet
   (B) should we not tell her the bad news yet
   (C) the bad news we should not tell her yet
   (D) yet we should not tell her the bad news

2. Money _____ in most cultures of the world.
   (A) the principal tool for trade is
   (B) is it the principal tool for trade
   (C) is the principal tool for trade
   (D) the principal tool for trade is

3. Although the colored television set _____, almost every American family now owns at least one.
   (A) a recent invention is
   (B) is a recent invention
   (C) recent, is an invention
   (D) is it a recent invention

4. Carpenters _____ to build cabinets.
    (A) woodworking, a variety of useful tools
    (B) use of a variety of woodworking tools
    (C) a variety of woodworking tools use
    (D) use a variety of woodworking tools

5. This dictionary _____ with all the definitions we need to know for the test on
    Tuesday.
    (A) can it provide us
    (B) us can provide
    (C) can provide us
    (D) it can provide us

6. Mars _____ vast oceans of dust.
    (A) is a planet covered with
    (B) a planet is covered with
    (C) covered with a planet is
    (D) is covered with a planet

G✔26   Check Word Order in Subordinate Clauses Beginning with Question Words

Question words such as *who, what, when(ever), where(ever), why, how(ever), how long, how much,* and *how many* occur in many English sentences. These words are most commonly found in information questions—questions which ask for specific information, not just for an answer of *yes* or *no*.

When question words are used in sentences asking direct information questions:

   1. the subject and the first part of the verb of the sentence are inverted, that is, the subject is placed after the first verb; and,

   2. a question mark (?) is placed at the end of the sentence.

Who	is		she?
Question word	*first (and only) V*		*S*

What	is	she	doing?
Question word	*first V*	*S*	*second V*

In sentences where there is no verb BE or other helping verb (a modal or *have*), the helping verb DO is used in making direct information questions. The helping verb DO becomes the first verb in the sentence and again, the first verb and the subject are inverted.

Where	does	she	live?
Question word	*first V*	*S*	*second V*

Question words are also used to begin subordinate clauses that do not ask a direct question. The sentences that contain these clauses are not followed by a question mark (?). In these clauses, the subject and the verb are *not* inverted. The helping verb DO is *not* used.

I don't know <u>who she is</u>.
         Noun clause

<u>When she arrives</u>, please show her in.
    Adverb clause

Tell me the reason <u>why she didn't come</u>.
         Adjective clause

The TOEFL tests your understanding of word order in subordinate clauses
    beginning with question words by:
1. using incorrect word order in these clauses; or,
2. adding the word DO to these clauses.

MODEL

Brian is having trouble understanding _____.
    (A)   how should he start this assignment
    (B)   this assignment how he should start
    (C)   should he start this assignment how
    (D)   how he should start this assignment

What is needed in this sentence?
Answer: A noun clause beginning with a question word

▼ Explanation ▲

In this question, a direct object is needed. Noun clauses beginning with question words can function as direct objects. Answer (A) contains a direct question, so it cannot function as the direct object in this sentence. Answers (B) and (C) contain noun clauses in which the word order is incorrect. Answer (D) is the correct answer to the question because it contains a noun clause with the correct word order.

☞ ON THE TOEFL TEST

- Check to see that the word order is correct in subordinate clauses beginning with question words.
- Check to see that DO is not added to these clauses when it is not needed.

EXERCISE 26A: Practice Identifying Word Order Errors

For each sentence, circle the question words. Then, on the line provided, put an *I* if the sentence is incorrect and a *C* if the sentence is correct.
    Correct each error.

   I   1. Marion is not sure (who) ~~does she want~~ *she wants* to ask to her party.

_____   2. Wherever she goes, he goes.

_____   3. Only Angela can tell you what is the recipe for this wonderful pie.

_____   4. Carlos is not sure how long will he stay in the United States.

_____   5. As the fall progresses, there are fewer hours every day when the sun shines.

_____   6. When is it baking, bread should not be disturbed.

_____ 7. I would like to know when do you make your final decision.

_____ 8. How does she plan to finish all of this work by tomorrow is a mystery to me.

_____ 9. It is not easy to decide exactly how we should proceed with this project.

_____ 10. Maybe they should try to figure out what does the baby want.

_____ 11. I have not been able to find the place where does she live.

EXERCISE 26B: More Practice with Word Order

Circle the correct answer.

1. Carol has just found _____.
   (A) what she thinks will be a very good job
   (B) what does she think will be a very good job
   (C) a very good job will be what she thinks
   (D) she thinks what will be a very good job

2. Please let me know _____.
   (A) when is it time to go
   (B) when time it is to go
   (C) when to go it is time
   (D) when it is time to go

3. _____ working at the hardware store, Vincent was never happy.
   (A) He was
   (B) When he was
   (C) When was he
   (D) Was he

4. The doctor has not yet determined _____.
   (A) what does Arlene have
   (B) what Arlene has
   (C) Arlene has what
   (D) what has Arlene

5. Peoples' attitudes and daily lifestyles are influenced by _____.
   (A) they see and hear what on television
   (B) on television what they see and hear
   (C) they see and hear on television what
   (D) what they see and hear on television

6. _____ incubating, a chicken's egg needs to be kept warm and dry.
   (A) When it is
   (B) Is it when
   (C) It is when
   (D) When is it

G✔27   Check Inverted Subject-Verb Word Order with Special Expressions and in Conditional Sentences

As discussed in G✔26, the standard word order of *subject + verb* (+ *object* and/or + *complement*) is not followed in all English sentences. In certain situations, inverted subject-verb word order is used. That is, the subject of a sentence is placed after the first helping verb or after BE. If there is no verb BE or if there is no helping verb, the helping verb DO is added as the first verb of the sentence. This inverted subject-verb word order is most common in direct questions, but it is also common in other situations.

1.   After special expressions of location:

> <u>On the beach</u>   were   <u>five beach umbrellas</u>.
> *Expression of location*   V   S

> <u>Nowhere</u>   <u>did</u>   <u>he</u> see her.
> *Expression of location*   *first V*   S

2. After special negative (*no, not,* and *never*) and almost negative (*hardly, rarely, scarcely, not only, at no time, barely, only, seldom,* etc.) expressions:

> <u>Never</u>   <u>had</u>   <u>I</u> seen such a glorious sight.
> *Negative*   *first V*   S

> <u>Only</u> after he saw her <u>did</u>   <u>he</u> understand.*
> *Almost negative*   *first V*   S

*NOTE: When the negative or almost negative expression is part of a subordinate clause, the subject and verb of the subordinate clause are not inverted. The subject and the verb of the main clause are inverted.

3. After the special expressions *so* and *neither*:

> <u>So</u> happy <u>was</u> <u>she</u> that she danced around the room.
>   V   S

> I liked the coffee, and <u>so</u> <u>did</u> <u>Mike</u>.
>   V   S

> I didn't like the coffee, and <u>neither</u> <u>did</u> <u>Mike</u>.
>   V   S

4. In conditional sentences that do not begin with *if*:

> With *if*:   If <u>he</u> <u>had seen</u> you, he would have greeted you.
>   S   V

> Without *if*:   <u>Had</u> <u>he</u> seen you, he would have greeted you.
>   *first V* S

▼▼▼

The TOEFL tests your understanding of inverted subject-verb word order with special expressions and in conditional sentences by:
1. using standard word order where inverted subject-verb word order is needed;
2. inverting subjects and verbs incorrectly; or,
3. using other structures where inverted constructions are needed.

MODEL

Rarely _____ happy.
- (A) John is ever
- (B) is John ever
- (C) ever John is
- (D) John ever is

What is needed in this sentence?
Answer: An inverted subject and verb

▼ Explanation ▲

In this question, *rarely* is the first word of the sentence. Inverted subject-verb word order occurs after *rarely*. Answer (B) is the correct answer to this question. It is the only answer choice that contains inverted subject-verb word order.

MODEL

_____, he would have understood the movie better.
- (A) Carl had read the book
- (B) The book had been read by Carl
- (C) Had Carl read the book
- (D) Read the book had Carl

What is needed in this sentence?
Answer: A conditional that does not begin with *if*

▼ Explanation ▲

In this question, each answer choice contains parts of a conditional without *if*. In these types of conditionals, inverted subject-verb word order is needed. Answer (A) does not contain inverted word order. Answer (B) contains a passive construction. This is not the inverted structure that is needed. Answer (D) contains inverted word order, but using the wrong part of the verb. Answer (C) is the correct answer to the question because it contains correct inverted subject-verb word order.

☞ ON THE TOEFL TEST

- Check to see that inverted subject-verb word order is used where it is needed in TOEFL questions.
- Check to see that subject-verb inversion is done correctly.

See the Grammar Appendix, #34, page 461 if you need more information on conditional sentences.

EXERCISE 27A: Practice with Inverted Subject-Verb Word Order with Special Expressions

In the sentences, underline the special expressions which signal a need for inverted subject-verb word order. Then, on the line provided, put an *I* if the sentence is incorrect and a *C* if the sentence is correct. Correct each error. Use inverted subject-verb word order in your corrections.

<u>C</u> 1. <u>So</u> tired was he that he couldn't keep his eyes open.

____ 2. Scarcely I had opened the door when the cat ran out.

____ 3. Not only he suffered from a cut on his forehead, but he also had several bruises on his left arm.

____ 4. Only once Harold had met Maude before they fell in love.

____ 5. Kate left the concert early, and so John did.

____ 6. In the basement were three old baseball bats and a glove.

____ 7. Only in Dr. Krankshaw's class do we have a quiz every day.

____ 8. Nowhere I can find the hat I want to wear to the party.

____ 9. We couldn't find your house, and neither could Walter.

____ 10. In the garage the broken lawn mower was.

____ 11. Rarely have I eaten so much at one meal.

EXERCISE 27B: Practice with Inverted Subject-Verb Word Order in Conditionals

Rewrite each conditional containing *if* as a conditional that does not contain *if*. To do this, delete the *if* and invert the subject and the first verb of the subordinate clause.

1. If I had found the book, I would have given it to you.

   Had I found the book, I would have given it to you.

2. If Jane had been more careful, she wouldn't have hurt herself.

   _____

3. If Alexander were here, he would help me with this homework.

   _____

4. If the fire fighters had not gotten here in time, the house would have burned down.

   _____

5. If they should ever change their minds, tell them to call me.

   _____

6. My father would settle this problem for me, if he were here.

EXERCISE 27C: More Practice with Inverted Subject-Verb Word Order

Circle the correct answer.

1. At one end of the street _____.
   (A) is a vacant lot
   (B) a vacant lot
   (C) a vacant lot is
   (D) is where a vacant lot

2. Not until several days after the accident _____ to remember what had happened.
   (A) John began
   (B) and John began
   (C) John beginning
   (D) did John begin

3. Domestic cats enjoy playing and sitting in the sun, _____ cats in the wild.
   (A) and so do
   (B) do so and
   (C) so do and
   (D) do and so

4. _____ that you borrowed his car, he would be very angry.
   (A) Ever were Matt to find out
   (B) Were Matt ever to find out
   (C) Matt were ever to find out
   (D) Were ever to find out Matt

5. _____ classes, even when the weather is bad.
   (A) Rarely this professor has cancelled
   (B) Has this professor rarely cancelled
   (C) Has cancelled this professor rarely
   (D) Rarely has this professor cancelled

6. Over the river and through the woods _____ my grandmother lives.
   (A) the house is where
   (B) where is the house
   (C) is the house where
   (D) where the house is

G✔28 Check Parallel Structure in Comparisons and in Series Joined by AND, BUT, or OR

When words, phrases, or clauses have parallel (similar) functions in English sentences, they should have parallel structure as well. It is important to maintain parallel structure in English sentences.

Clarice is <u>beautiful</u>, <u>smart</u>, and <u>talented</u>.
           Adj   *Adj*   *Adj*

You should be especially careful about parallel structure when:
1. words, phrases, or clauses are used in a series joined by *and, but,* or *or*; and,
2. comparisons are being made.

1. Parallel structure in words, phrases, and clauses used in a series joined by *and, but,* or *or*:

Incorrect:	He likes	<u>to swim</u>,	<u>to hike</u>,	and <u>riding</u> his bike.
		Infinitive	*Infinitive*	*Gerund*

Correct:	He likes	<u>to swim</u>,	<u>to hike</u>,	and <u>to ride</u> his bike.
		Infinitive	*Infinitive*	*Infinitive*

Incorrect: She went home because <u>she needed money</u> and <u>due to her mother's illness</u>.
                             Subordinate clause   *Prepositional phrase*

Correct: She went home <u>because she needed money</u> and <u>because her mother was ill</u>.
                      Subordinate clause   *Subordinate clause*

Incorrect: <u>Her cheerful outward manner</u> and <u>she told interesting stories</u> made her
                     Noun phrase   *Main clause*
very popular with her friends.

Correct: <u>Her cheerful outward manner</u> and <u>her interesting stories</u> made her very
                  Noun phrase   *Noun phrase*
popular with her friends.

2. Parallel structure with equative (*as...as*) and comparative (——*er than/more...than*) constructions and with other expressions of comparison (e.g., *similar to, the same as*):

Incorrect: <u>How to pronounce English</u> is more difficult than <u>reading it</u>.
              Infinitive phrase   *Gerund phrase*

Correct: <u>Pronouncing English</u> is more difficult than <u>reading it</u>.
            Gerund phrase   *Gerund phrase*

In comparisons, you must be especially careful that the two compared things are parallel in both meaning and structure.

Incorrect: The <u>shelves</u> in Durick Library are taller than <u>Norwich</u> <u>Library</u>.

In this sentence, *shelves* and *Norwich Library* are being compared. These two nouns are not comparable (parallel in meaning) even though they are parallel in structure.

Correct: The <u>shelves</u> in Durick Library are taller than <u>those</u> in Norwich Library.

In this sentence, *shelves* are being compared to *shelves*, referred to by the pronoun *those*. These two structures are parallel in meaning and in structure.

▼▼▼

The TOEFL tests your understanding of parallel structure in series and in comparisons by:

1. using structures that are not parallel in words, phrases, and clauses in series and in comparisons; or,

2. using structures in comparisons that are not parallel in meaning as well as in structure.

MODEL
Lance's efforts led to a promotion, _____, and an award of $10,000.
(A)   his peers recognized him
(B)   recognition by his peers
(C)   he received recognition from his peers
(D)   to receive recognition from his peers
What is needed in this sentence?
Answer: A noun phrase parallel to *a promotion* and *an award*

▼ Explanation ▲

In this sentence, noun phrases are being joined in a series with *and*. Answers (A) and (C) contain more than a noun phrase. They contain complete sentences. Answer (D) contains an infinitive phrase. Answer (B) is the correct answer to this question. It contains a noun phrase that is parallel in structure to *a promotion* and *an award*.

MODEL
Sleeping <u>well</u> is as important <u>to</u> good <u>health</u> as <u>to eat</u> well.
A   B   C   D
What is wrong with this sentence?
Answer: A comparison is being made between two structures which are not parallel.

▼ Explanation ▲

In this question, the gerund *sleeping* is compared to the infinitive *to eat*. These two structures are not parallel. Answer (D) is the correct answer to this question because *to eat* is incorrect.
Correction: *eating*

☛ ON THE TOEFL TEST
• Check to see that parallel structures are used in TOEFL questions that contain series and comparisons.
• Check to see that the parallel structures used in comparisons are parallel in meaning as well as in form.

See the Grammar Appendix, #32 and #33, pages 458–459 if you need more information about gerunds and infinitives. See G✔24 if you need more information about equatives and comparatives.

EXERCISE 28A: Practice with Parallel Structure in Words, Phrases, and Clauses in a Series

On the line provided, put an *I* if the sentence is incorrect and a *C* if the sentence is correct. Then, correct each error.

garbage to be emptied/garbage to empty

__I__   1.   There are dishes to do, floors to mop, and ~~that garbage should be emptied~~.

____   2.   The waitress brought me a plate of beans, a spoon, and she gave me a napkin.

____   3.   On weekends, they enjoy hiking, sailing, and to ride horseback.

____   4.   After our trip, we were tired but happy.

____   5.   Jake suggested that we take his car or walking to the auditorium.

____   6.   I need to write a short but it should be effective response to his letter.

EXERCISE 28B: Practice with Parallel Structure in Comparisons

On the line provided, put an *I* if the sentence is incorrect and a *C* if the sentence is correct. Then, correct each error.

__C__   1.   I think I have more work to do tonight than you do.

____   2.   The carrots in this soup are tastier than that soup.

____   3.   This house is bigger than we had before.

____   4.   Reading a good book can be as much fun as when you watch a movie.

____   5.   Paper sandwich bags are as good as plastic ones.

____   6.   Tonight's menu will be the same as last night.

EXERCISE 28C: More Practice with Parallel Structure

Choose the letter of the underlined part of the sentence that is incorrect. Then, correct the error.

hunting

__A__   1.   Fishing and ~~to hunt~~ are prohibited in this area; those who violate this regulation will be
                                  A

arrested and <u>punished</u>.
                      B

____   2.   My legs are <u>longer than yours</u>, which makes running and <u>to jump</u> easier for me than
                          A   B

they are for you.

____   3.   He has worked in a restaurant, <u>a bar</u>, and a gas station, so he has more work experience
                                                A

<u>than yours</u>.
     B

_____ 4. Life in this country is quite similar <u>to my country</u>, but I am not adjusting <u>as easily as</u> I
                                                    A   B

thought I would to my new environment.

_____ 5. We will go skiing <u>and sledding</u> today or <u>it will be tomorrow</u>.
                                 A   B

_____ 6. The shoes in this store are more expensive <u>than that store</u>, but they are not more
                                                                        A

attractive <u>or more durable</u>.
                 B

EXERCISE 28D: More Practice with Parallel Structure

Circle the correct answer.

1. Although your recipe for bread _____, the bread made with my recipe is as good as
   yours.
   (A) takes longer than my bread
   (B) it takes longer than mine
   (C) takes longer than my recipe
   (D) my recipe takes longer

2. Getting something is not always as easy as _____.
   (A) wanting it
   (B) when you want it
   (C) to want it
   (D) you want it

3. The combined population of the states of Montana, Idaho, and Wyoming is less than

   _____.
   (A) that of the city of Los Angeles
   (B) people who live in the city of Los Angeles
   (C) the city of Los Angeles
   (D) the city of Los Angeles has a population

4. In addition to being a successful mother, actress, and _____, Thelma is the president
   of her own company.
   (A) she writes
   (B) to write
   (C) writing
   (D) writer

5. Automobile accidents are far more frequent than _____.
   (A) having an accident in an airplane
   (B) airplanes have accidents
   (C) airplane accidents
   (D) when there are airplane accidents

6. Too much stress can cause sleeplessness, depression, and _____.
   (A) lack of appetite
   (B) you don't want to eat
   (C) lack of appetite is caused
   (D) to lack appetite

G✔29   Check Paired Expressions

There are pairs of expressions in English which can be especially confusing. These paired expressions are:

    both … and
    either … or
    neither … nor
    not only … but also

Paired expressions can act as clause markers, or they can function to join words or phrases.

> As clause markers:
>
> <u>Either</u> <u>he will go to the movie</u> <u>or</u> <u>he will go to the play</u>.
> CM   Clause   CM   Clause
>
> Joining phrases:
>
> He will go <u>either</u> <u>to the movie</u> <u>or</u> <u>to the play</u>.
>   CM   Prep phrase CM Prep phrase
>
> Joining words:
>
> He will go <u>either</u> <u>today</u> <u>or</u> <u>tomorrow</u>.
>   CM   Word CM   Word

Paired expressions need to be checked for a variety of things. Parallelism, as discussed above in G✔28, is important for paired expressions. The same grammatical form should follow each word of a paired expression.

> Incorrect: Laura <u>both</u> <u>enjoys</u> books <u>and</u> <u>music</u>.
>   Verb   Noun
>
> Correct: Laura enjoys <u>both</u> <u>books</u> <u>and</u> <u>music</u>.
>   Noun   Noun

It is also important to check subject-verb agreement, as discussed above in G✔11, with paired expressions.

When subjects are joined by *both … and*, they take a plural verb.

> Both Angela and her mother <u>are coming</u> to visit us.

When subjects are joined by *either … or*, *neither … nor*, or *not only … but also*, the verb agrees with the closer subject.

> Either the teacher or the students <u>are coming</u> to visit us.

> Either the students or the teacher <u>is coming</u> to visit us.

With paired expressions that contain negative words, inverted subject–verb word order, as discussed in G✔27, is also important.

Inverted subject–verb word order is needed only after the negative or almost negative parts of paired expressions.

> <u>Not only</u> <u>did</u> <u>he</u> buy her a diamond ring, <u>but</u> <u>he</u> <u>also</u> <u>bought</u> her a gold watch.
> Neg   V S   S   V
>
> <u>Neither</u> <u>did</u> <u>he</u> write <u>nor</u> <u>did</u> <u>he</u> call.
> Neg   V S   Neg V   S

Finally, it is important to check that paired expressions are formed correctly. The two parts of paired expressions must not be changed.

Incorrect: <u>Neither</u> her mother <u>or</u> her father was there.

Correct: <u>Neither</u> her mother <u>nor</u> her father was there.

▼▼▼

The TOEFL tests your understanding of paired expressions by:
1. using incorrect parallel structure, word order, or subject-verb agreement with parallel expressions; or,
2. combining parts of paired expressions incorrectly.

MODEL

We must _____ but also our clothes.
   (A)   not only pack our books
   (B)   pack not only our books
   (C)   our books not only pack
   (D)   not our only books pack

What is needed in this sentence?
Answer: The first half of a paired expression + a noun phrase

---

▼ Explanation ▲

In this question, the second half of a paired expression, *but also*, is present. *But also* is followed by the noun phrase *our clothes*. To keep parallel structure in this sentence, *not only* followed by a noun phrase is needed. Answers (A) and (C) contain *not only* followed by a verb. Answer (D) separates *not* from *only*, which creates an incorrect form. Answer (B) is the correct answer to the question because it contains *not only* followed by a noun phrase.

MODEL

Both Leo <u>also</u> Margaret <u>were waiting</u> <u>for</u> the bus <u>when</u> the storm began.
            A   B   C   D

What is wrong with this sentence?
Answer: A paired expression has been incorrectly formed.

▼ Explanation ▲

In this question, the first part of a paired expression, *both*, is used. However, the second part of this expression is missing and has been replaced by *also*. Answer (A) is the correct answer to the question because *also* is incorrect.
Correction: *and*

- Check to see that paired expressions are formed correctly in TOEFL questions.
- Check to see that word order, subject-verb agreement, and parallel structure are correct for paired expressions.

EXERCISE 29A: Practice with Paired Expressions

Choose the letter of the underlined part of the sentence that is incorrect. Use the choices provided to answer the question: *What is wrong with this sentence?* Choices:

      Subject-verb agreement
      Word order
      Parallel structure
      The form of a paired expression
    Then, correct each error.

                  will she
<u>A</u> 1. Not only <u>she will</u> wash the windows for you, but she will <u>also</u> vacuum the floors.
               A   B

What is wrong with this sentence? _____*Word order*_____

_____ 2. The city of Los Angeles suffers from <u>both</u> air pollution and <u>there is water</u> pollution.
                                            A   B

What is wrong with this sentence? _____

_____ 3. Neither <u>did he do</u> his chores <u>or</u> did he finish his homework.
              A   B

What is wrong with this sentence? _____

_____ 4. Either the cats <u>or</u> the dog <u>are making</u> a lot of noise downstairs.
                    A   B

What is wrong with this sentence? _____

_____ 5. Larry will <u>not only help</u> with the construction <u>but also</u> with the painting of the new
                    A   B

      barn.

What is wrong with this sentence? _____

_____ 6. Neither Jack nor Jane <u>are</u> interested in seeing either the play <u>or</u> the concert.
                             A   B

What is wrong with this sentence? _____

EXERCISE 29B: More Practice with Paired Expressions

Circle the correct answer.

1. Marcia has not only driven hundreds of miles to get here _____ as well.
   (A) and she has spent hundreds of dollars.
   (B) but also hundreds of dollars spent
   (C) but also spent hundreds of dollars
   (D) she has but also spent hundreds of dollars

2. Animals are classified as either cold-blooded _____.
   (A) or they have warm blood
   (B) or warm-blooded
   (C) nor warm-blooded
   (D) or being warm-blooded

3. Most authors feel that writing is _____ and enjoyable.
   (A) both essential
   (B) either essential
   (C) essentially both
   (D) essential both

4. Neither hard work _____ unrewarded in this company.
   (A) nor loyalty go
   (B) or loyalty goes
   (C) goes loyalty or
   (D) nor loyalty goes

5. _____ for her devotion to her family but also for her dedication to her job.
   (A) Not only Catherine is respected
   (B) Catherine is respected not only
   (C) Catherine, who is respected not only
   (D) Catherine, respected not only

6. We want to go either to the Bahamas _____ during our spring vacation from school this year.
   (A) or visiting New England
   (B) or to New England
   (C) we want or to visit New England
   (D) or New England to visit

G✔30   Check Confusing Words and Expressions

There are words and expressions in English which are especially confusing because they sound very much alike and/or because they have very similar functions in English sentences.

Incorrect: He was <u>formally</u> a teacher, but now he is a car dealer.

Correct: He was <u>formerly</u> a teacher, but now he is a car dealer.

Formally and *formerly* in this pair of sentences sound very much alike and have similar functions. However, their meanings are quite different. *Formally* means *officially* and does not have the meaning necessary for this sentence. *Formerly*, which means *before*, has the correct meaning for this sentence.

Incorrect: Melissa often <u>does</u> a cake for dessert.

Correct: Melissa often <u>makes</u> a cake for dessert.

Does and *make* in this pair of sentences do not sound alike. However, they both function as verbs, and they have some similarities in meaning. The verb DO, however, often expresses the idea of *performing* or *completing*. *Make* often expresses the idea of *creating* or *constructing*. The difference in meaning between *make* and *do* is great enough that they are not interchangeable. Since Melissa had *created* rather than *performed* the cake, *make* is the correct verb for this sentence.

The TOEFL tests your understanding of confusing words and expressions by:
1. incorrectly using words that sound alike; or,
2. incorrectly using words that have very similar meanings and functions in a sentence.

A comprehensive list of all of the confusing words and expressions in English is not possible. In the Grammar Appendix, #35, pages 461–468, however, you will find a list of the confusing words and expressions that are most commonly tested on the TOEFL. Refer to this list if you have difficulty completing the exercises below.

MODEL

The tests in <u>this class</u> are <u>less difficult than</u> tests <u>in</u> <u>another</u> classes.
 A   B   C D

What is wrong with this sentence?
Answer: A word that sounds like the correct word has been substituted for the correct word.

▼ Explanation ▲

In this question, *another* has been used to describe *classes*. However, *another* is used only with singular, countable, indefinite nouns. Answer (D) is the correct answer to this question because *another* is incorrect.
Correction: *other*

☞ ON THE TOEFL TEST

- Check to see that words that sound alike are not substituted for one another in TOEFL questions.
- Check to see that words with similar meanings and functions are not substituted for one another.

EXERCISE 30A: Practice with Confusing Words and Expressions

Circle the correct word or expression in each pair.

1. This decision will be made on the (basis/base) of test scores.

2. (Farther/Further) evidence is needed before we can make any judgments about this person.

3. The long-term (effects/affects) of this drug are unknown.

4. Clyde was (such/so) happy about his new job that he danced around the room.

5. Success (like/as) a teacher depends on your ability to understand students' needs.

6. (No/not) problem is too great to solve if we work diligently together.

7. Nancy enjoys playing tennis (and/also) riding her bike.

8. Western sculpture, (like/alike) Western painting, often immortalizes the cowboy.

9. On the one hand, Edward values the input of his staff; (on the other/on the contrary), he prefers not to have them involved in the final decision-making process.

10. Please (do/make) the dishes tonight after dinner so they don't pile up in the sink.

11. Carol likes these pants, but she doesn't like the (other/others).

12. Loretta was (very/too) industrious, and she finished all of her assignments last night.

13. Peter was (lying/laying) on the couch when I entered the room.

14. We must (accept/except) that there are certain things in life that we cannot do.

15. Please do not do anything (special/especially) elaborate for my birthday.

16. If you tell me (whose/who's) names should be on this list, I will type them for you.

17. The (costume/custom) of hiding eggs on Easter is practiced in many American homes.

18. Paul said that (almost/most) of the pie was eaten by the children.

19. Scientists feel that (they're/there) are several reasons to explore space.

20. The preparations for graduation have (already/all ready) been made.

21. The (first/former) book I read was easier than the other two.

EXERCISE 30B: More Practice with Confusing Words and Expressions

Choose the letter of the incorrect word or phrase in each sentence. Then, correct the error.

_A_ 1. The men <u>lied</u> *lay* quietly for several days in their tents, gathering energy before making the
        A

     <u>descent</u> from the top of the mountain.
     B

_____ 2. We should find a time when <u>it's</u> convenient to <u>set</u> down together and discuss this issue.
                                A   B

_____ 3. <u>Between</u> the three of them, they must come up with some sound <u>advice</u> for the
       A   B
     committee.

_____ 4. We <u>had better</u> account for the <u>number</u> of money that is missing from the vault.
          A   B

_____ 5. This <u>maybe</u> the <u>last</u> time I see you.
          A   B

____ 6. The ball rolled <u>passed</u> me and <u>through</u> the kitchen.
                      A   B

____ 7. <u>Beside</u> the three papers I have to write for history, I have one for philosophy, <u>too</u>.
          A   B

____ 8. <u>Your</u> professor has told me that you worked <u>hardly</u> on this assignment.
          A   B

____ 9. They <u>raised</u> the flag in a <u>quite</u> ceremony.
                A   B

____ 10. Please <u>remind</u> that Thomas is very <u>sensitive</u> to outside criticism.
               A   B

____ 11. The <u>imaginary</u> paper that John wrote for English class <u>nearly</u> won him a very
            A   B
prestigious prize.

Grammar Checkpoint Test Six for G✔25 through G✔30

Allow yourself 5 minutes to complete this checkpoint test. There are 11 questions on the test. Check your answers in the answer key. Next to each answer is the number of the checkpoint that is being tested in each of these questions. Use these numbers to determine which checkpoints, if any, you need to study again.

<u>Questions 1 through 7</u>

Circle the letter of the one word or phrase that best completes the sentence.

1. John Updike has published not only many novels and stories _____ four books of poems, a play, and numerous book reviews and other prose writings.
   (A) but he has also written
   (B) also
   (C) but also
   (D) in addition to writing

2. Fat _____ for the energy from food eaten in excess of need.
   (A) is the body's chief storage form
   (B) the body's chief storage form it is
   (C) is it the body's chief storage form
   (D) the body's is chief storage form

3. Not until several years after a war has ended _____ to feel the severe psychological damage it can cause.
   (A) do many of its veterans begin
   (B) many of its veterans begin
   (C) and many of its veterans begin
   (D) many of its veterans beginning

4. Over the past several decades, radio telescopes _____ of the universe from the one disclosed by ordinary telescopes.
   (A) have quite a different view given scientists
   (B) quite a different view have given scientists
   C) have they given scientists quite a different view
   (D) have given scientists quite a different view

5. Astronomers rely on measurements of mass and brightness to determine

   _____.
   (A) how old is a star
   (B) is a star how old
   (C) a star is how old
   (D) how old a star is

6. At one end of an amino acid _____.
   (A) an amine group is
   (B) is an amine group
   (C) an amine group is there
   (D) is where an amine group

7. Fats _____ and help insulate and protect the body.
   (A) an efficient storage material is formed
   (B) their efficient storage material is formed
   (C) form an efficient storage material
   (D) efficient storage material is formed

<u>Questions 8 through 11</u>

Circle the letter of the underlined part of the sentence that is incorrect.

8. The long-term <u>affects</u> of the American Civil War, <u>which</u> split families and friends apart, <u>are</u> still
               A   B   C
   being felt in the <u>twentieth century</u>.
                       D

9. Topology is <u>a branch of</u> mathematics <u>that</u> deals with the ways in which surfaces can be
                    A   B
   twisted, <u>bend</u>, pulled, or otherwise transformed <u>from</u> one shape to another.
             C   D

10. Scientists still know <u>little</u> either about <u>variations</u> in the moon's gravitational field <u>also</u> about <u>its</u>
                              A   B   C   D
    surface composition.

11. The ladybug beetle is <u>such</u> helpful in controlling other, more harmful insects, <u>that</u> it is <u>often</u>
                             A   B   C
    sold to gardeners <u>as</u> a natural method for pest control.
                           D

Structure and Written Expression Section Test

On the following pages you will find a practice section test for Section Two of the TOEFL.

Allow yourself only 25 minutes to complete this test.

Use the second part of the SECTION TESTS ANSWER SHEET from the General Appendix, #4, page 509 to record your answers.

When answering each question, use the strategies and skills you have just reviewed in the preceding chapter.

Score your test using *The Heinemann TOEFL Course Tapescripts and Answers*. Next to each answer in this key is the number of the checkpoint that is being tested in each of the Structure and Written Expression Section Test questions. Use these numbers to determine which checkpoints, if any, you need to study again.

Estimate your TOEFL score for this section test using Score Conversion Table 1 in the General Appendix, #3, page 505.

SECTION 2
STRUCTURE AND WRITTEN EXPRESSION

Time–25 minutes

This section is designed to measure your ability to recognize language that is appropriate for standard written English. There are two types of questions in this section, with special directions for each type.

<u>Directions:</u> Questions 1–15 are incomplete sentences. Beneath each sentence you will see four words or phrases, marked (A), (B), (C), and (D). Choose the <u>one</u> word or phrase that best completes the sentence. Then, on your answer sheet, find the number of the question and fill in the space that corresponds to the letter of the answer you have chosen. Fill in the space so that the letter inside the oval cannot be seen.

Example I   <u>Sample Answer</u>

    Most American families _____ at least one automobile.   ● Ⓑ Ⓒ Ⓓ
    (A) have
    (B) in
    (C) that
    (D) has

The sentence should read, "Most American families have at least one automobile." Therefore, you should choose answer (A).

Example II   <u>Sample Answer</u>

    _____ recent times, the discipline of biology has expanded rapidly   Ⓐ Ⓑ Ⓒ ●
    into a variety of subdisciplines.
    (A) It is since
    (B) When
    (C) Since it is
    (D) In

The sentence should read, "In recent times, the discipline of biology has expanded into a variety of subdisciplines." Therefore, you should choose answer (D).

After you read the directions, begin work on the questions.

1. _____ for drugs to act as antagonists to vitamins.
    (A) There is common
    (B) Because it is common
    (C) Common it is
    (D) It is common

2. The fairy slipper orchid _____ in relatively inaccessible mountain forest regions of North America.
    (A) can only finding
    (B) only to be found
    (C) found only
    (D) can only be found

GO ON TO THE NEXT PAGE ▶

3. _____ in nomadic societies is broadly defined.
   (A) The concept of family
   (B) As the concept of family
   (C) The concept of family that
   (D) Because the concept of family

4. _____ people to act recklessly, the color red is the background color of choice in gambling casinos.
   (A) It is thought to cause
   (B) Thinking about causing
   (C) Thought to cause
   (D) To think about causing

5. On a promontory overlooking the Pacific Ocean _____ of the University of California.
   (A) the Santa Barbara campus lies
   (B) lies there the Santa Barbara campus
   (C) lies the Santa Barbara campus
   (D) lies where the Santa.Barbara campus

6. Burce Barton, _____ was one of the most successful advertising men of the 1920s.
   (A) was the son of a minister
   (B) the son of a minister
   (C) whom the son of a minister
   (D) of the son of a minister

7. Few U.S. presidents have enjoyed_____ did John F. Kennedy.
   (A) as much as popularity
   (B) as much popularity as
   (C) as much popularity
   (D) the most popularity

8. It is difficult to determine exactly _____
   (A) what the center of the earth consists of
   (B) what does the center of the earth consist of
   (C) the center of the earth consists of what
   (D) what of the center of the earth consists

9. Though convinced that the economy was basically sound, _____.
   (A) President Hoover took steps to prevent the spread of depression
   (B) preventing the spread of depression took steps by President Hoover
   (C) the spread of depression was prevented by steps taken by President Hoover
   (D) steps were taken by President Hoover to prevent the spread of depression

10. Benjamin Franklin was indeed a practical man; _____ who gave a large part of his life to the service of the American colonies.
    (A) nevertheless, he was also an idealist
    (B) that he was also an idealist
    (C) also an idealist
    (D) also as an idealist

11. Cell biologists _____ in studying cells today.
    (A) sophisticated, a variety of useful chemical techniques
    (B) a variety of sophisticated chemical techniques use
    (C) use a variety of sophisticated chemical techniques
    (D) use of a variety of sophisticated chemical techniques

12. The overall strength of a country's economy is _____ determines the value of its currency.
    (A) that
    (B) whose
    (C) what
    (D) it

13. _____ recover from the setbacks they have experienced in recent years, the economy of the entire country would be positively affected.
    (A) American car manufacturers should ever
    (B) Ever should American car manufacturers
    (C) Should American car.manufacturers ever
    (D) American car manufacturers ever should

GO ON TO THE NEXT PAGE

14. ----------- witnesses is forbidden in the Federal Courts of the United States.
(A) Aggressively cross-examine
(B) Cross-examination aggressive
(C) Aggressive cross-examining
(D) The aggressive cross-examination of

15. The flora of the arid American Southwest is less varied than _____.
(A) the semi-tropical Southeast
(B) that of the semi-tropical Southeast
(C) the Southeast is semi-tropical
(D) it is semi-tropical in the Southeast

Directions: In questions 16-40, each sentence has four underlined words or phrases. The four underlined parts of the sentence are marked (A), (B), (C), and (D). Identify the one underlined word or phrase that must be changed in order for the sentence to be correct. Then, on your answer sheet, find the number of the question and fill in the space that corresponds to the letter of the answer you have chosen.

Example I   Sample Answer

The octopus is a unique animal because they has three functioning hearts.   Ⓐ Ⓑ ● Ⓓ
           A   B   C   D

The sentence should read, "The octopus is a unique animal because it has three functioning hearts." Therefore, you should choose answer (C).

Example II   Sample Answer

The beagle, one of the most ancient breeds of dog known, originating in England.   Ⓐ Ⓑ Ⓒ ●
            A   B   C   D

The sentence should read, "The beagle, one of the most ancient breeds of dog known, originated in England." Therefore, you should choose answer (D).

After you read the directions, begin work on the questions.

16. Once have built their nests, birds lay eggs and hatch their young.
    A   B   C   D

17. Moisturize in the air forms an effective insulating blanket over most of the earth.
    A   B   C   D

18. Competitive firms are always under pressure to reduce costs, improve quality, and catering to
    A   B   C   D
consumer preferences.

19. A sector of a circle is a pie-shaped regions bounded by a central angle, the arc it cuts off, and two
             A   B   C   D
radii.

20. Scientists often place the initial domestication of horses at around 4,000 years ago, basing them
              A   B   C
estimates on historical depictions showing horses used by military cavalry.
                                                        D

GO ON TO THE NEXT PAGE ▶

21. The <u>discovery</u> of a new primate species, the black-faced lion tamarin, will be <u>formerly</u> announced
         A   B

    <u>as soon as</u> scientists have <u>further</u> evidence of its existence.
       C   D

22. The Beartooth Highway crisscrosses the border <u>between</u> Montana and Wyoming,
                                                A

    <u>eventually climbing</u> to an elevation of <u>eleven thousand foot</u> at <u>scenic</u> Beartooth Pass.
          B   C   D

23. Water pollutants <u>are classified</u> either as <u>enriching</u> substances that cause eutrophication <u>nor</u> as
                   A   B   C

    poisonous materials <u>that</u> harm aquatic life.
                 D

24. In today's world, Americans <u>had depended on</u> the automobile <u>as</u> <u>their</u> <u>primary means</u> of
                                A   B C   D

    transportation.

25. Aspirin seems <u>helpfully</u> in reducing the risk of stroke in people <u>whose</u> upper heart chambers <u>beat</u>
              A   B   C

    <u>irregularly</u>.
       D

26. The sugar maple is a <u>popular</u> tree <u>in</u> New England <u>because</u> the sap which <u>they produce</u> can be
                       A   B   C   D

    converted into syrup.

27. <u>Fast</u>, obedient, and intelligent, <u>the</u> quarterhorse <u>is rode</u> in <u>many</u> rodeos.
     A   B   C   D

28. The computer, one of <u>man's</u> <u>most</u> recent creations, <u>have</u> revolutionized <u>the</u> world of information
                         A   B   C   D

    processing.

29. President Woodrow Wilson's <u>collapse</u> on October 2, 1919, was a <u>tragical</u> event <u>not only</u> for the
                               A   B   C

    president and his family <u>but also</u> for the nation.
                       D

30. Although <u>both</u> television and radio <u>lacks</u> the permanent quality that the printed word has, they
              A   B

    remain the <u>preferred</u> sources of entertainment and information <u>for</u> the majority of Americans.
                 C   D

31. Scholars of historical change <u>feels</u> <u>that</u> the velocity of history <u>has been</u> greatly accelerated by the
                               A B   C

    onward rush of science and technology <u>during</u> the twentieth century.
                                      D

GO ON TO THE NEXT PAGE

32. <u>No</u> nationwide survey has yet tried <u>assess</u> the extent of zinc deficiency in the United States or
    A   B
    Canada, <u>but</u> indications are <u>that</u> it does occur.
            C   D

33. <u>An</u> invention's chance <u>of being accepted</u> <u>depends of</u> its superiority to the method or object
    A   B   C
    <u>it is replacing</u>.
    D

34. Edgar Allan Poe, <u>creation</u> of the detective story at <u>the age</u> of thirty-two, <u>claimed to prefer</u> writing
                      A   B   C
    poetry <u>to writing</u> prose.
           D

35. In 1976, NASA <u>setted</u> up its Search for Extra-Terrestrial Intelligence program, which was designed
                  A
    <u>to seek out</u> evidence of <u>intelligent</u> life on <u>other</u> planets.
    B   C   D

36. Garlic, <u>who</u> is a member of the lily family, <u>is valued</u> both for its medicinal properties <u>and</u> <u>for</u> its
            A   B   C   D
    pungent flavor.

37. For the most part, <u>cook</u> vegetables <u>contain</u> fewer usable nutrients <u>than</u> <u>do</u> raw vegetables.
                       A   B   C   D

38. The powerful, <u>destroy</u> force of hurricanes, <u>common</u> in the Caribbean and southeastern United
                  A   B
    States, <u>sometimes</u> <u>reaches</u> as far north as New England.
            C   D

39. While solvent-based wall paints <u>offer</u> good coverage and sealing power, <u>they</u> are <u>most</u> difficult to
                                    A   B   C
    <u>clean up</u> than are water-based paints.
    D

40. Electronic games, <u>much of which</u> can be powerful <u>instructional</u> tools, are becoming
                      A   B
    <u>more and more prevalent</u> with the <u>proliferation</u> of computers in schools.
    C   D

THIS IS THE END OF SECTION 2

**IF YOU FINISH BEFORE TIME IS CALLED, CHECK YOUR WORK ON SECTION 2 ONLY.
DO NOT READ OR WORK ON ANY OTHER SECTION OF THE TEST.
THE SUPERVISOR WILL TELL YOU WHEN TO BEGIN WORK ON SECTION 3.
FOR MORE PRACTICE, TAKE A COMPLETE TEST FROM *THE HEINEMANN TOEFL PRACTICE TESTS*.**

STOP   STOP   STOP   **STOP**   STOP   STOP   STOP

VOCABULARY AND READING COMPREHENSION

The purpose of Section Three of the TOEFL is to test your knowledge of the meanings and uses of words in written English and your ability to understand a variety of reading materials. The vocabulary and reading topics in Section Three are taken from general and formal English. For the most part, informal and conversational language is not tested in this section. The questions based on the reading passages will not require you to have outside knowledge of the topics.

GENERAL STRATEGIES FOR SECTION THREE

1. Be familiar with Section Three instructions before you take the actual TOEFL test. Then, during the test, do not read the instructions. Move immediately to the first question and begin working.

2. Use your time wisely. You should spend 10 to 12 minutes on the complete vocabulary section. Plan to spend more time on the reading passages, where thinking about the questions will help you choose the correct answers.

3. Remember to change your overall approach. In Section Three Vocabulary you must select the correct word from the choices. This is different from the Written Expression questions, where you are asked to identify the mistake. Work quickly through this section. In most cases, you either know the answer or you don't.

Vocabulary and Reading Comprehension: Question Types

Section Three contains 60 questions which must be completed in 45 minutes. There are two parts to this section of the TOEFL.

Vocabulary (30 questions)
You read a sentence that has an underlined word or phrase. Then, you choose the word or phrase that is closest in meaning to the part underlined.

Reading (5 or 6 passages with a total of 30 questions)
You read a written passage, followed by several questions, and choose the correct written answers to those questions.

Before preparing for Section Three Vocabulary and Reading Comprehension questions, read the following notes about vocabulary on the TOEFL test.

Vocabulary Throughout the TOEFL

Vocabulary is an important part of all sections of the TOEFL. It is tested in different ways in each section of the test. Knowing how vocabulary is tested will help you to be better prepared throughout the TOEFL.

Vocabulary in the Listening Comprehension Section of the TOEFL

Words tested in this section are often informal and idiomatic. In this section of the test, the context of the word will give you clues to its meaning. Knowing the meaning will help you to answer the questions asked about the listening items.

Read the following tapescripts for examples of vocabulary on Section One of the TOEFL.

Restatements

After you hear a sentence, read the four choices and decide which *one* is closest in meaning to the sentence you heard.

MODEL

You will hear:
   That movie was a waste of time.

You will read:
   (A)   I really enjoyed that movie.
   (B)   Let's wait until it's time for the movie.
   (C)   The movie was very long.
   (D)   I don't think that going to that movie was worthwhile.

Answer:

▼ Explanation ▲

If you know that *a waste of time* means *the movie had little value*, then you can discount (A) and (B). You might choose (C) because of the words *long* and *time* if you don't know the meaning of *waste*. In order to answer the question correctly, you need to know that *worthwhile* and *waste of time* are opposite in meaning. Answer (D) is the correct answer to the question because *I don't think that movie was worthwhile* is closest in meaning to *That movie was a waste of time.*

Mini-Dialogues

After you hear a conversation and the question about it, read the four possible answers and decide which *one* is the best answer to the question you heard.

MODEL

You will hear:

    W: Say Sam, can you fill in for me this afternoon at the store? I need to keep an appointment.

    M: Sure, Sandy, if it's OK with the manager. When is your shift?

    Q: What does Sam agree to do?

You will read:

    (A) Set up an appointment for Sandy.

    (B) Meet Sandy at the store.

    (C) Substitute for Sandy at work.

    (D) Talk to the manager.

Answer:

▼ Explanation ▲

Situational vocabulary is important in this part of the TOEFL. The vocabulary clues in the conversation are *fill in* and *at the store*, which are similar in meaning to *substitute* and *at work* in answer (C). Other clues are the words *manager* and *When is your shift?* which are related to *at work*. Answer (C) is the correct answer to the question.

Talks and Longer Conversations

After you hear a talk and the questions about it, read the answer choices and decide which one is the best answer to each question you heard.

MODEL

You will hear:

Thank you for coming to this meeting for students who will be remaining on campus during the spring break. As the Resident Housing Supervisor, it is my responsibility to explain the vacation arrangements and have you fill out forms giving the dates that you will be on campus. Keening Hall will be the only dormitory open during the break period, and you all will be assigned a temporary room there. Please indicate on the housing portion of the form if you wish to share a room. Mark the dining portion if you want to participate in the temporary meal plan. All meals will be served in the snack bar, as the dining hall will be closed. Please pick up your new keys and move your belongings by the eighteenth, as you will not be able to enter regular dorms until they reopen after the break.

You will hear:

    1. Who is the speaker?

You will read:

    (A) The person in charge of on-campus housing.

    (B) The head of the student association.

    (C) The dean of students.

    (D) The director of Keening Hall.

Continued

You will hear:
 2. Which group of students is the speaker addressing?

You will read:
 (A) Those who need to finish their studies early.
 (B) Those who want to work in a special program.
 (C) Those who will stay on campus during a vacation period.
 (D) New students who will be moving on campus soon.

You will hear:
 3. What was said about food during this time?

You will read:
 (A) There is no provision for meals on campus.
 (B) Students can get a temporary meal plan for a smaller dining area.
 (C) Meals will be served as usual in the dining hall.
 (D) Students can prepare snacks in their rooms.

Answers:

▼ Explanation ▲

The correct answer to Question 1 is (A) *The person in charge of on-campus housing*. Clues to this are the terms *Resident*, which means *on-campus*, and *Supervisor*, which means *the person in charge*.

 The correct answer to Question 2 is (C) *Those who will stay on-campus during a vacation period*. Vocabulary clues are *spring break*, which means *a vacation period*, and *remaining on campus*, which is similar in meaning to *stay on campus*.

 The correct answer to Question 3 is (B) *Students can get a temporary meal plan for a smaller dining area*. Vocabulary clues for this question are *temporary meal plan*, which is repeated in answer (B), and the term *snack bar*, meaning a *smaller dining area*.

 Knowledge of vocabulary related to college life and academic studies is important for the Listening Comprehension Section of the TOEFL.

 Check the Listening Comprehension Checkpoints for further study of vocabulary tested in Section One of the TOEFL.

Vocabulary in the Structure and Written Expression Section of the TOEFL

Although vocabulary is not directly tested in the Structure and Written Expression Section, knowledge of vocabulary and word forms makes it easier to answer the questions in Section Two of the TOEFL. Knowing which words usually occur together will also help you in this section. In addition, the vocabulary used in the grammar items is similar to the formal vocabulary found in the Vocabulary and Reading Section of the TOEFL; knowing this vocabulary will help you prepare for Section Three of the TOEFL.

Read the following grammar items for examples of vocabulary in Section Two of the TOEFL.

MODEL

Choose the *one* word or phrase that best completes the sentence.

Red meat is an excellent source _____ protein.
(A)   of
(B)   by
(C)   about
(D)   on

Answer:

▼ Explanation ▲

Knowing that the noun *source* is often used with prepositional phrases introduced by *of* makes answering this item easier. Answer (A) is the correct answer to the question because the preposition *of* should introduce the noun *protein*.

MODEL

Identify the one underlined word or phrase that must be changed in order for the sentence to be correct.

Paul Revere <u>designed</u> the first <u>officially</u> seal of the thirteen <u>colonies</u>
               A   B   C
<u>as well as</u> the state seal now used by Massachusetts.
    D

Answer:

▼ Explanation ▲

Knowledge of word forms will assure that you understand that the adjective form *official* is needed, not the adverb form *officially*. Answer (B) is the correct answer to the question because *officially* is the incorrect word form.

Vocabulary in the Reading Comprehension Section of the TOEFL

In the reading passages, questions often ask what a word could be replaced by or what a word means. In Section Three, the context of the word in the sentence and in the whole passage will provide clues to its meaning.

Read the following passage for an example of vocabulary in context.

MODEL

Read the following passage and choose the *one* best answer to the question.

The situation for the Wadden Sea seal population is becoming increasingly worse. Already endangered by years of market hunting for skins and mounting pollution, the population of seals in the sanctuary is
line threatened again by a mysterious plague which has swept down on the
(5) animals. One seal after another got sick, grew weak, and died. The culprit was a virus, its origin unknown, that ultimately killed thousands of harbor seals along the entire North Sea coastline.

In line 5, the word "plague" probably means
  (A) storm
  (B) epidemic
  (C) expedition
  (D) pollution

Answer:

▼ Explanation ▲

The passage tells us that the seal population is in danger, and the answer choices *storm* and *pollution* are related to this negative concept. However, the sentences following the word *plague* give further information about its meaning. The phrases *got sick, grew weak, and died*, and *virus...that ultimately killed* indicate that *epidemic* is the best choice. The answer *expedition* can be discounted because it has no relation to either the negative concept or the clarifying information. Answer (B) is the correct answer to the question because *epidemic* is closest to the contextual meaning of *plague*.

Check the Vocabulary and Reading Comprehension Checkpoints for further study of vocabulary tested in this section of the TOEFL.

Vocabulary

The vocabulary tested in the Vocabulary and Reading Comprehension Section of the TOEFL is general and formal. The words are often taken from academic topics. You will NOT be tested on idioms, technical words, proper names, or words that refer to a specific referent, such as *chair* or *elephant*.

All choices in the vocabulary questions are grammatically correct, so grammatical clues will not help you to choose the best word. The sentences in this section will not provide you with contextual clues to meaning. You need to know the vocabulary item being tested and make automatic responses to the choices.

In the Vocabulary Section of the TOEFL there are 30 sentences with an underlined word or phrase. You have between 20 and 30 seconds to read each sentence and the four answer choices, and choose the word or phase that is closest in meaning to the underlined part.

You should complete the vocabulary questions in 10 to 12 minutes to allow more time for the reading comprehension questions, where context will help you to decide on the correct answer.

Read the following question for an example of items in the vocabulary part of Section Three of the TOEFL.

MODEL

Circle the letter of the word that is closest in meaning to the underlined word or phrase.

Though whistling swans live mainly in the tundra regions of the north, they winter in large <u>flocks</u> on the Chesapeake Bay.
- (A) islands
- (B) ice floes
- (C) numbers
- (D) preserves

Answer:

▼ Explanation ▲

In order to answer this question correctly, you need to know that *flocks* is a term used to refer to large *numbers* of birds. Grammatical clues don't help since all choices are nouns, which is the grammatical form needed. Contextual clues are not helpful in this type of question either. The relation of *islands* to *the Chesapeake Bay* is possible, as is the relation of *ice floes* to both the *Bay* and *northern tundra regions*. *Preserves* could also be possible, since many birds are protected in certain areas of the country. Answer (C) is the correct answer to the question because *numbers* is closest in meaning to *flocks*.

In this section of the TOEFL an extensive knowledge of English vocabulary is important. You need to know what the underlined words and phrases and choices mean and make a quick match.

To prepare for the Vocabulary Section of the TOEFL you need to acquire a wide vocabulary. One of the best and most enjoyable ways to increase your vocabulary is to listen to and read English as much and as often as possible. Study of the Vocabulary Checkpoints in *The Heinemann TOEFL Preparation Course* will give you help in general vocabulary preparation for the TOEFL. In addition, it will be helpful to practice answering vocabulary questions in a TOEFL format in a timed situation.

VOCABULARY QUESTION STRATEGIES

1. Read the underlined word and scan the choices. Match the word with the choice which is closest in meaning. Quickly read the sentence to be sure that the word or phrase fits the meaning of the sentence.

2. Complete your word and choice matches first.

3. If you cannot make a match, go back and re-read the sentence. Try to determine the general meaning of the sentence. If you do not know the underlined word or phrase, you can sometimes predict which of the choices is correct from the general meaning of the sentence by using logical reasoning.

4. Do not spend time trying to find grammatical or contextual clues in the sentence. Remember that in this section of the TOEFL grammatical and contextual clues will not help you much.

5. Use your time wisely. You should only spend 20 seconds on each vocabulary question.

6. Guess if you don't know the answer to a question. **Unanswered questions on the TOEFL are marked wrong.** Choose the word that you feel might be correct, but beware of TOEFL tricks—words that have the same form or the same root but have a different meaning from the word underlined.

✔ VOCABULARY CHECKPOINTS

Following is a list of Vocabulary Checkpoints covered in the Vocabulary Checkpoint Study. If the Diagnostic Test on pages 20–41 indicated that Vocabulary was your weak area, you should carefully complete these checkpoints. You should also review the Vocabulary Appendix charts.

While you should give special attention to the Vocabulary Checkpoints if it was your weak area, we recommend that you review all of the Vocabulary and Reading Checkpoints in this book.

A comprehensive Section Test follows the Reading Comprehension Checkpoint Study. This test should be taken after you have studied all the Vocabulary and Reading Comprehension Checkpoints.

The most important thing you can do for success on the Vocabulary Section of the TOEFL is to work systematically on vocabulary development. To develop your vocabulary, work on the following Vocabulary Checkpoints and Vocabulary Checkpoint Tests.

✔ VOCABULARY CHECKPOINT STUDY

Vocabulary Checkpoint Test One

Allow yourself a maximum of four minutes to complete this checkpoint test. There are ten questions on the test. Remember to use the Vocabulary Question Strategies.

Circle the letter of the word that is closest in meaning to the underlined word or phrase.

1. The teacher remarked <u>emphatically</u> that there would be no extension on the due date for the last assignment.
   (A) pleasantly
   (B) forcefully
   (C) disdainfully
   (D) eagerly

2. Some people believe that <u>dusk</u> is the nicest time of the day.
   (A) morning
   (B) dawn
   (C) twilight
   (D) noon

3. Children are cautioned to <u>avert</u> their eyes to avoid looking directly at the sun.
   (A) shade
   (B) close
   (C) blink
   (D) turn aside

4. One of the most important <u>components</u> of a healthy lifestyle is getting enough exercise.
   (A) suggestions
   (B) attitudes
   (C) measures
   (D) parts

5. A primary requirement for a productive vegetable garden is <u>fertile</u> soil.
   (A) rich
   (B) fine
   (C) irrigated
   (D) sandy

6. A smoldering log may suddenly <u>burst</u> into flames when it reaches a certain temperature.
   (A) change
   (B) erupt
   (C) flicker
   (D) endure

7. The news reporter was reprimanded for writing <u>a biased</u> article about the citywide strike.
   (A) an inaccurate
   (B) a prejudiced
   (C) an uninteresting
   (D) a lengthy

8. Many public radio stations are partially <u>funded</u> by contributions from listeners.
   (A) directed
   (B) influenced
   (C) financed
   (D) programmed

9. People who are trying to lose weight must <u>overcome</u> their urge to eat more than they really need to satisfy their hunger.
   (A) control
   (B) outlive
   (C) obey
   (D) understand

10. Dwarfism is a condition which is associated with the <u>lack</u> of a growth hormone produced by the pituitary gland.
    (A) appearance
    (B) amount
    (C) absence
    (D) benefit

V✔1   Read Widely and Concentrate on Vocabulary

The TOEFL tests your ability to quickly recognize vocabulary words similar in meaning to the underlined word in a sentence.

You have only 20 to 30 seconds to read the underlined word and select the word closest in meaning from the four choices. This means you need to develop a large recognition vocabulary in English. The words in your recognition vocabulary are those that you recognize and understand when you read or listen but do not necessarily use in your writing or speech. In order to be successful on the TOEFL Vocabulary Section, you should have a vocabulary of about 5,000 to 10,000 words in English, including both general and academic words.

Developing your vocabulary does not happen quickly, and trying to learn word lists a few weeks before you take the TOEFL won't help you very much. The best way to acquire a large vocabulary is to read a lot of English books and magazines. You should establish a reading program for yourself and read regularly in English. Read general and formal English in special topic magazines, academic textbooks, and magazine sections of newspapers. Read informal English in popular magazines, newspapers, novels, short stories, and plays which contain vocabulary of daily routines and idioms. You should try to read as much authentic English as possible since words tested on the TOEFL come from authentic English materials. Authentic English is English written for native speakers and not adapted or simplified for special ESL textbooks or study materials.

Read academic textbooks in English for upper secondary or first-year American college courses: textbooks in history, geography, chemistry, biology, natural science, psychology, economics, business, physics, geology, astronomy, art, and literature. The introductory chapters in these textbooks are especially useful for new vocabulary. Read these first. Most libraries have copies of course books in these areas.

Read magazine and newspaper articles about art, architecture, music, dance, religion, theater, film, medicine, current events, and famous people.

Magazines: *Reader's Digest, International Wildlife, Life, Smithsonian, Science News, Time, Newsweek, US News and World Report.*

Newspapers with good magazine sections: *The New York Times, Washington Post, Los Angeles Times, and Miami Herald.*

While you are reading a text for the first time, concentrate on understanding the meaning (see Reading Appendix #1). However, to increase your English vocabulary you should read the text a second time and pay special attention to new words and their meanings. Use an English/English dictionary to look up new words. Use a thesaurus to find words with related meanings, synonyms, and antonyms. Record the meanings of all new words and review them often. See Vocabulary Checkpoints V✔3, V✔9, and V✔10 for ways to work with new words you find in your reading. Always find the meanings of words used in *The Heinemann TOEFL Preparation Course* and *The Heinemann TOEFL Practice Tests*. These words are especially common on TOEFL tests.

EXERCISE 1A: Intensive Reading for New Vocabulary

Read the following passage QUICKLY for general understanding. Then, read the passage a second time and circle words that you don't know and cannot guess from the context of the passage. The words you circle will be used in the exercises for V✔3.

> The trail west lasted long indeed. From the Missouri River to the West Coast, it ran 2,000-odd zigzag miles, with constant detours for pasture or water. But the distance in miles mattered less than the distance in time. It usually took about four and a half months
> *line* to reach the Far West, and the trip became a race against the seasons, in which sure timing
> (5) made the difference between success and failure.
>
> Late April or early May was the best time to get rolling, though the departure date had to be calculated with care. If a wagon train started too early in the spring, there would not be enough grass on the prairie to graze the livestock. Then animals would start to sicken, slowing up the train and causing alterations of schedule that might bring trouble
> (10) later. On the other hand, a train that pushed off after other trains were already on the trail found campsites marked by trampled grass and fouled water holes.
>
> Worse still, an emigrant company that dallied too long could get trapped at the far end of the journey by early winter blizzards in the coastal mountains. Obviously it was important to get to the departure point on the Missouri at the right moment, and keep
> (15) pretty close to schedule.

☛ BEFORE THE TOEFL TEST

- Read widely in many areas and concentrate on words and their meanings.
- Use a good English/English dictionary and an English thesaurus.

V✔2   Use Special ESL Vocabulary and Idiom Textbooks

The following textbooks and reference books offer special help in vocabulary and idiom study. Use them as part of your general language preparation, as well as for study for the TOEFL.

Longman Dictionary of Contemporary English, New York: Longman, 1978.

Longman Lexicon of Contemporary English, T. McArthur. London: Longman, 1981.

Oxford Advanced Learner's Dictionary of Current English, A.S. Hornby. Oxford University Press, 1980.

Cambridge English Lexicon, R. Hindmarsh. Cambridge: Cambridge University Press, 1980.

The Random House Thesaurus: College Edition. New York: Random House, 1984.

Advanced English Vocabulary: Workbook Series, Helen Barnard. Cambridge, MA: Newbury House Publishers, 1975.

Words for Students of English: A Vocabulary Series for ESL, Vols. 1–6, Holly Deemer Rogerson, Gary Esarey, Linda Schmandt, and Dorolyn Smith. Pittsburgh, PA: University of Pittsburgh Press, Pitt Series in English as a Second Language, 1988.

Developing Vocabulary Skills, Dennis Keen. Cambridge, MA: Newbury House, 1985.

Checklists for Vocabulary Study, Richard Yorkey. New York: Longman, 1981.

Lexicarry: An Illustrated Vocabulary-Builder for Second Languages, Pat Moran. Brattleboro, VT: Pro Lingua Press, 1986.

In Other Words: Life Skills Vocabulary in Context, Kathleen Santopietro. San Diego, CA: Dormac, 1989.

A Dictionary of American Idioms. Woodbury: Barron's Educational Series, 1975.

Attitudes Through Idioms, Tom Adams and Susan R. Kuder. Cambridge, MA: Newbury House Publishers, 1985.

☛ BEFORE THE TOEFL TEST

• Establish a regular program of vocabulary study.

Exercises 2A–2C are examples of vocabulary exercise types commonly found in vocabulary and idiom textbooks.

EXERCISE 2A: Sample Vocabulary Exercise

Put a plus sign (+) if the person mentioned is happy. Put a minus sign (-) if the person is sad.

__+__ 1. Martin was offered a job at both companies that he interviewed with. He's on *top of the world*.

_____ 2. Sandra has to study all weekend and can't go to the party. She's really *down in the dumps*.

_____ 3. Ken found the wallet he had lost last week. Now he *feels like a million bucks*.

EXERCISE 2B: Sample Vocabulary Exercise

The following group of words contains *one* word that does not logically fit with the others. Cross out that word, and write the general category the rest of the words belong to.

1. prosperous   wealthy   ba̶n̶krupt   well-to-do   rich

    _____*all the words describe a good economic position*_____

2. mountain   valley   mesa   river   delta   marsh

    _____

3. solitude   isolation   propensity   seclusion

    _____

EXERCISE 2C: Sample Vocabulary Exercise

Complete each sentence with the correct vocabulary word.

   diligent   adept   innate

1. The thief was ____*adept*____ at finding ways to enter locked cars.

2. Martin rarely gets lost because of his _____ sense of direction.

3. Joan mastered the violin after hours of _____ practice.

V✔3   Make and Use Vocabulary Flash Cards

In order to develop your vocabulary in English, you need to regularly review the new words that you find in your reading.

One good way to review new vocabulary is to make sets of vocabulary flash cards. To do this, use any firm, blank cards. Use three-by-five-inch note cards, if available. Make and use vocabulary flash cards in the following way:

1. On one side of the card write the new word or phrase; on the bottom of this side put the different forms of the word.
   (See V✔9 for practice with word forms.)

2. On the back side of the card write synonyms or related words and a sentence in English illustrating the use of the word in context.

3. Organize your words in some meaningful way, and set aside several times a week to review them. Look at the new word and recall a synonym or use the word in a sentence.

4. Put the words that you know in one pile and those that you don't know in another. Review those that you don't know more often.

5. If you find the new word in another sentence in your reading, put the new sentence on the card to help you in your review.

6. Some students prefer to include the native language equivalent of the new word on the flash card. If you do use the native language word or phrase, note it on the bottom of the back side of the card. Concentrate on the information you put down in English.

   NOTE: Some students write words in lists in a notebook; however, most students agree that it is much easier to use and review vocabulary flash cards. You can't separate a list into those words that you know and those you don't know as you can with flash cards.

☛ BEFORE THE TOEFL TEST

Studying vocabulary flash cards helps you to develop automatic responses to words that will help you in the Vocabulary Section of the TOEFL.

• Make and use vocabulary flash cards.

EXERCISE 3A: Making Vocabulary Flash Cards

Sample words used for this exercise are found in the reading for Exercise 1A in V✔1.

　　Study the model vocabulary flash card and use it as an example for your own flash cards. The word *detours* appears in the sample reading comprehension passage on page 253.

Front

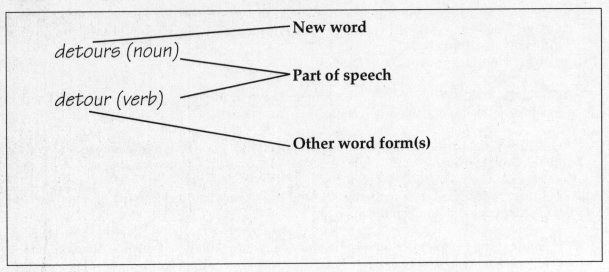

Back

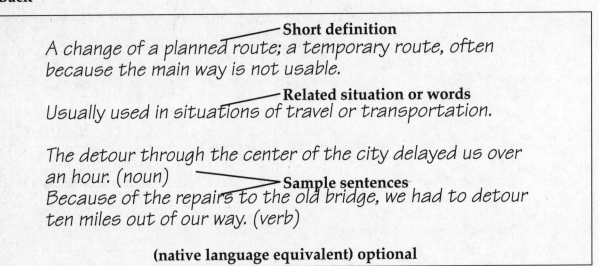

EXERCISE 3B: Practice Making Vocabulary Flash Cards

Fill in the flash cards for each of the words below. Use a dictionary to help you.

1.   prairie (found in the reading passage on page 253)

Front

prairie

Back

2. fouled (found in the reading passage on page 253)

Front

Back

3. blizzards (found in the reading passage on page 253)

Front

Back

Complete several more flash cards for other new words from the reading in Exercise 1A for V✔1. As you work with other reading passages during your preparation for the TOEFL, make and use vocabulary flash cards.

V✔4   Practice with Adverbs with Related Meanings

An adverb is a word which functions to modify a verb, an adjective, or another adverb. Adverbs are often formed by adding the ending ——*ly* to adjectives.

> quick   →   quickly
> The child ran *quickly* to the door.

Learning the meaning of adverbs will help you to identify synonyms on the Vocabulary Section of the TOEFL and to read the passages in the Reading Comprehension Section with more understanding.

There are several types of adverbs that are commonly tested on the TOEFL Vocabulary Section:

adverbs that limit
adverbs of speed
adverbs that reflect how often
adverbs that show how well something is done
adverbs of degree and effort
adverbs that show in what way something was done

The following lists of adverbs and related exercises will give you practice in building your vocabulary with adverbs.

☞ BEFORE THE TOEFL TEST

- Learn the meanings of adverbs of different types.

Adverbs that limit

Group A	Group B	Group C
almost	scarcely	rather
practically	hardly	roughly
virtually	barely	
essentially	just	
	merely	

EXERCISE 4A: Adverbs that Limit

Study the following explanations and model sentences. Pay attention to the meaning of each adverb.

almost, practically   a limited amount, a little bit; not completely but somewhat; just about, nearly.

She saved *almost* no money last year.
She saved *practically* no money last year.

The actress won *practically* all the awards.
The actress won *almost* all the awards.

virtually, essentially   almost completely; almost entirely; for the most part.

The accident victims escaped *virtually* unharmed.
The accident victims escaped *essentially* unharmed.

Jon and Will are doing *essentially* the same experiment.
Jon and Will are doing *virtually* the same experiment.

scarcely   emphasizes a narrow margin, below satisfactory performance; very little ability or possibility; barely, hardly; a negative word and often followed by *any* or *enough*.

The child can *scarcely* read.
John didn't study and *scarcely* passed the test.
We had *scarcely* enough food to feed the family.
There was *scarcely* any light in the old tunnel.

hardly   with great effort; with little likelihood, almost not at all; emphasizes the difficulty involved; barely or scarcely; a negative word.

It was snowing so much that we could *hardly* see the road.
I could *hardly* stand because I was very tired.
It is *hardly* possible to save money when you are in school.

barely   only meeting the minimum condition; emphasizes the narrow margin of achieving or having something; scarcely or hardly; a negative word.

I have *barely* any money.
We had *barely* arrived when the movie began.
I have *barely* enough money to pay the tuition.
It is *barely* 11:00. We can't eat lunch yet.

just   immediate past; only; the minimal amount possible.

She *just* finished the test.
I have *just* one more test to take.
Don't come to the review session; *just* study at home.

merely   used to limit an extreme condition; and nothing more; simply.

I didn't break the glass, I *merely* dropped it.
I wasn't worried about missing the bus. I *merely* walked to school.
The child can't talk yet. She's *merely* a baby.
She did not mean to forget you; it was *merely* an oversight.

rather   somewhat, a little bit.

I am *rather* broke.
She is *rather* shy.
It is *rather* cloudy today.

roughly   approximately, used with numbers.

I have *roughly* one dollar in coins.
The scientists have completed *roughly* two dozen experiments.
Mary wears *roughly* a size ten dress.

EXERCISE 4B: Practice with Adverbs that Limit

Fill in each blank with the appropriate adverb from the choices given. Use each word only once.

1. almost/merely/rather

   She is ___*rather*___ pretty.

   She was ___*merely*___ late, not absent.

2. practically/barely/rather

   I can't leave yet. Work finishes at 5:30 and it is _____ 5:00.

   We can go home soon. Our work is _____ completed.

3. merely/hardly/virtually

   I don't think we should cancel the picnic. The sun is coming out and it is _____ raining.

   We'll never get to shore. The wind has died; there's _____ no breeze.

4. rather/practically/just

   Don't bother to clean up. _____ lock the door.

   Take a sweater. It is _____ cold today.

5. merely/roughly/almost

   I didn't mean to insult him. I _____ said he was overweight.

   There was so much traffic that we _____ missed the plane.

6. scarcely/virtually/roughly

   I'm not really sure. I think there are _____ 200 people invited to the reception. It's sure to be crowded.

   I give up! This job is _____ impossible.

7. rather/just/essentially

   Because of the fire, the house was _____ destroyed. They have to rebuild everything.

   The concert had _____ started when we arrived. We didn't miss much at all.

8. almost/hardly/roughly

   Please wait for me. I have _____ finished the assignment.

   Don't bother waiting. I've _____ begun.

9. practically/rather/barely

Joan was in such a hurry that she _____ ran through the store.

It was _____ impolite of her to eat and run.

10. barely/rather/virtually

We were sitting so far from the speaker that we could _____ hear the talk.

I didn't buy the dress because it was _____ expensive.

11. practically/merely/scarcely

The temperature in the room was so cold that I could _____ see my breath in the air.

The survivors had been missing for twenty days and were _____ alive when they were rescued.

Adverbs of speed

quickly	with speed or promptness; in a short time
hastily	in a hurry; speedily; too quickly to be careful
promptly	without delay; in a timely manner; at once
slowly	with little speed; unhurriedly; taking a long time
lethargically	drowsily; without energy; with apathy or dullness
tardily	late; not prompt or on time

EXERCISE 4C: Adverbs of Speed

The following pairs of words show opposite meaning. Study the sentences which illustrate the meaning.

quickly/slowly

Tom wanted to get to the football game on time, so he did his work carefully but *quickly*.

Sally was not in a hurry to reach the library, so she walked *slowly* and window-shopped along the way.

hastily/lethargically

When Martha found that her mother was coming to visit in an hour, she *hastily* cleaned the house, not bothering to polish the silver.

The children seemed tired and sleepy as they *lethargically* put their toys away.

promptly/tardily

The two sisters are quite different. Elena always tries to be on time and arrives for class *promptly* at 8:30.

Nelly, however, arrives at about 8:40 and always enters the class *tardily*.

EXERCISE 4D: Practice with Adverbs of Speed

Fill in each blank with an appropriate adverb from those listed in Exercise 4C. Use each adverb only once.

1. Try to do your exercises __*promptly*__ after class so that you don't forget information the teacher gave you.

2. Not having time for conversation, Joan _____ greeted her friends and rushed on, hardly hearing what they said.

3. The snow and ice make driving _____ an important aspect of winter travel.

4. The tennis player took the ball, concentrated for a moment, and _____ stepped up to the line to serve.

5. Since I lost your address, I'm afraid that you will receive this note somewhat _____.

6. Awakening in the spring after a long hibernation, bears move about _____ for several hours.

Adverbs that reflect how often

constantly	continually; without pause
steadily	continuing forward in an even, regular manner
regularly	in evenly spaced intervals; habitually
intermittently	sporadically; recurrently; irregularly
occasionally	once in a while; not often; infrequently
periodically	routinely; at fixed intervals or times
annually	once a year
daily	once a day
weekly	once a week

EXERCISE 4E: Adverbs that Reflect How Often

Study the frequency of occurrence of the following groups of adverbs.

constantly:	//					
steadily:	/ /					
regularly:	/ / / / / / / / / / / / /					
occasionally:	/	/	/	/		
intermittently:	/	/ /	/ /	/	/	/
periodically:	2:00	6:00	8:00	10:00	12:00	
annually:	1990	1991	1992	1993	1994	1995	1996
daily:	Mon	Tues	Wed	Thur	Fri	Sat	Sun
weekly:	Mon		Mon		Mon		Mon

EXERCISE 4F: Practice with Adverbs that Reflect How Often

Fill in each blank with the best adverb from the list above. Use each adverb only once. Note the words in bold print for clues.

1. **We didn't see him every day;** he only stopped in ___*occasionally*___.

2. Although the team had no long runs, they progressed _____ down the field. **Slowly but surely,** they approached the goal line.

3. It is hard for the secretary to get much work done because the telephone rings _____. **She never gets a minute to herself.**

4. The accountant visits the office **once a year;** she checks the books _____.

5. The doctor ordered the overweight man to take long walks **every day**. He needed to exercise _____.

6. The captain went on the deck _____ to talk to the passengers. He thought it was important to be available to them **at certain times during the day**.

7. The rain showers occurred _____ throughout the day. **No one knew when to expect another downpour.**

8. In order to be in top condition a horse needs to be exercised _____, **not just when it seems convenient.**

9. The news program is broadcast **every Saturday**. It can be viewed _____ on Channel 6.

Adverbs that show how well something is done

correctly	conscientiously	deftly
effectively	concisely	erroneously
efficiently	precisely	sloppily

EXERCISE 4G: Adverbs that Show How Well Something is Done

Study the adverbs and short definitions. Then, read the sentences which illustrate the meaning.

correctly   without errors

  If you don't read the directions *correctly*, you might make a mistake in assembling the model.

effectively   meeting a need

  You should see a drop in the fever within a few hours after taking this medicine; it works very *effectively*.

efficiently   without waste

  The furnace heats more *efficiently* if the damper is properly regulated. You use less fuel and have a more constant temperature.

conscientiously   thoughtfully, with care

> Before leaving the office every day the manager *conscientiously* checks for messages, turns off the lights, and locks the door.

concisely   briefly and clearly

> Sylvan impressed his boss by *concisely* describing the nature of the problem in just a few minutes.

precisely   to the point, accurately

> The chef cooks the dishes *precisely* as the recipes direct, and the results are always the same.

deftly   skillfully

> The young gymnast continued her routine, *deftly* executing the movements to the applause of the crowd.

erroneously   incorrectly

> John *erroneously* turned on the hot water instead of the cold and burned his hand badly.

sloppily   without care, carelessly

> Compositions that are written *sloppily* and handed in without being proofread will always receive low grades.

EXERCISE 4H: Practice with Adverbs that Show How Well Something Is Done

Read the following situations and fill in each blank with an appropriate adverb from the list above. Use each adverb only once.

1. This letter should be shorter and to the point. It should be ___*concisely*___ written.

2. These craftsmen do an excellent job on woodwork. Their tableware is _____ carved.

3. Martina never takes a day off and always arrives at work on time. She does her job very _____.

4. I can't accept this application. Be more careful. This is _____ done.

5. The correct date for the meeting is February 22. It was _____ printed in the newspaper as February 20.

6. Marty does all his shopping and household errands on one day and drives to town only once a week. He plans his week very _____.

7. Spelling is a very exact skill. You have to think very _____.

8. We have planted trees and constructed a canopy. This _____ shades our outdoor patio.

9. Marcia received the highest grade in the class. She answered all of the questions _____.

Adverbs of degree and effort

ultimately	finally; in the end
urgently:	with great need; very seriously
marginally	barely
more and more	increasingly
enormously	immensely; tremendously
assuredly	certainly; positively
mildly	somewhat; moderately
laconically:	briefly; concisely

EXERCISE 4I: Adverbs of Degree and Effort

Read the following sentences and study the meaning of the adverbs.

1. It was his greed that *ultimately* ended the thief's career.

2. After the earthquake, medical supplies were *urgently* needed.

3. Taking orders in advance didn't help much; it was only *marginally* useful in marketing the product.

4. As different criteria were added to the selection process, the decision became *more and more* difficult.

5. Thanks so much for your advice. You've been *enormously* helpful.

6. Traveling by air is *assuredly* the fastest mode of transportation.

7. Because of the advance preparations for the storm, the homes in our area were only *mildly* affected.

8. Even though the newscaster spoke *laconically* on the topic and did not elaborate much, the broadcast was quite informative.

EXERCISE 4J: Practice with Adverbs of Degree and Effort

Match each adverb on the left with a word or phrase of similar meaning on the right.

____ 1. ultimately	A. to a limited extent
____ 2. urgently	B. tremendously, very much
____ 3. marginally	C. not seriously
____ 4. more and more	D. finally
____ 5. enormously	E. concisely, briefly
____ 6. assuredly	F. increasingly
____ 7. mildly	G. certainly
____ 8. laconically	H. compellingly

Adverbs that show in what way something was done

frankly	directly, in a straightforward manner
explicitly	in an exact and detailed way
peculiarly	oddly, strangely
impartially	without favor
typically	in the usual manner
readily	without hesitation
willingly	with pleasure

EXERCISE 4K: Adverbs that Show in What Way Something was Done

Read the following sentences and study the meaning of the adverbs.

1. People who speak *frankly* are often criticized for their lack of tact.

2. The photograph of the demonstration depicted the scene *explicitly*; nothing was left to the imagination.

3. The *peculiarly* acrid smell in the basement caused the man to check for hot electrical wires.

4. The judge was known for making her decisions *impartially* even though her personal views might differ.

5. Driving in the city is always difficult. During our last trip to the city we got stuck in the *typically* congested rush hour traffic.

6. The director puts telephone numbers of major clients in a file on her desk where they are *readily* available.

7. Children *willingly* get up early on Christmas Day, anticipating the gifts waiting for them under the tree.

EXERCISE 4L: Practice with Adverbs that Show in What Way Something was Done

Read the following situations and then fill in each short rejoinder using an appropriate adverb from the list above.

1. The neighbors were glad to be able to help the family rebuild the barn after the fire.

    They helped ___*willingly*___.

2. The cook arranged her spices and ingredients so that they were close at hand and convenient for her to use.

    The spices and ingredients were _____ found.

3. The ambassador did not beat around the bush but came right to the point and stated things clearly.

    The ambassador spoke _____.

4. The patient wandered through the halls at all hours and talked constantly about her money.

   The disease made her act _____.

5. The teacher always reads the composition without looking at the name of the writer. Then he gives a grade.

   The teacher grades the compositions _____.

6. James first read the directions. Then he carefully followed each step of the instructions.

   He followed the directions _____.

7. The children put on raincoats and rubber boots before they left the classroom for recess.

   They were dressed for the _____ rainy weather that occurs in New England during the spring.

EXERCISE 4M: Practice with Adverbs of Different Types

Work QUICKLY to select the adverb with a similar meaning. Circle the correct answer.

1. normally
   (A) summarily
   (B) evidently
   (C) typically
   (D) actually

2. frankly
   (A) modestly
   (B) faithfully
   (C) directly
   (D) indiscreetly

3. carefully
   (A) impishly
   (B) conscientiously
   (C) provisionally
   (D) solitarily

4. essentially
   (A) barely
   (B) totally
   (C) basically
   (D) dismally

5. unquestionably
   (A) assuredly
   (B) perplexedly
   (C) jointly
   (D) marginally

6. merely
   (A) delicately
   (B) quite
   (C) usually
   (D) just

7. skillfully
   (A) faintly
   (B) quickly
   (C) deftly
   (D) playfully

8. constantly
   (A) intermittently
   (B) continually
   (C) variably
   (D) attentively

9. hastily
   (A) flexibly
   (B) accurately
   (C) laconically
   (D) speedily

10. steadily
    (A) traditionally
    (B) incessantly
    (C) markedly
    (D) forcefully

11. laconically
    (A) concisely
    (B) collectively
    (C) dangerously
    (D) unlikely

12. rather
    (A) sometimes
    (B) often
    (C) somewhat
    (D) practically

Vocabulary Checkpoint Test Two for V✔4

Allow yourself no more than four minutes to complete this checkpoint test. There are ten questions on the test. Check your answers in the *Tapescripts and Answers*.

Circle the word which is closest in meaning to the underlined word in the sentence.

1. The exam began at <u>precisely</u> 5:00.
   (A) vaguely
   (B) exactly
   (C) roughly
   (D) belatedly

2. The message stated that his presence was <u>urgently</u> required.
   (A) usually
   (B) willingly
   (C) compellingly
   (D) rather

3. To the embarrassment of the police, the suspect was <u>erroneously</u> identified.
   (A) temporarily
   (B) promptly
   (C) assuredly
   (D) incorrectly

4. The reservoir was <u>virtually</u> empty by the end of the summer.
   (A) completely
   (B) essentially
   (C) regularly
   (D) ultimately

5. The grant from the government was made <u>annually</u>.
   (A) occasionally
   (B) steadily
   (C) yearly
   (D) traditionally

6. Manufacture of the new product was delayed because the resources were not <u>readily</u> available.
   (A) infinitely
   (B) immediately
   (C) appropriately
   (D) intactly

7. The weather was <u>fairly</u> warm for the season.
   (A) completely
   (B) intermittently
   (C) rather
   (D) tardily

8. The lions stretched <u>lethargically</u> in the warm sun.
   (A) happily
   (B) drowsily
   (C) enthusiastically
   (D) enormously

9. The formation was <u>efficiently</u> completed within the time allowed.
   (A) capably
   (B) promptly
   (C) hardly
   (D) partially

10. The audience could <u>barely</u> hear the actors when the sound system broke down.
    (A) usually
    (B) scarcely
    (C) effortlessly
    (D) really

V✔5   Practice with Adjectives with Related Meanings

Adjectives are descriptive words that modify nouns and noun structures.

Picasso was a *famous* painter.

Adjectives are often formed by adding adjective suffixes or word endings to nouns and verbs. (See V✔10 for an extensive list of adjective-forming suffixes.)

Noun	Adjective suffix	New word
hero	——ic	heroic
operation	——al	operational
Verb		
investigate	——ive	investigative
desire	——able	desirable

Learning the meanings of adjectives will help you to quickly identify synonyms on the Vocabulary Section of the TOEFL. Knowing adjectives which have related meanings will also help you to read the TOEFL Reading Comprehension passages with better understanding. The following lists of adjectives and related exercises will give you practice in working on building your vocabulary with adjectives.

☛ BEFORE THE TOEFL TEST

- Learn the meanings of adjectives.

EXERCISE 5A: Adjectives with Related Meanings

Study the following list of pairs of adjectives with opposite meanings and the sentences which illustrate their meaning.

Learn the synonyms as well as the adjectives in italics.

adequate/deficient	energetic/listless
assured/insecure	innocent/guilty
bold/cautious	lively/dull
capable/inept	robust/weak
competent/incompetent	meek/assertive
eager/indifferent	zealous/apathetic

adequate   enough; sufficient
deficient   lacking; not enough

The school supervisors provided the children with *adequate* supervision during recess.

They also made sure that the classrooms were not *deficient* in instructional materials.

assured   poised
insecure   uncertain

The lawyer appeared confident and *assured* as she defended her client.

The defendant, however, looked puzzled and *insecure* as he took the stand.

bold	daring; presumptuous
cautious	fearful; wary

The officer's *bold* plan included a midnight raid.

The more *cautious* general favored a traditional attack.

capable	expert; adept
inept	inexpert; unskilled

The boy showed that he was *capable* of sailing by skillfully navigating the boat into the harbor.

The youngsters were enthusiastic about boating, but they were *inept* at rigging the sails and required the captain's help.

competent	qualified; skilled
incompetent	unqualified; inexperienced

If you are not a *competent* bookkeeper, please do not apply for the job at the bank.

The previous clerk was so *incompetent* at simple arithmetic that he could not make correct change for a sale.

eager	avid; enthusiastic
indifferent	apathetic; nonchalant

Being *eager* to see the newest movie, we arrived at the theater quite early.

No one was *indifferent* to the story; even the adults were smiling.

energetic	active; vigorous
listless	torpid; lethargic

We had the *energetic* support of the whole team, who worked around the clock to meet the deadline.

By the next morning everyone was tired and *listless* and not prepared for a full day of work.

innocent	guiltless; inculpable
guilty	blamable; culpable

Since there was no evidence to support the charge, the man was presumed *innocent*.

Another suspect admitted he was *guilty* and confessed to the crime.

lively	active; spirited
dull	monotonous; boring

The *lively* discussion continued far into the night.

Joan much preferred that to a *dull* evening at home alone.

robust	vigorous; healthy
weak	frail; powerless

The athlete had been training for three months and his *robust* good health was obvious.

At the end of the race several runners were too *weak* to cross the finish line.

meek	submissive; acquiescent
assertive	domineering; willful

The role of women in the eighteenth century was to be *meek* and subservient to their husbands.

On the other hand, women today are less submissive and more *assertive* both at home and at their jobs.

zealous	enthusiastic; fervent
apathetic	indifferent; unresponsive

Only the most *zealous* skiers were on the mountain in the subzero temperatures.

It is hard to be *apathetic* about the sport when there is such breathtaking scenery and beautiful weather.

EXERCISE 5B: Practice with Adjectives with Related Meanings

Match each adjective on the left with a word of similar meaning on the right.

<u>C</u> 1. robust   A. fervent

_____ 2. meek   B. lethargic

_____ 3. deficient   C. vigorous

_____ 4. competent   D. lacking

_____ 5. listless   E. daring

_____ 6. bold   F. submissive

_____ 7. dull   G. monotonous

_____ 8. eager   H. apathetic

_____ 9. zealous   I. unskilled

_____ 10. inept   J. qualified

_____ 11. cautious   K. avid

_____ 12. indifferent   L. wary

EXERCISE 5C: Practice with Adjectives of Positive and Negative Attributes

Read each sentence and decide if the adjective in italics expresses a positive or negative attribute. Use a plus sign (+) for positive words and a minus sign (-) for negative words. If you do not know the word, use the context of the sentence to help you.

After you complete the exercise, use your dictionary to find more precise meanings of new words. Then, make a vocabulary flash card with the new word and its synonyms.

polite	belligerent	dismal	vivacious
forlorn	callous	benign	coy
jealous	reliable	jovial	enraged
optimistic	altruistic	apprehensive	humble

1. Being a *polite* young man, Tom opened the door for the girls.

   __+__   polite

2. The child was close to tears as she stood in the middle of the store, looking lost and *forlorn*.

   _____   forlorn

3. Although Marty had a perfectly good doll, she was *jealous* of her sister, whose doll was bigger and newer.

   _____   jealous

4. The group was *optimistic* about the next day's weather, and packed bathing suits for the trip to the beach.

   _____   optimistic

5. The drunken man was in a *belligerent* mood and wanted to fight with anyone he met.

   _____   belligerent

6. Those who are raised in the midst of civil war seem to be more *callous* to destruction than others more fortunate.

   _____   callous

7. Hank was highly recommended as a hardworking and *reliable* employee.

   _____   reliable

8. The family gave money for a new orphanage and has been involved in other *altruistic* endeavors.

   _____   altruistic

9. The sight of the smoldering remains of the factory was a *dismal* reminder of the previous night's fire.

   _____   dismal

10. The old man's *benign* behavior with animals made him a favorite with the neighborhood kids as well.

    _____   benign

11. Telling funny stories and singing silly songs make our annual campout a *jovial* affair.

    _____   jovial

12. Because the appointment had been cancelled twice before, Jane was *apprehensive* about calling again.

____ apprehensive

13. Her *vivacious* spirit and warm smile endeared my aunt to all of us.

____ vivacious

14. Her *coy* manner made her seem even more attractive to the young men at the party, but alienated the young women.

____ coy

15. After being shot in the shoulder the *enraged* bear attacked the campers.

____ enraged

16. The scientist accepted his award with no more than a *humble* thank-you.

____ humble

EXERCISE 5D: Practice with Adjectives and Their Synonyms

Match the adjective on the left with a synonym on the right.

Group A

_C_ 1. polite   A. discouraging

____ 2. forlorn   B. charitable

____ 3. vivacious   C. courteous

____ 4. optimistic   D. lonesome

____ 5. dismal   E. flirtatious

____ 6. coy   F. lively

____ 7. enraged   G. very angry

____ 8. altruistic   H. hopeful

Group B

____ 1. reliable   A. cautious

____ 2. humble   B. spirited

____ 3. benign   C. aggressive

____ 4. jovial   D. trustworthy

____ 5. jealous   E. unpretentious

____ 6. callous   F. insensitive

____ 7. apprehensive   G. kind

____ 8. belligerent   H. envious

EXERCISE 5E: Practice with Adjectives of Amount

Put the following adjectives of amount into two groups: small and large.

> ample, copious, sparse, dearth, abundant lavish, scant, profuse, meager, scarce

Small	Large
	ample

EXERCISE 5F: Practice with Adjectives of Size

Put the following adjectives of size into two groups: small and large.

> diminutive, bulky, gigantic, huge, stunted, immense, massive, microscopic, portly, miniature, petite, slight, prodigious, dainty, vast, voluminous, puny

Small	Large
diminutive	

EXERCISE 5G: Practice with Adjectives of Smell and Taste

Match the following smells and tastes with their sources.

_C_ 1. smelly   A. medicine

___ 2. bitter   B. sauce

___ 3. scented   C. old sneakers

___ 4. savory   D. perfume

___ 5. fragrant   A. smoke

___ 6. putrid   B. a soft drink

___ 7. tangy   C. decaying meat

___ 8. acrid   D. flowers

___ 9. rotten   A. curry

___ 10. spicy   B. unsalted crackers

___ 11. tasty   C. garbage

___ 12. bland   D. cake

V✔6   Predict Meaning Using Latin and Greek Roots

The knowledge of Latin and Greek roots of English words is very important to building a large vocabulary and developing vocabulary skills. A root is the basic part of a word to which prefixes and suffixes can be added to form many other words. The root of a word gives its basic meaning. Knowing just twenty-five roots can help you to figure out the basic meaning of hundreds of other English words.

Latin root	Area of meaning
belli	war

English words	English meaning
belligerent	ready to fight
rebellion	armed resistance to authority
bellicose	warlike

Knowing the meaning of the roots of English words is an especially important vocabulary building aid if your language is not based on Latin and Greek roots, as is English. If you do not know a word in English, knowing its root can help you to predict its probable meaning. (See V✔9, Make and Study Word Form Charts for practice forming words from Latin and Greek roots.)

☞ BEFORE THE TOEFL TEST

- Learn the most common roots of English words.

Use the list of Latin and Greek roots below to become familiar with roots and their areas of meaning. Practice alone or with a friend to work with the example words in this list.

Here are several ways to practice with the following roots, their areas of meaning, and the example words.

1. Cover the root column. Look at the example words and the area of meaning. Circle the root in each example word.
2. Cover the area of meaning column. Look at the root and example words. Write down the area of meaning on a separate paper.
3. Cover the example words. Look at the root and area of meaning. Write down several words that contain the root. If you think of words that are not listed, add them to the example word column.
4. Find a reading passage in another book or use the sentences from exercises in Sections One and Two in this book. Make a list of words that are new for you and try to guess the meaning of each word by analyzing the root of the word. Use your dictionary to confirm your guess.

ROOT	AREA OF MEANING	EXAMPLE WORDS
Group 1		
act	do	action, react
agro	field	agriculture, agrarian
anthr	human	anthropology, philanthropist
aqua	water	aquarium, aqueous
arch	chief	monarch, architect
art	skill	artist, artisan, artifact
belli	war	bellicose, rebellion
biblio	book	bibliography

ROOT	AREA OF MEANING	EXAMPLE WORDS
Group 2		
bio	life	biography, biology, biopsy
cede, ceed	go, yield	proceed, concede, succeed
cert	sure	certain, certify, certificate
chron	time	chronological, synchronize
clar	clear	clarify, declare
cogn	know	recognize, cognition
corp	body	corporation, corpus, corpse
cum	heap	cumulative, accumulate
Group 3		
dem	people	democracy, demography
dict	speak	dictate, predict, verdict
don, donat	give	donation, pardon, donate
duct	lead	conduct, educate
fac, fact	do, make	factory, manufacture
fer	bear, carry	transfer, ferry
fig	form	figure, effigy, figment
gen	birth, race	generation, genocide, progeny
Group 4		
gnos	know	agnostic, diagnostic, prognosis
grad, gress	step	graduation, progress
graph	write	telegraph, phonograph
greg	gather	gregarious, congregation
homo	man	homicide, homage
iatr	medical care	psychiatry, podiatry
jus	law	justice, justify
lab	work	labor, laboratory, collaborate
Group 5		
loc	place	location, allocate
lum	light	luminous, illuminate
lys	break down	analysis, paralysis
man	hand	manual, manufacture, manuscript
mech	machine	mechanic, mechanize
mem	mindful	memory, remember, commemorate
min	small, lesser	minute, minor, minimize
mit, miss	send	submit, remit, transmission
Group 6		
mov	move	remove, movement
nat	born	natal, native, innate
nav	ship	navy, naval, navigate
neo	new	neoclassic, neonatal
nomen, nym	name	nomenclature, pseudonym
ocu	eye	oculist, binocular
ortho	straight, right	orthodontist, orthodox
phil	love	philosophy, philanthropist

ROOT	AREA OF MEANING	EXAMPLE WORDS

Group 7

ROOT	AREA OF MEANING	EXAMPLE WORDS
photo	light	photograph, photosynthesis
plic, plex	fold	complex, implication, perplex
pon, pos	put, place	opponent, postpone, disposal
pop	people	populace, population, popular
port	carry	transport, import, porter
psych	mind, soul	psychology, psyche, psychopath
pul	urge	compulsory, expulsion, repulse
put	think	reputation, computer, deputy

Group 8

ROOT	AREA OF MEANING	EXAMPLE WORDS
ras	scrape	erase, abrasive, rasp, razor
rid	laugh	ridiculous, deride, derisive
scribe, script	write	describe, description
sens, sent	feel	sensation, sensitive, dissent
spir	breath	respiration, conspire, inspire
sta	stand	status, stationary, stagnant
struct	build	structure, instruct
tact, tang	touch	tangible, tactile, intact
tain	hold	detain, container, restraint

Group 9

ROOT	AREA OF MEANING	EXAMPLE WORDS
ten	have, hold	tenure, tenuous, intent
terr	land	terrain, territory, terrace
the	god	theology, atheism, monotheism
therm	heat	hypothermia, thermostat
tract	pull, drag	tractor, traction, intractable
urb	city	urban, suburb, urbane
vene, vent	come	convention, advent, convene
vict, vinc	conquer	victim, conviction
vid	see	video, evidence, provide
viv, vit	live	vivid, vitality

EXERCISE 6A: Practice with Roots

Give the meaning for each root. Then, give some English word(s) of your own containing the root. Use the list of example words on page 277 if you need help.

1. mem _____*mindful*_____ _____*memory, remind, remembrance*_____

2. agro _____ _____

3. aqua _____ _____

4. bio _____ _____

5. cert _____ _____

6. chron _____ _____

7. dem _____ _____

8. greg _____ _____

9. jus   _____   _____

10. min   _____   _____

11. mov   _____   _____

12. put   _____   _____

13. viv   _____   _____

EXERCISE 6B: Practice Using Roots to Predict Meaning

Work QUICKLY to select the word that has a similar meaning to the word given. Circle the best choice. Then, circle the root you find in the given word.

1. circumvent
   (A) retrieve
   (B) bypass
   (C) locate
   (D) insist

2. convincingly
   (A) persuasively
   (B) rebelliously
   (C) exclusively
   (D) appropriately

3. collaborate
   (A) evaluate
   (B) assign
   (C) invent
   (D) cooperate

4. concede
   (A) yield
   (B) advance
   (C) devise
   (D) insist

5. stationary
   (A) fixed
   (B) entirely
   (C) divided
   (D) essential

6. repulsive
   (A) isolated
   (B) rival
   (C) disgusting
   (D) normal

7. neonatal
   (A) innovative
   (B) newborn
   (C) showy
   (D) damp

8. ridicule
   (A) mature
   (B) incline
   (C) humiliate
   (D) notice

9. urbanized
   (A) light
   (B) citified
   (C) analyzed
   (D) proven

10. reputable
    (A) trustworthy
    (B) conspicuous
    (C) illuminated
    (D) manual

11. demographic
    (A) suspicious
    (B) intelligible
    (C) population
    (D) negligent

12. synchronized
    (A) calibrated
    (B) paralyzed
    (C) restricted
    (D) mandatory

Vocabulary Checkpoint Test Three for V✔6

Allow yourself four minutes to complete the checkpoint test.

Work quickly to choose the word that is closest in meaning to the underlined word in the sentence. Circle the best choice.

1. Drought, floods, and invasions of insects are all factors which affect <u>an agrarian</u> society.
   (A) an impoverished
   (B) a utilitarian
   (C) an agricultural
   (D) a populated

2. After hatching the eggs, the female of the species seems to lose interest in her <u>progeny</u>.
   (A) mate
   (B) nest
   (C) offspring
   (D) welfare

3. The instructions in the letter asked for <u>remittance</u> by mail.
   (A) compensation
   (B) reduction
   (C) acceptance
   (D) inquiry

4. The <u>gregarious</u> nature of the politician made him a popular campaigner.
   (A) sincere
   (B) convincing
   (C) astute
   (D) sociable

5. The terms of the loan <u>dictate</u> the amount of payment per month.
   (A) submit
   (B) decree
   (C) reject
   (D) total

6. <u>Rebellion</u> of any sort is likely to be an unpleasant way to initiate change.
   (A) Consensus
   (B) Insurrection
   (C) Mitigation
   (D) Realignment

7. A yearly physical examination is required for most sports to <u>certify</u> the players' health.
   (A) check
   (B) support
   (C) verify
   (D) acknowledge

8. Most American families <u>allocate</u> one quarter of their income for housing.
   (A) budget
   (B) earn
   (C) generate
   (D) invest

9. The child reminded us all of our youth in some <u>intangible</u> way.
   (A) joyous
   (B) preposterous
   (C) elusive
   (D) remarkable

10. An <u>aqueous</u> substance leaked from the battered package.
    (A) repulsive
    (B) squeamish
    (C) rubbery
    (D) watery

V✔7   Predict Meaning Using Prefixes

A prefix is a part of a word that is attached before the word root and changes the meaning of the word.

Prefix	Meaning	Word
im——	not	possible

New word: impossible
New meaning: not possible

Prefixes in English have areas of meanings, and knowing prefixes will help you to add more words to your vocabulary. Although there are many prefixes, knowing the most important ones should be part of your preparation for the TOEFL.

☞ BEFORE THE TOEFL TEST

- Learn the most common prefixes in English.

Use the following lists of prefixes in English to become familiar with each prefix, its area of meaning, and some example words.

Study the words in Column A. Complete Exercises 7A and 7B to fill in Column B.

		Column A Example word	Column B Example word of your own
Prefixes for negation			
a——	not	amoral	_____
dis——	not	disassociate	_____
il——	not	illiterate	*illegal*
im——	not	impossible	_____
in——	not	inactive	*indecisive*
ir——	not	irrational	_____
mis——	wrong	misgiving	_____
non——	not	nonexistent	_____
un——	not	unintentional	*unimportant*
Prefixes for number and size			
demi——	half	demitasse	_____
hemi——	half	hemisphere	_____
semi——	half	semicircle	_____
mon——, *mono*——	one	monologue	_____
uni——	one	unification	_____
prot——	first	prototypical	_____

poly——	many	polygamy	_____
olig——	few	oligarchy	_____
_bi_——,			
bin——	two	bilingual	_____
tri——	three	trimester	_____
dec——,			
deci——	ten	decade	_____
cent——,			
hect——	hundred	centennial	_____
myria——	ten thousand	myriameter	_____

Prefixes for very small

| _milli_—— | thousandths | milligram | _____ |
| _micro_—— | small | microscope | _____ |

Prefixes for very large

macro——	large	macroeconomics	_____
mega——	large	megalomania	_____
kilo——	tens	kilogram	_____
magni——	great	magnificent	_____

Prefixes for time

ante——	before	antebellum	_____
pre——	before	pre-industrial	_____
pro——	before	progeny	_____
_re_——	again	regain	_____
after——	after	aftertaste	_afterthought_
post——	after	postgraduate	_postpone_
epi——	after	epilogue	_epitaph_

Prefixes for where

_ad_——	to, toward	addiction	_____
_ac_——	to, toward	accrue	_____
_af_——	to, toward	affirm	_____
_ag_——	to, toward	aggressive	_____
_an_——	to, toward	annotate	_____
_as_——	to, toward	aspire	_____
_by_——	near	bystander	_____

em——,			
en——	in	envelope	_____
im——	into	immerse	_____
intra——	within	intramural	_____
intro——	inside	introspection	_____
enter——	among	entertain	_____
inter——	among	interstate	_____
epi——	upon	epidermis	_____
e——	out, away	emigrate	_____
ex——	out	exit	_____
extra——	outside	extraterrestrial	_____
de——	from, down	demerit	_____
off——	from	offspring	_____
tele——	distant	telecommunications	_____
mid——	middle	midsummer	_____
on——	on	onshore	_____
para——	beside	paralegal	_____
per——	throughout	pervasive	_____
circu——	around	circumvent	_____
peri——	all around	periphery	_____
trans——	across	transcontinental	_____
dia——	through	diagonal	_____
pro——	forward	proceed	_____
re——	back	retract	_____
retro——	back	retroflex	_____
sub——	under	subzero	_____
under——	below	underachiever	_____
with——	back away	withdraw	_____
super——	over	supervisor	_____

Prefixes for amount

hypo——	too little	hypoglycemic	_____
under——	less than	underweight	_____
hyper——	too much	hyperactive	_____
extra——	excessive	extravagant	_____
out——	surpassing	outdo	_____

ultra——	beyond	ultramodern	_____
pene——	almost	peninsula	_____
omni——	all	omnipresent	_____

Prefixes for relationship of together or separate

self——	self	self-sufficient	_____
auto——	self	autocratic	_____
ab——	away from	abdicate	_____
col——	with	colleague	_____
com——	with	commune	_____
con——	with	connect	_____
co——	together	coordinate	_____
sym——	together	symphony	_____
syn——	together	synthesis	_____

Prefixes that make a judgment

anti——	against	antisocial	_____
contra——	against	contraception	_____
dys——	bad	dysfunction	_____
mal——	bad	maladjusted	_____
mis——	wrong	misfortune	_____
bene——	good	benefactor	_____
eu——	good	euphoria	_____
pro——	for	pro-education	_____

Other prefixes

ambi——	both	ambivalent	_____
amphi——	around	amphitheater	_____
be——	make	befriend	_____
hetero——	different	heterodox	_____
homo——	same	homogeneous	_____
pseudo——	false	pseudonym	_____
meta——	change	metabolism	_____
neo——	new	neoclassicism	_____

EXERCISE 7A: Practice with Prefixes

Each of the following listed words has a prefix. Put each word into one of the given groups according to the meaning of the prefix. Look up in your dictionary any words that you don't know.

Then, write each word on one of the blank lines in Column B of the lists of prefixes on pages 282–285. If you can, add a word of your own in Column B, too.

The first list of words has been done for you.

1. **after**thought, **un**important, **epi**taph, **in**decisive, **post**pone, **il**legal

Negative	**After**
unimportant	*afterthought*
indecisive	*epitaph*
illegal	*postpone*

2. **sym**phony, **ad**here, **a**scend, **an**nex, **co**operate, **ac**cess, **syn**thesis

   Where (to, toward)   **Together**

3. **im**migrate, **anti**war, **pre**amble, **contra**dict, **pro**logue, **intra**state, **ante**cedent, **intro**vert, **retro**active, **re**call

   Where (into, inside)   **Judgement (against)**

   Time (before)   **Where (back)**

4. **uni**verse, **hyper**active, **myri**ad, **trans**continental, **mega**phone **mon**arch, **dia**meter, **out**number, **ultra**sensitive, **circum**vent **magni**ficent

   Large   **Too much, excessive**

   Through, across   **One**

EXERCISE 7B: More Practice with Prefixes

Give the meaning of each prefix in the following list. Then, give a sample word for each prefix. Use your dictionary if necessary. Add this word to the list of example words in Column B, pages 282–285.

Prefix	Meaning	Example Word
1. poly-	*not*	*unpopular*
2. poly-		
3. bi-		
4. cent-		
5. macro-		
6. neo-		
7. re-		
8. mis-		
9. hemi-		
10. micro-		
11. deci-		
12. homo-		
13. under-		
14. ante-		
15. inter-		

V✔8   Predict Meaning Using Suffixes

A suffix is a part of an English word that attaches to the end of the word. Suffixes change the part of speech of a word, as well as mark general areas of meaning. Knowledge of English suffixes will help you to identify the part of speech of a word in a sentence and to predict its probable area of meaning.

Noun	Verb	Adjective	Adverb
accuracy	X	accurate	accurately
instruction	instruct	instructional, instructive	instructively
agreement	agree	agreeable	agreeably
satisfaction	satisfy	satisfactory	satisfactorily
west	X	western	westward

☞ BEFORE THE TOEFL TEST

• Learn the forms and meanings of English suffixes.

See G✔20 for more information on forming nouns, verbs, adjectives, and adverbs by adding suffixes. You will get more practice using suffixes by completing the Word Form Charts for V✔10, pages 299–304 and Vocabulary Appendix #2, pages 470–488.

Use the following lists of suffixes to become familiar with suffixes, their area of meaning, and example words.

Study the following charts to learn the forms and meanings of English suffixes and some sample words.

Noun Suffixes

The following suffixes are added to nouns to show:

The one who practices

——ist	socialist, biologist
——cian	magician

The one who works with

——man	cameraman
——wright	playwright

Art or skill

——ship	showmanship, craftsmanship

Females

——ess, ——stress, ——tress	hostess, seamstress, actress
——enne	comedienne, equestrienne
——ette	usherette, majorette
——ine	heroine
——trix	aviatrix

A trade or occupation

——ery	surgery, robbery
——ry	dentistry, husbandry
——er, ——or	teacher, mentor
——eer	engineer
——ite	socialite
——ant, ——ent	applicant, occupant, correspondent

An action or process

——ade	blockade, parade
——age	marriage, pilgrimage
——ation	vacation, visitation
——cy	accuracy, truancy
——ism	baptism, heroism
——ment	amusement, agreement
——ure	tenure, seizure, failure

A product or thing

——ade	orangeade
——ery, ——ry	mastery, jewelry
——ment	adornment, instrument
——mony	harmony, matrimony

Material

——ing	lining, stuffing, siding

Place for

——arium	aquarium, planetarium
——ary	infirmary, library

——orium	sanatorium, auditorium
——ory	laboratory, observatory

Small things

——cle	particle, icicle
——cule	molecule, minuscule
——et	bonnet, sonnet
——ette	kitchenette, cigarette
——let	owlet, pamphlet
——ling	duckling, fledgling

The study of

——ology	biology, physiology

Scientific or social systems

——ics	physics, statistics

Surgical removal of

——ectomy	tonsillectomy, appendectomy

Inflammation of

——itis	tonsillitis, appendicitis

State or quality of

——ance, -ence	admittance, dependence
——ancy, -ency	buoyancy, insurgency
——ation	demonstration, registration
——cy	infancy, primacy
——dom	freedom, kingdom
——ery, ——ry	treachery
——hood	boyhood
——ion	companion, passion
——ism	socialism, feudalism, racism
——ity	brevity, inequity
——ization	commercialization, civilization
——ment	advertisement, enjoyment
——ness	happiness, friendliness, rashness
——or	horror, terror, stupor
——ship	friendship, hardship
——sion	dimension, apprehension
——th	length, width, warmth
——tion	partition, confirmation
——tude	rectitude, attitude
——ty	felicity, obscurity

Adjective Suffixes

The following suffixes are added to nouns and verbs to form adjectives which mean:

Full of

——ful	joyful, hopeful
——ose	verbose, grandiose
——ous	anxious, joyous
——ulent	turbulent

Lacking or without

——less	hopeless, joyless

Relating to

——al, ——an	natural, urban
——ary	honorary
——esque	picturesque
——etic	pathetic
——ical	identical
——ic	barbaric
——ian	agrarian
——ial	congenial
——ine	bovine
——ish	childish
——like	lifelike
——ly	comely, sisterly
——oid	celluloid
——ular	popular

Made of

——en	earthen, flaxen

Capable of

——able,——ible	fixable, desirable, intelligible

Inclined to

——acious	tenacious
——ant, ——ent	observant, prudent
——ative	talkative
——ble	inhabitable
——ive	responsive
——some	quarrelsome

State or quality of

——ate	temperate
——id	lucid, splendid
——ile	hostile, docile
——ious	ambitious
——und	moribund
——uous	sensuous
——y	wealthy, sunny

Adverb Suffixes

The following suffixes attach to adjectives and nouns to form adverbs of:

Manner

——ily (spelling change)	happily, speedily
——ly	quickly, jointly
——wise	clockwise
——ways	sideways

Extent

——ly	urgently, extremely

Verb Suffixes

The following suffixes form verbs with the meanings:

To make

——ate	liberate, activate
——en	brighten, broaden
——fy	nullify, satisfy
——ize	popularize, generalize

Action or process

——ade	invade
——age	scrimmage, pillage
——er	badger, deliver
——ish	flourish, nourish
——ure	endure, censure

Repeated action

——ble	fumble, mumble, stumble

These English suffixes should be reviewed often as you fill in the Word Form Charts in V✔9. If you are not sure of a form, use your dictionary.

EXERCISE 8A: Practice with Suffixes

Identify each suffix listed below as a noun, verb, adjective, or adverb suffix. Then, give a sample word for each suffix.

Suffix	Part of Speech	Example Word
1. ——ment	*noun*	*disagreement*
2. ——ic		
3. ——ant		
4. ——ize		
5. ——ary		
6. ——ish		
7. ——acious		
8. ——ily		
9. ——fy		
10. ——wise		
11. ——ular		
12. ——cy		

EXERCISE 8B: More Practice with Suffixes

Match the phrase on the left with the appropriate word from the column on the right. Use the lists on pages 288–291 if you need help.

____	1. Inflammation of the appendix	A.	powerless
____	2. Material for covering a roof	B.	arrogantly
____	3. Diminutive: dining furniture set	C.	roofing
____	4. Capable of being broken	D.	appendicitis
____	5. Someone who works in biology	E.	dinette
____	6. Related to riding horses	F.	biologist
____	7. Without power	G.	breakable
____	8. In an arrogant manner	H.	equestrian

EXERCISE 8C: More Practice with Suffixes

Use the suffix given for the phrase to find the correct word. Write the word in the blank. Use the lists on pages 288–291 if you need help.

1. A woman who acts on stage   -tress   _____

2. Having many clouds   -y   _____

3. To make dark   -en   _____

4. The quality of having ambition   -ious   _____

5. To make popular   -ize   _____

6. Place for scientific experiments   -ory   _____

7. To repeatedly fall when walking   -ble   _____

8. Anxious; without rest   -less   _____

EXERCISE 8D: More Practice with Suffixes

Give the correct word for the phrase. Use the lists on pages 288–291 if you need help.

1. Something that makes you worry is   _____

2. A person who writes plays   _____

3. Time of life as an infant   _____

4. The state of being friends   _____

5. Full of wishes   _____

6. A person who practices medicine   _____

7. Having a lot of wind   _____

8. A drink of lemons, sugar, and water   _____

EXERCISE 8E: Practice Using Roots, Prefixes, and Suffixes to Predict Word Meaning

When working with roots, prefixes, and suffixes, follow these steps:

A. Separate the word into prefixes, roots, and suffixes and give the area of meaning for each. Refer to your lists of roots, prefixes, and suffixes in V✔6, V✔7, and V✔8. Identify the part of speech by noting the suffix.

B. Write your predicted meaning of the word based on your knowledge of the roots, prefixes, and suffixes.

C. Use your dictionary to look up the specific meaning of the word and write it below your predicted meaning.

D. Use the word in a sentence of your own.

1. philanthropist

   A.   phil   anthr   opist   Noun
       (love)   (human) (person)

   B. Predicted meaning: *A person who loves mankind.*

   C. Dictionary definition: *A person who shows affection for humankind, especially by giving money, property, or doing work for the needy and poor.*

   D. *The philanthropist Andrew Carnegie gave millions of dollars to establish libraries.*

2. manufacture

   A.

   B.

   C.

   D.

3. induction

   A.

   B.

   C.

   D.

4. activate

   A.

   B.

   C.

   D.

5. optician

   A.

   B.

   C.

   D.

6. prediction

   A.

   B.

   C.

   D.

7. urban

   A.

   B.

   C.

   D.

8. autograph

   A.

   B.

   C.

   D.

9. popular

   A.

   B.

   C.

   D.

10. transportation

    A.

    B.

    C.

    D.

Vocabulary Checkpoint Test Four for V✔7 and V✔8

Allow yourself four minutes to complete this checkpoint test. There are ten questions on the test.

Circle the letter of the word that is closest in meaning to the underlined word or phrase in the context of the sentence.

1. The chairman introduced the speaker with a few <u>laudatory</u> remarks.
   (A) explanatory
   (B) complimentary
   (C) brief
   (D) introductory

2. The river of molten lava flowing steadily toward the town was an <u>awesome</u> sight.
   (A) heartwarming
   (B) encouraging
   (C) astonishing
   (D) amusing

3. Businesses sometimes establish firms in foreign countries to <u>circumvent</u> local restrictions.
   (A) avoid
   (B) compensate for
   (C) adjust to
   (D) comply with

4. The American author Mark Twain was popular in part because of his gift as a <u>humorous</u> public speaker.
   (A) a sincere
   (B) an amusing
   (C) an interesting
   (D) a provocative

5. The senator's aide was reprimanded because of his <u>outspoken</u> criticism of the proposed legislation.
   (A) unusual
   (B) unjustified
   (C) straightforward
   (D) clever

6. The harpsichord was <u>antecedent</u> to the pianoforte as an early musical instrument.
   (A) prior to
   (B) reminiscent of
   (C) insidious to
   (D) imitative of

7. The decision to increase the degree requirements was seen as <u>contradictory</u> to the program's stated goals.
   (A) supportive of
   (B) complimentary to
   (C) germane to
   (D) inconsistent with

8. Remains of nuts and seeds indicated that a family of squirrels had been recent <u>occupants</u> of the attic eaves.
   (A) visitors to
   (B) inhabitants of
   (C) assailants of
   (D) protectors of

9. Female members of one African tribe wear neck rings not only as <u>an adornment</u> but also as signification of their status as married.
   (A) a requirement
   (B) a precaution
   (C) a decoration
   (D) a peculiarity

10. The professor pointed out that much important information can be found in the <u>prologue</u> of a play.
   (A) contents
   (B) introductory remarks
   (C) appendix
   (D) bibliography

V✔9   Make and Study Word Form Charts

A word form chart is a chart in which a word with the same root is listed according to its part of speech in English. The forms of a word that are listed in a word form chart are noun, verb, adjective and adverb. These word forms are created in English by adding suffixes to the root of a word.

Noun	Verb	Adjective	Adverb
conservation	conserve	conservative	conservatively

A word form chart is a useful study aid for building your vocabulary. It will give you at a glance a review of different forms of words with similar meanings. Word form charts require that you understand the forms and meanings of English suffixes that change the part of speech of a word. Review V√8 for information and practice with English suffixes.

Word form charts will help you to increase your ability to identify different forms of words and to predict their probable meaning. Knowledge of word forms is tested in the Written Expression part of Section Two of the TOEFL. Refer to G✔20–G✔22, pages 447–451 for information on word forms as they are tested in TOEFL Section Two. In the Reading Comprehension part of TOEFL Section Three, knowing different forms of words and their meanings will help you to read faster with comprehension. In the Test of Written English, the ability to use words in different forms will allow you to write more precisely and in more detail.

Word form charts are provided in the Vocabulary Appendix. These charts correspond to the word category charts that you will learn about in V✔10. Practice with word forms using these charts. Look up new words in your English dictionary to find the different forms of the word, and fill out the word form charts. Review the charts often and practice recalling the different forms of the words.

Additional word form charts are found in the Vocabulary Appendix for you to fill out as you work with vocabulary in *The Heinemann TOEFL Preparation Course* and *The Heinemann TOEFL Practical Tests*. Make additional charts yourself based on your outside reading for further study with word forms.

☛ BEFORE THE TOEFL

- Use word form charts to build your vocabulary.

EXERCISE 9A: Word Forms and Their Functions

Study the following information about word forms and functions.

1. Verbs in English often function as adjectives when the suffixes ——*ed*, ——*d*, ——*en*, and ——*ing* are added to the verb stem.

mystify	mystified	a mystified look
decorate	decorated	a decorated cake
break	broken	a broken cup
linger	lingering	a lingering headache

   Irregular past participle forms are also used for this adjective function.

   The *slain* policeman was given the city's highest honor.

   See Grammar Appendix, #14, pages 442–445 for a list of irregular verb forms.

---

2. Nouns in English form plurals by adding the suffixes ——s, ——es, ——ies, ——i, and ——a. Note the form of the noun plural as you fill out the word form charts below and in the Vocabulary Appendix.

Singular	Plural
cup	cups
dish	dishes
baby	babies
stimulus	stimuli
medium	media

    See Grammar Appendix, #4, page 436 for rules on noun plurals and irregular noun plural forms.

3. Noun forms in English often function as adjectives: *guest*
    Noun: The distinguished *guest* was seated at the head table.
    Adjective: The *guest* list was prepared weeks ahead of the dinner.

    The meaning is similar in both functions.
    On the word form charts below and in the Vocabulary Appendix, the word appears in the noun function.

4. Gerunds are nouns formed by adding the suffix —*ing* to verb stems.
    Verb: *ship*
    Gerund: *shipping*

            Shipping is an important component of the manufacturing industry.

    Gerunds need not be added to word form charts, but you need to remember their function and meaning.

5. Many words in English have the same form for different functions.

    The word *ship* could function as a noun:
            I traveled by *ship*.

    or a verb:
            The company will *ship* the necessary parts.

    The function of the word form depends on its use in the sentence. However, most times there will be a similar or related meaning of the words. Being aware of this change of function but relationship of meaning will help you to read with better understanding.
    Add the same word form to different functions on word form charts as you complete them.

6. In English different forms of a word may have the same function.
    Nouns: *ship*   We traveled by *ship*.
                       shipment   We received the *shipment* of parts.
                       shipper   The major *shipper* of the parts is located in Boston.

    Add the different forms of a word with the same function to the word form charts as you complete them.

EXERCISE 9B: Making Word Form Charts

Study the sample word form chart for *air transportation* to learn how to make a word form chart.

Sample Word Form Chart: Air Transportation

Noun	Verb	Adjective	Adverb
convenience	X	convenient	conveniently
aviation	X	X	X
aviator	X	X	X
aviatrix	X	X	X
airliner	X	X	X
airline	X	X	X
reservation	reserve	reserved	X
flight	fly	X	X
departure	depart	X	X
arrival	arrive	X	X
terminal	terminate	X	terminally
termination	X	X	X
confirmation	confirm	confirmed	X
assignment	assign	assigned	X
security	secure	X	securely
mechanics	mechanize	mechanical	mechanically
fuel	fuel	X	X
control	control	X	X
landing	land	X	X
	board	boarding	X
turbulence	X	turbulent	turbulently
schedule	schedule	scheduled	X
	reschedule	X	X
	bump	bumped	X
	overbook	overbooked	X
delay	delay	delayed	X
	lose	lost	X
connection	connect	connecting	X

NOTE: You will practice with an additional word form chart in Exercise 10E.

V✔10   Make and Study Word Category Charts

In order to develop the ability to recognize words quickly and easily, it is helpful to put words into a chart that shows their relationship. A word category chart is a chart that groups words from a general topic area into related categories. The Vocabulary Appendix provides word category charts for the topics most commonly tested in the TOEFL.

Developing and using word category charts will be helpful for both the Vocabulary Section and the Reading Comprehension Section of the TOEFL. Other sections of the TOEFL that test your knowledge and use of vocabulary are the Listening Comprehension Section and the Test of Written English. In addition, the word category charts will be useful preparation for any future study in English. A wide vocabulary in English is necessary for academic and professional success.

To use word category charts effectively as you study and read, do these four things:

1. Add more words and categories to the lists in the Vocabulary Appendix.
2. Use your dictionary and thesaurus to find the meaning of new words.
3. Make new flash cards to practice quick recall of the words.
4. Use the new words. Write sentences and short compositions in which the new words are used.

The following word category charts with related word form charts appear in the Vocabulary Appendix. The topics for the charts are selected to give you practice in areas often included in the Reading Comprehension Section of the TOEFL. Complete the word category charts and exercises for additional practice in vocabulary development after studying V✔10.

Business
Arts and Literature
Natural Science and Biology
Health and Medicine
Social Studies and History
Geography
Science
Descriptive Words

☞ BEFORE THE TOEFL

- Use word category charts to systematically study vocabulary.

EXERCISE 10A: Using a Word Category Chart

Below is a sample word category chart for words related to *air transportation*. Study this chart and note how it can be used as a study aid.

Word Category Chart: Air Transportation

Transport
airplane
jet
airliner
shuttle

_____

_____

People
pilot
copilot
stewardess
steward
flight attendant
air traffic controller
mechanic

_____

_____

Places
airport
terminal
ticket counter
runway
gate
baggage claim area
landing strip
airfield
control tower
security system

_____

_____

Possible problems
missing the flight
missing the connections
losing the baggage
overbooking
delays
crashing
being bumped
rough weather
turbulence
the expense

_____

Other terms
aviation
airlines
travel
fly
flight
arrival
departure
takeoff
landing
fueling
altitude
outbound
incoming
radar
schedule
carry-on
baggage
luggage
seat assignment

Activities
reserve
confirm
reschedule
check the bags
board

_____

_____

_____

_____

_____

_____

_____*Advantages*_____

_____*fast*_____

_____*comfortable*_____

_____

_____

_____

_____

_____

_____

EXERCISE 10B: More Practice with Word Category Charts

Add more words to the categories on the blanks provided in Exercise 10A. You can also add more categories. In Exercise 10A, the category *Activities* has been added to the original chart. You add the category *Advantages* and words for that category in the space provided in Exercise 10A.

EXERCISE 10C: Practice Using Words from the Word Category Chart

Fill in the blanks with words from the word category for *air transportation*.

Traveling by air is one of the major conveniences of the twentieth century. The whole field of _____ is geared to meet our needs for safe, efficient, and fast transportation. After a recent trip on a major _____ a passenger wrote the following account:

I began preparations for my trip early by calling the airline and making _____. A few days later I received my ticket telling me my _____ number and the times of _____ from my city and _____ at my destination. I was advised to arrive at the airline _____ an hour before takeoff in order to _____ for my flight, receive my seat _____, and _____ my baggage. It is important not to be late, or you might _____ the flight. On the day of my flight, I went to the ticket _____ where I was directed to the waiting area of the _____ from which my airplane would depart. As I entered this area I was checked through the _____ system. While I was waiting, I noticed how busy everyone was. The _____ were checking the plane for last minute repairs, and a large truck was _____ the plane with gasoline to make it ready for takeoff.

People in the _____ tower of the airport have a lot of responsibility. These _____ must supervise incoming and _____ flights and carefully monitor _____ and takeoffs. They must be sure that the _____ are clear and that weather conditions are relayed to the _____ of the airplanes using the _____.

When my flight was called I _____ the airplane. I was pleasantly greeted by the _____ and offered reading material and, after take-off, drinks and food. The weather was good, and there was no air _____ to cause us worry or discomfort. Although my flight was trouble free, during the holidays air travel becomes more hectic. Often airlines sell too many tickets for a flight and are then _____. Some unlucky passengers will be _____ and asked to reschedule on a later flight. Bad weather might also cause a later takeoff, and this _____ often results in missed _____ at the next stop. One of the most annoying aspects of air travel at holiday season is the possibility of _____ your luggage. I always try to carry on with me enough clothing for several days. On the whole, however, air travel is worth the expense. It is fast, safe, and usually reliable.

EXERCISE 10D: More Practice with Word Category Charts

The following word category chart for *music* is partially completed. Study the chart to recognize the categories listed. Then, read the list of music words that follows the chart and add these words to the appropriate categories in the spaces provided.

      NOTE: Words followed by an asterisk (*) are included in the word form chart for *music* in Exercise 10E.

Word Category Chart: Music

Types of music
blues
country western
heavy metal
hymns
modern
ragtime
reggae
spirituals
symphony*

_____

_____

_____

_____

_____

Musical groups
a marching band
a dance band
a concert artist: solo
an ensemble
small groups: duet, trio, quartet
a chorus*

_____

_____

_____

Attributes of musicians
talented*
gifted*
dedicated*
recognized*
praised*

_____

_____

_____

Types of performances
a cantana
a concert

_____

_____

_____

Musical instruments
a violin
a viola
drums*
a flute
a saxophone
a trumpet
a French Horn

_____

_____

_____

_____

_____

_____

_____

Musical activities
play
practice
audition*
accompany*

_____

_____

_____

Musical features
melody*
tone*

_____

_____

Places of performance
a music hall
a recital hall
a club
a performing arts center
a theater*
a coffeehouse

_____

_____

_____

Types of voice
alto
bass
contralto

_____

_____

_____

Other terms
lyrics of a song
a score of music
tune

_____

_____

_____

Add the following words to the categories for music in the chart. Use your dictionary if you don't know the meaning of the word.

an oboe*
concert hall
soprano
classical
a musical
jazz
rehearse*
a harp
rhythm*
an opera house
rock
debut*
a recital

tenor
a choir
a bass
sing*
a trombone
an orchestra*
folk
a clarinet
an oratorio
a piano
popular
harmony*
ballads
drums*

EXERCISE 10E: More Practice with Word Form Charts

The following word form chart for *music* has been partially filled in. Words followed by an asterisk in the word category chart for *music*, Exercise 10D, page 302, have been placed in the word form chart according to their different parts of speech. Fill in each blank space with the appropriate form of the word given. If there is no blank line, then there isn't a word for that part of speech. Use your dictionary if you need help.

Noun	Verb	Adjective	Adverb
hymn, hymnal	X	X	X
symphony	X		
chorus	X	choral	
orchestra	orchestrate		
audition		X	X
accompanist	accompany	X	X
_____	rehearse	X	X
debut	debut	X	X
_____	sing	singable	X
_____	X	talented	X
gift	X	gifted	X
_____	dedicate	dedicated	X
_____	recognize	recognized	X
praise	_____	praised	X
melody	X	_____	melodically
tone, tonality	tone	_____	tonally
X	X	atonal	_____
harmony	_____	harmonic	harmonically
rhythm	X	_____	rhythmically
piano, pianist	X	X	X
oboe, oboist	X	X	X
drum,_____	_____	X	X
theater	X	theatrical	_____

The Vocabulary Appendix #2, page 470, contains additional word form charts for you to use as you continue to increase your vocabulary for the TOEFL.

Reading Comprehension

The purpose of the Reading Comprehension Section of the TOEFL is to measure your ability to quickly read and understand a variety of short reading passages. You have approximately 30 minutes to read five or six passages and answer 30 multiple-choice questions about their meaning.

The topics of the reading passages in Section Three of the TOEFL are often academic in nature. Popular topics are the physical sciences (biology, physics, geology), American history (events and people), business, art and dance, literature, medicine, and the social sciences (sociology and psychology). Other topics for reading passages are general information about people and places in the United States. Whatever the topic, the style of the reading passages is formal English and they are written to give information appropriate for a first-year college student.

The questions about the reading passages can all be answered using information in the passages themselves. Outside knowledge of the subject matter is not necessary.

The biggest factor in the Reading Comprehension Section of the TOEFL is time. You should spend no more than 6 minutes on each passage and its questions.

Success in the Reading Comprehension Section will also depend on your knowledge of English vocabulary. In this section of the TOEFL, knowing the meaning of formal and academic words in English will help you to better understand the meaning of the reading passages. To develop your vocabulary for the Reading Comprehension Section of the TOEFL, you should work carefully through the Vocabulary Section of this book and read widely with attention to vocabulary. See the Vocabulary Appendix, pages 469–488 for more practice with vocabulary development.

Remember:
- Reading passages on the TOEFL are written in formal English and are general and academic in nature.

- Reading quickly with comprehension is the key to being successful on the Reading Comprehension Section of the TOEFL.

- A large vocabulary in English is very important for success on the Reading Comprehension Section of the TOEFL.

The passages and exercises in this part of the chapter use topics, language, and questions similar to those on the TOEFL. The following reading strategies and Reading Checkpoints will help you to develop your reading skills to be successful in the Reading Comprehension Section of the TOEFL.

1. Use your time wisely. You have only 30 to 35 minutes to read all the passages and answer 30 questions. This means you should spend only 6 minutes on each passage and its questions. Concentrate and work quickly.

2. Acquire a large vocabulary of formal and academic English to help you to better understand the meaning of the reading passages.

3. Read actively and concentrate on reading for information. Active reading is the most important strategy you can develop for this part of the TOEFL. See R✔1 and R✔2 to practice reading actively.

4. Identify the types of questions you will need to answer before you read the passage. Knowing what the questions are will help you to read more effectively and with a purpose. See R✔3–R✔8 for practice with question types on the TOEFL.

Reading Comprehension: Question Types

In the Reading Comprehension Section there are five or six passages that have 200 to 400 words. Each passage is followed by three to seven questions. There are 30 questions in the Reading Comprehension Section, and the most difficult passages are those at the end of this section.

MODEL

The following is a model reading comprehension passage and questions. Read the passage and answer the questions. Then read the explanation.

The dingo, Australia's wild dog, was first spotted on the northwest shores of the subcontinent in the late seventeenth century. The arrival of the dingo brought about substantial changes in the the continent's ecosystem. It is noted that with the establishment of dingoes, native predators declined. Among the animals probably displaced from the mainland by the dingo was the Tasmanian tiger, a recently extinct wolf-like marsupial.

1. What is the main point the author makes in this passage?
    (A) The dingo caused changes in Australia's balance of nature.
    (B) The dingo is not native to Australia.
    (C) The dingo is similar to a dog.
    (D) The dingo came to Australia in the 1600s.

2. According to the passage, after the dingoes arrived in Australia the Tasmanian tiger
    (A) took on the characteristics of a wolf
    (B) began hunting the dingo
    (C) began to die out
    (D) moved to the south of the continent

Continued

3. We can infer from the passage that the dingo
   - (A) is becoming extinct
   - (B) was not domesticated in large numbers
   - (C) lives in a particular part of Australia
   - (D) befriended many native animals

Answers:

▼ Explanation ▲

The correct answer to Question 1 is (A). Although all four choices are true, the main point of the passage is (A) *The dingo caused changes in Australia's balance of nature*. The passage states *The arrival of the dingo brought about substantial changes in the continent's ecosystem*. This point is then supported by information in the next two sentences.

The correct answer to Question 2 is (C). None of the choices is true from the information in the passage except (C) *began to die out*. The last sentence in the passage states: *Among the animals that the dingo probably displaced was the Tasmanian tiger, a recently extinct wolf-like marsupial*. The words *displaced* and *recently extinct* are similar in meaning to the choice *began to die out*, which is the correct answer.

The correct answer to Question 3 is (B). We do not have enough information in the passage to infer any of the choices except (B) *was not domesticated in large numbers*. We can infer this because in the first sentence of the passage the dingo was described as *Australia's wild dog*. We know that *wild* is similar in meaning to *not domesticated*, which makes (B) the best answer.

The TOEFL will test your ability to read a passage quickly for information and to answer questions about the meaning of the passage. This is the same type of reading that you will be asked to do in an academic course or in job-related tasks. In order to develop your ability to read well in English you need to develop effective reading skills and strategies. The following strategies will help you with the questions in the Reading Comprehension Section of the TOEFL.

READING COMPREHENSION QUESTION STRATEGIES

1. Read the first and last sentences of the passage to establish the topic and main idea. Skim the passage for the key concepts and vocabulary. Answer the first question. See R✔2 to practice this strategy.

2. Read the questions following the passage to find out what information you are looking for. DO NOT read the answer choices at this time; just read the questions.

3. Read the passage carefully, keeping in mind the questions you will have to answer.

4. Answer the questions. Use key words and phrases in the questions to scan the passage for the correct answer. When you find the answer in the passage, match it with one of the answer choices.

5. **Guess if you do not know the correct answer.** Use any clues in the question and passage to make your best guess. If you finish the Reading Comprehension Section before the time is up, you can go back to questions that you were not sure about.

Reading Appendix #1, pages 489–498, contains a special section, **A Good Overall Reading Strategy**. This section is meant to give additional practice in the reading skills and strategies that you should use in the reading that you do outside *The Heinemann TOEFL Preparation Course*. Becoming a good reader takes time and practice beyond the scope of this book. Complete Reading Appendix #1 if you need additional work on developing good reading strategies.

✔ READING COMPREHENSION CHECKPOINTS

Following is a list of the Reading Comprehension Checkpoints which are included in the Reading Checkpoint Study. Page numbers are provided for easy reference. If the Diagnostic Test on pages 19–41 indicated that reading comprehension was your weak area, work carefully through these checkpoints. The Reading Checkpoint Study will help you to develop good reading skills and strategies as you prepare for the Reading Comprehension Section of the TOEFL.

✔ READING COMPREHENSION CHECKPOINT STUDY

R✔1   Build Good Reading Skills: Skim and Scan

The reading skills of skimming and scanning are very important when you need to read quickly for information.

Skimming means reading quickly for general meaning. You skim reading material to find out about the topic, the main ideas, and the general organization of a passage.

Scanning means knowing what information you need to find before you read. Then your eyes move quickly to find that particular information. You scan when you are looking for a fact or a detail or a particular vocabulary word.

The reading skills of skimming and scanning will be very useful to you in the Reading Comprehension Section of the TOEFL. Because the TOEFL is a timed reading situation, reading quickly for meaning is extremely important in order to finish the test and to answer questions correctly.

☞ BEFORE THE TOEFL TEST

- Skim and scan as you practice reading the short passages in this book and in your outside reading.

As you practice skimming and scanning with reading materials, you will develop an active reading strategy.

Think about the following reading passages and questions. Answer each question before you read the explanation.

MODEL

People are still reading books, and lots of them. The number of new books published keeps growing—90,000 new titles in the United States during the last year by the latest industry count. The number is double the total output two decades ago. Reading is still an important part of our lives.

1. What is this passage about?
   - (A) The amount of reading people do
   - (B) Book reviews
   - (C) Leisure time activities
   - (D) A popular new book

2. How many new books were published in the United States last year?
   - (A) 60,000
   - (B) 900
   - (C) 9,000
   - (D) 90,000

Answers:

▼ Explanation ▲

The correct answer to Question 1 is (A) *The amount of reading people do*. By reading the first sentence of the passage you find the phrases *reading books* and *lots of them*. As you quickly read the rest of the paragraph you find these words and ideas repeated in different ways. You could answer the question by quickly skimming the passage for the general idea.

The correct answer to Question 2 is (D) *90,000*. The question asks how many, and this tells you to look for a number. By scanning the passage for a number, you are able to find the correct answer of *90,000*.

MODEL

The average book reader spends more than one hour a day poring over the pages, often just before bed. Readers are not an idle lot. They are busy people, tennis players, skiers, gardeners. "TV isn't really a problem," insists John Y. Cole, director of the Center for Books. Reading experts say that television programs based on books actually stimulate book sales. People find time to read because they enjoy reading, and they adjust their schedules to include time to pursue this activity.

3. This paragraph is about
   (A) the continued popularity of reading
   (B) favorite programs of TV viewers
   (C) busy people
   (D) popular outdoor sports

4. Who is John Y. Cole?
   (A) A TV viewer
   (B) A tennis player
   (C) Director of the Center for Books
   (D) A book salesman

Answers:

▼ Explanation ▲

The correct answer to Question 3 is (A) *the continued popularity of reading*. By skimming the first sentence of the passage you find the phrases *average book reader* and *more than one hour a day*. By skimming the last sentence you find this idea repeated in the phrases *find time to read* and *adjust their schedules to include time to pursue this activity*.

The correct answer to Question 4 is (C) *Director of the Center for Books*. The question asks about a name. By scanning the passage to find the name you locate the information to answer the question.

EXERCISE 1A: Practice Skimming for General Information

Skim the passage in 30 seconds. DO NOT spend more than this amount of time on your first reading of the passage. Then, read each question, and circle the correct answer.

Sometimes called puma, panther, or mountain lion, the agile cougar has a greater natural range than any other mammal in the Western Hemisphere except humans. However, long viewed as a threat to livestock, it has been intensively hunted since the arrival of European colonists to the Americas and was almost extinct by the early twentieth century. While protective measures have been implemented in the United States, humans continue to destroy the cougar's habitat, further endangering this solitary cat.

1. This passage is about
    (A) a person
    (B) a place
    (C) an animal
    (D) a time

2. This passage discusses
    (A) a problem
    (B) a solution
    (C) an opinion
    (D) a policy

3. The author of this passage expresses
   (A) love
   (B) concern
   (C) joy
   (D) anger

EXERCISE 1B: Practice Scanning for Details

Allow yourself one minute to do this exercise. Read the questions below about the passage in Exercise 1A. Then, using the related words in bold print below, QUICKLY scan the passage to find the answer to each question. Circle the answer when you find it in the passage.

1. The cougar is known by how many **other names**?

2. In what **part of the world** does the cougar live?

3. At what point in time did the cougar face **extinction**?

4. What **country** has measures to **protect** the cougar?

EXERCISE 1C: More Practice Skimming

Skim this passage in 45 seconds. DO NOT spend more than this amount of time on your first reading of the passage. Then, read each question, and circle the correct answer.

> In marine habitats, a number of small creatures are involved in a "cleaning symbiosis." At least six species of small shrimp, frequently brightly colored, crawl over fish, picking off parasites and cleaning injured areas. This is not an accidental occurrence, because fish are observed to congregate around these shrimp and stay motionless while being inspected. Several species of small fish (wrasses) are also cleaners, nearly all of them having appropriate adaptations such as long snouts, tweezer-like teeth, and bright coloration. Conspicuous coloration probably communicates that these animals are not prey.

1. This passage is mainly about
   (A) a process of marine life
   (B) a place in the sea
   (C) a species of marine life
   (D) a mystery of marine life

2. The habitat described in this passage is
   (A) an aquarium
   (B) an island
   (C) the ocean
   (D) a laboratory

3. The "cleaning symbiosis" discussed in the passage is
   (A) unimportant
   (B) harmful
   (C) predatory
   (D) beneficial

EXERCISE 1D: More Practice Scanning

Allow yourself two minutes to do this exercise. Read the questions below about the passage in Exercise 1C. Then, using the related words in bold print below, scan the passage to answer each question. Circle the answer when you find it in the passage.

1. What **two types of marine life** are involved in "**cleaning** symbiosis"?

2. What **two jobs** are accomplished in this activity?

3. What type of fish are "**cleaners**"?

4. How are fish that act as "**cleaners**" **especially equipped** to do this job?

5. What **protects** these fish from **being eaten by other fish**?

EXERCISE 1E: More Practice Skimming

Skim this passage in 60 seconds. **Do not** spend more than this amount of time on the first reading of the passage. Then, read each question, and circle the correct answer.

The northern lights, or the aurora borealis, is one of nature's most dazzling spectacles. When it appears, there is often a crackling sound coming from the sky. A huge, line luminous arc lights up the night, and
line this arc is constantly in motion. Sometimes, the brilliant rays of light
(5)   spread upward in the shape of a fan. At other times, they flash here and there like giant searchlights, or move up and down so suddenly that they have been called "the merry dancers." Farther north the aurora frequently looks like fiery draperies which hang from the sky and sway to and fro while flames of red, orange, green, and blue play up and down the moving
(10)   folds.
According to scientific measurements, this discharge of light takes place from 50 to 100 miles above the earth. But it doesn't reach its greatest brilliance at the North Pole. It is seen at its best around the Hudson Bay region in Canada, in northern Scotland, and in southern Norway and
(15)   Sweden. It may sometimes be seen even in the United States as it flashes across the northern sky.
Science is still not certain regarding exactly what these lights are and what causes them. But it is believed that the rays are due to discharges of electricity in the rare upper atmosphere. The displays seem to center about
(20)   the earth's magnetic poles, and electrical and magnetic disturbances often occur when the lights are especially brilliant.

1. This passage is about
   (A) a scientific phenomenon
   (B) a natural disaster
   (C) an architectural monument
   (D) a natural landform

2. This passage discusses the findings of
   (A) teachers
   (B) scientists
   (C) northerners
   (D) artists

3. In which part of the passage does the author discuss what the aurora borealis looks like?
   (A) Paragraph 1
   (B) Paragraph 2
   (C) Paragraph 3
   (D) Whole passage

4. Paragraph 2 mainly discusses northern lights in relation to their
   (A) size
   (B) colors
   (C) location
   (D) cause

5. From Paragraph 3 we learn that the cause of northern lights is
   (A) uncertain
   (B) beyond belief
   (C) uninvestigated
   (D) well established

EXERCISE 1F: More Practice Scanning

Allow yourself up to one minute to do this exercise. Read the questions below about the passage in Exercise 1E. Then, using the related words in bold print below, scan the passage to answer each question. Circle the answer when you find it in the passage.

1. Why have the northern lights been called **"the merry dancers"**?

2. **How many miles** above the earth does the aurora borealis take place?

3. In what part of **Canada** can the northern lights best be seen?

4. What do scientists believe is **discharged in the earth's atmosphere** to cause the aurora borealis?

☛ BEFORE THE TOEFL TEST

- Practice the skills of skimming and scanning whenever you read for information. Practice with these skills will make you a better active reader and more confident when you are reading in the TOEFL test.

The questions about the reading passages in Section Three of the TOEFL can be classified into seven general types. Each of the Checkpoints R✔2–R✔8 corresponds to one of the seven question types. Use the skills of skimming and scanning that you learned about in R✔1 as you complete the following Reading Comprehension Checkpoints on TOEFL question types.

R✔2   Check the Topic, Main Idea, and Title of a Passage

Almost all TOEFL passages contain one question about either the topic or subject, the main idea, or the best title of a reading passage. This type of question is usually the first question about the passage. These questions ask about the whole passage, not just a part of the passage. In order to correctly answer these questions, you should use the skimming and scanning strategies practiced in R✔1.

To answer questions on the TOEFL about the topic, the main idea, or the best title of a passage, follow these steps:

1. Read the first several sentences for the topic and main idea.
2. Read the last sentences for the conclusion and a possible restatement of the topic and main idea.
3. Skim the rest of the passage for the key words that will confirm the topic and the main idea and show the organization of the passage.
4. Read the first question about the passage and answer it.
5. Read the answer choices. Eliminate any answers that are definitely wrong, and choose the best answer from the remaining ones.

Think about the following passage. Answer the questions before you read the explanation.

In the critical area of food production, new cooperative efforts in agricultural research and development are paying off. Food scientists are discovering that humankind is nowhere near the limits of plant, livestock, and soil productivity. There is still room to boost yields and learn how to use more efficiently the earth's acreage for animal and crop husbandry. Investigation of irrigation procedures, pest control, intercropping, and multicropping are several areas that are providing useful information for the world's farmers.

1. What is the topic of this passage?
    (A) Agricultural research and food production
    (B) Farmers throughout the world
    (C) Food scientists
    (D) Investigation of irrigation procedures

2. The main idea of this passage is
    (A) new information from agricultural research can increase world food production
    (B) food production is declining around the world
    (C) agricultural research and development will be expensive
    (D) irrigation procedures, pest control, intercropping and multicropping are important areas of investigation

3. Which of the following is the best title for this passage?
    (A) Food in Different Parts of the World
    (B) New Hope for the World's Farmers
    (C) Food Scientists
    (D) Using the Earth's Resources

Answers:

▼ Explanation ▲

The correct answer to Question 1 is (A) *Agricultural research and food production*. This question asks you about the topic of the passage, which is the most general statement you make about a passage. In the first sentence of this passage the phrases *food production* and *agricultural research and development* give you this basic concept. The rest of the information in the passage supports the statement in the first sentence. Answers (B), (C), and (D) are too specific to be the topic of the passage. Answer (A) is the most general statement in the passage.

The correct answer to Question 2 is (A) *new information from agricultural research can increase world food production*. This question asks you about the main idea of the passage. The main idea of a passage tells you something more about the topic. In this passage the author tell us that *efforts of agricultural research and development in the area of food production are **paying off***, which means they are beneficial. Other key words that develop this concept are: *nowhere near the limits of...productivity; boost yields...use more efficiently; investigation...useful information for the world's farmers*. Answer (B) is not true; answer (C) is not mentioned in the passage; and answer (D) is supporting information, not the main idea.

The correct answer to Question 3 is (B) *New Hope for the World's Farmers*. This question asks you to identify the best title for the passage. The best title will usually restate parts of both the topic and the main idea. Answer (A) does not include ideas mentioned in the passage. Answers (C) and (D) are both too specific. Answer (B) includes the topic by referring to *World's Farmers* and also includes the main idea with the paraphrase *New Hope*.

Read About the Topic

The topic of a passage is what the passage is mainly about. It can usually be stated in a few words and is the most general statement that can be made about the passage. To identify the topic of a passage, read the first and last sentences of the passage. Skim through the passage and notice the words that are repeated exactly or are repeated as synonyms or pronouns many times throughout the passage. These key words should give you a clue to the topic.

TOEFL questions about the topic of a passage are often worded as follows:

What is the topic of this passage?
This passage mainly discusses...
What does this passage mainly discuss?
This passage deals mainly with...
What is the subject of this passage?

☛ ON THE TOEFL TEST
• Remember that topic questions ask about the whole passage.

NOTE: The terms *subject* and *topic* are often used interchangeably in questions on the Reading Comprehension Section of the TOEFL test.

EXERCISE 2A: Practice Predicting the Topic from the Key Words

Read the following key words to predict the probable topic of the reading passage from which they were taken. Circle the letter of the probable topic.

1. Reservations, February, snow conditions, ski pass, rentals, ice skating, sauna, on the other hand, water temperature, beach, swimming, suntan, fishing.
   (A) Recreational activities
   (B) Two types of winter vacations
   (C) Learning to ski
   (D) Choosing a pastime

2. Basic document, seismogram, literature of the earthquake, analyze the waves, calculate, power, duration, surface location, precise origin, movement along the fault, piece of paper, piece of tape.
   (A) Recording an earthquake
   (B) Predicting an earthquake
   (C) Photographing an earthquake
   (D) The structure of the earth

3. Sweet corn, home gardens, warm weather crop, plant early, August harvest, corn-on-the-cob, canning, freezing, relishes, eating pleasure, good nutrition.
   (A) The history of sweet corn
   (B) Where to grow sweet corn
   (C) Common corn recipes
   (D) Sweet corn as a garden vegetable

4. Radio, AM transmitters, high signal, 1920s, at first, mass listening, earphones, Pittsburgh, Chicago, pioneer, later on, loudspeaker, living room, weekly broadcasts, favorite shows.
   (A) Radio programming
   (B) The development of AM radio
   (C) Early communications
   (D) The first radio stations

5. Form, space, light, architect, superficial effects, International Style, box-like, inhibiting to spatial freedom, devoid of any organic relationship with nature, peas in a pod.
   (A) Architectural criticism
   (B) Restrictive building codes
   (C) Garden vegetables
   (D) Natural forms in housing

Read About the Main Idea

The main idea of a passage is a statement about the topic which indicates a point of view about the topic. While the topic is stated as an answer to the question "What is the passage about?" the main idea answers the question "What is important about the topic?" A main idea is most often a full sentence which contains a statement about the topic. To identify the main idea of a sentence, look for key words that show a relationship to the topic and are repeated throughout the passage. The main idea is often restated in the conclusion of the passage.

TOEFL questions about the main idea are often worded as follows:

What is the main idea of this passage?
What is the author's main point in this passage?

EXERCISE 2B: Practice Identifying the Topic, Main Idea, and Details in a Series of Statements from a Reading Passage

Skim all four statements for each question. Label each statement: *T* for topic, *MI* for main idea, or *D* for details.

_D_ 1. Electrical failure is a constant concern to both engineers and ground control.

_T_   Problems with the NASA space program

_MI_   Technical problems have consistently delayed progress in the NASA space program.

_D_   Fuselage leaks caused postponement of the latest shuttle flight.

____ 2. The technique involves inserting genetic instructions into the bacteria, which follow the instructions.

____   Producing human insulin

____   Humulin is the first substance made by gene-splicing approved by the U.S. government for human use.

____   The instructions involve creating the two necessary ingredients to make insulin.

_____ 3. With the Appalachian Trail following the state line along the ridge, this is a wonderful place to hike from spring to fall.

_____ Each season will offer visitors to the park an array of sights and activities.

_____ Smoky Mountain National Park

_____ Mountain laurel and flame azalea bloom in early June to mid-July.

_____ 4. Fungal foods, of which corn smut is perhaps the ugliest, may soon become part of American *nouvelle cuisine*.

_____ Most people in the United States view corn smut with revulsion because they question the safety of fungal foods in general.

_____ The mushroom-like fungus has long played a part in the diet of Native American cultures.

_____ New uses for "corn smut"

_____ 5. For instance, air freight may be much more expensive than rail transport, but shipping everything from a single warehouse may cut other costs.

_____ The cost of transportation

_____ Many companies today use the total physical distribution concept, maximizing the efficiency of physical distribution activities while minimizing their cost.

_____ The company will make cost tradeoffs between the various physical distribution activities.

Read About the Title

A TOEFL question about the best title for a short reading passage will test your understanding of both the topic and the main idea. The best title for a passage will include the key words of the topic. It will often include key words from the main idea. In some cases the exact words for the main idea will be replaced by synonyms or a paraphrase. Words that indicate the organization of the passage may also occur in the title. Very often the last sentences of a passage will be a summary of the topic and main idea and provide important clues for a title question.

In answer choices for TOEFL questions about the title of a passage, the title is written using capital letters for the main words. A title is often stated as a collection of key words from the passage, and not as a complete sentence.

TOEFL questions on the title are often worded as follows:

What is the best title for the passage?
Which of the following is the best title for the passage?

To be successful at selecting the best title for a short reading passage follow these steps:

1. Skim and scan to establish the topic and main ideas, and to find the key words.
2. Read the answer choices to match the key words from the passage with those in the answer choices.
3. Eliminate wrong answer choices.
4. Select the best choice from those remaining.

EXERCISE 2C: Practice Predicting the Best Title for a Reading Passage Based on Main Ideas from the Passage

Read the key sentences. Circle the letter of the best title for a passage containing these key sentences.

1. All caged birds need a home that is large and roomy.

    Most finches need a cage with narrow spaces between the bars.

    Almost any garden setting is ideal for an aviary, as long as it is out of the wind's path.

    A. Caged Birds
    B. The Proper Home for Your Bird
    C. Finding the Right Bird

2. Deciduous forest communities once formed a continuous band across eastern North America.

    In its natural state it is rich in species, net production is high, and the structure of the ecosystem is stable.

    Today much of this area is occupied and utilized by human beings, so that the biome rarely is found in its original state.

    A. Forest Ecosystems
    B. The Changing Deciduous Forest
    C. Human Influence on Biomes

3. Numerology begins with your name and your birthdate.

    During the time of Pýthagoras, the famous Greek mathematician and philosopher, numerology was reserved for the rulers, who often used it to make critical decisions.
    Sometimes understanding yourself is just as important as understanding someone else.

    A. Personality Disorders and Their Cure
    B. Ancient Mathematicians
    C. Describing You Through Numbers

4. Early in the seventeenth century, settlers from western France came to what is now Nova Scotia's fertile Annapolis Basin.

    Their new homeland of Acadie fell under British rule in 1755, and 10,000 Acadians were deported, captured, or detained.

    By 1765 a few hundred had settled in Louisiana, while 2,500 impoverished Acadians congregated in French maritime ports.

    In 1785 the Spanish king transported about 1,600 Acadians to Louisiana; this has been called the largest single transatlantic migration up to that time, the end of a 30-year exile.

    A. The Early Settling of North America
    B. Acadians on the Move
    C. A Transatlantic Migration

5. The art of judo lies not so much in great strength as in skillful use of the body and mind.

Judo involves a complex system of physical and mental skills that help produce both mental and physical fitness.

Consisting of hundreds of techniques, every movement in judo has a definite meaning and purpose.

A. Judo: More Than a Sport
B. Judo and Physical Fitness
C. Disadvantages of Judo

EXERCISE 2D: Practice Identifying the Topic, Main Idea, and Best Title of a Reading Passage

Read the passage and answer the questions. Circle the correct answer to each question.

Sometimes called puma, panther, or mountain lion, the agile cougar has a greater natural range than any other mammal in the Western Hemisphere except humans. However, long viewed as a threat to livestock, it has been intensively hunted since the arrival of European colonists to the Americas and was almost extinct by the early twentieth century. While protective measures have been implemented in the United States, humans continue to destroy the cougar's habitat, further endangering this solitary cat.

1. What is the topic of the passage?
   (A) The cougar
   (B) Mammals of the Western Hemisphere
   (C) Endangered species
   (D) A threat to livestock

2. What is the main idea of the passage?
   (A) The cougar has a large natural habitat.
   (B) The cougar is still an endangered animal.
   (C) The cougar is a threat to livestock.
   (D) The cougar was almost extinct in the early twentieth century.

3. What is the best title for the passage?
   (A) The Habitat of the Cougar
   (B) The Cougar: A Threat to Livestock
   (C) Protecting the Cougar
   (D) The Endangered Cougar

EXERCISE 2E: More Practice Identifying the Topic, Main Idea, and Best Title

Read the passage and answer the questions. Circle the correct answer to each question.

In marine habitats, a number of small creatures are involved in a "cleaning symbiosis." At least six species of small shrimp, frequently brightly colored, crawl over fish, picking off parasites and cleaning injured areas. This is not an accidental occurrence, because fish are observed to congregate around these shrimp and stay motionless while being inspected. Several species of small fish (wrasses) are also cleaners, nearly all of them having appropriate adaptations such as long snouts, tweezer-like teeth, and bright coloration. Conspicuous coloration probably communicates that these animals are not prey.

1. What is the topic of this passage?
   (A) Marine life
   (B) Why fish need to be cleaned
   (C) How certain sea creatures clean other fish
   (D) How fish are adapted to be cleaners

2. What is the main idea of the passage?
   (A) Some fish need to be cleaned.
   (B) Cleaning symbiosis is an important aspect of marine life.
   (C) Certain fish are better adapted to be cleaners than others.
   (D) Cleaner fish are brightly colored.

3. What is the best title for the passage?
   (A) Shrimp and Fish
   (B) Nature's Cleaners of the Deep
   (C) Protective Coloration for Fish
   (D) Why Fish Are Cleaners

EXERCISE 2F: More Practice Identifying the Topic, Main Idea, and Best Title

Read the passage and answer the questions. Circle the correct answer to each question.

> The northern lights, or the aurora borealis, is one of nature's most dazzling spectacles. When it appears, there is often a crackling sound coming from the sky. A huge, line luminous arc lights up the night, and
> *line* this arc is constantly in motion. Sometimes, the brilliant rays of light
> *(5)* spread upward in the shape of a fan. At other times, they flash here and there like giant searchlights, or move up and down so suddenly that they have been called "the merry dancers." Farther north the aurora frequently looks like fiery draperies which hang from the sky and sway to and fro while flames of red, orange, green, and blue play up and down the moving
> *(10)* folds.
>
> According to scientific measurements, this discharge of light takes place from 50 to 100 miles above the earth. But it doesn't reach its greatest brilliance at the North Pole. It is seen at its best around the Hudson Bay region in Canada, in northern Scotland, and in southern Norway and
> *(15)* Sweden. It may sometimes be seen even in the United States as it flashes across the northern sky.
>
> Science is still not certain regarding exactly what these lights are and what causes them. But it is believed that the rays are due to discharges of electricity in the rare upper atmosphere. The displays seem to center about
> *(20)* the earth's magnetic poles, and electrical and magnetic disturbances often occur when the lights are especially brilliant.

1. What is the topic of this passage?
   (A) What the northern lights look like
   (B) The northern lights
   (C) The cause of the northern lights
   (D) Where to best see the northern lights

2. What is the author's main point in Paragraph 2?
   (A) The northern lights can be best seen in northern skies at some distance from the North Pole.
   (B) The northern lights are brightest at the North Pole.
   (C) The distance from earth of the discharge of light can be measured by scientists.
   (D) The northern lights are observable in the United States.

3. What is the best title for the passage?
   (A) Lights in the North
   (B) The Northern Lights: Nature's Fireworks
   (C) Brilliant Electrical Discharges
   (D) Where to See the Northern Lights

EXERCISE 2G: More Practice Identifying the Topic, Main Idea, and Best Title

Read the passage and answer the questions. Circle the correct answer to each question.

Coral reefs are to the seas what rain forests are to the land. Teeming with life, these ecosystems depend upon sunlight and an intricate relationship between plant and line animal to survive.

line
(5)   The brilliant blue of the Red Sea is an unexpected sight within the dry expanse of the Middle Eastern desert. Even more unexpected, however, is the myriad of colorful marine creatures which thrive in its shallow reefs and deep slopes.Half a world away in Australia's Coral Sea, a pair of clownfish will find protection in the reef as they patiently guard their eggs until they hatch. Strangely enough, these fish are actually poor swimmers
(10) and seldom stray far from the protective cover provided by the sea anemones which dwell in their coral reef homes.

Another colorful addition to coral reefs appears as a rose-like creation. It is actually a ribbon of thousands of tiny nudibranch eggs. Nudibranches are a variety of very colorful, strangely shaped gastropods which can be
(15) found in the world's warm seas and which feed on sponges, hydroid polyps, sea anemones, moss animals, or sea squirts.

1. What is the topic of this passage?
   (A) Colorful fish
   (B) Rain forests
   (C) Coral reefs
   (D) Ecosystems of the world

2. What is the author's main point in this passage?
   (A) Coral reefs provide an ecosystem to support fish and plant life.
   (B) Coral reefs are found in warm waters of the world.
   (C) Fish found in coral reefs are very colorful.
   (D) Coral reefs are different from rain forests.

3. What is the best title for this passage?
   (A) Plant Life in a Coral Reef
   (B) Facts About Fish
   (C) Comparative Ecosystems
   (D) Colorful Ecosystems of the Sea

See the Reading Appendix #2, pages 489–498, for more information on the Topic, Main Idea, and Title of a reading passage. In the Tapescripts and Answers Book, *you will find explanations for the answers to the questions in Exercises 2D–2G.*

R✔3   Check Purpose and Organizational Patterns

Some TOEFL Reading Comprehension questions ask about the author's purpose for the passage or about the organization of the passage.

The purpose of a passage is the reason the author wrote the passage, or the intent of the author in writing the passage. The organizational pattern of a reading passage is the way that the author arranges the information to carry out his or her purpose or intent in writing the passage. TOEFL questions about the general organizational pattern of a passage ask you about the style the author uses in his or her writing rather than the purpose of the whole passage.

Think about the following passage and questions. Answer the questions before reading the explanation.

MODEL

The art of writing itself is a good example of what students of the past call independent invention, since systems of writing have evolved in isolation at different times in different parts of the world. For example, one
line system—the Chinese ideogram—can be traced to its origin in archaic signs
(5) engraved on the scapular bones of sheep or the shells of turtles in the second millennium B.C. as a means of asking questions of heaven. Roughly 1,000 years later an entirely independent system of writing arose halfway around the world in Mesoamerica. It combined a simple system of numerical notation with complex hieroglyphs and was principally used to
(10 indicate the dates of various events according to an elaborate calendrical system.

1. What is the purpose of this passage?
   (A)   To show that writing is an example of independent invention.
   (B)   To explain the origin of writing.
   (C)   To describe two systems of writing.
   (D)   To compare writing in China to writing in Mesoamerica.

2. Which of the following best describes the organization of the passage?
   (A)   A comparison of two competing systems
   (B)   An examination of a problem
   (C)   A statement supported by examples
   (D)   A chronological development

3. Where in the passage does the author describe the early writing system of Mesoamerica?
   (A)   Lines 1–3
   (B)   Lines 3–7
   (C)   Lines 6–8
   (D)   Lines 8–11

Answers:

▼ Explanation ▲

The correct answer to Question 1 is (A). The sentence *Writing is an example of independent invention* contains both the topic and main idea of the passage. The use of examples to support this is represented by *To show that*. Answers (B) and (C) are not true, and answer (D) is not specific enough for this passage.

The correct answer to Question 2 is (C). The first sentence of the passage states that *systems of writing have evolved in isolation at different times in different parts of the world*. From this we understand the topic (systems of writing) and the main idea (evolved in isolation). The second sentence begins with *For example, one system...* in lines 3–4, which repeats the topic. In line 7, *an entirely independent system...arose* introduces the second example, again repeating the topic and the main idea. Answer (C) *A statement supported by examples* correctly represents the organization of the passage. Answer (A) is incorrect because there is no comparison made and the systems of writing are not competing. Answer (B) is incorrect because the main idea is not a problem but a statement of fact. Answer (D) is incorrect because although dates and years are mentioned in the passage, they are used to support the main idea and not as the organizational pattern.

The correct answer to Question 3 is (D). In line 8 we find the word Mesoamerica. The question asks about the description of the writing system of Mesoamerica, which is found in lines 8–11. In lines 6–8, preceding the word Mesoamerica, the passage states when and what happened in Mesoamerica rather than describing the writing system. Lines 1–3 are the topic and main idea, and lines 3–7 describe the origin of the Chinese ideogram.

TOEFL questions about the purpose of a whole passage are often worded as:

What is the purpose of this passage?
The main purpose of this passage is to...
What is the author's main purpose in the passage?

In addition to asking questions about the purpose of the whole passage, TOEFL Reading Comprehension questions may also ask you about specific purposes within the passage.

TOEFL questions about a specific purpose within a passage are often worded as:

Why does the author mention X in the passage?
In the X paragraph the author mentions Y in order to...
In line X why does the author mention Y?

Common verbs used in answer choices for TOEFL questions about purpose are:

to discuss	to warn
to tell about	to discredit
to summarize	to describe
to tell how	to praise
to explain	to advocate
to present	to predict
to show	to persuade
to illustrate	to convince
to classify	to compare and contrast

Words often used in the answer choices that describe these specific purposes are:

to prove
to verify
to support
to underscore
to point out

Use your dictionary to find the meaning of these verbs.

EXERCISE 3A: Practice with Verbs Used in Questions About Purpose

Match each verb on the left with the correct definition on the right.

_E_	1. to predict	A. to support, to plead in favor of
____	2. to illustrate	B. to inform of possible trouble or problems
____	3. to contrast	C. to emphasize
____	4. to persuade	D. to show that something is true
____	5. to praise	E. to tell in advance; to foresee
____	6. to warn	F. to express approval or admiration
____	7. to classify	G. to influence or convince a person to believe in a certain way
____	8. to advocate	H. to arrange in order by class or category
____	9. to discredit	I. to examine by argument; to comment on
____	10. to discuss	J. to give additional evidence
____	11. to underscore	K. to destroy confidence in
____	12. to verify	L. to show the differences
____	13. to support	M. to make clear by example

TOEFL questions about the organizational pattern of a reading are often worded as follows:

Which of the following best describes the organization of the passage?
Which of the following best describes the format of the passage?
Where in the passage does the author (compare, classify, describe) X?

Words in the answer choices that describe these organizational patterns are:

a description
an illustration
an introduction
a classification
a comparison
a summary
a criticism
an explanation
giving a set of instructions
showing through examples

a process
a definition
a contrast
cause and effect
chronological order
a response
a hypothesis

Some words that signal organizational patterns are:
>   for example
>   on the other hand, in contrast
>   similarly, likewise
>   therefore, thus, as a result
>   (dates), by the time, later

See the Reading Appendix, #3, pages 497–498 for a more complete list of signal words for organizational patterns.

EXERCISE 3B: Practice Identifying Organizational Patterns

Read the following phrases from reading passages. Then, choose the appropriate organizational pattern from the list below, and write it in the space provided.

>   a process   further definition
>   a classification   chronological order
>   cause and effect   a comparison
>   a contrast

1. The major kinds of, fundamental characteristics, clearly distinguishable features, insignificant differences

    _____*a classification*_____

2. Later, subsequently, during that time, afterwards, as an adult

    _____

3. Likewise, in the same way, correspondingly, another resemblance

    _____

4. On the other hand, unlike, even so, however, differ from

    _____

5. Consequently, thus, due to, owing to, it follows that

    _____

6. Initially we will..., the next step, the projected results, a foreseeable outcome,

    _____

7. To clarify, in other words, by...is meant, to restate

    _____

Very often the organizational pattern of a passage is not signaled by the use of specific words or phrases. In these cases you must reason logically to understand the organizational pattern used.

EXERCISE 3C: Practice Identifying the Purpose and Organizational Patterns of a Reading Passage

Look again at the reading passage in Exercise 2D, page 319. Read the passage and circle the letter of the best answer to each question.

1. What is the purpose of the passage?
   (A) To warn readers about the threat of the cougar to livestock
   (B) To discuss the natural range of the cougar
   (C) To inform readers about the continued endangerment of the cougar
   (D) To describe the history of the cougar in the Western Hemisphere

2. Why does the author mention in the passage that the cougar was almost extinct by the early twentieth century?
   (A) To emphasize that the cougar is an endangered animal
   (B) To show similarities between the cougar and other endangered animals
   (C) To indicate that the colonists were skilled hunters
   (D) To prove that the cougar is a dangerous animal

EXERCISE 3D: More Practice Identifying the Purpose and Organizational Patterns of a Reading Passage

Look again at the reading passage in Exercise 2E, page 320. Read the passage and circle the letter of the best answer to each question.

1. The main purpose of the passage is to
   (A) describe a biological process of association in a marine habitat
   (B) discuss activities of certain sea creatures
   (C) contrast cleaning activities of shrimp and fish
   (D) describe adaptations of fish for particular jobs

2. Which of the following best describes the format of this passage?
   (A) A hypothesis followed by support
   (B) A statement followed by a description
   (C) A response to a question
   (D) An extended definition

EXERCISE 3E: More Practice Identifying the Purpose and Organizational Patterns of a Reading Passage

Look again at the reading passage for Exercise 2F, page 321. Read the passage and circle the letter of the best answer to each question.

1. What is the purpose of the passage?
   (A) To discredit scientists for not knowing the cause or the exact nature of the northern lights
   (B) To discuss the general characteristics of the northern lights
   (C) To describe the appearance of the northern lights
   (D) To tell readers where the northern lights may best be seen

2. Why does the author use the term "merry dancers" in line 7?
   (A) To suggest the feeling that watching the lights would bring about
   (B) To compare the movement of the lights to movements of dancers
   (C) To encourage people to view the aurora borealis
   (D) To point out that the lights are not a serious scientific phenomenon

EXERCISE 3F: More Practice Identifying the Purpose and Organizational Patterns of a Reading Passage

Read the passage and answer the questions. Circle the letter of each correct answer.

The potato is probably one of the most important vegetable crops in the United States today. The potato's original home is in the mountainous regions of South America, although it is referred to as the Irish potato. It
line was cultivated rather extensively by the Inca Indians of Peru as far back as
(5) 200 A.D. Early explorers after Columbus introduced the potato to Europe between 1532 and 1550.

Not until the potato was introduced into Ireland was it recognized for its great food value rather than as a curiosity, and by the 1600s it was cultivated extensively in that country. For approximately 250 years the
(10) potato was a major source of food in most of Europe. In fact the majority of the population in Ireland depended on this crop for its existence.

When the late blight disease came from America into Ireland (1845–1847), it caused a national disaster. Destruction of the vines and decay of the tubers caused a complete loss of the crop nationwide. The
(15) result was the Irish famine in which thousands starved to death.

A colony of Presbyterian Irish who settled in New Hampshire introduced the potato to America in 1719. Soon after the Irish famine the potato gained importance in the United States.

1. What is the purpose of this passage?
   (A) To compare agriculture in Ireland and the United States
   (B) To convince us of the value of the potato
   (C) To inform us about the history of the potato
   (D) To clarify that the potato came from South America

2. Which of the following best describes the organization of the passage?
   (A) Random presentation of facts about the potato
   (B) An explanation of the popularity of the potato
   (C) A discussion of chronological events concerning the potato
   (D) A description of the use of potatoes

3. Why does the author mention the Irish famine in the passage?
   (A) To illustrate the importance of the potato as a source of food
   (B) To indicate the effect of vegetable diseases
   (C) To show how the potato got to the United States
   (D) To familiarize us with the history of Ireland

   See Tapescripts and Answers *for an explanation of the answers for Exercises 3C–3F.*

Reading Comprehension Checkpoint Test One for R✔1 through R✔3

Allow yourself 15 minutes to complete this checkpoint test. There are three passages and 15 questions. Circle the letter of the correct answer to each question.

Questions 1–5

line
(5)

(10)

Today, going to the beach is not as simple as it used to be. Our shorelines are becoming an environmentalist's nightmare—and a threat to swimmers, too. How can you line decide if a beach is clean? One place to look for help is the local health department of a coastal community. It often monitors chemical and bacterial levels in water which are usually undetectable to the naked eye. Also, consider the amount and type of beach debris. Although there's no evidence linking debris with water pollution that could harm humans, thousands of marine animals die every year after eating or becoming tangled in plastic six-pack containers, fishnet, and other synthetic matter. Plastics on the beach mean you may find dead marine life in the water.

1. What is the topic of this passage?
   (A) Beaches
   (B) Water pollution
   (C) Dead marine life
   (D) Deciding if a beach is clean

2. What is the main idea of this passage?
   (A) Beach debris is harmful to marine life.
   (B) There are two ways to decide if a beach is clean.
   (C) The country's shores are in environmental danger.
   (D) The local health department monitors a community's beaches.

3. Which of the following would be the best title for this passage?
   (A) A Day at the Beach
   (B) Cleaning Our Beaches
   (C) Beach Debris: A Swimmer's Hazard
   (D) Caution! Dangers at the Beach

4. The main purpose of this passage is to
   (A) publicize the condition of beaches today
   (B) present suggestions for determining the condition of the beach
   (C) give an account of the danger of beach debris to marine animals
   (D) suggest methods of detecting bacterial levels in the water

5. The audience for this passage would most likely be
   (A) microbiologists
   (B) environmentalists
   (C) health department officials
   (D) potential beach-goers

Questions 6–10

The grizzly bear is one of the largest North American brown bears. In the
Rocky Mountains, frosted long hairs on the shoulders give this brown bear
a "grizzled" appearance, and thus the name grizzly bear. Though classed

line
with the carnivores, the grizzly bear is largely vegetarian and rarely eats
(5) flesh. During the summer these bears are avid fishers, and comb the waters
of mountain streams and rivers to catch salmon swimming upstream.

Even though the name refers to the bear's appearance rather than to its
temper, it can be an imposing and even terrifying beast. Tragic
confrontations between people and the grizzly have led to its reputation as
(10) an animal to be feared and even destroyed. The grizzly plays a big role in
the legends of the North American pioneer, and today visitors to national
parks must be cautious when they enter the grizzly's habitat. The grizzly
bear is an animal best observed from afar; cohabitation with man is not in
its nature.

6. What is the topic of this passage?
(A) Bears
(B) Habitats of bears
(C) How bears catch fish
(D) Grizzly bears

7. The main point of this passage is
(A) the grizzly bear is named for its vicious nature
(B) grizzly bears should be destroyed
(C) grizzly bears can be dangerous and should be respected by humans
(D) grizzly bears like to eat fish

8. Which of the following would be the best title for this passage?
(A) A Type of Brown Bear
(B) Facts About the Grizzly Bear
(C) How the Grizzly Bear Catches Fish
(D) The Legend of the Grizzly

9. What is the author's main purpose in the passage?
(A) To scare readers about the grizzly bear
(B) To inform readers about the grizzly bear
(C) To describe the grizzly's habitat
(D) To warn tourists in national parks about grizzly bears

10. Where in the passage does the author give the reason for the bear's name?
(A) Lines 2–3
(B) Lines 8–10
(C) Lines 4–6
(D) Lines 7–8

Money is an international commodity that moves across continents almost as fast as it moves across the street. One of the things that lures money across international borders is the rate of interest. If interest rates
line are higher abroad than at home, American businesses and investors will
(5) move their money out of the USA and into countries with higher interest rates. When domestic interest rates are higher, the flow of money will reverse.

These international money flows are another constraint on monetary policy. Suppose the federal government wants to slow the economy by
(10) limiting money-supply growth. Such tight-money policies will tend to raise interest rates in the USA. A higher interest rate is supposed to curb domestic investment and consumer spending. But those higher U.S. interest rates will also be an attraction for foreign money. People holding dollars abroad will want to move more money to the United States, where
(15) it can earn higher interest rates. Foreigners will also want to exchange their currencies for dollars, again in order to earn higher interest rates.

As international money flows into the United States, the money supply will expand more quickly than the government desired. This will frustrate the government's policy objectives and may force it to tighten the money
(20) supply even more. Capital inflows will also tend to increase the international value of the dollar, making it more difficult to sell U.S. exports. In sum, the internationalization of money is one more problem the federal government has to worry about when it conducts monetary policy.

11. This passage mainly discusses
(A) international politics
(B) U.S. banking
(C) international money and monetary policy
(D) interest rates for foreign investors

12. The main idea of the passage is that
(A) money is an international commodity
(B) interest rates determine the flow of international money
(C) the Fed controls the international money market
(D) internationalization of money will affect monetary policy

13. Which of the following would be the best title for this passage?
(A) Foreign Money in the USA
(B) Higher Interest Rates: A Cure for Financial Problems?
(C) International Constraints on Monetary Policy
(D) Take Your Money Abroad

14. What is the purpose of the passage?
(A) To discourage foreign investment
(B) To gain support for the federal government
(C) To argue for lower interest rates
(D) To discuss the effect of the flow of international money

15. Which of the following best describes the organization of the passage?
(A) A classification of monetary policies
(B) A criticism of current monetary policy
(C) A response to a proposal for a change in monetary policy
(D) An explanation of an issue in monetary policy

R✔4   Check Reference Words

The Reading Comprehension Section of the TOEFL often includes questions on reference words. Reference words are those words in a passage that refer back to concepts (words or phrases) mentioned earlier in the passage or refer forward to words or phrases that will be introduced. We use reference words in English to avoid repeating the same word.

> The man paid the bill when the man received the man's check.
> The man paid the bill when *he* received *his* check.

Reference words also help to tie together the whole passage so that it is easier to understand. Reference words are usually pronouns, but may also be possessive adjectives or specified items. Some examples of reference words are:

Subject Pronoun	Object Pronoun	Possessive Pronoun	Demonstrative Pronoun	Indefinite Pronoun	Specified Item
it	it	its	this	one	this concept
they	them	theirs	that	some	that dilemma
he	him	his	these	another	these works
she	her	hers	those	several	those ideas

In determining the referent (the word or phrase that reference words refer to), you should use both the structure and the meaning of the sentence.

Think about the following passage and questions. Answer the questions before you read the explanation.

MODEL

(1)   Throughout the year, chimpanzee food is quite varied, but it is mainly
(2) vegetable material. At times, however the Gombe Park is loaded with
(3) insects—termites, ants, caterpillars—and the chimpanzees will eat huge
(4) numbers of them. The chimpanzees' really remarkable behavior appears
(5) when they gather termites. According to Suzuki and van Lawick-Goodall,
(6) when chimpanzees see that termites have pushed open their tunnels on the
(7) surface, they will go off to find a suitable termiting tool. It may look
(8) simple, but the job takes skill and patience.

1. The word "their" in line 6 refers to
  (A)   the termites'
  (B)   the tunnels'
  (C)   the chimpanzees'
  (D)   Suzuki's and van Lawick-Goodall's

2. The pronoun "they" in line 7 refers to
  (A)   Suzuki and van Lawick-Goodall
  (B)   termites
  (C)   tools
  (D)   chimpanzees

3. The pronoun "It" in line 7 refers to
  (A)   a suitable termite tool
  (B)   the job
  (C)   skill
  (D)   patience

Answers:

▼ Explanation ▲

The answer to Question 1 is (A) *the termites'*. This question might be confusing because you know that *their* can refer to a plural noun. In the sentence, *Suzuki and van Lawick-Goodall, chimpanzees, and termites* are all plural concepts. Logical reasoning will tell you that termites are the ones that live in tunnels, and that the correct answer must be (A).

The answer to Question 2 is (D) *chimpanzees*. In this case, the plural pronoun *they* could refer to either chimpanzees or termites. The meaning of the whole passage, however, makes it clear that the chimpanzees are looking for a tool to gather termites, and *they* refers to *chimpanzees*.

The answer to Question 3 is (B) *the job*. The pronoun *it* could possibly refer to any singular object, and at first glance you might choose *a suitable tool*. However, as you read on, it becomes clear that what *looks simple* is *the job*. In this sentence the pronoun refers forward.

EXERCISE 4A: Practice Identifying Referents

Read the following passage. The numbered reference words in bold print are listed after the passage. In the space next to each reference word in the list, write the word that it refers to.

> Throughout the year, chimpanzee food is quite varied, but **it** is mainly vegetable material. At times, however, the Gombe Park is loaded with insects—termites, ants, caterpillars—and the chimpanzees will eat huge numbers of **them**. The chimpanzees' really remarkable behavior appears when **they** gather termites. According to Suzuki and van Lawick-Goodall, when chimpanzees see that termites have pushed open their tunnels on the surface, they will go off to find a suitable termiting tool. A foot-long, rather thin, straight twig is best, and it may take quite a while to choose suitable sticks; then extraneous side branches and leaves must be carefully cleared off. The ape may even select and prepare **several** at a time, carrying **them** all back to the termiting hill firmly cupped in the closed palm of the hand while **it** knuckle-walks. The chimpanzee will lie down on its side next to the termite hill, and with skill and care, stick the twig into one of the open tunnels. The stick is wiggled, then slowly withdrawn; if **it** has termites adhering to **it**, the chimp licks **them** off the tool, and does **it** again. The job may look simple, but it takes skill to maneuver the stick through the twisting termite corridors.
>
> **This** is a complex learned behavior, involving the manufacture of an implement.

1. **it** *chimpanzee food*

2. **them** _____

3. **they** _____

4. **several** _____

5. them _____

6. it _____

7. it _____

8. it _____

9. them _____

10. it _____

11. this _____

EXERCISE 4B: Practice Matching Reference Words with Their Referents

Underline the referent of the word or words in bold print. Draw a line to connect the two.

1. In <u>her first collection of poems</u>, Isabella Pupurai Matsikidze combines her frankly feminist views with personal narratives and descriptions of the society and politics in her native Zimbabwe. **This work** shows that Matsikidze is a significant new poetic voice in the world of African letters.

2. Biophysics is a branch of biology in which the methods and principles of physics are applied to the study of living things. **This science** has grown up in the twentieth century alongside the development of electronics.

3. The most striking anatomical features of birds are **those** associated with flight. The forelimbs are modified as wings and are associated with enormous breast muscles which make powered flight possible. Even in flightless birds such as the penguin and ostrich it is clear that the forelimbs were once used as wings. **The latter**, however, are now adapted to be runners, with strong legs rather than predominant wings.

4. Punishment and reward belong properly in the autocratic social system. Here, the authority, enjoying a dominant position, had the privilege of meting out rewards or punishment according to merits. It was **his** privilege to decide who was deserving of rewards and who of punishment. **Such behavior** can be observed today by watching some parents deal with their children.

5. The small child looked up at the candy canes dangling from the tree's branches and took **one**. He quickly stuffed it in his pocket, and while no one was watching, reached for another.

6. It was a beautiful winter morning when the hikers left the base camp. The first part of the climb was accomplished easily, and the group planned to stop for lunch at a prearranged spot. As **they** approached the shelter where food and provisions were stored, the weather had begun to change. The valley below was covered with clouds, and the wind was howling furiously. To make matters worse, the shelter had been blown over and the food, ropes, and blankets were gone. **This dilemma** left them feeling apprehensive and unsettled.

7. A horse dislikes it when its rider comes off. Such an upset is also bad for a young horse psychologically, as once **it** discovers that it can get rid of its rider, it may form the habit of deliberately trying to unseat him. **One** then has the makings of a potential bucking bronco.

EXERCISE 4C: More Practice with Reference Words

Read the following passage. Then, circle the letter of the correct answer to each question.

> Thomas Jefferson's liberal views of democracy were first proposed in his draft of the Bill of Rights in 1776. Unfortunately, the Virginia Convention used only the preamble of this draft in the more conservative document
> *line* that they accepted, which had been drafted by George Mason. Much of
> (5) what Jefferson wanted was, however, obtainable as ordinary legislation, and when he took his seat in the new legislature, it was with a view of putting through a definite program of reforms. In this he had the support of such men as Mason, George Wythe, and James Madison, against the strenuous opposition of such leaders of the old order as Edmund Pendleton
> (10) and Robert Nicholas Carter. These men had much to lose if Jefferson's ideas were carried out.

1. The words "this draft" in line 3 refer to
   (A) the draft Jefferson wrote.
   (B) the draft that George Mason wrote.
   (C) the preamble.
   (D) the draft that was accepted.

2. The pronoun "he" in line 6 refers to
   (A) George Mason.
   (B) Thomas Jefferson.
   (C) a member of the Virginia Convention.
   (D) a member of the legislature.

3. The pronoun "this" in line 7 refers to
   (A) the implementation of the Bill of Rights.
   (B) the acceptance of Jefferson's original draft.
   (C) putting through a program of definite reforms.
   (D) carrying out Jefferson's liberal views.

4. The phrase "these men" in line 10 refers to
   (A) Mason, George Wythe, and James Madison.
   (B) the members of the legislature.
   (C) the members of the Virginia Convention.
   (D) Edmund Pendleton and Robert Nicholas Carter.

See Tapescripts and Answers *for an explanation of the answers to Exercise 4C.*

R✔5   Check Details and Factual Information

A large number of questions on the Reading Comprehension Section of the TOEFL ask about the details and facts in reading passages. These questions are usually asked in the order that the information appears in the passage. Your understanding of the topic and main idea and the overall organization of the passage will help you to answer these questions.

There are two types of fact and detail questions on the TOEFL: questions about what IS true according to the information and questions about what IS NOT true. Answer choices for questions about facts and details may use the exact words of the passage, but more often they are restatements of the information and require that you know synonyms and related words.

Think about the following passage and questions. Answer the questions before reading the explanation.

MODEL

Throughout the year, chimpanzee food is quite varied, but it is mainly vegetable material. At times, however, Gombe Park is loaded with insects—termites, ants, caterpillars—and the chimpanzees will eat huge numbers of them. The chimpanzees' really remarkable behavior appears when they gather termites. According to Suzuki and van Lawick-Goodall, when chimpanzees see that termites have pushed open their tunnels on the surface, they will go off to find a suitable termiting tool. It may look simple, but the job takes skill and patience.

1. According to the passage, which of the following are NOT mentioned as part of the chimpanzee's diet?
    (A) Termites
    (B) Vegetable material
    (C) Ants
    (D) Mosquitoes

2. The author states in the passage that the chimpanzees' most remarkable behavior can best be seen
    (A) when they are hungry.
    (B) as they are resting.
    (C) when they are looking for termites.
    (D) in the spring.

3. According to the author, when chimpanzees gather termites they show
    (A) a dependence on each other.
    (B) remarkable strength.
    (C) understanding and caring.
    (D) ability and persistence.

Answers:

▼ Explanation ▲

The correct answer to Question 1 is (D) *Mosquitoes*. This question asks you to identify the answer that is NOT in the passage. By knowing where in the passage the food that chimpanzees eat is mentioned, you can quickly look at those sentences and match the items in the sentence with those in the answer choices. Mosquitoes are not mentioned in the passage.

NOTE: In questions that ask what is NOT in the passage, information that is true is not the correct answer.

The correct answer to Question 2 is (C) *when they are looking for termites*. To answer this question you need to match the words *chimpanzees' most remarkable behavior* in the question with those words in the passage. This will tell you in what part of the passage you will find the answer. After careful reading of the sentence, you can match the information in the passage with the answer choice. In this case the passage states *when they gather termites*, and a restatement of this is found in answer choice (C).

The correct answer to Question 3 is (D) *ability and persistence*. In this question you are asked to find what chimpanzees *show* rather than *do* when they gather termites. The last sentence of the passage states that the job (of gathering termites) *takes skill and patience*. Scanning the answer choices will tell you that the best restatement of the information in the passage is *ability and persistence*.

Questions about details and facts are often worded in the following ways:

About information that IS in the passage:

According to the passage, who
                          why
                          where
                          when
                          how, etc....?
According to the author,...
The author states in the passage that...
The author indicates that...
The author refers to which of the following as...
It is stated in the passage that...

About information that IS NOT in the passage:

All of the following are mentioned in the passage as...EXCEPT...
According to the passage all of the following are true about...EXCEPT...
Which of the following is NOT mentioned in the passage as...?
Which of the following is NOT stated in the passage?

To be successful at answering questions about facts and details in a short reading passage, follow these steps:
1. Read the question and identify the key words and controlling idea. REMEMBER that the questions will be in order of the information in the passage.
2. Scan the passage for the key words and controlling ideas. REMEMBER that you should look for synonyms and related words as well as exact words.
3. Carefully read this part of the passage to answer the question.
4. Scan the answer choices to match the information in the passage with the correct answer choice.
5. Be careful to look for the information that is not true in a TOEFL question worded with NOT and EXCEPT.

EXERCISE 5A: Practice Scanning for Facts and Details

Read the following passage QUICKLY. Read the question and scan for the lines of the passage that would answer the question. Write the number of the lines in the spaces provided.

When we think of time, we think of clock time. Action all around the world is synchronized by clock time, starting with train schedules, worldwide plane schedules, navigation, astronomy, worldwide
line telecommunication, etc. These depend completely on accurate timing. The
(5) accuracy standards of time keeping devices have been increasing rapidly due to the demands for more and more accurate timing for space communication, navigation, astronomy, etc. Rather than use mechanical clocks, we are relying nowadays on "atomic clocks." This is not a clock in the usual sense but a device that uses the very stable oscillation of the
(10) cesium atoms as a standard for timekeeping.

From grandfather clocks to wristwatches, all these clocks are supposed to chop up for us the 24 hours of the day more or less reliably into hours, minutes, and seconds. Let's call this kind of time "objective" since everybody's watches are supposed to cut time into slices of even thickness.
(15) However, we know from personal experience that time does not "feel" as passing evenly under different circumstances. When pursuing some interesting activity, time "flies"; while waiting in the dentist's office, it "drags." When Einstein was once asked about this "psychological time," he replied with a now famous observation: "When you spend two hours
(20) with a nice girl, you think it's only a minute. But when you sit on a hot stove for a minute, you think it's two hours." Realizing the relativity of time, let us see, then, how this subjective time can be put to some use.

Limit yourself to 30 seconds for this part of the exercise. In what lines would you find information about:

1. schedules and clock time: _____Lines 2–4_____

2. accuracy standards: _____

3. how atomic clocks work: _____

4. how objective time is measured: _____

5. how time "feels": _____

6. Einstein's ideas of time: _____

EXERCISE 5B: Practice Answering Questions About Facts and Details

Write the answer to each question about the passage from Exercise 5A in the space provided.

1. How many types of actions mentioned in the passage depend on accurate timing?

   _____

2. What has happened as a result of the demands for more accurate timing by space
   communication, navigation, and astronomy?

   _____

3. What does the atomic clock use as a standard for timekeeping?

   _____

4. What is the defining characteristic of objective time?

   _____

5. What does our personal experience with time tell us?

   _____

6. When does time "feel" longer?

   _____

   When does time "feel" shorter?

   _____

7. Did Einstein think that objective and subjective time were similar or different?

   _____

**EXERCISE 5C: Practice Answering Questions About Facts and Details As They
                  Appear on the TOEFL**

Answer the following questions about the passage in Exercise 5A. Circle the correct answer.

1. According to the passage, which of the following is NOT an example of accurate timing?
   (A) Clock time
   (B) Psychological time
   (C) Atomic clock time
   (D) Objective time

2. According to the passage, demands for more accurate timing have resulted in
   (A) the growth of telecommunications, navigation, and astronomy
   (B) the development of better mechanical clocks
   (C) the improvement of accuracy standards for timekeeping devices
   (D) the dependence on atomic power

3. The author states in the passage that because of the need for more accurate standards of timekeeping, today we are
   (A) thinking about time in a different way
   (B) revising schedules of trains and planes
   (C) relying more on atomic clocks
   (D) enjoying more leisure time

4. According to the passage, a defining characteristic of objective time is that
   (A) it divides time evenly for everyone
   (B) it is different from clock time
   (C) it seems to pass quickly
   (D) it uses a 24-hour system

5. According to the passage, personal experience tells us that for different circumstances
   (A) different clocks should be used
   (B) our impression of how quickly time passes will vary
   (C) different standards of accuracy will apply
   (D) more interesting activities should be chosen

6. According to the passage, Einstein, when asked about psychological time,
   (A) declined to answer
   (B) commented on its stability
   (C) said that socializing was more time-consuming than tending the fire
   (D) observed that time seems to pass quickly or slowly according to our activity

EXERCISE 5D: More Practice Answering Questions on Facts and Details

Read the following passage. Circle the correct answer to each question.

The world above the forest floor can be observed by all of us. Rarely, however, do we take the time to notice the teeming life and bustling activity that occurs beneath the ground we walk on.

line   Of all soil-dwelling creatures, the most abundant are mites and
(5) springtails, insect-like creatures that literally eat their way through caverns of subterranean vegetation. The tiny, eight-legged mites lay their eggs on plant matter, which their larvae eat and convert into fresh soil. The bright-colored springtails are named for their ability to leap long distances during their search for decomposed plant matter to eat.

(10)   Both mites and springtails are prey to a host of soil-dwelling predators. They thus anchor one end of the food chain that extends to higher forms of forest "lowlife," such as moles that feed on earthworms and shrews that eat beetles.

      Those mammals, in turn, dig tunnels that function as underground
(15) byways for other subterranean species. Hibernating chipmunks, turtles, and salamanders sift and mix the soil when they burrow to winter dens. Cottontails and gray foxes excavate shallow dens as sanctuary from predators and harsh weather, while gray squirrels, hiding acorns for the lean season, further blend the earth. From microbe to people, thousands of
(20) species work the land upon which all life depends.

1. The passage states that which of the following are the most numerous inhabitants of the soil?
   (A) Foxes and cottontails
   (B) Earthworms and ants
   (C) Mites and springtails
   (D) Shrews and moles

2. According to the passage, all of the following are true about mites and springtails EXCEPT
   (A) they make new soil
   (B) they resemble insects
   (C) they form the lower end of the food chain
   (D) they hibernate for the winter

3. An example of predator and prey given in this passage is
   (A) mites and springtails
   (B) turtles and salamanders
   (C) moles and earthworms
   (D) grey squirrels and acorns

4. Which of the following are mentioned in the passage as living underground during the winter?
   (A) Shrews
   (B) Foxes
   (C) Squirrels
   (D) Salamanders

5. According to the author, the contribution that all the animals mentioned in the passage make to their habitat is
   (A) they form the food chain
   (B) they work the soil
   (C) they find safety in the soil
   (D) they convert plant material to new earth

EXERCISE 5E: More Practice Answering Questions on Facts and Details

Read the following passage. Circle the correct answer to each question.

line

(5)

(10)

(15)

Only humans have a spoken, symbolic language; scientists have long thought that nonhuman primates had much less sophisticated communication systems. True, but line chimpanzees use gestures and many voice sounds in the wild, while other apes use sounds to communicate territorial information. Chimpanzees seem to have a natural talent for learning symbolic language under controlled conditions. A famous chimpanzee named Washoe was trained to communicate with humans, using no less than 175 sign language gestures similar to those of the American Sign Language. After more than a year Washoe could associate particular signs with activities, such as eating and drinking. Another chimpanzee named Sarah was taught to read and write with plastic symbols and acquired a vocabulary of 130 different words, to the extent that she obeyed sequences of written instructions given with the symbols. But such experiments in communication with primates are a far cry from the versatility and grace of human speech.

1. According to the passage, all of the following are true of chimpanzee communication EXCEPT
   (A) it is less sophisticated than human language
   (B) it is observable in the wild
   (C) it uses gestures
   (D) it is as versatile as human communication

2. The passage states that the ability of chimpanzees to learn symbolic language in certain situations is due to
   (A) their territoriality
   (B) their use of gestures and voice sounds in the wild
   (C) their natural talent
   (D) their use of the American Sign Language

3. According to the passage, the chimpanzee Washoe
   (A) was able to associate some signs with activities after a year
   (B) used fewer than 175 signs to communicate
   (C) was fluent in the American Sign Language
   (D) could read and write

4. The passage states that Sarah's ability to read and write was judged by
   (A) the size of her vocabulary
   (B) her dexterity in using the plastic symbols
   (C) her obedience to instructions given in the symbol language
   (D) the number of symbol sequences that she could manipulate

5. According to the author, spoken, symbolic language is
   (A) not a sophisticated communication system
   (B) only available to humans
   (C) shared by both humans and chimpanzees
   (D) similar to the language used by chimpanzees

   See Tapescripts and Answers *for an explanation of the answers to Exercises 5D and 5E.*

R✔6   Check to Make Inferences

Questions on the Reading Comprehension Section of the TOEFL often ask you to use your understanding of the facts and details which are directly stated in a reading passage to make an inference (a prediction or conclusion) about the passage. Information that is not directly stated in the passage is said to be implied by the author. Questions about implied information may be about a part of the passage or about what came before or will come after the passage. You may be asked to draw conclusions about the passage itself, or to make predictions about another related situation.

Think about the following sentence and questions:

> In last year's competition, of the five contestants chosen, one was from White Springs, two from other towns in Idaho, and the rest from neighboring areas of the Pacific Northwest.

Using the facts of the text itself, we can make several inferences (conclusions based on facts) about this sentence.

▼ Explanation ▲

1. What or where is White Springs?
   We can infer that White Springs is a town in Idaho based on the phrase *other towns in Idaho*.
2. Where is Idaho?
   We can infer that both White Springs and Idaho are in the Pacific Northwest based on *from neighboring areas of the Pacific Northwest*.
3. How many contestants are from the rest of the Pacific Northwest?
   We can infer that there were two contestants from the neighboring areas of the Pacific Northwest by using simple arithmetic.
4. What type of competition might this be?
   We can infer something about the competition or contest. We can guess that it was a regional competition, rather than national, since all the contestants came from the same geographic area.

5. What probably preceded this sentence?
   We can infer that the information given before this sentence was probably about the contestants in this year's competition, based on the phrase *In last year's competition*.

Questions that ask you to make an inference or to predict are often worded in the following ways:

It can be inferred from the passage that…
Which of the following can be inferred from the passage?
The author implies in the passage…
Which of the following is the most likely…?
What did the paragraph preceding the passage most probably discuss?
What will the paragraph that follows this passage most likely discuss?
Which of the following generalizations is supported by the passage?

or occasionally:

Which of the following CANNOT be inferred from the passage?
REMEMBER: In this type of question, true answers are NOT correct.

Questions that ask you to make inferences are usually in order according to the information in the passage. Use skills of skimming and scanning to locate the information in the passage that you are asked to understand. Then look for the relationships in the stated information. Also, use your understanding of the author's purpose and organization of the passage. Use logical reasoning to draw conclusions and make predictions about the passage from information which is not specifically stated.

EXERCISE 6A: Practice Making Inferences by Identifying Statements That Can Be Inferred from a Passage

Read the passages. Circle ALL of the answers that can be inferred from a passage.

1. When the Pilgrims arrived from England in 1620, they found the native American communities devastated by a plague that eventually wiped out between 90 and 96 percent of the native inhabitants of southern New England.

   What can be inferred from the passage?
   (A) The Pilgrims arrived in southern New England.
   (B) The Pilgrims were also afflicted by the plague.
   (C) The native Americans offered little resistance to the Pilgrims.
   (D) The plague began in England.

2. The fossils that have led to this new view of dinosaurs as migratory creatures have been found in Alaska, Canada, Greenland, and the Soviet Union, as well as in Antarctica and southern Australia. At the time dinosaurs thrived near the poles, conditions there were radically different from those today. The planet was warmer, especially in these polar regions.

   What can be inferred from the passage?
   (A) Dinosaurs are usually thought of as sedentary creatures.
   (B) Dinosaurs migrated from Alaska to Australia.
   (C) The fossils have been found in polar regions.
   (D) The temperature at the poles today is cold.

3. A good source of vitamin B is kale. Spinach and escarole are other green leafy vegetables that provide this essential vitamin. Enjoy your daily salad, and you'll have your vitamin B as well.

   What can be inferred from the passage?
   (A) Kale is a green leafy vegetable.
   (B) Vitamin B is the most essential vitamin.
   (C) Eating salad will guarantee good health.
   (D) Kale, spinach, and escarole can be used in salads.

4. A popular vacation spot during summer months is Nags Head; its beaches, excellent surf fishing, and nearby historical sites make it one of North Carolina's most popular seaside towns. Other resorts in neighboring southern states may provide more night life, but Nags Head attracts families year after year.

   What can be inferred from the passage?
   (A) Nags Head is in the South.
   (B) You can see many children in Nags Head in July.
   (C) Nags Head has many nightclubs and discotheques.
   (D) Nags Head is on the coast.

5. A popular color for spring fashions is chartreuse. Gone are the dark and dreary browns and blacks of winter; "bright" is the tone for spring. Another green that is being shown this spring is moss green, with a somewhat softer hue.

   What can be inferred from the passage?
   (A) Chartreuse is a bright color.
   (B) Brown is a good color for spring fashions.
   (C) Chartreuse is a type of green color.
   (D) Brown and black were popular colors in the winter.

6. From the dunes you get a view of the whole area, and the constant winds on the bluff provide today's sky-gliders the same advantage afforded Orville and Wilbur Wright in 1900 as they prepared for the world's first powered flight.

   What can be inferred from the passage?
   (A) The dunes are located higher than other land forms of the area.
   (B) The dunes have served those interested in flying for many years.
   (C) The Wrights had trouble sky-gliding and used power.
   (D) Good winds are necessary for sky-gliding.

7. The first recorded European visit to the Outer Banks was made by Verazzano, who was in search of a route to the West. The area was referred to by Verazzano and his crew as Annunciata, which means "to announce." But the name did not prevail because neither maps nor permanent settlements were made. When the English increased their visits to the area, they referred to it as New Brittaine, and then later as Arcadia. The name Arcadia was taken from the ancient Greek city where the people had a simple, rustic lifestyle. However, this was the name given by people who did not reside in the Outer Banks. The name Arcadia didn't stick.

   What can be inferred from the passage?
   (A) The Outer Banks are west of Europe.
   (B) Verazzano had hopes for European settlements in the Outer Banks.
   (C) The Outer Banks offers a simple, rustic lifestyle today.
   (D) The English made permanent settlements in Arcadia.

8. The term "not worth a continental" became a popular reference to things of little value as a result of the inability of the government of the United States to pay for the Revolutionary War. Specifically, the federal government had no power to levy taxes that might transfer resources from the private sector to the public sector. To pay for needed weapons and soldiers, the federal government had only two other options, either (1) borrow money or (2) create new money. When loans proved to be inadequate, the Continental Congress started issuing new paper money—the "continental" dollar—in 1775. By the end of 1779, Congress had authorized issuance of over $250 million in Continental dollars. Fortunately, the war ended before the economy collapsed.

What can be inferred from the passage?
(A) The option of creating new money was not entirely successful.
(B) Two expenses of the Revolutionary War were weapons and soldiers.
(C) Most of the money at that time was held by the private sector.
(D) The federal government did not consider the option of loans.

9. Fundamental to the theory of plate tectonics is the assumption that while all the plates seem to be moving at different relative speeds—ranging from a fraction of an inch to a maximum of five inches a year—the whole jigsaw puzzle of plates is interlinked. No one plate can move without affecting others, and the activity of one can influence another thousands of miles away: The Atlantic Ocean could not be getting wider—as it is with the spreading of the African Plate away from the South American Plate—if the Pacific sea floor were not being consumed in deep oceanic trenches faster than it is created at the Pacific ridges. The plates move rapidly by geological standards: two inches per year—to pick a typical speed—up to 30 miles in one million years. It took only 150 million years for a mere fracture in an ancient continent to turn into the Atlantic Ocean.

What can be inferred from the passage?
(A) As the Atlantic is getting wider, the Pacific Ocean is getting narrower.
(B) Plate tectonics is a complex, interrelated system.
(C) The Atlantic Ocean used to be a continent.
(D) Geological standards of time are faster than normal standards of time.

10. During the Great Depression of the 1930s, unemployment affected as much as twenty-five percent of the labor force. Today's federal system of social welfare programs did not exist then, so the families of most of the unemployed went hungry. Since that time, we have progressed both in maintaining higher levels of employment and in providing support services to the unemployed. However, unemployment is still a threat in certain industries and for certain groups, especially among minority youth first entering the labor force. Unemployment is a waste of human resources, and represents a drain on public budgets and on the life savings of individual families.

What can be inferred from the passage?
(A) Unemployment caused many hardships for families during the Great Depression.
(B) Figures for today's unemployment are higher than in the 1930s.
(C) Unemployment is a special threat to a black teenager.
(D) Programs to support the unemployed are funded by the federal government.

To be successful answering TOEFL questions that ask you to make inferences, use your knowledge of signal words. Words that signal relationships between ideas in a reading passage give valuable clues about information that is not directly stated in a reading passage. Review the signal words studied in R√4 and those listed in the Reading Appendix, #3, pages 497–498.

EXERCISE 6B: **Practice Identifying and Understanding Words That Signal Relationships in a Reading Passage**

Use the words to predict what information will follow. Circle the letter of the answer that would best complete each statement.

1. **Whereas** the fiscal policy of Keynes required the federal government to spend large amounts of money, economists today
   (A) are looking for ways to utilize the private sector.
   (B) are in favor of even more government spending.

2. High-impact aerobics has been associated with high injury rates, and recently instructors have begun teaching low- impact aerobics. **However**, it appears that low-impact aerobics is not void of injuries. **In short**,
   (A) low-impact aerobics offers people a good alternative for safer exercise programs.
   (B) no exercise program is entirely injury-free.

3. Herbicides, like all chemicals sprayed in the environment, have some adverse affects. **Not only** have earthworms and other soil microorganisms been killed by some herbicides, but also
   (A) much needed insect predators have been destroyed by these chemicals.
   (B) these chemicals are often used in powder form.

4. **However** dismal the outlook for world peace today may seem,
   (A) people will continue to search for alternatives to global warfare.
   (B) peace will not occur in the next decade.

5. Noam Chomsky, **apart from** his work as a linguist,
   (A) continues to lecture on language theory.
   (B) is well known for his outspoken views in politics.

6. The talks between the labor union and the company's owners seemed hopeless. **Even** protests from the workers themselves
   (A) failed to resolve the issues.
   (B) helped to bring about a compromise solution.

7. When FM broadcasting began to develop, the industry treated it as a minor novelty. Its success today is due to its technical superiority to AM. **In particular**,
   (A) FM stations are virtually static-free and transmit music with greater fidelity in stereophonic sound.
   (B) FM stations can target their programming to audience segments with special listening interests.

8. At present, the 30,000 tons of trash Burlingtonians generate each year are collected by 14 individual companies. Critics contend this system is irrational, since certain streets are served by as many as four different carters. Their new proposal suggests that the trash removal system be revised **in such a way as to**
   (A) collect more trash.
   (B) reduce the number of carters involved.

9. What is disturbing about the projected tax plan is **not so much** the amount of money to be raised **but** the type of tax being proposed. Taxpayers, **therefore**, are asking for more information about
   (A) what the tax monies will be spent for.
   (B) who will be asked to pay the taxes.

10. Students in today's undergraduate colleges are being asked to specialize before they have acquired the general cultivation that would acquaint them with the ideas and disciplines that are the components of culture. **Moreover**,
    (A) the humanities, as currently taught and studied, are as much addicted to specialized scholarship as are the scientific departments to highly specialized research.
    (B) the cultural events that are a part of every college campus are today widely diversified and give a good overview of both our past and our future.

EXERCISE 6C: Practice Making Inferences and Understanding Implied Information

Read the following passage. Circle the correct answer to each question.

Only two spiders found in the continental United States are deadly to humans: the black widow and the brown recluse. The black widow is found in all the 48 contiguous states, more commonly in the South and
line West than in the North. Crabill describes it as "a shy and retiring spider
(5) that doesn't go looking for trouble." The black widow's bite is excruciatingly painful. "Sometimes even morphine won't knock out the pain." Crabill says.

But at least a black widow's bite can be treated; there is no effective treatment for a brown recluse's bite. This spider, sometimes called the
(10) violin spider because of a violin-like marking on its upper body, is found predominantly in the South, especially in the Gulf States, and in the West. They are far more to be feared than the U.S. tarantula. Crabill explains:

"All tarantulas native to the United States are not known to be hazardous to life, although they will bite. As you get down into the New
(15) World tropics, some are extremely dangerous, and here is where you get into trouble with tarantulas as pets. The only safe rule is: If you don't know where it came from, don't handle it."

1. All of the following could be inferred from the passage about the brown recluse EXCEPT
   (A) it is more deadly than the black widow
   (B) it can be handled easily
   (C) it is more common in the southern states
   (D) it is distinctively marked

2. It can be inferred from the passage that morphine is
   (A) good for killing black widow spiders
   (B) a painkiller
   (C) a total cure for a spider bite
   (D) sold mostly in the South and West

3. The author implies in the passage that tarantulas
   (A) are found only in the New World tropics
   (B) make good pets
   (C) are a kind of spider
   (D) should never be handled by humans

4. It can be inferred from the passage that Crabill
   (A) has never seen a tarantula
   (B) is an expert on spiders
   (C) probably has a New World tarantula as a pet
   (D) would not use morphine for a spider bite

EXERCISE 6D: More Practice Making Inferences and Understanding Implied Information

Read the passage. Circle the correct answer to each question.

line
(5)

(10)

Elements may be the basic building blocks of matter, but what—if anything—makes up the elements? In other words, what would be the result of taking an element, a piece of gold, for example, and cutting it in half, and in half again, ad infinitum. We would soon reach the point of having such a small piece of gold that it would be beyond our ability to cut it. It is at times like these when scientists must use their knowledge about how elements react to continue the experiment in their minds. Scientists have done just that and have agreed that if they continue to cut a piece of gold in half, they would eventually reach a particle called the atom (in this case, an atom of gold). The atom is the smallest part of an element that retains the chemical properties of the element. One gold atom is so small that billions of them are required to make a tiny speck of gold that can be seen with a microscope. The atom, therefore, is the basic particle which constitutes the elements. Gold is composed of gold atoms, iron of iron atoms, and oxygen of oxygen atoms.

1. What did the paragraph preceding this one most probably discuss?
   (A) Elements as they are essential to matter
   (B) Minerals other than gold
   (C) The scientific method of inquiry
   (D) Scientific experiments

2. All of the following can be inferred from the passage EXCEPT
   (A) matter is made up of atoms
   (B) each element is composed of its own type of atoms
   (C) the gold atom is the smallest particle known to science
   (D) one atom of gold cannot be seen with a regular microscope

3. The author implies in the passage that scientists
   (A) apply their knowledge through abstract thinking
   (B) are more concerned with atoms than with elements
   (C) had difficulty cutting the gold in half
   (D) don't often agree with each other

4. This passage would most likely appear in which of the following course books?
   (A) A history book
   (B) A biography of a scientist
   (C) An introductory chemistry book
   (D) A book on mineralogy

EXERCISE 6E: More Practice Making Inferences and Understanding Implied Information

Read the passage. Circle the correct answer.

> Trucks rank high in meeting the transportation needs of most manufacturers. They are the most frequently used form of transportation, for two reasons: (1) they offer door-to-door delivery from the manufacturer
>
> *line* to the customer without intermediate unloading, and (2) they operate on
>
> *(5)* public highways that do not require an expensive terminal or right-of-way as airlines and railroads do. The main drawback of trucks is that they cannot carry all types of cargo. Federal regulations limit weight loads and truck dimensions, so trucks cannot cost-effectively haul heavy, bulky commodities like steel or coal.
>
> *(10)* Trucks can now carry larger loads on interstate highways, thanks to a 1983 law permitting the use of tandem trailers—two trailers hooked together and pulled by a single cab. Even with this change in federal rules, however, certain types of cargoes, such as gases, are difficult to handle by truck. Other types of transportation are more suited to these cargoes.

1. It can be inferred from the passage that truck transportation would be LEAST effective for which of the following commodities?
   (A) Computers
   (B) Iron ore
   (C) Canned food
   (D) Paper products

2. It can be inferred from the passage that trucks meet all of the following criteria for transportation EXCEPT
   (A) direct delivery of product
   (B) low expenses for handling product
   (C) low overhead for storage of product
   (D) diversified cargoes

3. The author implies in the passage that federal regulation of trucks
   (A) is stricter today than ever
   (B) is paid for by the manufacturers
   (C) has been more lenient since 1983
   (D) forbids trucks to handle gases

4. The passage following this one will most likely discuss
   (A) more specific federal regulations on trucks
   (B) other transportation systems
   (C) interstate truck routes most commonly used
   (D) cargoes shipped by tandem trailers

See Tapescripts and Answers *for an explanation of the answers to Exercises 6C–6E.*

Reading Comprehension Checkpoint Test Two for R✔1 through R✔6

Allow yourself 18 minutes to complete this checkpoint test. There are three passages and 20 questions.

Circle the letter of the correct answer to each question.

<u>Questions 1–8</u>

Spiders produce three basic types of webs. The sheet web is a two-dimensional layer of threads seemingly laid out at random. The space web is a three-dimensional, wispy structure. The orb web, by far the most familiar, is the two-dimensional cartwheel pattern.

line
(5)   Of the 30,000 spider species, some 6,000 are orb spinners. For three decades Dr. Peter N. Witt has studied orb spinners, especially a species called *Areneus diadematus*, and their webs. Witt is a German-born medical doctor and self-taught arachnologist, whose passion is to understand the ways of spiders. Witt has delved deeply into the behavior of spiders and
(10)   vastly expanded our knowledge about orb spinners and their webs. Some of his findings have even amazed other arachnologists.

"We have actually compared human building activities to spider building and we find an enormous amount of parallel between the two," Witt says. For one thing, just like their human counterparts in the building
(15)   trades, orb spinners erect a form of removable scaffolding as they weave their webs.

Orb spinners are solitary creatures who dwell one to a web. The web is home, food source, and mating ground, and it is guarded aggressively. When a male arrives at mating time, the courtship ritual is an intricate set
(20)   of advances and retreats until the female is finally won over and no longer tries to kill her would-be lover.

Orb spinners each weave a new web every day, working in the predawn darkness and executing the distinctive pattern of concentric circles and radial lines in a half hour or less. "There is nothing as important as web
(25)   building, because without the web there is no food," Witt says.

1. The topic of this passage is
   (A) spiders
   (B) different types of webs spiders make
   (C) Dr. Peter N. Witt
   (D) orb spinners and their webs

2. According to the passage, the difference between the sheet web and the orb web is
   (A) the pattern
   (B) the size
   (C) the texture
   (D) the length of threads spun by the spiders

3. We can infer from the passage that an arachnologist is
   (A) a photographer
   (B) a medical doctor
   (C) a person who studies spiders
   (D) a person who intensely dislikes spiders

4. The word "their" in line 14 refers to
   (A) humans who build
   (B) other arachnologists
   (C) Witt and his associates
   (D) orb spinners

5. According to the passage, web-making by spiders and human building activities are
   (A) both dependent on removable scaffolding
   (B) hard to compare
   (C) simple to analyze
   (D) lengthy procedures

6. The word "it" in line 18 refers to
   (A) the web
   (B) the food source
   (C) the female spider
   (D) the mating ground

7. We can infer that one thing the female orb spinner is NOT is
   (A) hard-working
   (B) cautious
   (C) solitary
   (D) easily wooed

8. We can conclude from the passage that the purpose of webs is
   (A) to initiate courtship of spiders
   (B) to engage spiders in useful activity
   (C) to provide a way for spiders to entrap food
   (D) to display artistic talents of spiders

Questions 9–16

For any business, the cost of transportation is normally the largest single item in the overall cost of physical distribution. It doesn't necessarily follow, though, that a manufacturer should simply pick the cheapest available form of transportation. Many companies today use the total
line available form of transportation. Many companies today use the total
(5) physical distribution concept, an approach that involves maximizing the efficiency of physical distribution activities while minimizing their cost. Often, this means that the company will make cost tradeoffs between the various physical distribution activities. For instance, air freight may be much more expensive than rail transport, but a national manufacturer
(10) might use air freight to ship everything from a single warehouse and thus avoid the greater expense of maintaining several warehouses.

When a firm chooses a type of transportation, it has to bear in mind its other marketing concerns—storage, financing, sales, inventory size, and the like. Transportation, in fact, can be an especially important sales tool. If the
(15) firm can supply its customers' needs more quickly and reliably than its competitors do, it will have a vital advantage: so it may be more profitable in the long run to pay higher transportation costs, rather than risk the loss of future sales. In addition, speedy delivery is crucial in some industries. A mail-order distributor sending fruit from Oregon to Pennsylvania needs
(20) the promptness of air freight. On the other hand, a manufacturer shipping lingerie from New York to Massachusetts may be perfectly satisfied with slower (and cheaper) truck or rail transport.

9. The main idea of this passage is that
   (A) businesses should use the least expensive form of transportation
   (B) transportation is an important aspect of business
   (C) rail transportation is less expensive than air freight
   (D) most manufacturers choose the fastest form of delivery

10. According to the passage all of the following would influence the type of transportation that a company might choose EXCEPT
    (A) the type of goods to be shipped
    (B) the expense of the shipping
    (C) the time it takes for delivery
    (D) the size of its warehouses

11. The author states in the passage that the total physical distribution concept
    (A) is based on the capability and cost-effectiveness of a transportation system
    (B) advocates the use of air freight because of its efficiency
    (C) suggests trading goods for transportation services
    (D) relies on using warehouses for storing goods

12. It can be inferred from the passage that transportation is
    (A) important to continued successful sales
    (B) independent of other business concerns
    (C) not used effectively by businesses
    (D) too expensive for most mail-order industries to use

13. We can conclude from the passage that a business that deals in perishable goods would probably choose to ship by
    (A) rail
    (B) truck
    (C) air freight
    (D) any type of cheap transport

14. The word "its" in line 15 refers to which of the following?
    (A) competitors
    (B) firm
    (C) customers
    (D) sales tool

15. This passage would probably be assigned reading in which of the following academic courses?
    (A) Marketing
    (B) Statistics
    (C) Mechanical engineering
    (D) History

Questions 16–20

      Insect control is only one of the problems being addressed by cooperative agricultural research teams. Besides the problem of pests, great quantities of food are lost by improper threshing methods and by poor

line handling, storage, and food preservation.

(5)   Fermentation and mold during wet-season crop harvesting and badly organized drying and milling facilities lose much grain. Grain dryers that work for North America may be useless in tropical climates. Grain bins designed for gentle prairie winds are no good for Africa's blazing sun. Developing the right storage facilities for local conditions is a great need.

16. This passage mainly discusses
    (A) insect control
    (B) food harvesting and storage
    (C) tropical climates
    (D) grain loss

17. According to the passage, one problem leading to crop loss is
    (A) Poor planting methods
    (B) Damage from vandals
    (C) Proper transportation of food products
    (D) Harvesting procedures during rainy seasons

18. What did the paragraph preceding this passage most probably discuss?
    (A) proper threshing methods
    (B) food preservation
    (C) insect control
    (D) agriculture in North America

19. It can be inferred from the passage that
    (A) agricultural facilities used in North America are not appropriate in all parts of the world
    (B) drying food is easy in tropical climates
    (C) African storage facilities are superior to North American ones
    (D) Pest control is the biggest problem facing agricultural research today

20. The author implies in the passage that agricultural research
    (A) disregards climatic conditions in its studies
    (B) is making insignificant contributions to tropical agriculture
    (C) will continue to investigate storage facilities for food
    (D) is primarily taking place in North America

R✔7   Check Vocabulary in Context

Questions on the Reading Comprehension Section of the TOEFL often ask you about the meaning of words or expressions used in the reading passage. This type of question asks you to know synonyms, as in the Vocabulary Section; however, in the Reading Comprehension Section, you can use the context of the passage to help you understand what the words mean. When you answer this type of question about a word in the passage, you need to scan to find the sentence that the word is in, read it carefully, and reason logically.

Think about the following passage and question. Answer the question before reading the explanation.

MODEL

(3)   The hippopotamus spends as much time in the water as on land. It swims and dives well, but prefers to spend its days submerged in the water with only its eyes and ears sticking out. It lives in the swamps, streams and marshes of tropical Africa.

As used in line 2, the phrase "submerged in the water" means that the animal is
- (A)   swimming in the water
- (B)   standing covered with water
- (C)   floating on the water
- (D)   wading in water

Answer:

▼ Explanation ▲

Since all of the answer choices involve the water, you must read carefully for context clues in the sentence. The sentence states that it *spends its days ...in water with only its eyes and ears sticking out.* Using the full context of the sentence, we read that the *hippo swims and dives well, but prefers to spend its days submerged...*; therefore answer (A) *swimming...* is not the same as submerged. You know that answers (C) *floating on the water* and (D) *wading in the water* both expose more than the eyes and ears of the hippo, and are incorrect. The correct answer choice is (B) *standing covered with water*. You reach this conclusion by inferring information from the passage and from the answer choices and by using logical reasoning.

Questions about the meaning of a word in a passage are often worded as follows:

In line 0 the phrase *XXX* refers to…
As used in line 0, the word *XX* could best be replaced by which of the following?

EXERCISE 7:   Practice Understanding Vocabulary in Context

Read the following short passages. Circle the correct answer to each question.

1. The colonists may have headed north toward the Chesapeake Bay area and there established a
settlement inland of the Bay. The native Americans of this area, the Chesapeakes, line were a
small group of no more than 1,000 people. If assimilation occurred, the settlers would have
line adopted Indian ways of living to a considerable extent, perhaps transforming their village into
(5) an Indian-style one or even amalgamating with Skicoac or another community. With the
opportunities for hunting, fishing, and agriculture that the area afforded, such a village, no
doubt separately organized at first, could enjoy a good living, given the absence of war,
internal dissension, and epidemic disease, none of which can be eliminated.

As used in line 5, the phrase "amalgamating with" could best be replaced by which of the
following words?
(A) changing
(B) joining with
(C) competing with
(D) supervising

The word "afforded" as used in line 6 could best be replaced by the word
(A) offered
(B) charged
(C) engaged
(D) entertained

2. Though classed with the carnivores, the grizzly bear is largely vegetarian and rarely eats flesh.
During the summer these bears are avid fishers and comb the waters of mountain streams and
rivers to catch salmon swimming upstream.

As used in line 1, a "carnivore" is most probably
(A) a vegetable eater
(B) a flesh eater
(C) a fisherman
(D) a type of bear

As used in line 2, the phrase "comb the waters" means that grizzlies
(A) search thoroughly
(B) enjoy fishing
(C) are usually unsuccessful
(D) enter the water

3. How can you decide if a beach is clean? One place to look for help is the local health
department of a coastal community. The local health departments monitor chemical and
bacterial levels in water which are usually undetectable to the naked eye.

The phrase "undetectable to the naked eye" as used in line 3 means
(A) easy to see if you look
(B) not able to be seen without a microscope
(C) hard to imagine
(D) the cause of eye problems

4. In the critical area of food production, new cooperative efforts in agricultural research and development are paying off. Food scientists are discovering that humankind is nowhere near the limits of plant, livestock, and soil productivity.

The phrase "paying off" as used in the first sentence could best be replaced by which of the following?
(A) costing a lot
(B) attracting attention
(C) showing success
(D) hard work

5. When the Pilgrims arrived from England in 1620, they found the native American communities devastated by a plague that eventually wiped out between 90 and 96 percent of the native inhabitants of southern New England.

As used in line 2, the phrase "wiped out" can best be replaced by which of the following?
(A) affected
(B) completely destroyed
(C) restored
(D) reinstated

6. The fossils that have led to this new view of dinosaurs as migratory creatures have been found in Alaska, Canada, Greenland, and the Soviet Union, as well as in Antarctica and southern Australia. At the time dinosaurs thrived near the poles, conditions there were radically different from those today. The planet was warmer, especially in the polar regions where four months of constant daylight and phenomenal plant growth allowed the huge beasts constant grazing.

The word "thrived" as used in line 3 could best be replaced by
(A) wandered
(B) existed
(C) summered
(D) flourished

7. When the English increased their visits to the area, they referred to it as New Brittaine, and then later as Arcadia. The name Arcadia was taken from the ancient Greek city where the people had a simple, rustic lifestyle. However, this was the name given by people who did not reside in the Outer Banks. The name Arcadia didn't stick.

As used in line 4, the expression "the name didn't stick" refers to the fact that
(A) the name is no longer used
(B) there were really no sticks in Arcadia
(C) the name Arcadia was replaced by New Brittaine
(D) Arcadia was too far from Greece to be a place name

8. Unemployment is still a threat in certain industries and for certain groups, especially among minority youth first entering the labor force. Unemployment is a waste of human resources, and represents a drain on public budgets and on the life savings of individual families.

As used in line 3, the phrase "a drain on" could best be replaced by which of the following?
(A) a misuse of
(B) a depletion of
(C) a lien against
(D) a neglect of

9. Herbicides, like all chemicals sprayed in the environment, have some adverse affects. Not only have earthworms and other soil microorganisms been killed by some herbicides, but also much needed insect predators have been destroyed by these chemicals.

   As used in line 1, the word "adverse" could best be replaced by which of the following?
   (A) unusual
   (B) interesting
   (C) harmful
   (D) notorious

10. Students in today's undergraduate colleges are being asked to specialize before they have acquired the general cultivation that would acquaint them with the ideas and disciplines that are the components of culture. Moreover, the humanities, as currently taught and studied, are as much addicted to specialized scholarship as are the scientific departments to highly specialized research.

    As used in line 4, the phrase "addicted to" may best be replaced by which of the following?
    (A) given over to
    (B) accustomed to
    (C) in need of
    (D) evaluated by

11. The black widow is found in all the 48 contiguous states, more commonly in the South and West than in the North. Crabill describes it as "a shy and retiring spider that doesn't go looking for trouble." The black widow's bite is excruciatingly painful. "Sometimes even morphine won't knock out the pain," Crabill says.

    As used in line 3, the word "excruciatingly" could best be replaced by which of the following?
    (A) somewhat
    (B) barely
    (C) mildly
    (D) unbearably

12. Trucks rank high in meeting the transportation needs of most manufacturers. They are the most frequently used form of transportation, for two reasons: (1) they offer door-to- door delivery from the manufacturer to the customer without intermediate unloading and (2) they
line operate on public highways that do not require an expensive terminal or right-of-way as
(5) airlines and railroads do. The main drawback of trucks is that they cannot carry all types of cargo. Federal regulations limit weight loads and truck dimensions, so trucks cannot cost-effectively haul heavy, bulky commodities like steel or coal.

    As used in line 5, the word "drawback" may best be replaced by which of the following?
    (A) design flaw
    (B) influence
    (C) disadvantage
    (D) mission

R✔8   Check the Attitude of the Author and the Tone of the Passage

A question on the TOEFL that asks about the attitude of the author or the tone of the passage requires that you think about the whole passage. Most often reading passages on the TOEFL give information in an objective way, and the author's point of view is neutral. The tone of these passages is informational. However, in some passages the author may express how he or she feels about the topic, the ideas, or the issues that he or she has written about. In these passages you should look for words that show an emotion or a strong point of view. Recognizing these words will help you to understand the attitude of the author and the tone of the passage.

MODEL

We must realize the futility of trying to impose our will upon our children. No amount of punishment will bring about lasting submission. Today's children are willing to take any amount of punishment in order to assert their "rights." Confused and bewildered parents mistakenly hope that punishment will eventually bring results, without realizing that they are actually getting nowhere with their methods. At best, they gain only temporary results from punishment. When the same punishment has to be repeated again and again, it should be obvious that it does not work.

1. Which of the following best describes the author's attitude toward punishment in the passage?
   (A) Sympathetic
   (B) Indifferent
   (C) Approving
   (D) Critical

2. What is the tone of the passage?
   (A) Descriptive
   (B) Sarcastic
   (C) Cautionary
   (D) Informational

Answers:

▼ Explanation ▲

The correct answer to Question 1 is (D) *Critical*. Key words and phrases in the passage that will help you to understand the author's attitude are *the futility of trying to impose our will*, *No amount of punishment will bring about lasting submission*, *parents mistakenly hope...getting nowhere with their methods*, *At best...temporary results*, and *it does not work*. The author's statements about punishment show that he or she is against punishment and thinks punishment is ineffective. You can discount answers (A), (B), and (C) because they do not restate the author's attitude.

The correct answer to Question 2 is (C) *Cautionary*. Throughout the passage the author is warning parents not to use punishment because it is ineffective. The tone of the passage reflects this warning. Answers (A), (B), and (D) do not describe a warning.

Exercise 8A: Words Describing the Author's Attitude and the Tone of a Passage

Match the word on the left with the best explanation on the right. Then, write the letter of the correct explanation in the space provided. Use your dictionary if you need help.

_F_ 1. emotional   A. disinterested; neutral

____ 2. informative   B. trying to change an attitude, an opinion, or a behavior

____ 3. humorous   C. objective; factual reporting; neutral

____ 4. descriptive   D. angry

____ 5. sarcastic   E. giving chronological facts about the past

____ 6. complimentary   F. showing emotion; happy, sad

____ 7. critical   G. making fun of something

____ 8. indifferent   H. disagreeing with something

____ 9. sympathetic   I. giving reasons and support for a point

____ 10. cautionary   J. funny

____ 11. persuasive   K. worried; very interested; distressed

____ 12. explanatory   L. agreement with a point; showing understanding

____ 13. outraged   M. describing something—a process, a place, a person

____ 14. concerned   N. giving a warning

____ 15. historical   O. showing approval or praise

Exercise 8B: Practice Identifying the Author's Attitude and the Tone of a Passage

Read the sentences. Then, from the list below, choose the word that best states the attitude or tone of the passage and write it in the space provided. Use each word only once.

descriptive   explanatory
concerned   critical
approving   advisory
historical

1. Jefferson, although elected a member of the Virginia Convention, had not wished to delay longer his return to Philadelphia, where he took his seat again on May 14. On the following day, May 15, Congress passed a resolution recommending that the separate colonies establish for themselves the new forms of government of their choice.

_____ _historical_ _____

2. Travelers with a history of motion sickness—including nausea, dizziness, and cold sweats—may want to take steps to avoid these uncomfortable symptoms. Avoid heavy meals, dairy products, and alcohol just before your trip.

_____

3. The African elephant, earth's largest land animal, is under unprecedented assault. Elephant numbers have been reduced from an estimated 1.2 million in 1981 to approximately 750,000 in 1988. The disastrous decline of elephant populations, primarily due to poaching and illegal trade in ivory, is one of the major conservation problems facing Africa.

   _____

4. Horses are timid by nature. Their natural defense lies in speed of flight—which is why a frightened horse tries to bolt. If cornered, they will defend themselves by biting, or by turning around and kicking. Stallions, by nature, are more prone to rear up and strike out with their forelegs, while mares are more likely to kick out with their hind legs and to be uncertain in temperament, especially when in season.

   _____

5. The term "mother earth" is not only self-limiting, but it also conflicts with the relationship we need to develop with our planet. After all, we leave our mothers, and as women our mothers are often exploited and abused. The built-in biases associated with "mother" should not be passed on to the earth.

   _____

6. In her first poem, the commonplace is transformed into art. Her poetic voice becomes distinctive and quite possibly distinguished. This poem points to the direction in which her best poetry is likely to move as her voice matures.

   _____

7. The great blue heron is a picturesque, aristocratic, long-legged wading bird. Many people call it the Blue Crane. But although it bears some resemblance to this family, it is not a crane, for cranes fly with necks outstretched like geese. The great blue heron flies with its long neck looped and the slender, black-crested head resting almost on the shoulders. In flight, long legs trail straight behind the short tail. Powerful wings beat slowly, steadily, almost rhythmically. When standing on stilt-like legs, the heron reaches a height of four feet, although it weighs something less than eight pounds.

   _____

EXERCISE 8C: More Practice Identifying the Author's Attitude and the Tone of a Passage

Read the passage and answer the questions about the author's attitude and the tone of the passage. Circle the correct answer to each question.

Our forebears had a deep respect for tradition and the accepted way of doing things. It was their complete adherence to rules that enabled them to do many things so well. Because all people helped with the construction of
line their own house, I assume that building knowledge was passed from
(5) generation to generation. Often, in the crudest early implements there can be found a beading or indented decoration worthy of the most sensitive artisan; in the simplest house framing one can see touches in hand-hewn beams that show a knowledge of classic architecture. Ira Allen, brother of Ethan Allen, wrote of Vermont, "I am really at a loss in the classification of
(10) the inhabitants here. They are all farmers, and again every farmer is a mechanic in some way or other, as the inclination leads or necessity requires. The hand that guides the plow most frequently constructs it."

1. What is the author's attitude toward the workmanship of people who lived in the past?
   (A) Indifferent
   (B) Critical
   (C) Admiring
   (D) Sarcastic

2. What is the tone of the passage?
   (A) Sad
   (B) Complimentary
   (C) Critical
   (D) Humorous

EXERCISE 8D: More Practice Identifying the Author's Attitude and the Tone of a Passage

Read the passage and answer the questions about the author's attitude and the tone of the passage. Circle the correct answer to each question.

There is reason today to reflect on the state of higher learning in America in its mission to teach the ordinary student to be a cultured person. The trouble is not simply that the sciences have displaced the humanities. The
line humanities, as currently taught and studied, are as much addicted to
(5) specialized scholarship as are the scientific departments to highly specialized research. The trouble rather is that the broadly educated generalist has become an endangered species. The ever-increasing specialization of knowledge in all fields has almost completely displaced the generalist.
(10) In most of our colleges, the elective system reigns supreme. Its only requirement—the choice of a major in one field of subject matter and a minor in another—compels students to specialize before they have acquired the general cultivation that would acquaint them with the ideas and disciplines that are the components of human culture.

1. What is the author's attitude in the passage toward higher education in America?
   (A) Understanding
   (B) Disinterested
   (C) Disapproving
   (D) Emotional

2. What is the tone of the passage?
   (A) Neutral
   (B) Concerned
   (C) Descriptive
   (D) Inspirational

See Tapescripts and Answers *for an explanation of Exercises 8C and 8D.*

Reading Comprehension Checkpoint Test Three for R✔1 through R✔8

Allow yourself 18 minutes to complete this checkpoint test. There are three passages and 20 questions on the test. Circle the letter of the correct answer to each question.

Noise is a given in our everyday lives. From the moment the alarm clock buzzes or the garbage trucks rouse us, to the time we fall asleep despite the neighbor's stereo, we accommodate noisy intrusions.

line
(5) Studies suggest that we pay a price for adapting to noise: higher blood pressure, heart rate, and adrenaline secretion—even after the noise stops; heightened aggression; impaired resistance to disease; a sense of helplessness. In terms of stress, unpredictability is an important factor. Studies suggest that when we can control noise, its effects are much less damaging.

(10) Although there are no studies on the effects of quiet in repairing the stress of noise, those who have studied the physiological effects of noise believe that quiet provides an escape. Most people who work in a busy and fairly noisy environment love quiet and need it desperately.

We are so acclimated to noise that complete quiet is sometimes
(15) unsettling. You might have trouble sleeping on vacation in the mountains, for example, without the background sounds of traffic. But making the effort to find quiet gives us a chance to hear ourselves think, to become attuned to the world around us, to find peacefulness and calm. It provides a serene antidote to the intrusively loud world we live in the rest of the day.

1. This passage mainly discusses
   (A) life in the city
   (B) the effect of noise on our lives
   (C) diseases related to stress
   (D) why quiet is hard to find

2. What is the best title for this passage?
   (A) Noise and Disease
   (B) Finding Quiet in a Noisy World
   (C) The Causes of Noise
   (D) Getting Rid of Noise

3. We can infer from the passage that the author is writing for which group of people?
   (A) People who live in the country
   (B) Vacationers
   (C) City-dwellers
   (D) Doctors

4. What is the author's attitude toward noise in the passage?
   (A) Humorous
   (B) Critical
   (C) Emotional
   (D) Indifferent

5. According to the passage, noise causes all of the following EXCEPT
   (A) oversleeping
   (B) stress
   (C) higher blood pressure
   (D) heightened aggression

6. The author indicates in the passage that stress from noise occurs mainly
   (A) in the morning
   (B) when we can't control it
   (C) in the mountains
   (D) from traffic

7. The phrase "pay a price for" in line 4 could best be replaced by which of the following?
   (A) suffer from
   (B) lose money because of
   (C) work hard
   (D) indulge in

8. The word "unsettling" in line 15 could best be replaced by which of the following?
   (A) rewarding
   (B) necessary
   (C) unavoidable
   (D) disturbing

line

(5)

(10)

(15)

(20)

(25)

(30)

The killer sea waves known as tsunamis are so quiet in their approach from afar, so seemingly harmless, that until recently their history has been one of surprise attack.

Out in the middle of the ocean, the distance between tsunami wave crests can be 100 miles and the height of the waves no more than three feet: Mariners can ride one and suspect nothing. At the shoreline, the first sign is often an ebbing of the waters that leaves fish stranded and slapping on the bottom. However, this is not a retreat but rather a gathering of forces. When the great waves finally do strike, they rear up and batter harbor and coast, inflicting death and damage.

These seismic sea waves—or tidal waves, as they are sometimes called—bear no relation to the moon or tides. And the word "tsunami," Japanese for "harbor wave," relates to their destination rather than their origin. The causes are various: undersea or coastal earthquakes, deep ocean avalanches or volcanism. Whatever the cause, the wave motion starts with a sudden jolt like a whack from a giant paddle that displaces the water. And the greater the undersea whack, the greater the tsunami's devastating power.

In 1883, Krakatoa volcano in the East Indies erupted, and the entire island collapsed in 820 feet of water. A tsunami of tremendous force ricocheted around Java and Sumatra, killing 36,000 people with walls of water that reached 115 feet in height.

In 1946 a tsunami struck first near Alaska and then, without warning, hit the Hawaiian islands, killing 159 people and inflicting millions of dollars of damage. This led to the creation of the Tsunami Warning System, whose nerve center in Honolulu keeps a round-the-clock vigil with the aid of new technology. If the seismic sea waves are confirmed by the Honolulu center, warnings are transmitted within a few hours to all threatened Pacific points. While tsunami damage remains unavoidable, lives lost today are more likely to be in the tens than in the thousands. Tsunamis have been deprived of their most deadly sting—surprise.

9. The author's main point in this passage is that
   (A) seismic sea waves today are carefully monitored and cause less damage than in the past
   (B) tsunamis can do little damage when they strike
   (C) there is little possibility of avoiding tidal waves once they are in motion
   (D) we need better equipment to track the movements of tsunamis

10. According to the passage, seismic sea waves
   (A) are easily detected by fishermen
   (B) are named "tsunami" for the origin of the wave in the harbor
   (C) are called tidal waves because of their relation to the moon
   (D) originate far from the place where they strike

11. In line 16, why does the author mention "a giant paddle"?
   (A) To make a comparison
   (B) To give a definition
   (C) To draw a conclusion
   (D) To make a suggestion

12. According to the passage, all of the following are possible causes for seismic sea waves EXCEPT
   (A) earthquakes near a coastline
   (B) tides
   (C) avalanches underwater
   (D) volcanos

13. The phrase "a round–the–clock vigil" in line 26 could best replaced by which of the following?
(A) a good count
(B) a constant watch
(C) a careful record
(D) an open line

14. The tone of this article can best be described as
(A) informative
(B) exaggerated
(C) indignant
(D) humorous

15. According to the passage, the Tsunami Warning System was created because of
(A) the availability of new technology
(B) the nervous state of people in Honolulu
(C) the occurrence of the 1946 tsunami
(D) the loss of millions of lives

Questions 16–20

For several decades, psychologists have been doing extensive research on a subject that affects millions of us: hobbies. According to their findings, a person's choice of hobby can be almost as revealing as his reaction to an
line ink blot.
(5)   Investigators found that a clearly distinguishable pattern exists between hobby preferences and personality. Scientists now say that they are in a position to study your hobby and come up with a fairly accurate estimate of your emotional maturity, level of intelligence, and distinguishing personality traits.
(10)   This is because people generally pick a hobby of their own free will. As a parallel, a person choosing a mate employs a method of selection that reflects his or her intellectual and emotional maturity; the same process is at work in choosing a hobby.
    A hobby is never a task, but a form of living expression that
(15) complements and augments one's own personality.

16. The best title for this passage is
(A) Hobbies: A Glimpse of the True You
(B) A Psychologist's Hobby
(C) How to Choose a Hobby
(D) The Importance of Choosing the Right Hobby

17. It can be inferred from the passage that a reaction to an ink blot
(A) is used to reveal a person's personality
(B) is one kind of hobby
(C) is being extensively investigated today
(D) is the author's favorite hobby

18. The author implies in the passage that hobbies are
(A) only for the emotionally mature
(B) something most people have
(C) as important as a mate
(D) very time-consuming endeavors

19. According to the passage, a person's choice of hobby can tell scientists about all of the following EXCEPT
(A) level of intelligence
(B) probable choice of mate
(C) emotional maturity
(D) special personality traits

20. As used in line 15, the word "augments" can best be replaced by
(A) reveals
(B) misconstrues
(C) extends
(D) affects

Vocabulary and Reading Comprehension Section Test

On the following pages you will find a practice section test for Section Three of the TOEFL Vocabulary and Reading Comprehension.

Allow yourself 45 minutes to complete this test.

Use the third part of the SECTION TESTS ANSWER SHEET, numbers 1–60, from the General Appendix, #4, page 509 to record your answers.

When answering each question, use the strategies and skills you have reviewed in the preceding chapter.

Score your test using *The Heinemann TOEFL Preparation Course Tapescripts and Answers*. Next to each answer in this key is the number of the checkpoint that is being tested in the corresponding Vocabulary and Reading Comprehension Section Test questions. Use these numbers to determine which checkpoints, if any, you need to study again.

Estimate your TOEFL score for this section test using Score Conversion Table 1 in the General Appendix, #3, page 505.

SECTION THREE
VOCABULARY AND READING COMPREHENSION SECTION TEST

Time—45 minutes

This section is designed to measure your comprehension of standard written English. There are two types of questions in this section, with special directions for each type.

Directions: In questions 1–30, each sentence has an underlined word or phrase. Below each sentence are four other words or phrases, marked (A), (B), (C), and (D). You are to choose the one word or phrase that best keeps the meaning of the original sentence if it is substituted for the underlined word or phrase. Then, on your answer sheet, find the number of the question and fill in the space that corresponds to the letter you have chosen. Fill in the space so that the letter inside the oval cannot be seen.

Example   Sample Answer

Ladybugs, small brightly colored beetles,   ● Ⓑ Ⓒ Ⓓ
feed on plant aphids and have considerable
economic value in controlling pest populations.

    (A) limiting
    (B) finding
    (C) increasing
    (D) ruling

The best answer is (A) because "Ladybugs, small brightly colored beetles, feed on plant aphids and have considerable economic value in limiting pest populations" is closest in meaning to the original sentence. Therefore, you should choose answer (A).

After you read the directions, begin work on the questions.

1. The Mississippi River begins its journey to the sea in Minnesota, meandering southward some 2,500 miles to empty into the Gulf of Mexico.
   (A) flowing
   (B) winding
   (C) rushing
   (D) inching

2. Oprah Winfrey's troubled childhood was cheered periodically by extended visits to a benign aunt and uncle.
   (A) distant
   (B) rich
   (C) kindly
   (D) reclusive

3. The book's success was judged to be due in part to the collaboration of the author and the editors.
   (A) hard work
   (B) cooperation
   (C) inspiration
   (D) financial backing

4. The young of most species eat voraciously for the first few weeks of their lives.
   (A) regularly
   (B) ravenously
   (C) intermittently
   (D) quickly

GO ON TO THE NEXT PAGE ➤

5. Before landing the plane, the pilot checked with the tower for <u>verification</u> of her coordinates.
   (A) confirmation of
   (B) guidance with
   (C) information about
   (D) mention of

6. The speaker concluded with a few <u>terse</u> comments in response to the reporter's question.
   (A) hysterical
   (B) abrupt
   (C) anecdotal
   (D) leading

7. With the invention of the telephone we see the end of <u>an epoch</u> in which personal correspondence was a part of a gentleman's daily life.
   (A) an event
   (B) a tradition
   (C) an era
   (D) a distinction

8. Matthew has the reputation for <u>consistently</u> being late for class.
   (A) rarely
   (B) once in a while
   (C) constantly
   (D) conspicuously

9. <u>Irate</u> behavior does little to solve problems or assuage feelings.
   (A) uninformed
   (B) silly
   (C) reticent
   (D) angry

10. A career in medicine does not appeal to those who are <u>squeamish about</u> dissecting laboratory animals.
    (A) confused about
    (B) inexperienced in
    (C) uneasy about
    (D) inept at

11. In Victorian England it was traditional for gentlemen to <u>adjourn to</u> the library after a formal dinner.
    (A) retire to
    (B) call
    (C) return to
    (D) read in

12. Be sure to send in the <u>requisite</u> information with the application form.
    (A) questionable
    (B) necessary
    (C) important
    (D) enclosed

13. To achieve success in most laboratory courses, one must approach a task <u>analytically</u>.
    (A) diplomatically
    (B) indiscriminately
    (C) systematically
    (D) assertively

14. To overcome the <u>insurgency</u>, special forces were moved to the area.
    (A) disaster
    (B) rebellion
    (C) invasion
    (D) alienation

15. Patchwork quilts are known for the <u>variegated</u> pieces used in their construction.
    (A) symmetrical
    (B) well-worn
    (C) carefully chosen
    (D) many-colored

16. Psychologists note that to be able to resume normal life after the loss of a loved one, people must have time to <u>grieve</u>.
    (A) recover
    (B) talk
    (C) mourn
    (D) adjust

GO ON TO THE NEXT PAGE

17. Early prehistoric cave paintings contain
    <u>figures</u> of animals in motion.
    (A) forms
    (B) remains
    (C) numerals
    (D) apparitions

18. The victim of the mugging was able to give
    <u>a lucid</u> account of the attack.
    (A) a clear
    (B) a sketchy
    (C) an immediate
    (D) an emotional

19. Some parents believe that the best way to
    handle obstreperous children is to <u>ignore</u> their
    behavior.
    (A) reward
    (B) restrain
    (C) punish
    (D) pay no attention to

20. <u>Lacking</u> the complete specifications for the
    job, we completed the drawings as best we
    could.
    (A) Using
    (B) Missing
    (C) Interpreting
    (D) Requiring

21. A <u>range</u> of questions was included on the
    examination to assure that the topic was
    adequately covered.
    (A) large number
    (B) list
    (C) variety
    (D) taxonomy

22. The city that we had <u>initially</u> planned to visit
    was Seattle.
    (A) eventually
    (B) previously
    (C) hopefully
    (D) originally

23. The defendant appeared to be <u>devoid of</u>
    feelings as the sentence was read by the
    judge.
    (A) overcome by
    (B) without
    (C) devastated by
    (D) wrestling with

24. The corporation spent money <u>effusively</u> after
    receiving news of the upcoming merger.
    (A) sparingly
    (B) randomly
    (C) lavishly
    (D) selectively

25. The campers awoke as the rain <u>permeated</u>
    their tent.
    (A) fell unto
    (B) resounded on
    (C) seeped through
    (D) dripped from

26. A monopoly was formed when the company
    gained <u>proprietorship</u> of the three smaller
    firms.
    (A) control
    (B) influence
    (C) ownership
    (D) allegiance

27. The crash of the airliner was caused by a
    <u>minute</u> crack in the fuselage.
    (A) discernible
    (B) tiny
    (C) disastrous
    (D) crucial

28. One method of treating lower back pain is to
    <u>fuse</u> the vertebrae in the lower spinal column.
    (A) medicate
    (B) manipulate
    (C) support
    (D) join

GO ON TO THE NEXT PAGE ➤

29. The request for a voluntary pay freeze was met with <u>skepticism</u> on the part of the workers.
    (A) anger
    (B) distrust
    (C) disdain
    (D) compliance

30. A child who is the subject of neglect and <u>derision</u> may never achieve a healthy self–image.
    (A) ridicule
    (B) punishment
    (C) isolation
    (D) malnutrition

<u>Directions:</u> In the rest of this section you will read several passages. Each one is followed by several questions about it. For questions 31–60, you are to choose the <u>one</u> best answer, (A), (B), (C), or (D), to each question. Then, on your answer sheet, find the number of the question and fill in the space that corresponds to the letter of the answer you have chosen.

Answer all questions following a passage on the basis of what is <u>stated</u> or <u>implied</u> in that passage.

Read the following passage.

The flamingo is a beautiful water bird with long legs and a curving neck like a swan's. Most flamingos have deep red or flame-colored feathers with black quills. Some have pink or white feathers. The long legs and webbed feet are well suited for wading. The flamingo
line eats in a peculiar manner. It plunges its head underwater and sifts the mud with a fine
(5) hairlike "comb" along the edge of its bent bill. In this way, it strains out small shellfish and other animals. The bird nests on a mound of mud with a hollow on top to hold its single egg. Flamingos are timid and often live together in large colonies. The birds once lived in the southern United States, but plume hunters killed them faster than they could breed, and the flamingo no longer lives wild in the United States.

Example I   <u>Sample Answer</u>

The flamingo can eat shellfish and other animals because of its   Ⓐ ● Ⓒ Ⓓ
    (A) curved neck
    (B) specially formed bill
    (C) long legs
    (D) brightly colored feathers

According to the passage, the flamingo sifts mud for food with "a fine hairlike 'comb' along the edge of its bent bill." Therefore, you should choose answer (B).

GO ON TO THE NEXT PAGE ➤

Example II   <u>Sample Answer</u>

How many young would you expect the flamingo to raise at one time?   Ⓐ Ⓑ ● Ⓓ
   (A)   Several
   (B)   Two
   (C)   One
   (D)   Four

The passage states that the flamingo nests on a mound of mud with a "single" egg. Therefore, you should choose answer (C).

After you read the directions, begin work on the questions.

<u>Questions 31–35</u>

One of the most mysterious things in nature is the ability of certain creatures to find their way home, sometimes from great distances. Birds are not the only ones who can do this. Bees, eels, and salmon are able to return to a particular place after long journeys, too.
line   Many experiments have been made with birds in an attempt to find out what guides them on
 (5)   their way home. In one case, seven swallows were taken 400 miles from home. When they were set free, five of them returned to their nests. In another case, a certain kind of sea bird was taken from its nest off the Welsh coast to Venice by plane. When it was released, it made its way home to its nest, a distance of 930 miles if it flew in a straight line.
Migrating birds offer an even more amazing example of this ability. There are swallows that
(10) migrate from England to South Africa every year. They not only return to England the next spring, but many of them come back to nest in the very same house where they nested the year before. They fly the incredible distance of 6,000 miles, one way.
Certain types of butterflies migrate, too, and find their way home over long distances. In the tropics one can sometimes see great mass flights of butterflies all flying steadily in one
(15) direction. They may go a thousand miles and more, and then return again in another season.
Despite all the efforts that have been made to explain how these creatures find their way home, we still have no sure explanation. Since many of the birds fly over great bodies of water, we can't explain it by saying they use landmarks to guide them. Just to say they have an "instinct" doesn't really explain the right conditions. The reason they do it may be to obtain food or to reproduce under the right conditions. But the signals and guideposts they use on their flights are still a mystery to us.

31. What is the main idea of this passage?
    (A) We know little about how migratory creatures find their way home
    (B) Many different types of creatures migrate annually
    (C) Creatures migrate to find food and to reproduce
    (D) Migratory birds travel long distances during migration

GO ON TO THE NEXT PAGE ▶

32. In paragraph 4 the author mentions butterflies in order to
    (A) include the tropics in the discussion of migration
    (B) give another example of migratory creatures
    (C) show that these small flying creatures don't get lost
    (D) show that butterflies cover long distances when migrating

33. In line 9 the phrase "this ability" refers to
    (A) the ability to fly long distances
    (B) the ability to build nests year after year
    (C) the ability to find their way home
    (D) the ability to fly in a straight line

34. According to the passage, swallows traveling from South Africa to England
    (A) cover a relatively short distance
    (B) often return to precisely the same point each year
    (C) may not return for a number of years
    (D) rebuild the same type of nest in similar locations each spring

35. The attitude of the author toward the ability of certain creatures to find their way home may best be expressed by which of the following?
    (A) Confused
    (B) Sympathetic
    (C) Admiring
    (D) Indifferent

Questions 36–41

Medical research on the prevention of strokes has recently made several breakthroughs. The researchers studied strokes that are caused by an irregular heart rhythm that produces blood clots. When those clots get lodged in an artery that supplies blood to the brain, they
line reduce blood flow and produce a stroke. The use of the blood- thinning drug warfarin cut
(5) the risk of stroke by 67 percent. Up to 75,000 Americans who have strokes each year suffer from irregular heart rhythms. The data also suggest that aspirin is effective and is a reasonable alternative. Doctors might feel more comfortable prescribing aspirin because of the slight possibility that warfarin may lead to internal bleeding.
   In separate studies with patients with severe narrowing of the carotid artery, one of the
(10) most common causes of a stroke, a form of surgery now exists which effectively prevents strokes. The surgery involves the removal of a portion of the carotid artery in the neck when it is partially blocked by cholesterol deposits. When the blocked portion has been removed, the artery is reconnected with an artificial tube or a vein from elsewhere in the body.
(15) The research on stroke prevention has showed such dramatic results that doctors have abruptly halted the studies to make the information available to all patients.

36. Which of the following would be the best title for this passage?
    (A) Surgery to Prevent Strokes
    (B) Strokes and Their Causes
    (C) New Measures for Preventing Strokes
    (D) Doctors Halt Studies

37. According to the passage, which of the following is NOT true of the drug warfarin?
    (A) It might possibly lead to internal bleeding
    (B) It has been effective in preventing strokes
    (C) It has been used in research studies on people with irregular heartbeats
    (D) It eliminates cholesterol deposits in arteries

GO ON TO THE NEXT PAGE

38. It can be inferred from the passage that strokes are a result of
    (A) reduced blood flow to the brain
    (B) expansion of the carotid artery
    (C) taking too many aspirin
    (D) internal bleeding

39. According to the article, the data about aspirin suggest that
    (A) it is not as useful as warfarin
    (B) it is linked to internal bleeding
    (C) it could be used instead of warfarin
    (D) it is a substitute for surgery of the carotid artery

40. The word "it" in line 11 refers to
    (A) neck
    (B) carotid artery
    (C) surgery
    (D) a stroke

41. We can conclude from the passage that the attitude of doctors toward the results of the stroke prevention research is
    (A) cautious
    (B) positive
    (C) frustrated
    (D) indifferent

Questions 42–45

For a brief interlude in American history, between the passing of the Indian and the buffalo and the entry of the farmer and the barbed-wire fence, the Great Plains witnessed the most picturesque industrial drama ever staged—the drama of the open range and the cattle ranch.
line If the Southern planter could once claim that cotton was king, the Western cattlerancher
(5) could proclaim with equal fervor that grass was king. For the time being, at least, the plains were one limitless, fenceless, gateless pasture of rich, succulent, and ownerless grass that was there for the taking. Within an incredibly short period the herds of bison had been replaced and outnumbered by the herds of cattle.

42. The author's main point in this passage is that
    (A) this was a profitable time for western cattleranchers
    (B) the Great Plains is a good place for cattle grazing
    (C) cotton was as important to the South as grass to the West
    (D) during this time the pastureland was industrialized

43. According to the passage, a notable characteristic of the Great Plains at this time was
    (A) its lack of industry
    (B) the large number of buffalo found there
    (C) its openness
    (D) its opportunities for farmers

44. All of the following can be inferred from the passage EXCEPT
    (A) there were more cattle on the range during this period than buffalo
    (B) grass was the most important commodity for the cattlerancher
    (C) grazing land at this time was free
    (D) cotton was important in Western agriculture

45. The author implies in the passage that the character of the Great Plains
    (A) remains unchanged today
    (B) changed with the coming of the farmer
    (C) is no longer picturesque
    (D) is similar to that of the South

GO ON TO THE NEXT PAGE

Questions 46–50

Tomatoes are probably the most popular garden vegetable grown in the United States. This can be attributed to their unique flavor, attractiveness, richness as a source of vitamins C and A, and versatility as a food. The popularity of peppers can be attributed to the same
line factors, although they are usually not consumed in large enough quantities to make them an
(5) important nutritional factor in the diet.

The cultivated tomato originated in the Andes mountains of South America. It was introduced to other areas of the world by Indians and European travelers. The first report of the tomato in North America was in 1710 where it was grown primarily as an ornamental plant. Tomatoes began gaining wide acceptance as a food plant in the United States between
(10) 1820 and 1850.

Peppers are also native to tropical America and were grown by American tribes in both North and South America over 2,000 years ago. The small red hot peppers were discovered by Columbus in the West Indies and introduced into Europe where they became popular before gaining widespread acceptance in the United States. Peppers became one of the first.
(15) New World foods used commercially in Europe.

46. The topic of this passage is
   (A) food discoveries of early Europeans
   (B) the nutritional value of garden vegetables
   (C) tomatoes and peppers
   (D) why tomatoes are more popular than peppers

47. According to the passage, why are peppers not an important nutritional factor in a diet?
   (A) People don't eat enough of them
   (B) They lack the necessary vitamins
   (C) They are less tasty than tomatoes
   (D) Peppers are found in tropical climates

48. It can be inferred from the passage that tomatoes were first used in North America
   (A) for food
   (B) as decoration
   (C) in place of peppers
   (D) for nutritional purposes

49. All of the following can be inferred from the passage about peppers EXCEPT
   (A) peppers became popular in the United States later than in Europe
   (B) peppers were bought and sold in Europe
   (C) red peppers are highly spiced
   (D) peppers originated fairly recently in North and South America

50. Which of the following best describes the format of this passage?
   (A) A hypothesis supported by evidence
   (B) A general introduction followed by chronological development
   (C) A response to a criticism
   (D) A question and subsequent answers

GO ON TO THE NEXT PAGE

Questions 51–56

What makes science fiction the literature choice for so many? Arthur C. Clarke, the novelist and scientist, gave a good answer once, when asked why he chose to write in this

line genre: "Because," he said, "no other literature is concerned with reality."

line   Clarke didn't say what sort of reality he had in mind, but there are two that suggest

(5) themselves. One of those significant realities of our time is science and technology.   Those are the things that have made this century move so fast, in ways that earlier generations could hardly even imagine, and science fiction has played some part in accelerating their progress. In the 1930s there was no television, radio showed little interest in science, even the daily newspapers covered it scantily and not very well; but science-fiction magazines

(10) were exploring in every pulpwood issue the latest concepts from genetics and nuclear physics to cosmology. I think it is fair to say that a majority of the world's leading scientists today were first turned on to their subjects by reading science-fiction stories.

The other reason for a fascination with science fiction is that the central fact of contemporary life is rapid, ever-accelerating change, change that alters the rules of all our

(15) lives all the time. And science fiction is, in essence, the literature of change.

51. Which of the following would be the best title for this passage?
(A) Why Read Science Fiction?
(B) How Science Relates to Reality
(C) Popular Literature of the 1930s
(D) Topics in Science Fiction

52. What is the author's main purpose in this passage?
(A) To explain the popularity of science-fiction literature
(B) To show the need for science-fiction literature
(C) To classify different types of literature
(D) To discuss the work of Arthur C. Clarke

53. According to the passage, which of the following carried news of science and technology to the public in the 1930s?
(A) Radio broadcasts
(B) Science-fiction magazines
(C) Television programs
(D) Newspaper coverage

54. The author mentions all of the following as being part of the reality with which science fiction is concerned EXCEPT
(A) change
(B) publication
(C) science
(D) technology

55. The phrase "turned on to" as used in line 12 could best be replaced by which of the following?
(A) employed by
(B) introduced to
(C) disenchanted with
(D) changed by

56. The attitude of the author toward science-fiction literature can best be described as
(A) critical
(B) approving
(C) wary
(D) cold

GO ON TO THE NEXT PAGE

Questions 57–60

    Among the more than 1.5 million species of living things that have been described and
named, the human species is unique in that its members adapt to the environment primarily
by a complicated form of learned behavior called culture, which is transmitted from
line generation to generation by the symbol system of language. For all practical purposes,
(5) geographic variation in our species is now irrelevant because people adapt to the
environment primarily by means of behavior, whose biological basis is in the brain and is not
reflected in superficial differences in body surfaces. When they first evolved, people who
had dark- colored skins were better adapted to climatic conditions near the equator than
those who had light-colored skins, but few human beings now live under natural conditions.
(10) Also, technological advances have assured that at the present time, human beings of various
races are as likely to reproduce in one environment as in another. The superficial differences
between existing human races are thus largely relics of the past and are not of much
functional significance today.

57. The author's main point in this passage is that
   (A) the differences between human races
       today are not very important
   (B) language is important to the human
       species
   (C) people with dark-colored skins were
       better adapted to living near the
       equator
   (D) geographic variation plays an important
       part in the human species

58. According to the passage, the human species
is unique because of
   (A) having different colored skins
   (B) adaptation to the environment through
       cultural behavior
   (C) technological advances in human
       reproduction
   (D) not living in natural conditions

59. It can be inferred from the passage that
members of the human species
   (A) don't live near the equator
   (B) are biologically different from each other
   (C) transmit their learned behavior through
       language
   (D) cannot reproduce between races

60. The tone of this passage can best be described
as
   (A) informational
   (B) hypothetical
   (C) pessimistic
   (D) critical

THIS IS THE END OF SECTION 3

**IF YOU FINISH BEFORE TIME IS CALLED, CHECK YOUR WORK ON SECTION 3 ONLY.
DO NOT READ OR WORK ON ANY OTHER SECTION OF THE TEST.**
FOR MORE PRACTICE, TAKE A COMPLETE TEST FROM *THE HEINNEMANN TOEFL PRACTICE TESTS.*

STOP   STOP   STOP   **STOP**   STOP   STOP   STOP

SECTION FOUR

TEST OF WRITTEN ENGLISH

The purpose of The Test of Written English (TWE) is to test your ability to write in standard written English. The writing tasks you are asked to perform on the TWE are similar to those required of students in academic courses in universities in North America. In your TWE essay you will be evaluated on your ability to:

Generate and organize ideas on paper.
Support those ideas with evidence or examples.
Use the conventions of standard written English.

The Test of Written English requires that you write for 30 minutes on one topic. Your essay is read by at least two readers and assigned a score based on a six-point, criterion-referenced scoring guide. (See W✔3 page 388 for information on the criteria used to score TWE essays.) Your score on the TWE is not included in your total TOEFL score, but is reported separately on the TOEFL score report. Colleges and universities that require the TWE will expect a score of 4, 5, or 6 on the essay. The TWE is not given on every TOEFL testing date. Check the *Bulletin of Information for TOEFL and TSE* for the dates that the TWE will be administered.

GENERAL STRATEGIES FOR SECTION FOUR

1. Understand the question. Know what the question is asking you to do.

2. Spend about five minutes thinking and organizing your ideas. Write your notes on the TOEFL question sheet. You will write your essay on the lined pages provided in the test book.

3. Be sure that you give adequate support for the major points that you make. Write only on the points in the question. DO NOT include irrelevant or unnecessary information.

4. Use vocabulary and structures with which you are familiar. Try to express yourself simply and clearly. Use vocabulary and structures of organization to introduce and to connect your ideas.

5. Write legibly and concisely. You have only two pages on which to write a 200–300 word essay. Extra pages are not provided.

6. Spend three to five minutes at the end reading your essay for careless mistakes of spelling, grammar, and punctuation.

Test of Written English: Question Types

The writing task given on the TWE will be one of two types.

Type One: Compare and Contrast Essay
You are given a short statement about an issue and asked to compare and contrast the points of the issue. You are asked to give specific reasons or support in your answer and to state your own position.

Type Two: Interpretation of Charts and Graphs
You are given a chart or graph and asked to describe and interpret the information on it. You are asked to draw conclusions and to support them with details and facts from the charts and graphs.

Examples of some common topics for TWE essays include:

COMPARISON AND CONTRAST TOPICS
Universal issues
   education
   use of leisure time
   raising children
   health and medicine
   the past and the present
Science and technology
   computers and people
   space exploration
Social issues
   gun control
   government spending
Personal issues
   choosing a job
   friends and family
Environmental problems
   pollution
   world population

INTERPRETATION OF CHARTS AND GRAPHS
Spending money
   government
   individual
Attitudes and values
   from surveys
Population figures
Spending time
Trends over time
   periods (e.g. climatic changes, health improvement)

Test of Written English: Vocabulary

The more you have read about and have thought about topics like these listed above, the more ideas you will have to use in your response to a TWE question. The kind of writing that you will do on the TWE is similar to the academic writing that you will be required to do if you attend an American college or university or if you need to use written English for professional reasons. In order to express yourself adequately in an academic writing task you must use vocabulary that appropriately develops the topic. The best way to gain a large and varied vocabulary is to read a lot in many different areas. Refer to the Vocabulary Appendix Word Category Charts pages 470–485 for more practice with vocabulary development.

✔ WRITING CHECKPOINTS

Below is a list of Writing Checkpoints which are included in the Writing Checkpoint Study. Page numbers are provided for your easy reference. The Writing Checkpoint study will help you to develop good writing skills and strategies as you prepare for the Test of Written English (TWE).

✔ WRITING CHECKPOINT STUDY

W✔1 Practice Prewriting for TWE Essays

There are several important steps for prewriting for Type One Questions, Compare and Contrast, and for Type Two Questions, Interpreting Charts and Graphs.

Type One Questions: Comparison and Contrast

Step I. Understand the question and know what it asks you to do.
Type One Questions for the TWE are about topics that most students are familiar with. A question that asks you to compare and contrast gives an issue and the context in which it is found, then a task (a problem to resolve). The response to the question (the solution to the problem) should include a discussion of the issue and your position regarding the issue.

MODEL

Question One:
Some people think that cities are the best places to live. Others prefer to live in a rural area. Compare the advantages of living in the city to the advantages of living in the country. Where would you prefer to live? Give reasons for your choice.

Before you begin to write about this question, be sure that you understand the issue and know what you are being asked to do. What is the issue and its context? What is the task? What will the response include?

Issue: Some people think that cities are the best places to live. Others prefer to live in a rural area.

TASK
Part 1: Compare the advantages of living in the city to the advantages of living in the country.
Part 2: Where would you prefer to live?
Response: Discussion of the advantages of living in the city and of living in the country.
Personal choice of where to live: development of reasons for this choice.

Step 2.   Generate ideas.

To answer Question One you first need to come up with ideas about the issue of living in the city versus living in a rural area. Task Part 1 asks you to compare the advantages of living in both places. Two common ways to put your ideas on paper are to make an idea map or to make a list. As you put ideas about the issue on paper, you will begin to think about how you will organize your main points. Here are examples of two possible ways to put your ideas about Question One on paper during pre-writing:

Make a LIST

City: Advantages
Better job/more money
Conveniences
Cultural opportunities
Entertainment

Country: Advantages
Close to nature
Little stress
Healthy Environment
Safe place to live

Make an IDEA MAP

Entertainment

Better jobs: more money

Living in the City

More conveniences

Cultural opportunities

Little stress

Safe place to live

Living in the Country

Close to nature

Healthy environment

The ideas in the LIST and IDEA MAP above are only examples of points to include for advantages of living in a city and advantages of living in the country. You may have other points that you think are more important for your list or idea map.

Some students think that an idea map is easier to refer to when they are writing an essay. If you choose to use the list form of making notes, be sure to organize your supporting points as you generate ideas.

Step 3.   Use adequate support for main points.

An answer to a comparison and contrast question must also include support for the main points. Examples, details, facts, and personal experiences strengthen the main points of an essay. Readers of TWE essays look for specific support of the points you make. As you generate ideas, add the details and facts that you think support your main ideas. Here are some examples of possible support for Question One.

City: Advantages
Better job/more money
  Support: engineering, sales, business

Conveniences
  Support: transportation, bus, subways
  stores (different types and price ranges)
  better schools and universities

Cultural offerings
  Support: libraries, museums, theaters

Entertainment
  Support: nightclubs, discos, restaurants

Country: Advantages
Closer to nature
  Support: beautiful, more peaceful

Fewer people
  Support: less traffic, no lines in stores,
  more personal relationships

Less stress and safer
  Support: time for enjoying other people,
  less crime and no drugs

Healthier environment
  Support: Clean air, family relationships

Support in an IDEA MAP:

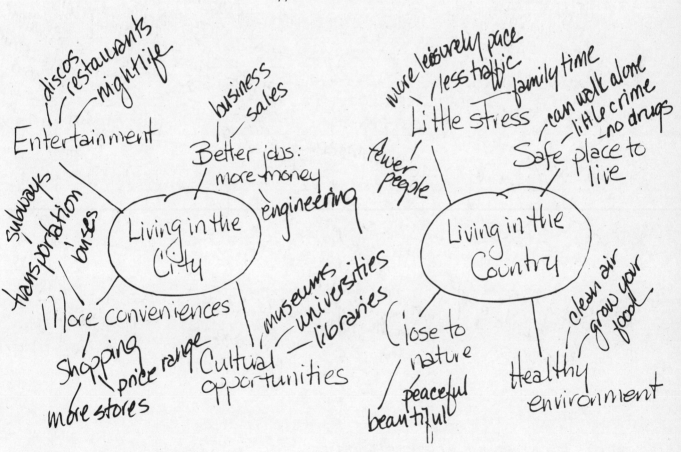

Step 4. Organize your ideas.

After you have your ideas on paper, you need to put them in the order that you will discuss them in the essay.

Clear organization is extremely important for a reader to be able to follow the ideas in an essay. When you have enough time, an outline of the points of the essay should be developed to guide you through the writing process. However, in the TWE you will not have time to go through outline writing, so you should go back to your list or map and number, use arrows, etc. to organize your ideas for writing. Here are examples of organization techniques for Question One:

Organization Techniques for a LIST

If you choose to generate your ideas in a list, the best way to show your organization is to number the main points in some order. You might put what you consider the most important points at the beginning in a response to Question One.

City: Advantages	Country: Advantages
2. Better job/more money	1. Close to nature
1. Conveniences	4. Safe place to live
3. Cultural offerings	3. Little stress
4. Entertainment	2. Healthy environment

Organization Techniques for an IDEA MAP

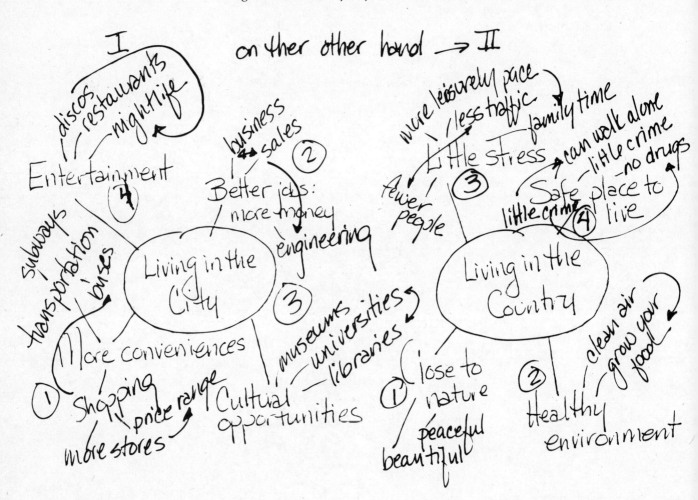

Step 5. *Take a position on the issue and defend it.*

An important part of the contrast and comparison essay is the second part of the task. The question may ask you to take a position on the issue and support it. If the question does not clearly ask you to take a position, you will be expected to come to a conclusion based on your discussion of the issue.

In some questions it will be quite clear to you what your position is. In other questions, you may feel that it is possible to choose either side of the issue. In this case, use your discussion of the points of the issue to lead you to a logical conclusion. This part of the essay does not need to be long, but it should include clear support for the position you take. Be sure to make a clearly supported statement at the end of the essay.

I prefer living in the city.
    Support: Give reasons and show contrast to living in the country.

More exciting, better job opportunities, availability of modern conveniences, etc.

I prefer to live in the country.
    Support: Give reasons and show contrast to living in the city.

Close to nature, no stress from crowds and traffic, no pollution, time to enjoy yourself, etc.

Type Two Questions: Interpretation of Charts and Graphs

Step 1:   Understand the question and know what it asks you to do.
Type Two Questions ask you to interpret information contained in charts and graphs and draw conclusions based on this information. You must understand the question and understand the information before you begin writing your response.

MODEL

Question Two:
    The two pie charts below show the proportion of time that is spent on several major aspects of college life by two students. What do the graphs tell you about the lifestyles of the two students? What conclusions can you come to about the two students?

How Two Students Spend Their Time in College

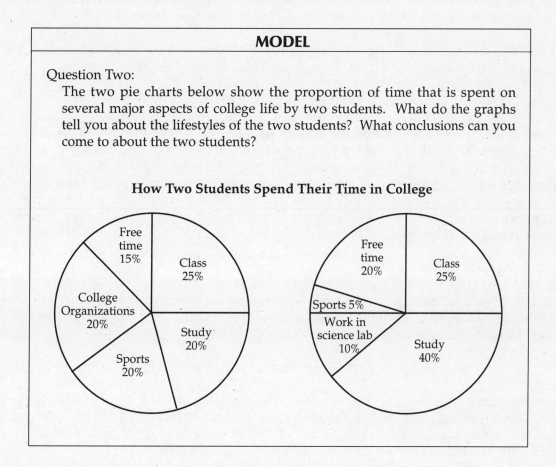

Before you begin to write about this question, be sure that you understand what type of information is given in the chart and what you are asked to do with it.

Issue: How two different students spend their time while in college.

Type of Information on Pie Charts: Percentage of time spent in class, study, sports, college activities, laboratory work, and free time.

TASK:
Part 1: Summarize the information from the chart about each student.
Part 2: Draw conclusions about the lifestyles of the two students and support them.
Possible Response: In this question an interpretation of the information is called for. As you describe the time spent on the activities you should begin to make a comparison between the students.

Give specific conclusions based on a comparison of time spent on each activity and support them with information from the chart.

Step 2: *Generate ideas by sorting out the facts.*
In a question which asks you to interpret information from charts and graphs it is important to note the basic information. As you do this you begin to see relationships between the facts.

Notes on Question Two:
Both students spend 25% of their time in class.
Student B spends twice as much time studying as Student A. Student B also spends time working in the science lab.
Student A spends the majority of his time on sports, college organizations, and free time.
Student B spends little time on sports, but has a little more free time than Student A.

Step 3: *Use adequate support by showing relationships between facts and conclusions.*
Use the basic facts that you have collected and try to find relationships between them.

Expanded notes to include support

Both students spend the **same amount of time** in class, but after this they show differences. The fact that Student B studies and works in the science lab for **half of his time** shows his interest in academic activities. He doesn't seem much interested in sports and has no college organizational activities. Student A is busy when he is not in class or studying; he devotes **equal time** to sports and college activities. Both students have **little free time**. By analyzing the charts you see two very different lifestyles. Be sure to provide data from the charts in your response and to write to answer the question.

Step 4: *Organize your ideas.*
In a Type Two Question, it is more interesting to do your interpretation as you write about the basic information in the charts or graphs. To factually describe each activity for each student before an interpretation of the information would also be very repetitive. TWE readers will look for both facts and interpretation throughout this type of essay.

Possible organization for Question Two

In organizing a response to Question Two, you may want to use the activities as the central points. Then, you could begin with the time spent by each student on academic activities and move to nonacademic activities, ending with free time. In this organization, your conclusion would further elaborate points of comparison that you make throughout your essay.

You could also organize this essay by discussing each student and his time expenditure separately. The comparison of life styles would then occur in the conclusion to the essay.

The most important point to remember when considering the organization of an essay is that it should be consistent throughout and only address the issue addressed in the question.

Step 5: *Draw specific conclusions.*

During prewriting, outline the points you want to include in your conclusion to the TWE essay question. As you write the final paragraphs of an essay responding to interpretation of charts and graphs, you should include specific conclusions based on your previous discussion and support these conclusions. In this part of the essay you may go further than the information given and make a personal statement or a prediction. This may follow up a line of logical reasoning or may be your prediction of the results or the consequences of the information.

Possible Conclusion for Question Two

In the conclusion of a response to Question Two, you might suggest that Student A is more socially oriented, while Student B is more academically oriented. You might also conclude that both students are actively involved in college life, without an overabundance of free time. In any case, provide support for your conclusions.

Importance of Time in Prewriting

Remember that you have only 30 minutes to complete your TWE essay. The prewriting steps listed above should be completed in five to eight minutes. As you practice responding to TWE essay questions, limit yourself to this amount of time for prewriting. Use abbreviations and note form as you put your ideas on paper. DO NOT spend time in prewriting complete sentences.

W✔2   Practice Writing a TWE Essay

There are several important steps for writing TWE essays. When you begin to write your essay, refer to your notes to remind yourself of your main points and supporting details and facts.

Well thought out and well organized notes will save you valuable time while you are writing the essay. Follow Steps 6–9 for both Type One Questions and Type Two Questions.

Step 6:   Use neat and legible handwriting.

Neat and legible handwriting will make your TWE essay easier for the reader to read. Although you will not be scored on your handwriting, it will influence the reader and create an overall impression. If you need to practice your handwriting, refer to the Writing Appendix, page 499.

Step 7:   Use correct grammar, appropriate vocabulary, and essay form.

Grammar

Your essay will be evaluated for the correct use of grammar, correct expression of syntactical relationships, and use of appropriate rhetorical forms of English. As you write, keep in mind the correct use of English grammar and sentence patterns. Refer to the Grammar Appendix, pages 435–468, to review basic English usage.

Vocabulary

Your essay will also be evaluated for the use of appropriate vocabulary. Readers will expect you to use vocabulary that clearly reflects the ideas that you present. The best way to insure that you are prepared to use adequate vocabulary in your TWE essay is to read in the topic areas that TWE questions address, and to use the Vocabulary Strategies discussed in Section Three of *The Heinemann TOEFL Preparation Course*. Refer to V✔10, Word Category Charts, for help in developing a good academic vocabulary.

Essay Form

An essay, which responds to an academic writing task in English, follows a basic organization which allows the reader to easily follow the development of the essay.

1. Each main point is contained in a separate paragraph.

   Paragraph One   Introduction (Restatement of the issue)
   Paragraph Two   **Main Point 1**
       Supporting statement
       Supporting statement
       Etc.
   Paragraph Three **Main Point 2**
       Supporting statement
       Supporting statement
       Etc.
   Paragraph Four   Conclusion (Your position statement)
       Supporting statement
       Supporting statement
       Concluding statement

2. The introduction of an essay contains a thesis statement, which restates the issue to be discussed.

   Introduction
       Thesis statement

3. Each paragraph contains a topic sentence, which states the main point.

   Paragraph One (Introduction)
       Thesis statement
   Paragraph Two
       Topic Sentence
   Paragraph Three
       Topic Sentence
   Paragraph Four
       Topic Sentence

4. Each paragraph contains supporting statements which add details and facts about the main point.

   Paragraph Two
       Topic Sentence
           Supporting statement
           Supporting statement
   Paragraph Three
       Topic Sentence
           Supporting statement
           Supporting statement

5. An essay contains a conclusion which may
   - state your position on the issue
   - draw a logical conclusion from the discussion

   The essay should end with a concluding statement.

   Paragraph Four (Conclusion)
      Topic sentence
         Supporting statement
         Supporting statement
         Concluding statement

Step 8: Use vocabulary signals to show organization.

The main points of your essay should be logically connected to show the organization of the essay. A good academic essay contains words and phrases that: (1) introduce and/or connect the main points of the essay; and, (2) signal supporting and concluding statements. Readers rely on these signals to make the essay easy to understand. Use words and phrases that clearly express your purpose and your organization.

Some examples of introductory words, signal words, and phrases are:

There are (three) main reasons for…
In addition, also, another point is, a second reason is…
On the other hand, in contrast…
The data shows that, from the chart we can see that…
Therefore, in conclusion…
Personally, my opinion is…

☞ ON THE TOEFL TEST

- Careful use of these words and phrases will result in a better essay and a higher TWE score.

Refer to the Reading Appendix #3, pages 497–498, to review vocabulary for organization and connection of ideas.

Step 9: Check your essay for spelling, punctuation, and grammar mistakes.

Allow yourself three to fives minutes at the end of the writing process to quickly reread your essay and check for careless mistakes. TWE readers will evaluate your essay for the mechanics of writing: correct spelling, punctuation, and grammar. Although the clarity of your ideas and the organization of your essay are the most important, correct spelling, punctuation, and grammar will affect your TWE essay score.

Now practice writing essays for Type One and Type Two questions. Find the TWE Answer Sheets on pages 511 and 512 in the General Appendix and make seven photocopies of each page. You will use these copies for the two TWE Writing Practice Questions on pages 386–387, for the four TWE Practice Essay Questions on pages 399–402, and for the Test of Written English on page 426.

TWE Writing Practice I: Type One Question

Before you begin to write your essay, review W✔1 and W✔2 for strategies to use when writing a Type One Question.

EXERCISE 1:   Practice Writing a Comparison and Contrast Essay

Allow yourself 30 minutes to write an essay on the following question.

Question One
> Some people think that cities are the best places to live. Others prefer to live in a rural area. Compare the advantages of living in the city to living in the country. Where would you prefer to live? Give reasons for you choice.

Use the rest of this page to make notes before writing. Write your essay on the photocopies you made of the TWE Answer Sheets, found on pages 511 and 512 in the General Appendix.

TWE Writing Practice II: Type Two Question

Before you begin to write your essay, review W✔1 and W✔2 for strategies to use when writing a Type Two Question.

EXERCISE 2: Practice Writing an Essay that Interprets Charts and Graphs

Allow yourself 30 minutes to write an essay on the following question.

Question Two

The two pie charts below show the proportion of time that is spent on several major aspects of college life by two students. What do the graphs tell you about the lifestyles of the two students? What conclusions can you come to about the two students?

How Two Students Spend Their Time in College

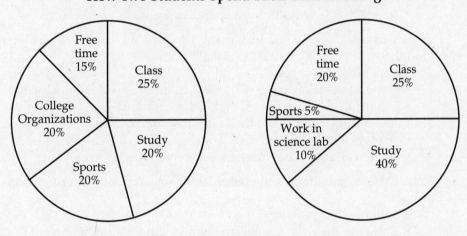

Use the rest of this page to make notes before you write. Write your essay on the photocopies you made of the TWE Answer Sheets, found on pages 511 and 512 in the General Appendix.

W✔3　Practice Self-scoring Your TWE Essays

TWE Scoring Guide

The readers who score the essays written for the TWE use the following Scoring Guide. The criteria in the Scoring Guide are followed by all readers. Become familiar with the criteria in order to self-score your own practice essays.

Scores

Score 6　Demonstrates clear competence in writing on both the rhetorical and syntactic levels, though it may have occasional errors.
　　　　A paper in this category
- effectively addresses the writing task,
- is well organized and well developed,
- uses clearly appropriate details to support a thesis or illustrate ideas,
- displays consistent facility in the use of language,
- demonstrates syntactic variety and appropriate word choice.

Score 5　Demonstrates competence in writing on both the rhetorical and syntactic levels, though it will probably have occasional errors.
　　　　A paper in this category
- may address some parts of the task more effectively than others,
- is generally well organized and well developed,
- uses details to support a thesis or illustrate an idea,
- displays facility in the use of language,
- demonstrates some syntactic variety and range of vocabulary.

Score 4　Demonstrates minimal competence in writing on both the rhetorical and syntactic levels.
　　　　A paper in this category
- addresses the writing topic adequately but may slight parts of the task,
- is adequately organized and developed,
- uses some details to support a thesis or illustrate an idea,
- demonstrates adequate but possibly inconsistent facility with syntax and usage,
- may contain some errors that occasionally obscure meaning.

Score 3　Demonstrates some developing competence in writing, but it remains flawed on either the rhetorical or syntactic level, or both.
　　　　A paper in this category has
- inadequate organization or development,
- inappropriate or insufficient details to support or illustrate generalizations,
- a noticeably inappropriate choice of words or word forms,
- an accumulation of errors in sentence structure and/or usage.

Score 2　Suggests incompetence in writing.
　　　　A paper in this category is seriously flawed by one or more of the following weaknesses:
- serious disorganization or underdevelopment,
- little or no detail, or irrelevant specifics,
- serious and frequent errors in sentence structure or usage,
- serious problems with focus.

Score 1　Demonstrates incompetence in writing
　　　　A paper in this category
- may be incoherent,
- may be undeveloped,
- may contain severe and persistent writing errors.

It is important for you to write essays on topics similar to those used on the TWE in order to practice writing quickly and carefully in a limited time period. It is also very useful for you to self-score your practice TWE essays. Self-scoring will help you to find your weak areas and to work on these in your next practice essay. Before you write and self-score your own essays, practice scoring student responses to the Type One and Type Two questions discussed in this chapter.

Practice Scoring Essays

Complete Exercises 1 and 2 to practice scoring essays.

EXERCISE 1:   Practice Scoring a Type One Question

The essays below have been written by students and scored using the TWE criteria. You will notice that these essays contain many errors commonly made by students when they write compositions. The essays have been scored using TWE criteria and there is one essay included for each score, 1–6. However, they are not presented in order of their rank. Work with the student essays in the following way:

1. Read each essay and decide what TWE score it should receive.
2. Read and score all six essays before you check your scoring with the correct answers on page 393.
3. Read the critique of each essay and compare it with your own assessment.
4. Self-score the essay you wrote for the Type One Question in the Writing Practice, p. 386.

All six essays below were written as answers to the question:
Some people think that cities are the best places to live. Others prefer to live in a rural area. Compare the advantages of living in the city to living in the country. Where would you prefer to live? Give reasons for your choice.

Essay 1A

City is a place where you can find everything you want or need. Rural area has something different compared with cities.

Since I borned I live in rural area. I love live in rural area because it is quiet, more space. I live in a place that it is twenty minutes from the capital. You can go to the capital by train, bus or car. I don't go frecuently because city is crowd, noise, everbody walk like a crazy because they don't have enough time to do what they are doing and sometimes dangerous. The small town where I live is not very big. But you can find everything you need, like food and personal things. The most thing I like is all the people know each other. The people there are generous, passive, and good workers. However, some of my friend prefere to live in the city because they can meet more people and find good jobs.

Finally, all depende because if you live in a big country is difficult to go to the city and prefered live in there.

Essay 1B

Nowadays a lot of people, especially young people think that cities are the best place to live. But there are also many people who prefer to live in rural areas. Living in the city and living in the country both have advantages and disadvantages.

Living in the city is very convenient. First, the transportation such as buses and trains are very good. Second, there are a lot of shopping places where we can get whatever we want. And also the city lives give us a lot of fun and make us very happy.

On the other hand, living in the country is very good to people, because of beautiful nature that give us beautiful air and water. And we don't have to be like the city people who always hurry and be busy because of caring their time and money.

I lived in the big city in Japan before I came over here. I know both ways of living in the city and country. Sometimes I miss the city life even though I don't miss my country and my parents. Just I miss the city life. Because I love shopping very much. Whenever I go to downtown in this small place, I am disappointed about that, and I don't like to take the buses. The buses are not just on time and only in the cities. So I prefer to live in the big cities like Tokyo.

Essay 1C

I think it's difficult to compare. To live in the country means quiet, peace. If you live in a little village you ma never be in a traffic jam. That's because there are only few cars. When you walk along the street, you can hear the birds singing. You know all the people you meet. Also live in the country mean healthfully. The products you eat are being produced by you or by your neighbors. People used to be friendly, so you are able to asking them for anything you want.

Instead of that kind of life take the other one. Live at the city means that you are always in a hurry. If you live in a flat maybe you don't know your neighbors probably. All the time you are hearing horns, engines and all types of noise that you can imagine. Also you have to take care when you walk along the streets because someone can steal your pocket money.

I don't want to write only about the bad face of living in a city. It's a very exciting to live at, because you can going to many places to visit. Places like cinemas, theatres, pubs. Also if you are a business man you can easier find your job. For me I like the peace of the country but I will live in the city for work and go to country for weekends.

Some people think that cities are the best places to live, while others like to live in the country. Both places have advantages and disadvantages.

From the daily life point of view, there are a number of stores or department stores in the cities, which give people a convenient life. They can get everything whenever they want. There are hospitals so that people don't have to worry about "What shall we do when we get sick?" While there are few stores in the country, if a village is located near the sea, people can get fresh fish, and if a town is located in the fields, they can get fresh vegetables or fruit.

When we think about culture, people enjoy going to a movie theater, to an art museum or to a concert. They can get much culture in the city. People living in the country get culture through TV or books. When it comes to socialization, the population in cities is large, so it is easier to be in contact with people. People can meet in a restaurant or a coffee shop. People in the rural areas may live far away from each other, and may have to drive a car for thirty minutes or so to go to a neighbor house. However, the relationships in the rural areas might be much closer and warmer.

Think about education; there are many schools, small schools and big schools, in the cities. Big schools have many books and good facilities. Schools in the country are small, but on the other hand a teacher-student relationship may be closer.

In my case, I prefer to live in the city. I feel relax and comfortable when I walk on the busy streets. I like tall buildings and enjoy looking at the city from the top of a tall building. I prefer to see buildings to see mountains. Above all, I can go to an art museum and a concert whenever I want to. I can enjoy an exciting life in the city. Many people say that living in the city causes people frustration and makes them tired. However in my case those things happen when I am in the rural area.

Essay 1E

I'm from Japan. I like in Japan, but I visited in Singapore, Taiwan, Malaysia and United States. I like in Singapore and Malaysia because it's very beautiful, and kind person. Then many things is very cheap. However Japan is best one because the food is very delicious. It's sushi, tempura, sukiyaki, udo and sashimi. I don't like American food because it isn't fish food. I like fish food. I also like Japanese food very much. Because I like to eat very much.

Essay 1F

My friends and I sometimes talk about the city life and the country life. They prefer to live in the city, like New York or Tokyo, but I have never thought to live in such a big city. For me just to stay for a few days is enough. The city is a place to visit, not to live in.

There are some advantages to live in a city. First of all, the transportation system is developed. You can go wherever you want whenever you want, even if you don't have your own car. If you live in the country you will get in trouble with transportation. There is no bus late at night. How can you survive without cars? Second, there are many places you can go to enjoy shopping and have fun. You can go to see movies, have delicious food at the restaurants, or enjoy a music concert. Though there are few places like this in the country, you can enjoy country life and relax yourself in a beautiful nature. You can go hiking, fishing, swimming in a river or lake, or climb a mountain. There is no air pollution problem or water pollution problem. Moreover, the country has much space for one person to own. In a city children have a lot of dangerous places and can't play outside. In the country they can play outside with beautiful nature. They will learn many things from nature.

The best life style for me is to live in a rural area like a suburb of a middle-size city, so that I can go to the city on weekends easily to enjoy shopping.

Scores for student essays, Type One question.

Essay 1A ......Score 2   Essay 1D..........Score 6
Essay 1B.......Score 4   Essay 1E ....Score 1
Essay 1C ......Score 3   Essay 1F............Score 5

Critiques for TWE student essays, Type One question.

Read the comments on each of the student responses and compare them with your own assessment of the essays.

Critique of Essay 1E: Score 1

The student who wrote this essay did not understand what the question asked him/her to do. Perhaps the writer misinterpreted the concept of "country" and got off on the wrong track. The simple statements and lack of development of the ideas show that this student was not ready to write a more complex essay, which is what the TWE requires.

Critique of Essay 1A: Score 2

The writer of this essay has responded to part of the question, but the essay lacks organization and sufficient development of the supporting points. The number of mistakes in usage and sentence structure greatly distracts from the content of the essay. Vocabulary is also very simple and often misused in the context of the question.

Critique of Essay 1C: Score 3

This essay shows an attempt to organize the main ideas, but topic sentences are missing and the points are neither fully developed nor introduced by appropriate transitions. The conclusion contains information about living in the city, with only one sentence stating the author's opinion. In addition, this essay has many mistakes in usage and structure. Although it is possible to understand the meaning, the essay suffers from awkward wording and lack of control of the language structures.

Critique of Essay 1B: Score 4

This essay shows a clearer division of ideas than Essay 1C. There are topic sentences and transition devices to introduce and link supporting ideas. However, the main points need to be supported with more details. The essay is very brief, and TWE readers expect ideas to be more fully developed. The length of the essay will be a significant factor in receiving a score of 4 or above on a TWE essay. Mistakes in structure and mechanics are evident, and the conclusion contains details that are irrelevant, which detracts from the overall impression of coherence in the essay.

Critique of Essay 1F: Score 5

This essay shows clear organization, uses several transition devices to link ideas and provides examples to support main points. Although there are several mistakes in structure and wording, they don't interfere with the understanding of the essay. In order for this essay to receive a higher score, more points should be discussed and the conclusion should be more fully developed.

Critique of Essay 1D: Score 6

This essay is clearly organized according to points of comparison for the city and the country. A number of points are discussed and there is good use of supporting details and examples. A few mistakes occur with structure, but the vocabulary is well chosen and covers a wide range. The overall impression given by this essay is that it is well organized and developed, and that the writer has a point of view that is clearly expressed in the conclusion.

Self-score the essay that you wrote for the Type One Question in Writing Practice, Exercise 1, page 386.

Exercise 2: **Practice Scoring a Type Two Question**

The essays below are student responses to the TWE Type Two question discussed in this chapter.

1. Read each essay and decide what TWE score it should receive.
2. Read and score the following six essays before you check your scoring with the correct answers on page 398.
3. Read the critique of each essay and compare it with your own assessment.
4. Self-score the essay you wrote for the Type One Question in the Writing Practice, page 387.

All six essays were written as answers to the question:

> The two pie charts below show the proportion of time that is spent on several major aspects of college life by two students. What do the graphs tell you about the life styles of the two students? What conclusions can you come to about the two students?

How Two Students Spend Their Time in College

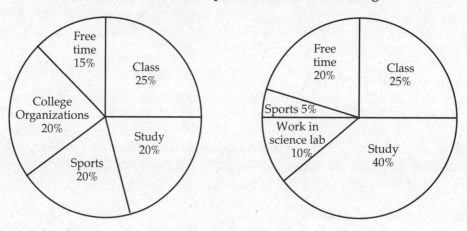

Essay 2A

If I look to the two Pie Charts I'll see that student B study more thin student A. Also student B work in science lab, but student A didn't spend any time in the lab. She spend 25% in class, but student A have 20% for sports but student B have just 5%, so I think student B is worker more thin student A. Also I think student B is study a science what need more work then any other major that why he spend 40% studying. But student A I think his major is more easy then student B because spends just 20% to study.

Essay 2B

Students in college spend their time in the way they prefer. The way they distribute this time is their lifestyle. The most of them have different lifestyles. Some give more emphasis their free time and other ones give more emphasis to academic time.

For example in comparing Student A and Student B we can observe that Student A has given more emphasis to his leisure time because he spend 35% practicing sports, reading, resting and watching T.V. On the other hand, Student B has 5% for sports and 20% for free time. This student prefers to read and make another activities instead of practice sports. Besides student A likes participating in college organizations and he dedicates to it 20% while student B doesn't like this kind of activities.

In addition to dedicate different quantities of time in their leisure time they also don't distribute their academic life in the same way. Student A gives 25% for class, 20% for study. It means 45% for academic time. While Student A spends 45% for his studies in general, student B spends 75% for this time. He has distributed it in 25% for classes, 40% for study and 10% for work in science lab. There is a big difference between a 45% and 75% which shows us the different way both students take advantage of their academic time.

In concluding, while student B spends the most of his time, 75% studying, taking classes and working in science lab, student A spends most of the time, 55%, in free time, practicing sports and participating in college organizations. Student B just gives 25% for leisure time and sports, and student A gives 45% for academic time.

Essay 2C

Time, a very important factor for college students, is administrated in different proportions according to personal interests. By looking at the preceding diagrams, we realize that student A has different personal interests than student B. While student A takes 45% of the 16 hours to attend classes and to study, student B uses 75% for the same activities. Student B also spends 10% of his time for working in the lab; therefore, he might be a science major. His major may require more time for studying.

On the other hand, student A has set time to participate in college organizations. The time he spends in these activities is as much as the time he uses for studying out of classes. He also shows more interest than student B in practicing sports. However, student A has less free time than student B.

These charts may give us an idea of why some students achieve higher grades than others, or why some students are better students. Nevertheless, there are other aspects that the graphs do not show. For instance, the charts do not mention if both students are in the same year or if they are taking the same number of classes or subjects. We do not know if both students are full time. And even if they are in the same year and they are taking the same number of classes, we still need to consider how different their classes are. If student A has an art major, his subject might not require too much time as student B, who probably is a science major.

What can we understand from the charts is that the two students choose to use their time in different ways. Student A seems to be more social and active, while student B appears to be more academically oriented.

Essay 2D

Looking at the pie chart, it seems that the two students spend their time differently, even if they have the same number of class hours.

Student A seems to have a balanced life; he spends approximately the same numbers of hours in each category. He probably likes very much sports. His participation in college organizations shows that he likes the social activities. He probably studies not more than average student.

Student B seems very dedicated to his courses. Including his lab, he studies two hours for each hour of class. He probably studies science. He does not like sports because he spends only 5% on it. He does not appear to like social activities; he might be shy. Having 20% of free time, he does not manage very well his life outside of his courses.

These two students have very different personalities. While student A is active and social, student B is reserved and dedicated to his studies

Essay 2E

I can see two kinds of people on these diagrams. The student A is extrovert, I think. He likes to be with people and spends 55% his time for that. These are sports, college organizations, and free time. Sports take 20% of his day time. I think it is kind of sport there a lot of students participate together, like American football, basket ball and so on. Study takes only 20% of his time and this shows us that it is not so important for him. I could try to presume which kind of subjects this student is studying. It can be literature or drama, language or art, maybe psychology, but I can't be sure.

The student B has only 25% of free time. The study plus work in sciene lab takes 50% of his day time. Sports take only 5-10% of his time and I can think that it is kind of individual sport, like jogging or swimming. This person must be introvert because the most part of his time he is with himself, without others. He works in science lab and it shows us that his position about study is very serious. He can study biology or chemistry, physics or math. And I can be absolutely sure that are two different people.

Essay 2F

We cannot put in compare two different students because sometimes one could be lazy and the other very study person. Student A doesn't spent a lot of time study, maybe because he doesn't need to study and he has the capacity of take everything fast in his mind. Another case of him could be that he preferred to do another things than study. Student B differents with Student A is because he needs to have more time to concentrate or has problems and need to study more. Sometimes is depend what classes are you taking. Some classes you have to spend a lot of time while the other are easy. Every thing in your studies is to be organized and study everyday what did you see in class. Sports is very necessary to have a good health and relax the mind. Student A is busy he has to many things to do day by day. He is an active person and must be athletic person. Student B is probably a serious person who thinks to have only time to study. Everyone has different style to spend the time.

Scores for student essays, Type Two Question.

Essay 2A...........Score 1   Essay 2D...........Score 5
Essay 2B ....Score 4   Essay 2E ....Score 3
Essay 2C ....Score 6   Essay 2F...........Score 2

Critiques for TWE student responses to Type Two Question.

Read the comments on each of the student responses and compare with your assessment of the essays

Critique of Essay 2A: Score 1

This essay suffers from an incomplete response to the question and consequent lack of organization and development of main points. There is a serious lack of control of the structure and vocabulary needed. This short piece shows that the writer is not prepared to write at the level of an interpretive essay.

Critique of Essay 2F: Score 2

This essay lacks organization and development of the topic.
There is only one paragraph and points are randomly developed.
There are many errors in sentence structure and usage, which contributes to the impression of lack of linguistic competence.

Critique of Essay 2E: Score 3

This essay shows a beginning effort in both organization and topic development. However, supporting statements are often not relevant to the main points of the essay. The essay is linguistically weak, and the conclusion to the essay is not developed.

Critique of Essay 2B: Score 4

This essay begins with a clear thesis followed by paragraph organization for each main point. However, language usage is weak, and although the charts are described, there is a lack of interpretation of the information. The conclusion is confusing, with no clear summary statement.

Critique of Essay 2D: Score 5

This essay, although brief, shows a clear thesis and development of the main points. There are a few structure mistakes but on the whole the essay demonstrates linguistic competence and a range of vocabulary use. The conclusion expresses an opinion based on an interpretation of the information developed in the body of the essay.

Critique 2C: Score 6

This essay has a clearly stated thesis which is well developed throughout the rest of the essay. Points from the charts are adequately described and interpreted. The writer also discusses aspects of lifestyle that cannot be assumed from the charts, and concludes with a clear summary statement connecting the main points of the essay. There are few mistakes with language usage, and discourse devices have been used effectively.

Self-score the essay that you wrote for the Type Two Question in Writing Practice, Exercise 2, page 387.

TWE PRACTICE ESSAY QUESTIONS

Practice writing TWE essays for the four questions below. Follow the test conditions as closely as possible. Allow yourself only 30 minutes to write each essay. Be sure to spend time prewriting and rereading at the end of the essay. Use the TWE Scoring Guide criteria to self-score your essay.

Practice Essay Question 1
Time: 30 minutes

The chart below shows the distribution of population in urban areas of the United States over the past forty years.
What does the chart tell you about the population shift?
What might you predict about the effects of these population changes?

Population Distribution in Major Urban Areas 1950–1990			
	1950	**1970**	**1990**
City center	60%	40%	10%
Suburbs	30%	40%	60%
Rural areas within 100 miles of a city	10%	20%	30%

Use the rest of this page to make notes before writing. Write your essay on the photocopies you made of the TWE Answer Sheets, found on pages 511 and 512 in the General Appendix.

Practice Essay Question 2
Time: 30 minutes

Some people believe that preschool education for children ages four and five should be supported by the government and available to all children. Others believe that preschool education should be privately funded and paid for by families that choose to send their children to these schools. Discuss these views. Which view do you agree with? Explain why.

Use the rest of this page to make notes before writing. Write your essay on the photocopies you made of the TWE Answer Sheets, found on pages 511 and 512 in the General Appendix.

Practice Essay Question 3
Time: 30 minutes

Some people think that studying a foreign language in the country where the language is spoken is the best way to learn the language. Others think that learning a foreign language while living in your own country is preferable. Discuss both situations. Which point of view do you agree with? Give your reasons.

Use the rest of this page to make notes before writing. Write your essay on the photocopies you made of the TWE Answer Sheets, found on pages 511 and 512 in the General Appendix.

The graph below shows the economic activity index for three economic sectors of country X over a 12-year period. Discuss the changes shown in the graph. What suggestions would you make for economic planning and development? Why?

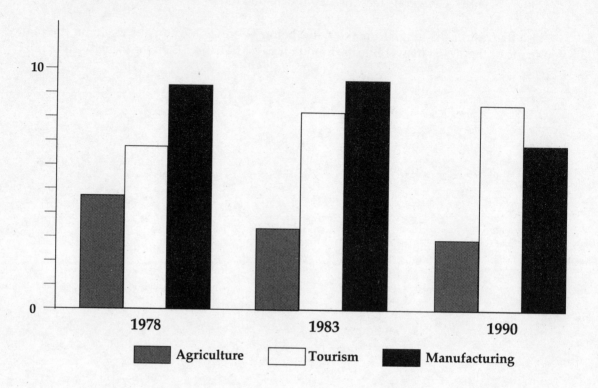

Use the rest of this page to make notes before writing. Write your essay on the photocopies you made of the TWE Answer Sheets, found on pages 511 and 512 in the General Appendix.

Complete Practice TOEFL Test

On the following pages, you will find the Complete Practice TOEFL Test for this course book. This test includes a Test of Written English.

The Complete Practice TOEFL Test is the same length as an actual TOEFL exam, and it contains all of the item types covered on a TOEFL. It takes approximately two hours to complete the first three sections of the test. Then, it takes an additional 30 minutes to complete the Test of Written English. If possible, you should take the entire test at one sitting. If this is not possible, you can take each section separately. If you choose this method, do not look ahead at the sections you have not yet completed. If you look ahead, you will not get good results when you actually complete each section as a test.

Steps to follow when taking the Complete Practice TOEFL Test:

1. Find the Complete Practice TOEFL Test Answer Sheet on page 510 in the General Appendix, #4. Mark your answers on this sheet.

2. Find the photocopies you made of the TWE Answers Sheets on pages 511 and 512 of the General Appendix. Write your essay on these answer sheets.

3. Set up a tape player with the audio cassette for Section One of the Complete Practice TOEFL Test.

4. As much as possible, simulate an actual TOEFL test-taking situation. Sit at a comfortable desk in a room that is quiet. Take the test at a time when you will not be interrupted.

5. Take the test according to the time limits set for official TOEFL tests. Section One will last 30–40 minutes and will be self-timed by the audio cassette that accompanies it. Allow yourself 25 minutes to complete Section Two, 45 minutes to complete Section Three, and 30 minutes to complete the Test of Written English.

6. Score the first three sections, using *The Heinemann TOEFL Course Tapescripts and Answers*.

7. Convert your score on the first three sections to a TOEFL score using Score Conversion Table 1 in the General Appendix, #3, page 505.

8. Score your TWE essay using the guidelines provided in W✔3, page 388.

9. Compare your score to your Diagnostic Test and Section Test scores, noting any continued areas of TOEFL strength and weakness.

When you are ready to start the Complete Practice TOEFL Test, begin the tape.
Do not go on to the next page until the tape tells you to do so.

SECTION I

LISTENING COMPREHENSION

In this section of the test, you will have an opportunity to demonstrate your ability to understand spoken English. There are three parts to this section, with special directions for each part.

Part A

Directions: For each question in Part A, you will hear a short sentence. Each sentence will be spoken just one time. The sentences you hear will not be written out for you. Therefore, you must listen carefully to understand what the speaker says.

After you hear a sentence, read the four choices in your test book, marked (A), (B), (C), and (D), and decide which <u>one</u> is closest in meaning to the sentence you heard. Then, on your answer sheet, find the number of the question and fill in the space that corresponds to the letter of the answer you have chosen. Fill in the space so that the letter inside the oval cannot be seen.

Example I   <u>Sample Answer</u>

You will hear: Ⓐ Ⓑ ● Ⓓ
You will read: (A)   Greg didn't bother to leave a tip.
                          (B)   Greg thought about typing a letter to his brother.
                          (C)   Greg didn't like to type.
                          (D)   My typing bothered Greg.

The speaker said, "Greg thought typing was a bother." Sentence (C), "Greg didn't like to type," is closest in meaning to the sentence you heard. Therefore, you should choose answer (C).

Example II   <u>Sample Answer</u>

You will hear: Ⓐ ● Ⓒ Ⓓ
You will read: (A)   Everyone will be able to take this exam later.
                          (B)   Students should bring a calculator to this exam.
                          (C)   This test will be part of every student's final grade.
                          (D)   No one can calculate the grades for this test.

The speaker said, "Everyone needs a calculator for this test." Sentence (B), "Students should bring a calculator to this exam," is closest in meaning to the sentence you heard. Therefore, you should choose answer (B).

GO ON TO THE NEXT PAGE ➡

1. (A) Did Carolyn like the book?
   (B) I liked Carolyn's book.
   (C) Did Carolyn write the book?
   (D) Carolyn should write a book.

2. (A) Isn't that a note in your book?
   (B) That notebook on the table isn't yours, is it?
   (C) Your note is in the book on the table.
   (D) Isn't the notebook on the table yours?

3. (A) I took Sally home from work.
   (B) Sally gave me a check for the work I did at her house.
   (C) I'll ask Sally to look over my assignment.
   (D) Sally is at home working.

4. (A) Let's look for a trail through here.
   (B) We've gotten lost going this way.
   (C) We must finish this.
   (D) Doing things this way isn't much fun.

5. (A) Ed was at a dry cleaner's.
   (B) Ed was in a clothing store.
   (C) Ed was in a restaurant.
   (D) Ed was in a shoe store.

6. (A) Forty-two cars have been removed this year.
   (B) Carl has lived in the city for forty-two years.
   (C) The city wants to remove those two cars.
   (D) Carl doesn't want to live in the city any more.

7. (A) Why did you go around the world like that?
   (B) How can we stop that from harming the earth?
   (C) Why did the girl buy that hat?
   (D) That wasn't a very smart thing to do.

8. (A) We could not get out of the elevator.
   (B) We'll see you there later.
   (C) Someone hit us from behind.
   (D) We put the stack in the elevator.

9. (A) This month we must pay our rent on the thirteenth.
   (B) Each month on the thirtieth we must pay our rent.
   (C) Every month when I check, this apartment is the dirtiest.
   (D) There were thirty apartments for rent when I checked.

10. (A) She didn't invent the job.
    (B) She didn't catch up on her work.
    (C) She wore make up to work.
    (D) She didn't miss any work.

11. (A) I responded to Harry's short letter.
    (B) Harry left my letter on the seat.
    (C) Harry sent me a brief, direct response.
    (D) Harry's short response was better than mine.

12. (A) We were seated at six, but we ate later.
    (B) They all felt sick after they ate.
    (C) Although there were eight seats, only six were taken.
    (D) More people came than I had expected.

13. (A) I can't seem to work any faster.
    (B) I am too busy to meet this deadline.
    (C) I still miss them a lot, but I'm feeling better.
    (D) If I don't hurry up, I won't finish on time.

14. (A) I was not very pleased.
    (B) Please don't give me any more.
    (C) I was very happy.
    (D) It has been a pleasure to meet you.

15. (A) Tom didn't bring the books after all.
    (B) Jackie did not bring Tom the books.
    (C) Jackie thought Tom bought the books.
    (D) Jackie bought the books, but Tom didn't.

GO ON TO THE NEXT PAGE ➤

16. (A) He has been late to work a lot lately.
    (B) He goes for a walk when he has the time.
    (C) He has stopped exercising.
    (D) He doesn't work outdoors anymore.

17. (A) My brother's rival received the prize.
    (B) My brother came unexpectedly.
    (C) I surprised my brother when I arrived.
    (D) I gave my brother the prize when he arrived.

18. (A) Doctor Sparks doesn't think this lab is equipped for his needs.
    (B) Experiments in this lab must be carefully set up and conducted.
    (C) Doctor Sparks will type up his lab experiment results tonight.
    (D) Doctor Sparks wants to conduct experiments in this lab.

19. (A) I didn't study enough for this exam.
    (B) I can't stay to prepare for this test.
    (C) I must say that this exam wasn't prepared very well.
    (D) I was completely surprised by my grade on this test.

20. (A) We couldn't go to the picnic ourselves, but we sent some food.
    (B) We went to the picnic, but we didn't eat any food there.
    (C) All of the food that we took to the picnic got eaten.
    (D) Only some of our food was eaten at the picnic.

Part B

Directions: In Part B you will hear short conversations between two speakers. At the end of each conversation, a third person will ask a question about what was said. You will hear each conversation and question about it just one time. Therefore, you must listen carefully to understand what each speaker says. After you hear a conversation and the question about it, read the four possible answers in your test book and decide which one is the best answer to the question you heard. Then, on your answer sheet, find the number of the question and fill in the space that corresponds to the letter of the answer you have chosen.

Look at the following example.   Sample Answer

You will hear:
You will read: (A) At last winter is almost over.   Ⓐ Ⓑ ● Ⓓ
                  (B) She doesn't like winter weather very much.
                  (C) This winter's weather is similar to last winter's weather.
                  (D) Winter won't last as long this year as it did last year.

From the conversation you learn that the woman thinks the weather this winter is almost the same as the weather last winter. The best answer to the question "What does the woman mean?" is (C), "This winter's weather is similar to last winter's weather." Therefore, you should choose answer (C).

GO ON TO THE NEXT PAGE →

21. (A) She doesn't understand the instructions.
    (B) She lost the instructions she was reading.
    (C) She doesn't want to follow the directions.
    (D) She thinks they are lost.

22. (A) He will complete his paper this month.
    (B) The mine has been closed for a month.
    (C) It is taking him a long time to write his paper.
    (D) He can help the woman in a little while.

23. (A) It will be hard to find an ashtray.
    (B) There aren't any cigarettes here.
    (C) She can't see very well.
    (D) Smoking probably isn't permitted here.

24. (A) She'll take her work with her on vacation.
    (B) She and the man will have a good time on vacation.
    (C) She won't have time for a vacation.
    (D) She thinks she can finish her work on time.

25. (A) He'd like a larger piece this time.
    (B) He doesn't want any more.
    (C) His first piece was too large.
    (D) He'd like some more in a little while.

26. (A) She thinks he might be late to work.
    (B) His income isn't high enough.
    (C) She isn't sure he'll come to work today.
    (D) She'd like to talk to him, too.

27. (A) She has never seen such a long concert.
    (B) She enjoyed the concert very much.
    (C) She'll take the man along.
    (D) She didn't like the last song.

28. (A) It is not a bad idea to telephone the college.
    (B) She will call the college for the man.
    (C) Her eyes hurt, so she cannot see very well.
    (D) She will give the man's application to her colleagues.

29. (A) Gas station attendant.
    (B) Housekeeper.
    (C) Bank teller.
    (D) Airline stewardess.

30. (A) Ask someone to help him with his computer.
    (B) Read the instructions for setting up his computer.
    (C) Try to take his computer apart by himself.
    (D) Use his computer to help him set up his math project.

31. (A) She's trying to tie the bow.
    (B) She will call the man as soon as possible.
    (C) She is talking on the phone.
    (D) She hasn't gone home yet.

32. (A) The woman didn't want to deliver the invitation.
    (B) The woman would be gone on Saturday.
    (C) The woman would take the man to dinner.
    (D) He needed to take the invitation to the woman.

33. (A) Susan only has three glasses.
    (B) Susan knows about her third class.
    (C) He missed a class because of Susan.
    (D) Susan didn't attend one class.

34. (A) She'd like the man to pour her a glass of water.
    (B) It stopped raining three days ago.
    (C) It probably won't rain again for a few days.
    (D) The garden doesn't need any more water.

35. (A) He's looking forward to working with Fred.
    (B) They need to handle the photographs carefully.
    (C) Fred should be treated like a professional.
    (D) Their project will be the best.

GO ON TO THE NEXT PAGE ➤

Part C

Directions: In this part of the test, you will hear short talks and conversations. After each of them, you will be asked some questions. You will hear the talks and conversations and the questions about them just one time. They will not be written out for you. Therefore, you must listen carefully to understand what each speaker says.

After you hear a question, read the four possible answers in your test book and decide which <u>one</u> is the best answer to the question you heard. Then, on your answer sheet, find the number of the question and fill in the space that corresponds to the letter of the answer you have chosen.

Answer all questions on the basis of what is <u>stated</u> or <u>implied</u> in the talk or conversation.

Listen to this sample talk.

You will hear:

Now look at the following example.   <u>Sample Answer</u>

You will hear: ● Ⓑ Ⓒ Ⓓ
You will read: (A)   Only bumblebees can fertilize red clover plants.
                       (B)   Bumblebees protect red clover from plant eating insects.
                       (C)   Bumblebees bring water to red clover plants on their tongues.
                       (D)   Bumblebees keep mice and other animals away from red clover plants.

The best answer to the question "Why is it impossible to raise red clover where there are no bumblebees?" is (A), "Only bumblebees can fertilize red clover plants." Therefore, you should choose answer (A).

Now look at the next example.   <u>Sample Answer</u>

You will hear: Ⓐ Ⓑ Ⓒ ●
You will read: (A)   They both make honey.
                       (B)   They both build combs.
                       (C)   Both of them are found in underground nests.
                       (D)   They both live through the winter.

The best answer to the question "According to the speaker, in what way are the queen wasp and the queen bee similar?" is (D), "They both live through the winter." Therefore, you should choose answer (D).

36. (A) The man told her.
    (B) She received a call.
    (C) She read about it.
    (D) She organized the meeting.

37. (A) To plan a social event.
    (B) To talk about good health.
    (C) To discuss philosophy.
    (D) To make plans for raising money.

38. (A) She likes to work hard.
    (B) She doesn't have a job and can afford the time.
    (C) She thinks the Heart Association needs money.
    (D) She likes to dance.

GO ON TO THE NEXT PAGE ➤

39. (A) Go to the club meeting.
    (B) Organize a dance marathon.
    (C) Organize a raffle.
    (D) Participate in Spring Break.

40. (A) She will sell raffle tickets.
    (B) She will ask her aunt to give a big prize.
    (C) She will go to Florida for Spring Break.
    (D) She will work for the travel agency.

41. (A) He'd like to enjoy some good weather.
    (B) He has always wanted to fly an airplane.
    (C) He will have time off after the winter season.
    (D) He wants to see the fundraiser succeed.

42. (A) In a school.
    (B) At the post office.
    (C) On an airplane.
    (D) In a museum.

43. (A) He designed the first airplane to carry a passenger.
    (B) His work provided valuable information for inventors who came after him.
    (C) He was the first man to cross the Potomac River.
    (D) He put together an aeronautics collection.

44. (A) The Potomac River.
    (B) Several items of historical significance.
    (C) A steam engine.
    (D) One of Langley's inventions.

45. (A) Move into the next room.
    (B) Buy a commemorative stamp.
    (C) Take a ride in the Aerodrome #5.
    (D) Try to create a new model.

46. (A) She was taking a math test.
    (B) She had to fill out a survey after her class.
    (C) She was questioning Prof. Keene's premise in his lecture.
    (D) She was correcting quizzes for Prof. Keene.

47. (A) A psychology class.
    (B) A statistics class.
    (C) A science lab.
    (D) A history class.

48. (A) He is usually not prepared for his job.
    (B) He likes to have something to complain about.
    (C) He sets unrealistically high life goals.
    (D) A pessimist has the same luck as anyone else.

49. (A) It has little effect on shaping a person's outlook on life.
    (B) In the early years, too many failures may produce a pessimist.
    (C) A pessimist usually doesn't take advantage of life experiences.
    (D) The environment is unusually cruel to pessimists.

50. (A) Optimists use their consciences to their advantage.
    (B) Pessimists have a good relationship with their consciences.
    (C) The conscience plays a minor role in shaping one's outlook.
    (D) The pessimist follows the dictates of conscience, even though he might not want to.

THIS IS THE END OF THE LISTENING COMPREHENSION SECTION OF THE TEST

**THE NEXT PART OF THE TEST IS SECTION 2.
TURN TO THE DIRECTIONS FOR SECTION 2 IN YOUR TEST BOOK.
READ THEM, AND BEGIN WORK.
DO NOT READ OR WORK ON ANY OTHER SECTION OF THE TEST.**

STOP   STOP   STOP   **STOP**   STOP   STOP   STOP

SECTION 2
STRUCTURE AND WRITTEN EXPRESSION

Time—25 minutes

This section is designed to measure your ability to recognize language that is appropriate for standard written English. There are two types of questions in this section, with special directions for each type.

Directions: Questions 1–15 are incomplete sentences. Beneath each sentence you will see four words or phrases, marked (A), (B), (C), and (D). Choose the one word or phrase that best completes the sentence. Then, on your answer sheet, find the number of the question and fill in the space that corresponds to the letter of the answer you have chosen. Fill in the space so that the letter inside the oval cannot be seen.

Example I

Sample Answer

● Ⓑ Ⓒ Ⓓ

Most American families _____ at least one automobile.
   (A) have
   (B) in
   (C) that
(D) has

The sentence should read, "Most American families have at least one automobile." Therefore, you should choose answer (A).

Example II

Sample Answer

Ⓐ Ⓑ Ⓒ ●

_____ recent times, the discipline of biology has expanded
rapidly into a variety of subdisciplines.
   (A) It is since
   (B) When
   (C) Since it is
   (D) In

The sentence should read, "In recent times, the discipline of biology has expanded into a variety of subdisciplines." Therefore, you should choose answer (D).

After you read the directions, begin work on the questions.

GO ON TO THE NEXT PAGE ➤

1. _____ up to seven months.
   (A) Lasting New England winters
   (B) New England winters can last
   (C) Because a New England winter can last
   (D) The length of a New England winter

2. _____ discussion of group personality would be complete without a consideration of national character.
   (A) None
   (B) Not
   (C) No
   (D) Nothing

3. The Virginia strawberry, native to eastern North America, was used in pre-colonial times _____.
   (A) to flavor bread
   (B) bread flavoring
   (C) flavored bread
   (D) bread was flavored

4. There is evidence to suggest that, at certain times of the year, smog in the Arctic is thicker _____ anywhere else on earth.
   (A) of smog
   (B) that smog
   (C) smog
   (D) than smog

5. Studs Turkel has used what he learned _____ to produce taped oral histories of people and events.
   (A) when was he a radio talk show host
   (B) he was a radio talk show host when
   (C) when he was a radio talk show host
   (D) a radio talk show host when he was

6. _____ have a powerful influence on the shape of the entire magazine industry.
   (A) That economic principles
   (B) Why economic principles
   (C) Economic principles
   (D) Economic principles that

7. According to some records, Carl Sandburg, _____, was expelled from West Point Naval Academy because of deficiencies in English.
   (A) he was a poet and literary genius
   (B) his poetry and literary genius
   (C) poet and literary genius
   (D) whose poetry and literary genius

8. _____ two and one half hours to climb to the top of the Empire State Building.
   (A) Typically taking it
   (B) Typically takes it
   (C) It typically takes
   (D) To take it typically

9. The common crow, _____ one of the hardiest birds in existence, can live up to eighty years.
   (A) is considered
   (B) considered it
   (C) has been considered
   (D) considered

10. High and low atmospheric pressure systems are _____ cause changing weather patterns.
    (A) the
    (B) whose
    (C) which
    (D) what

11. _____ a sizable geographic area, it constitutes a biome.
    (A) That a group of plants and animals occupies
    (B) A group of plants and animals occupying
    (C) A group of plants and animals occupies
    (D) When a group of plants and animals occupies

GO ON TO THE NEXT PAGE ➤

12. Due primarily to _____, the Oneida Community broke up in 1880.
    (A) internal stresses
    (B) there were internal stresses
    (C) internal stresses of it
    (D) it had internal stresses

13. Starting in 1972, lightning fires in Yellowstone National Park _____ to take their natural course unless they threatened park facilities.
    (A) they allowed
    (B) allowing
    (C) allow
    (D) were allowed

14. Small microcomputers of today can process _____ their predecessors, which were twenty times their size.
    (A) in the same amount of information
    (B) and have the same amount of information
    (C) the information is the same as
    (D) the same amount of information as

15. By declining to run for presidential reelection in 1808, Thomas Jefferson _____ the two-term tradition still followed, with but a few exceptions, to the present day.
    (A) to help establish
    (B) helped the establishment
    (C) helped to establish
    (D) in helping to establish

Directions: In questions 16-40 each sentence has four underlined words or phrases. The four underlined parts of the sentence are marked (A), (B), (C), and (D). Identify the one underlined word or phrase that must be changed in order for the sentence to be correct. Then, on your answer sheet, find the number of the question and fill in the space that corresponds to the letter of the answer you have chosen.

Example I   Sample Answer

                                                                          Ⓐ Ⓑ ● Ⓓ

        The octopus is a unique animal because they has three functioning hearts.
                     A   B   C   D

The sentence should read, "The octopus is a unique animal because it has three functioning hearts." Therefore, you should choose answer (C).

Example II   Sample Answer

                                                                          Ⓐ Ⓑ Ⓒ ●

        The beagle, one of the most ancient breeds of dog known, originating in England.
                    A   B   C   D

The sentence should read, "The beagle, one of the most ancient breeds of dog known, originated in England." Therefore, you should choose answer (D).

After you read the directions, begin work on the questions.

GO ON TO THE NEXT PAGE ▶

16. Geothermal <u>energy</u>, <u>for example</u> the heat from <u>activate</u> volcanoes and geysers, <u>can be turned into</u>
          A   B   C   D
    electricity.

17. Serious research is <u>currently</u> being <u>undertook</u> to determine whether or not bee venom <u>may help</u>
                    A   B   C
    protect humans from the <u>discomfort</u> of arthritis.
                          D

18. The Massachusetts Institute of Technology is <u>an</u> university <u>known</u> for its programs in the sciences,
                                                A   B
    <u>but</u> it also offers students a well-rounded background in <u>the humanities</u>.
    C   D

19. The <u>short wave lengths</u> of ultraviolet light produce <u>luminescence</u> in the <u>crystalize</u> of <u>some</u>
              A   B   C   D
    minerals.

20. One traditional American <u>quilting</u> style makes use of a <u>patterns</u> of <u>interlocking</u> circles <u>to signify</u> the
                          A   B   C   D
    union of two people in marriage.

21. <u>Although</u> they have <u>found out</u> a great deal about its atmosphere, scientists <u>still</u> know very little
    A   B   C
    <u>around</u> variations in the moon's gravitational field.
    D

22. For the president of the United States, wisely <u>chooses</u> cabinet members <u>shortly after</u> election day <u>is</u>
                                        A   B   C
    crucial to a <u>successful</u> term in office.
            D

23. <u>In general</u>, banks are <u>heavily</u> regulated than are brokerage houses and <u>other</u> <u>financial</u> institutions.
      A   B   C D

24. The benefits to be <u>gaining</u> <u>from</u> daily exercise and proper diet <u>are</u> <u>indisputable</u>.
                       A   B   C   D

25. Small, <u>privately</u> owned ranches <u>become</u> <u>less and less common</u> during the <u>past</u> decade.
            A   B   C   D

26. Caste <u>is</u> a special form of social class <u>in which</u> membership <u>has determined</u> by birth and <u>fixed</u> for
        A   B   C   D
    life.

27. <u>In</u> recent years, steps <u>have been taken</u> to guarantee <u>equality</u> job opportunities to <u>the handicapped</u>
    A   B   C   D
    and to minorities.

GO ON TO THE NEXT PAGE ➤

28. The agricultural sector <u>in</u> the United States, with over two <u>million</u> farms, <u>have</u> a <u>highly</u> competitive
                 A   B   C   D
economic structure.

29. <u>Most</u> college-age students today are <u>interested in</u> finding universities in <u>which can</u> pursue <u>both</u>
    A   B   C   D
academic and athletic extra-curricular activities.

30. <u>Nationality</u> known Black activist LeRoi Jones <u>has also</u> <u>achieved</u> <u>recognition</u> for his powerful
    A   B   C   D
<u>separatist</u> poetry.
    D

31. The sulfur compounds <u>produced</u> when an onion <u>is sliced</u> are <u>too</u> strong that they cause
                      A   B   C
<u>burning and watering</u> of the eyes.
      D

32. Broccoli and <u>cauliflower taste</u> and smell <u>much like</u> cabbage, <u>from</u> which <u>it was</u> developed.
              A   B   C   D

33. The chlorophyll <u>in leaves</u> is a complex <u>organically</u> molecule capable of <u>converting</u> certain
                 A   B   C
wavelengths of light <u>into</u> chemical energy.
            D

34. Water and petroleum are the <u>only</u> two liquids <u>what</u> occur in <u>large</u> quantities <u>in</u> nature.
                         A   B   C   D

35. <u>Some</u> large birds, <u>such as</u> the ostrich and the cassowary, <u>is too</u> large and heavy to fly.
    A   B   C D

36. The <u>fastest</u> of all game fish is the sailfish, <u>that which</u> can travel at speeds of <u>up to</u> seventy
          A   B   C
<u>miles per hour.</u>
      D

37. It <u>believed is</u> that the galaxies of the universe <u>are receding</u> at <u>nearly half</u> the speed <u>of light.</u>
      A   B   C   D

38. <u>If</u> the personal computer had not been invented, <u>will</u> the information age have arrived <u>by</u> other
A   B   C
<u>means?</u>
   D

39. <u>Artificial</u> intelligence is the <u>simulation of</u> intelligent human behaviors, <u>such problem solving,</u>
    A   B   C
natural language communication, and <u>creativity.</u>
                                  D

GO ON TO THE NEXT PAGE ➤

40. The gypsy moth was <u>originally</u> introduced into the northeastern part of the United States by a
                         A

French <u>scientific</u> who hoped <u>to use</u> <u>it</u> to develop a new strain of silk.
        B   C   D

THIS IS THE END OF SECTION 2

**IF YOU FINISH BEFORE TIME IS CALLED, CHECK YOUR WORK ON SECTION 2 ONLY.
DO NOT READ OR WORK ON ANY OTHER SECTION OF THE TEST.
THE SUPERVISOR WILL TELL YOU WHEN TO BEGIN WORK ON SECTION 3.**

STOP   STOP   STOP   **STOP**   STOP   STOP   STOP

SECTION 3
VOCABULARY AND READING COMPREHENSION

Time– 45 minutes

This section is designed to measure your comprehension of standard written English. There are two types of questions in this section, with special directions for each type.

<u>Directions:</u> In questions 1–30 each sentence has an underlined word or phrase. Below each sentence are four other words or phrases, marked (A), (B), (C), (D). You are to choose the <u>one</u> word or phrase that <u>best keeps the meaning</u> of the original sentence if it is substituted for the underlined word or phrase. Then, on your answer sheet, find the number of the question and fill in the space that corresponds to the letter you have chosen. Fill in the space so that the letter inside the oval cannot be seen.

Example   <u>Sample Answer</u>

                                                ● Ⓑ Ⓒ Ⓓ

    Ladybugs, small brightly colored beetles, feed on plant aphids and
    have considerable economic value in <u>controlling</u> pest populations.
    (A) limiting
    (B) finding
    (C) increasing
    (D) ruling

The best answer is (A) because "Ladybugs, small brightly colored beetles, feed on plant aphids and have considerable economic value in limiting pest populations" is closest in meaning to the original sentence. Therefore, you should choose answer (A).

After you have read the directions, begin work on the questions.

1. The use of vaccines has <u>effectively</u> eliminated many childhood diseases.
   (A) partially
   (B) simply
   (C) successfully
   (D) quickly

2. Each species of firefly has its own signal pattern composed of light <u>flashes</u> lasting only a fraction of a second.
   (A) flickers
   (B) motions
   (C) marks
   (D) colors

3. In <u>an effort</u> to bring the American public back into the movie theaters, Hollywood began to produce longer and more expensive films.
   (A) a promise
   (B) a trend
   (C) an attempt
   (D) a motivation

4. The federal postal service extended free carrier service in the cities and <u>instituted</u> free rural delivery in 1897.
   (A) continued
   (B) cut back
   (C) proposed
   (D) began

GO ON TO THE NEXT PAGE ➤

5. The system of shorthand, which is any written system permitting the rapid transcription of speech, involves using symbols to represent <u>recurring</u> sounds.
(A) similar
(B) repeated
(C) melodious
(D) detected

6. Some animals have an even <u>keener</u> sense of taste than humans have.
(A) more discriminating
(B) more intelligent
(C) more limited
(D) more complex

7. In profit-sharing plans, pension funds are accumulated <u>annually</u> as a percentage of company profits.
(A) at cost
(B) assiduously
(C) regularly
(D) yearly

8. Edward Sapir, anthropologist and linguist, felt strongly that any study of language must <u>be accompanied by</u> a study of the culture of which it is a product.
(A) be preceded by
(B) occur with
(C) reflect
(D) document

9. With fewer <u>options</u> for inexpensive insurance being offered, most individuals hope to be covered through employment benefits.
(A) promises
(B) payments
(C) choices
(D) mandates

10. Political satirists make use of humor, irony and parody to <u>ridicule</u> a subject.
(A) belittle
(B) enhance
(C) describe
(D) benefit

11. Older bridges across the country are often closed because they are not structurally <u>sound</u>.
(A) balanced
(B) sturdy
(C) complete
(D) organized

12. The theory of plate tectonics <u>maintains</u> that sea-floor plates are continually being created at rifts along a global network of mid-ocean mountain ridges.
(A) requires
(B) simulates
(C) describes
(D) states

13. The male peacock has a train of up to 150 tail feathers, which can be erected in display to form <u>a showy</u> fan.
(A) an ordinary
(B) a large
(C) a striking
(D) a delicate

14. The earliest European universities were not specifically <u>founded</u>, but were spontaneous creations which evolved in the course of the 12th century.
(A) discovered
(B) administered
(C) endowed
(D) established

15. Since gelatin comes from animal bones, it is pure protein and easily digestible, which makes it a valuable food for <u>invalids</u>.
(A) babies
(B) the poor
(C) convalescents
(B) the aged

16. In the process of tatting, the craftsperson loops and knots cotton or linen thread that is <u>wound</u> around a small shuttle.
(A) spun
(B) wrapped
(C) threaded
(D) fastened

GO ON TO THE NEXT PAGE

17. Pneumonia is usually caused by bacteria and <u>rarely</u> results from pure virus infection.
(A) barely
(B) merely
(C) almost never
(D) possibly

18. In 1691 Plymouth Colony <u>merged</u> with Massachusetts Bay Colony to form Massachusetts.
(A) sided
(B) joined
(C) battled
(D) reformed

19. In the classical language of Sanskrit, dating from 1500 B.C., lies the <u>origin</u> of later Indo-European languages.
(A) understanding
(B) manuscript
(C) root
(D) measure

20. In recent years many invited nations have <u>boycotted</u> the Olympic Games as a protest against various political actions.
(A) ignored
(B) maligned
(C) not attended
(D) petitioned

21. Betsy Ross was an American <u>seamstress</u> who is said to have made the first American flag in 1776.
(A) artist
(B) inn keeper
(C) medical advisor
(D) clothing maker

22. All roundworms are long and thin, <u>tapering</u> at each end.
(A) bending
(B) rounding
(C) narrowing
(D) closing

23. A decorated top is more interesting to watch as its rotation slows and its images become <u>discernible</u>.
(A) clearer
(B) brighter
(C) larger
(D) more animated

24. Children of all ages <u>look forward to</u> the arrival of the holiday season.
(A) anticipate
(B) don't mind
(C) talk about
(D) misunderstand

25. The electric razor might not have been one of life's necessities, but it was one of the 20th century's electric <u>novelties</u>.
(A) mysteries
(B) failures
(C) gadgets
(D) breakthroughs

26. Old Faithful is the name given to a hot spring, or geyser, which erupts <u>intermittently</u> up to a height of 150 feet.
(A) magnificently
(B) forcefully
(C) briefly
(D) periodically

27. Laws against libel protect citizens from being <u>maliciously</u> attacked in print or on film.
(A) cunningly
(B) physically
(C) abusively
(D) decisively

28. With rapidly <u>appreciating</u> values of real estate, equity in a home is an excellent source of funds.
(A) fluctuating
(B) increasing
(C) engaging
(D) anticipating

GO ON TO THE NEXT PAGE

29. Fragile looking alpine flowers need <u>ingenious</u> adaptations to survive on the bleak mountain tundra.
   (A) scientific
   (B) seasonal
   (C) resourceful
   (D) predictable

30. Many discriminating readers choose a newspaper for its <u>impartial</u> treatment of the news rather than its sensational stories.
   (A) objective
   (B) slanted
   (C) brilliant
   (D) timely

<u>Directions:</u>   In the rest of this section you will read several passages. Each one is followed by several questions about it. For questions 31–60, you are to choose the <u>one</u> best answer, (A), (B), (C), or (D), to each question. Then, on your answer sheet, find the number of the question and fill in the space that corresponds to the letter of the answer you have chosen.

Answer all questions following a passage on the basis of what is <u>stated</u> or <u>implied</u> in that passage.

Read the following passage:

The flamingo is a beautiful water bird with long legs, and a curving neck like a swan's. Most flamingos have deep red or flame-colored feathers with black quills. Some have pink or white feathers. The long legs and webbed feet are well suited for wading. The flamingo eats
line in a peculiar manner. It plunges its head underwater and sifts the mud with a fine hairlike
(5) "comb" along the edge of its bent bill. In this way, it strains out small shellfish and other animals. The bird nests on a mound of mud with a hollow on top to hold its single egg. Flamingos are timid and often live together in large colonies. The birds once lived in the southern United States, but plume hunters killed them faster than they could breed, and the flamingo no longer lives wild in the United States.

Example I   <u>Sample Answer</u>
   The flamingo can eat shellfish and other animals because of its   Ⓐ ● Ⓒ Ⓓ
   (A) curved neck
   (B) especially formed bill
   (C) long legs
   (D) brightly colored feathers

According to the passage, the flamingo sifts mud for food with "a fine hairlike 'comb' along the edge of its bent bill". Therefore, you should choose answer (B).

Example II   <u>Sample Answer</u>
   How many young would you expect the flamingo to raise at one time?   Ⓐ Ⓑ ● Ⓓ
   (A) Several
   (B) Two
   (C) One
   (D) Four

The passage states that the flamingo nests on a mound of mud with a "single" egg. Therefore, you should choose answer (C).

After you read the directions, begin work on the questions.

GO ON TO THE NEXT PAGE ➤

Questions 31–37

By the mid-nineteenth century, in addition to its natural resources, the United States had accumulated enough capital in the form of factories to productively employ a large amount of labor, or human resources. A nation that still consisted largely of independent farmers
line could not provide an adequate labor supply for heavy industrialization. But millions of new
(5) workers came to the United States from abroad.

As we are all aware, not all these workers arrived voluntarily. Slaves were brought from Africa to the South; they were put to work on plantations to extract maximum harvests from the cotton fields. But in the North, the machines that turned that cotton into textiles were worked by massive waves of immigrants who came willingly from one part of Europe after
(10) another. This vastly expanded pool of labor allowed for large leaps in our national output.

A nation cannot grow forever by finding more natural resources and attracting more workers; thus, a country's extensive growth will eventually slow. But intensive growth gradually appears as better use is made of the labor force. In the United Sates in the mid-nineteenth century many of the newly arrived immigrants were unskilled and illiterate, but
(15) the education policy of their new land meant that their children all received an education, and many were trained in a skill. If a society gives workers more knowledge, they will be able to use machines in a more complex way and to follow more complex instructions, yielding manufactured goods of greater value; this process is often known as investing in human capital. In the late twentieth century, our physical capital is so abundant and our
(20) natural resources so limited that we are beginning to appreciate the importance of improving our human resources if we are to continue to grow.

31. This passage mainly discusses the national output in terms of
(A) the labor force
(B) natural resources
(C) factories
(D) immigration

32. Where did the necessary labor force for the nation's new industries come from?
(A) Unemployed farmers
(B) Europe and Africa
(C) The North
(D) The South

33. The phrase "massive waves of immigrants" in line 9 of the passage means that
(A) many immigrants came by ship
(B) many immigrants came at one time
(C) groups of immigrants came at different times
(D) groups of immigrants were greeted enthusiastically

34. From the passage, which of the following can be inferred about the United States in the first half of the nineteenth century?
(A) It was an underdeveloped nation.
(B) It was largely agricultural.
(C) It was fully industrialized.
(D) It was low in natural resources.

35. We can infer from the passage that an example of intensive growth is
(A) expansion of resources
(B) better use of the labor force
(C) educating the public
(D) limiting the human resources

36. According to the passage what is the end goal of an investment in human capital?
(A) Providing more valuable manufactured goods
(B) Educating immigrant families
(C) Training in use of complex machines
(D) Developing literacy for all

GO ON TO THE NEXT PAGE

37. We can infer from the passage that in the mid-nineteenth century the United States placed a high value on
    (A) European trade
    (B) education
    (C) agriculture
    (D) development of natural resources

Questions 38–42

      People have been playing with marbles for thousands of years. The first marbles were probably either river stones that happened to be naturally round enough to roll or, more likely, rounded globs of clay that were baked for hardness. Such very old clay marbles have
line been found in both Greek and Roman ruins, and quartzite spheres have been dated at
(5) around 6000 B.C.
      Harder and more durable marbles tend to inspire different kinds of games than soft clay marbles, which crack very easily. So with the advent of hand-rounded and polished marbles made of agate or some other rugged, igneous rock, the "golden age" of marbles and marble play flowered.
(10)   Stone marbles began to appear in the early 1800s in what is now the southern part of East Germany. Shortly after, handmade glass marbles appeared in the same part of Europe. For the next 120 years, marbles and marble playing—there were literally hundreds of games—flourished in both Europe and America.
      Marble players developed their own vocabulary for different sizes and materials of
(15) marbles, as well as for the many kinds of games to be played, and the way marbles were used in the games. For example, if you were going to play a game of Ring-Taw, one of the most popular and enduring marble games, you would *lag* for the first shot, and then *knuckle down* from the *baulk,* trying your best to get a *mib* or two with your opponent's *immie.*

38. The author makes the point in the passage that playing with marbles
    (A) has been going on since ancient times
    (B) is a relatively recent phenomenon
    (C) is losing popularity
    (D) is a very expensive pastime

39. According to the passage, which of the following was the least used substance for making marbles?
    (A) Agate
    (B) Rock
    (C) Glass
    (D) Clay

40. It can be inferred from the passage that the use of marbles became very popular in Europe and America
    (A) in the 18th century
    (B) in 6000 B.C.
    (C) in the 1970s
    (D) after glass marbles were developed

41. We can infer from the passage that marble playing
    (A) is a game only for children
    (B) has many variations in games
    (C) is played according to one set of rules
    (D) uses only one kind of marble

42. We can conclude from lines 17–18 of the passage that the terminology of marble playing is
    (A) specialized
    (B) easy to understand
    (C) used only by children
    (D) derived from the Greek language

GO ON TO THE NEXT PAGE

Questions 43–49

The log cabin, along with coonskin cap and Kentucky rifle, conjures up images of rugged pioneer days. Simple, one-room dwellings of logs, notched together at the corners, were introduced to America around 1638 by Swedish settlers in Delaware. Subsequently, German
line and Scotch Irish immigrants, as well as Russian explorers along the western coast and in
(5) Alaska, introduced their own forms of log construction. During the great westward expansion that began in the late 1700s, the log cabin was practically ubiquitous in timber-rich frontier areas; it could be built with only the aid of an axe, and required no costly nails. Intended to serve merely as way stations in the wilderness, cabins rarely became permanent homes. When families desired better housing with more amenities, they either abandoned
(10) their cabins—often to be occupied by new transients—incorporated them into larger dwellings, converted them into storage facilities, or in the South, used them as slave quarters. The myth of the log cabin as the sacrosanct birthplace of leaders, renowned for their honesty, humility, and other virtues, was inaugurated during the presidential campaign of 1840, when William Henry Harrison was touted throughout the country as a
(15) hard-cider swigging bumpkin who lived in a log cabin. His landslide victory over Martin Van Buren set a precedent for future presidential aspirants, but only a few such as "Honest Abe" Lincoln had bona fide claims to their humble origins. In the present day, the log cabin appears on such memorabilia as coins and postage stamps, and it is also the brand name of a popular syrup. The cabin is perpetuated architecturally in resorts, camps, inns, and
(20) restaurants along byways and highways.

43. According to the passage, who first introduced the log cabin structure in America?
(A) Russians in Alaska
(B) Pioneers in Kentucky
(C) Swedes in Delaware
(D) Germans in the West

44. We can infer from the passage that the log cabin originally
(A) was intended as a temporary home
(B) was comfortable and spacious
(C) was sold for large sums of money
(D) demonstrated the art of fine woodworking

45. The author implies that during the westward expansion the log cabin house
(A) diminished in popularity
(B) flourished
(C) became too costly
(D) required specialized tools

46. According to the passage which of the following did NOT happen when people moved into more luxurious housing?
(A) The cabin was abandoned.
(B) The cabin was sold for a high price.
(C) The cabin became part of a new home.
(D) The cabin was used for storage.

47. We can infer from the passage that after the presidential election of 1840
(A) wealth and social position became a positive campaign issue
(B) other presidential candidates professed to have lived in log cabins
(C) election campaigns were more honest
(D) people voted for a candidate based on his political party

GO ON TO THE NEXT PAGE

48. Why was William Henry Harrison mentioned in the passage?
    (A) As an example of an honest man
    (B) As an example of an underqualified candidate
    (C) To show how the log cabin myth began
    (D) To contrast his success with the defeat of Martin Van Buren

49. The author of the passage suggests that the log cabin house form has been
    (A) forgotten
    (B) romanticized
    (C) disparaged
    (D) simplified

Questions 50–56

   During the early twentieth century, there was a core of radical American artists who devoted themselves to exploring the potentials of modernism. Chief among them was Georgia O'Keeffe, the most famous woman artist of our time, who is best known for her dramatic paintings of gigantic flowers and sun-bleached desert bones.

line
(5)   A native of Wisconsin, O'Keeffe studied there, in Virginia, at the Art Institute of Chicago, and New York's Art Students League, and then earned her living as a public-school art teacher in Virginia and Texas. In 1915, at the age of twenty-eight, O'Keeffe arranged around her room all the art that she had produced so far, to evaluate it. Condemning each work as derivative, she destroyed them all, embarking on an entirely new series that she hoped
(10) would reflect only herself. The next year O'Keeffe sent some of her new work—remarkably spare, totally abstract charcoal drawings—to Anita Pollitzer, a friend living in New York. Pollitzer, impressed with the work, took the drawings to Alfred Stieglitz, the noted photographer, editor, dealer, and one of America's foremost promoters of modernist art. Stieglitz was also impressed; he became O'Keeffe's dealer, and later her husband. With
(15) Stieglitz's support and the help of positive reviews and significant sales, O'Keeffe was able to devote herself to painting: New York City scenes at night, at a time when the skyscrapers were brand-new; rural landscapes seen during summers at Lake George in upstate New York; and, finally, the blossoms and bones for which she became famous.

   By 1916 O'Keeffe was producing totally abstract drawings and water colors, many based
(20) on a series of simple lines and curved shapes. But she is known to far more viewers for her close-ups of flowers: red poppies, black irises, green orchids, pink-spotted lilies. Many theories have been advanced about the underlying meanings of these pictures. Much has been made of the "female qualities" of her blossoms; O'Keeffe, however always denied that there was any symbolism, sexual or otherwise, in her flower paintings. She claimed that their size was inspired by the skyscrapers being built all over New York and that what really interested her in a subject was not the flower, or the skulls, or the mountain, but the colors and shapes she saw as she looked at them.

50. According to the passage, what type of painter was Georgia O'Keeffe?
    (A) A portraitist
    (B) A miniaturist
    (C) A modernist
    (D) An expressionist

51. According to the passage, O'Keeffe is best known for her paintings of
    (A) objects
    (B) deserts
    (C) women
    (D) night scenes

GO ON TO THE NEXT PAGE ➤

52. According to the passage, why did O'Keeffe destroy her work in 1915?
    (A) She needed more space in her room.
    (B) She was unhappy with the medium in which she had been working.
    (C) She wanted to produce larger paintings.
    (D) She felt that her previous work was not original.

53. Why does the author cite Anita Pollitzer in the passage?
    (A) She was a noted art dealer.
    (B) She introduced O'Keeffe's work to Stieglitz.
    (C) She was a patron of O'Keeffe.
    (D) She was an acquaintance of O'Keeffe.

54. In line 11, the word "spare" could best be replaced by which of the following?
    (A) excessive
    (B) liberated
    (C) simple
    (D) modern

55. We can infer from the passage that O'Keeffe's new work promoted by Stieglitz
    (A) was well-received by the public
    (B) went relatively unnoticed
    (C) was criticized as too modern
    (D) dealt with the subject of flowers

56. According to the passage, O'Keeffe felt that her paintings of flowers had been influenced by all of the following EXCEPT
    (A) female qualities
    (B) the size of the New York skyscrapers
    (C) colors
    (D) shapes

GO ON TO THE NEXT PAGE ➔

Questions 57–60

Many of us forget that good teeth and gums are a significant part of good health. Without them we cannot eat many foods which provide important nutrients. Teeth are alive. Your saliva nourishes them through tiny passageways in the tooth. Poor nutrition can cause
line dental disease just as it causes other diseases of the body. Vitamins A and D, calcium,
(5) phosphorus and fluoride are important for tooth development. Reducing sugar in your diet is another way to keep your teeth healthy. Teeth are especially prone to decay in the six-month period after they come through the gums, before they are fully hardened.

Foods containing sugar cause tooth and gum decay in the following way. Certain types of bacteria found in saliva use sugar to make themselves a protective coating. This helps them
(10) cling to our teeth as a sticky substance called dental plaque which saliva cannot wash away. These bacteria, tiny organisms known as streptococci, multiply rapidly and produce large amounts of acids, which dissolve the enamel and irritate the gums, causing disease. To remove the plaque and prevent this decay, it's important to brush and floss our teeth daily.

57. What is the purpose of this passage?
   (A) To inform the reader about tooth decay and its prevention
   (B) To describe the dangers of dental plaque
   (C) To warn the reader about eating sweets and food with sugar
   (D) To tell the reader about bacteria in saliva

58. According to the author of the passage, when are teeth most susceptible to decay?
   (A) Shortly after they come through the gums
   (B) At night
   (C) When you are old
   (D) After eating

59. How does the author support the idea that we should brush our teeth daily?
   (A) By offering suggestions for prevention of tooth decay
   (B) By describing in some detail one cause of tooth decay
   (C) By elaborating on several causes of tooth decay
   (D) By stating nutritional information

60. According to the passage dental plaque is harmful because of
   (A) its sticky nature
   (B) the irritating acids it produces
   (C) the damage it does to the saliva
   (D) its unpleasant taste

THIS IS THE END OF SECTION 3

**IF YOU FINISH BEFORE TIME IS CALLED, CHECK YOUR WORK ON SECTION 3 ONLY.
DO NOT READ OR WORK ON ANY OTHER SECTION OF THE TEST.**

  STOP STOP STOP STOP STOP STOP

TEST OF WRITTEN ENGLISH

30 minutes

The graph below shows the annual energy consumption of office buildings since 1973. These buildings were converted to use solar heating and cooling devices and photovoltaics rather than fossil fuels for energy. What does the chart tell you about the reasons for energy use? What does it tell you about present energy consumption? Explain your conclusions, supporting them with details from the graph.

ANNUAL ENERGY CONSUMPTION

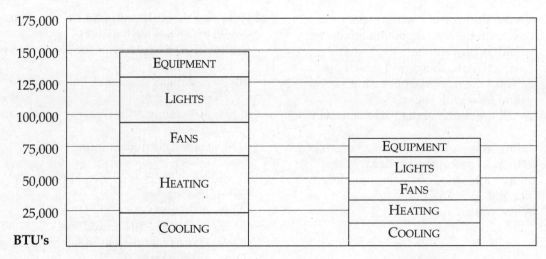

For more practice, take a complete test from *The Heinemann TOEFL Practice Tests*.

LISTENING APPENDIX

The Listening Appendix is meant to supplement the Listening Checkpoints treated in this text. Other books which may help students with their overall knowledge of the vocabulary, sounds, and spoken structures of North American English are listed below.

General Dictionaries:

Everyday American English Dictionary, edited by Richard A. Spears, Linda Schinke-Llano, and Betty Kirkpatrick. Lincolnwood, Illinois: National Textbook Company, 1987.

Longman Dictionary of American English. New York: Longman Inc., 1983.

Longman Lexicon of Contemporary English, Tom McArthur. Essex, England: Longman Group Limited, 1981.

Idiom Dictionaries and Workbooks:

Attitudes Through Idioms, Thomas W. Adams, and Susan R. Kuder. Rowley, Mass.: Newbury House Publishers, 1984.

A Dictionary of American Idioms. Project director Maxine Tull Boatner. Woodbury, New York: Barron's Educational Series, Inc., 1975.

The New Idioms in Action, George Reeves. Cambridge, Mass.: Newbury House Publishers, 1985.

Listening Skills Books (helpful audio cassettes accompany all of these books):

Clear Speech, Judy B. Gilbert. New York: Cambridge University Press, 1984.

Improving Aural Comprehension, Joan Morley. Ann Arbor: The University of Michigan Press, 1972.

Pronouncing American English, Gertrude F. Orion. New York: Newbury House Publishers, 1988.

Pronunciation Drills, new edition, Edith Crowell Trager and Sara Cook Henderson. Englewood Cliffs, NJ: Prentice-Hall, Inc., 1983.

This is a Recording, Barbara Fowler Swartz and Richard L. Smith. Englewood Cliffs, NJ: Prentice-Hall, Inc., 1986.

1. Word Category Charts

A. SCHOOL AND COLLEGE LIFE
General
advisor
application
apply to a university/college
assignment
assistantship
book
book bag
bookstore
campus
cancel/postpone a class/test
class
classmate
college
computer
conference
course
dean
dormitory (dorm)
exam
experiment
extension
fail
freshman
grade
graduation
handout
junior
laboratory
lecture
library
material
major
pass
photocopy
prerequisite
presentation
professor
program
project
professor
raise your hand
reference
requirement
roommate
scholarship
school
semester
seminar
senior

sophomore
student
student lounge
study
take a course
teaching assistant
teach
term
term project
test
text
text book
translate
tuition
type
typewriter
university
upperclassman
write a paper

_____

_____

_____

_____

_____

_____

_____

Fields of Study
administration
anthropology
astronomy
biology
business
chemistry
English
French
history
law
mathematics (math)
medicine
microbiology
physics
sociology
Spanish

Communications
address
conversation
copying machine
language
letter
local call
long distance call
mail
news
newspaper
package
phone
photocopies
post office
regulations
telephone

_____

_____

_____

_____

_____

_____

_____

_____

_____

B. DAILY LIFE
Clothing, Money, and Shopping
bank
change
charge
check
coat
credit card
department store
gift
housewares
jacket
shopping
shops
ski jacket
store
suit

_____

_____

_____

_____

_____

_____

_____

Food and Eating
cafeteria
cook
cup of coffee
dinner
meal
meal ticket
menu
napkin
pizza
recipe
restaurant
sandwich
silverware
soup

spicy
waiter
waitress

_____

_____

_____

_____

_____

_____

_____

_____

Health
appointment
dentist
doctor
eye doctor
glasses
injury
pain
pulled muscle
sore
tooth

_____

_____

_____

_____

_____

_____

_____

Home and Family
alarm
alarm clock
apartment
brother
children
cousin
daughter
father
house
lamp
mother
parents
shelf
sister
son

_____

_____

_____

_____

_____

_____

_____

Jobs and Occupations
agriculture
briefcase
director
industry
job
part-time
profession
salary
secretary
wages
work

_____

_____

_____

_____

_____

_____

_____

_____

_____

_____

_____

_____

_____

_____

Sports, Hobbies, and Entertainment

actor
actress
artist
baseball
boat
camera
cassette
concert
exercise
game
locker
movie
parade
photography
play
piano
sail
show
ski
sky diving
slide projector
solo
song
tape
tape recorder
television
tennis
tennis racket
theater
video
violin

_____

_____

_____

Time and Temperature

autumn
clear
cloudy
fall
fog
forecast
ice
midnight
noon
rain
snow
storm
summer
sunny
warm
weather
winter

_____

_____

_____

_____

_____

_____

_____

_____

Transportation and Travel
    airport
    baggage claim
    bus
    bus station
    gas
    gas station
    parking
    parking place
    passport
    plane
    reservation
    speeding ticket
    street
    suitcase
    taxi
    ticket
    trip

vacation
visa

_____

_____

_____

_____

_____

_____

_____

_____

2. Glossary of Idioms Used in the Listening Section of the Course

Please note that not all meanings of the idioms listed below are given. Only those meanings used in this text are discussed. For your reference, the exercise and question number are given for each idiom. Most occur in the tapescript; some occur in the answer choices.

ball of fire: person with great energy (Ex. 2A, #7)

to be/walk in someone else's shoes: to try to understand someone else or put oneself in that person's position (Ex. 9A, #19)

beat: very tired (Ex. 14B, #3)

to be short: not to have enough (Ex. 2A, #8)

to be tied up: to be busy (Ex. 2A, #9)

to be too much for someone: to be too difficult or overwhelming (Restatement Checkpoint Test, #12)

to blow the whistle: to tell secret information about (Ex. 2A, #10)

to break down: to become unusable because of breakage (Mini-Dialogue Checkpoint Test, #11)

can of worms: complex problem (Ex. 2A, #5)

to catch one's eye: to attract one's attention (Ex. 2C, #5)

coffee break: a short recess from work during which workers rest and drink coffee or other refreshment (Ex. 11A & B, #7)

to come up: to approach or come close (Mini-Dialogue Checkpoint Test, #10)

to cross one's mind: to be a sudden or passing thought (Diagnostic Test, #3)

to do one's best: to try very hard (Ex. 4D, #2)

to drop a class: to cancel one's enrollment in a class (Section Test, #5)

end of one's rope: the end of one's ability to cope or try (Section Test, #27)

to fall through: to fail (Ex. 2C, #4)

false start: an unsuccessful beginning (Restatement Checkpoint Test, #18)

to fill out: to complete (Section Test, #10)

to fill up the car: to put a full tank of gasoline in the car (Restatement Checkpoint Test, #7)

to get a hold of: to contact (Ex. 2C, #1)

to get along with: 1) to agree with; 2) to cooperate with (Model, page 44)

to get off the ground: to make a successful beginning (Ex. 2A, #6)

to get rid of: to give away or throw away (Diagnostic Test, #9)

to give a hand: 1) to applaud; 2) to help out (Explanation, page 49)

to go from bad to worse: to change from a bad condition to a worse one (Section Test, #24)

a good buy: a wise purchase (Restatement Checkpoint Test, #6)

to hang up: to place a telephone receiver back on its hook and break the connection (Ex. 11A and B, #9)

to have a hand in: to be partly responsible for (Model, page 49)

to have an edge on: to have an advantage over (Diagnostic Test, #11)

to have your hands tied: to be unable to help (Section Test, #18)

to hit the nail on the head: to be right about something (Ex. 2A, #1)

I'll say: I agree with this completely (Diagnostic Test, #34)

to keep something to oneself: to keep something secret (Ex. 2C, #7)

to knock oneself out: to work very hard at something (Example, page 43)

to land on one's feet: to get out of trouble without damage or injury and sometimes with a gain (Restatement Checkpoint Test, #18)

to learn the ropes: to gain experience (Ex. 2C, #11)

to look forward to: to expect with hope or pleasure (Example sentence, page 59)

to look on the bright side: to be optimistic (Ex. 2A, #2)

to make it: to go or to come to a place (Ex. 2C, #3)

not on your life: certainly not; not ever; not for any reason (Diagnostic Test, #30)

on foot: walking (Restatement Checkpoint Test, #7)

on sale: selling for a special reduced price (Model, page 117)

on the side: in addition to a main thing (Ex. 2A, #3)

on the whole: in most ways (Ex. 2A, #4)

to pick out: to choose (Ex. 9B, #7)

to pick up: to take on or away (Ex. 2C, #10)

to pull someone's leg: to tease someone (Ex. 2A, #11)

to put off: to postpone (Section Test, #30)

to receive with open arms: to welcome warmly or eagerly (Restatement Checkpoint Test, #14)

right away: immediately (Model, page 87)

to see to: to attend to, to take care of (Section Test, #2)

to see eye to eye: to agree with (Ex. 2C, #9)

to set aside: to separate, to make time for (Section Test, #14)

to set back: to cause something or someone to get behind schedule (Section Test, #6)

so long: good bye (Restatement Checkpoint Test, #1)

sold out: no longer available because all have been sold (Diagnostic Test, #27)

something else: stupendous, wonderful, so good as to be indescribable (Model, page 83)

to stop by: to visit on short notice or unexpectedly (Ex. 2C, #2)

to straighten up: 1) to tidy or clean up; 2) to improve one's behavior (Ex. 2C, #8)

to take a seat: to sit down (Ex. 4D, #1)

to take (a car) for a spin: to test-drive, to try out (Ex. 14B, #6)

to take into account: to consider, to remember and understand (Mini-Dialogue Checkpoint Test, #15)

to take it easy: to avoid hard work or worry; to rest (Diagnostic Test, #24)

to take part in: to join in, to have a part or share in (Diagnostic Test, #6)

to take place: to happen (Ex.17A, #2)

to turn up: to appear, to be found (Ex. 11D, #3)

to try on: to put something on to see if it fits (Section Test, #1)

to try out for: to try for a place on a team or a group (Ex. 16, #20)

to turn on: to start by turning a handle or moving a switch (Ex. 4C, #11)

GRAMMAR APPENDIX

CONTENTS

1. Subject
2. Object
3. Complement
4. Noun
5. Noun Structure
6. Article
7. Expression of Quantity
8. Pronoun
9. Number
10. Gender
11. Person
12. Adjective
13. Adverb
14. Verb
15. Verb Tense Form
16. Linking Verb
17. Transitive Verb
18. Intransitive Verb
19. Helping Verb
20. Agreement
21. Active and Passive Sentence Pairs
22. Modal or Modal-like Verb
23. Phrase
24. Preposition
25. Prepositional Phrase
26. Clause
27. Main Clause
28. Noun Clause
29. Adverb Clause
30. Adjective Clause
31. ——*ING* or ——*ED* Modifying Phrase
32. Gerund
33. Infinitive
34. Conditional Sentence
35. Confusing Words and Expressions

The Grammar Appendix is meant to supplement the Grammar Checkpoints treated in this text. It is not meant as a comprehensive review of English grammar. For students who need more grammar review, we would like to recommend the following books:

Understanding and Using English Grammar, Betty Schrampfer Azar. Englewood Cliffs, New Jersey: Prentice-Hall, 1989.

Modern English, A Practical Reference Guide, Marcella Frank. Englewood Cliffs, New Jersey: Prentice-Hall, 1972.

The Advanced Grammar Book, Jocelyn M. Steer and Karen Carlisi. New York: Newbury House, 1990.

1. **Subject (S):**   doer of the action in a sentence. In standard English word order, the subject comes first in a sentence.

   <u>Carol</u> will arrive tomorrow.
   S (Noun)

   <u>To know</u> her is to love her.
   S (Infinitive)

2. **Object (O)**
   A. direct receiver of the action of a sentence (DO).
   B. indirect receiver of the action of a sentence (IO).
   C. object of a preposition (O of prep).

   I handed <u>Andrew</u> <u>the scissors</u> that were on <u>the table</u>.
            IO   *DO*   *O of prep*

   In standard English word order, direct and indirect objects follow verbs.

   Objects of prepositions complete the idea of time, direction, etc. begun by a preposition and come at the end of a prepositional phrase.

3. **Complement (C)**
   A. subject identifier—noun complement after the verb BE (SC).

   Carol is <u>a teacher</u>.
        SC (Noun)

   What you see is <u>what you get</u>.
        SC (Noun clause)

   B. subject modifier —adjective complement after the verb BE and other linking verbs (SC).

   Jack is <u>happy</u>.
        SC (Adjective)

   C. object identifier—noun complement after the direct object of a sentence (OC).

   They made her <u>chairperson</u>.
        OC (Noun)

   D. object modifier—adjective complement after the direct object (OC).

   Her gift made me <u>happy</u>.
        OC (Adjective)

4. **Noun:** a word which names a person, place, thing, or idea.
   Countable noun: can be counted. Regular countable nouns end in ——*s* or ——*es* when they are plural.

   book......books   shoe......shoes
   boy......boys   dress......dresses

   Uncountable noun: cannot be counted. Most uncountable nouns are thought of as *wholes* that are made up of different parts.

   sugar   coffee
   bacon   wood
   homework money
   information rice

Many uncountable nouns are abstract concepts.

love	fun
happiness	music
freedom	peace
poverty	importance

Languages and fields of study are also uncountable nouns.

French	chemistry
Chinese	biology
English	engineering
Japanese	psychology

Nouns referring to natural phenomena are usually uncountable.

snow	rain
heat	weather
darkness	sunshine
wind	fire

Gerunds are uncountable nouns.

swimming	reading
walking	studying

Some uncountable nouns have countable meanings.

uncountable:	I like tea.
countable:	The teas of India are renowned for their full-bodied flavor.

uncountable:	We had chicken for dinner.
countable:	The chickens were making a lot of noise last night.

Indefinite noun: refers to things that are new or not known to either the listener or the speaker in a conversation or to either the reader or the writer in a text.

I want to buy a book.
In this sentence, no particular book has been mentioned. It is indefinite.

Definite noun: refers to things that are known or are made specific by their use in a sentence.

The book I want is entitled *Call of the Wild*.
In this sentence *book* has now become definite. It even has a title.

Note: In order to succeed on TOEFL questions that test nouns, it is helpful to be familiar with the irregular plural forms of the most common English nouns. Some of these include:

man	men	goose	geese
woman	women	mouse	mice
child	children	fish	fish
tooth	teeth	sheep	sheep
foot	feet	deer	deer

5. **Noun Structure:** a structure that functions as a subject, object, or complement in a sentence. Nouns and noun phrases (a noun plus all of its modifiers) are noun structures. Other noun structures include pronouns, gerunds, infinitives, and noun clauses.

<u>I</u>   like   <u>him</u>.
Pronoun   *Pronoun*
Subject   *Object*

<u>Reading</u> is my favorite pastime.
Gerund
Subject

I like <u>to read</u>.
    Infinitive
    Object

<u>What I want</u> is <u>whatever you want</u>.
Noun clause   *Noun clause*
Subject   *Complement*

Occasionally, but rarely, prepositional phrases function as noun structures. As the TOEFL does not specifically test this function of prepositional phrases, they are not included in the study of noun structures in this text.

6. **Article:** a word which comes before a noun and affects the meaning of the noun. There are two articles: *a/an* and *the*.

Article choice depends on the definite/indefinite categories of nouns as well as the countable/uncountable categories. The chart below classifies article and noun usage.

NOUNS AND ARTICLES

	Indefinite Nouns	Definite Nouns
Countable Singular Nouns	a boy an orange	the boy the orange
Countable Plural Nouns	_____ boys _____ oranges	the boys the oranges
Uncountable Nouns	_____ sugar	the sugar

The spelling of *a/an* is *a* before words beginning with a consonant sound. This includes the *y* sound as in the word *yellow*. Some words beginning with the vowel letter *u* actually begin with the consonant sound *y*. These words should be preceded by *a*. Some of these words are:

	unanimous	universe
	unicorn	university
	unicycle	uranium
	unification	usage
A	uniform	usable
	union	use
	unique	usual
	unit	utility
	unity	utopia
	universal	

The spelling of *a/an* is *an* before words beginning with a vowel sound. A few words begin with the consonant letter *h*, but actually begin with the vowel sound *uh* as in the word *up*. These words should be preceded by *an*. Some of these words are:

	heir	honor
	heirloom	honorable
An	homage	honorary
	honest	hour
	honesty	hourly

7. **Expression of Quantity:** a word or phrase which makes it possible to quantify a noun.

Some English expressions of quantity are used only with countable nouns. Other expressions of quantity are used only with uncountable nouns. Still other expressions of quantity are used with both countable and uncountable nouns. The chart below shows which expressions of quantity are used with countable and uncountable nouns.

USED WITH COUNTABLE NOUNS	USED WITH UNCOUNTABLE NOUNS
many	much
number of	amount of
few	little
a few	a little
fewer	less
none	none
some	some
any	any
a lot of	a lot of
one, two, three...	
several	

8. **Pronoun:** a word which replaces or refers to a noun or noun phrase.

PRONOUNS				
PERSONAL		**POSSESSIVE**		**REFLEXIVE**
SUBJECT	**OBJECT**	**ADJECTIVE**	**PRONOUN**	
I	me	my	mine	myself
you	you	your	yours	yourself
he	him	his	his	himself
she	her	her	hers	herself
it	it	its*	_____	itself
we	us	our	ours	ourselves
they	them	their	theirs	themselves
one	one	one's	_____	oneself

*NOTE: There is no apostrophe (') in this possessive form.

Subject pronouns are used:
A. as the subjects of main or subordinate clauses;

I like Clarence because <u>he</u> always smiles.

B. after the verb BE.

This is she.*

*NOTE: In current colloquial English, object pronouns are also acceptable in this position.

Object pronouns are used:
A. as indirect or direct objects of transitive verbs;

Jack's grandfather gave <u>him</u> an antique stopwatch.

B. as the objects of prepositions.

When Mary spoke to <u>me</u> she mentioned the party tonight.

Possessive adjectives are used to modify nouns and gerunds and show possession.

I thought <u>his</u> singing would be perfect for <u>our</u> ceremony.

Possessive pronouns are used:

A. in place of nouns functioning as subjects or objects;

   Since your car isn't running, let's take <u>mine</u>.

B. after *of* when it means possession;

   A son of <u>theirs</u> is a student at Cornell.

C. after the verb BE to indicate possession.

   This dress is <u>yours</u>.

Reflexive pronouns are used:

A. when the objects and subjects in a sentence are the same;

   Steve cut <u>himself</u> on some broken glass, and administered first aid to <u>himself</u>.

B. as objects of the preposition *by* to mean alone;

   Please try to do this exercise by <u>yourself</u>.

C.   for emphasis.

   The president <u>himself</u> visited our community.

9. **Number:** singular or plural. Nouns in English can be singular (one) or plural (more than one.) The pronouns that replace or refer to nouns can be singular or plural as well.

   That <u>girl</u> is a <u>student</u>. <u>She</u> likes being a <u>student</u>.
   Sing.   *Sing.*   *Sing.*   *Sing.*

   Those <u>girls</u> are <u>students</u>. <u>They</u> like being <u>students</u>.
   Plural   *Plural*   *Plural*   *Plural*

10. **Gender:** feminine, masculine, or neuter. Most English nouns are neuter. However, nouns which name female or male people (or sometimes other animals) are feminine or masculine. The pronouns that replace these nouns show feminine (she, her, hers, herself) or masculine (he, him, his, himself) gender.

    girl—she   boy—he

11. **Person:** first, second, or third.
    First person = the person or persons speaking (e.g., I, we)
    Second person = the person or persons spoken to (e.g., you)
    Third person = the person or persons spoken about (e.g., he, she, it, they, John, Mary)

12. **Adjective:** a word, phrase, or clause that modifies a noun or noun structure.

The big dog chased the little cat.
Adjective   *Adjective*

The baby playing in his crib is yours.
           Adjective phrase

The baby who is crying is mine.
           Adjective clause

13. **Adverb:** a word, phrase, or clause that modifies a verb, an adjective, or another adverb. An adverb tells manner (how), place (where), time (when), frequency (how often), degree (to what degree), or reason (why) an action takes place.

He ate quickly.
       Adverb of manner

He went home because he was tired.
           Adverb of reason

14. **Verb:** a word or phrase which expresses the action or state of being in a sentence. Some verb forms are referred to as finite verb forms. These are the forms of verbs which show tense and/or number. (e.g., is, was, has, had, goes, went, walks, walked). Other verb forms are referred to as nonfinite. These are the forms of verbs which do not show tense by themselves (e.g., going, to go, gone) and which can act as other parts of speech than verbs. The nonfinite verb forms in English are the infinitive (e.g., to go), the ——*ing* participle (e.g., going), and the past participle (e.g., gone).

The English verb has five principal finite and nonfinite parts.

PRINCIPAL PARTS OF SOME ENGLISH VERBS

Base Form	Present Participle	Present	Past Participle	Past
start	start(s)	starting	started	started
hope	hope(s)	hoping	hoped	hoped
study	study(ies)	studying	studied	studied
eat	eat(s)	eating	ate	eaten
give	give(s)	giving	gave	given
have	have (has)	having	had	had
be	am/is/are	being	was/were	been

Several of the verbs in the chart above have irregular parts, especially for their past and past participle forms. Below is a chart showing more irregular past and past participle forms.

IRREGULAR VERBS

Base Form	Past Form	Past Participle
arise	arose	arisen
be	was/were	been
bear	bore	borne/born
beat	beat	beaten
become	became	become
begin	began	begun
bend	bent	bent
bet	bet	bet
bid	bid	bid
bind	bound	bound
bite	bit	bitten
blow	blew	blown
break	broke	broken
bring	brought	brought
build	built	built
buy	bought	bought
catch	caught	caught
choose	chose	chosen
come	came	come
cost	cost	cost
cut	cut	cut
dig	dug	dug
do	did	done
draw	drew	drawn
eat	ate	eaten
fall	fell	fallen
feed	fed	fed
feel	felt	felt
fight	fought	fought
find	found	found
fit	fit	fit
fly	flew	flown
forbid	forbade	forbidden
forget	forgot	forgotten
forgive	forgave	forgiven
freeze	froze	frozen
get	got	gotten
give	gave	given
go	went	gone
grow	grew	grown
hang	hung	hung
have	had	had
hear	heard	heard
hide	hid	hidden
hit	hit	hit
hold	held	held

Base Form	Past Form	Past Participle
hurt	hurt	hurt
keep	kept	kept
know	knew	known
lay	laid	laid
lead	led	led
leave	left	left
lend	lent	lent
let	let	let
lie	lay	lain
lose	lost	lost
make	made	made
mean	meant	meant
meet	met	met
mistake	mistook	mistaken
pay	paid	paid
put	put	put
quit	quit	quit
read	read	read
rid	rid	rid
ride	rode	ridden
ring	rang	rung
rise	rose	risen
run	ran	run
say	said	said
see	saw	seen
seek	sought	sought
sell	sold	sold
send	sent	sent
set	set	set
shake	shook	shaken
shine	shined/shone	shined/shone
shoot	shot	shot
show	showed	showed/shown
shrink	shrank/shrunk	shrunk
shut	shut	shut
sing	sang	sang
sit	sat	sat
sleep	slept	slept
slide	slid	slid
speak	spoke	spoken
speed	sped/speeded	sped/speeded
spend	spent	spent
spin	spun	spun
spread	spread	spread
spring	sprang/sprung	sprung
stand	stood	stood
steal	stole	stolen
stick	stuck	stuck
sting	stung	stung
strive	strove	striven

Base Form	Past Form	Past Participle
struck	struck	stricken/struck
string	strung	strung
swear	swore	sworn
sweep	swept	swept
swim	swam	swum
swing	swung	swung
take	took	taken
teach	taught	taught
tear	tore	torn
tell	told	told
think	thought	thought
throw	threw	thrown
thrust	thrust	thrust
understand	understood	understood
undertake	undertook	undertaken
upset	upset	upset
wake	woke/waked	waked/woken
wear	wore	worn
weave	wove	woven
weep	wept	wept
win	won	won
wind	wound	wound
withdraw	withdrew	withdrawn
wring	wrung	wrung
write	wrote	written

15. **Verb Tense Form:**   the five principal verb parts discussed in number 14 are used in forming the English tenses.

NAME OF TENSE	HOW IT IS FORMED
Simple Present	Base Form (+*s* in third person singular) He <u>walks</u> to school every day.
Simple Past	Past Form He <u>walked</u> to school every day.
Simple Future	*will* + Base Form of main verb He <u>will walk</u> to school every day.
Present Continuous	*am/is/are* + Present Participle of main verb He <u>is walking</u> to school right now.
Past Continuous	*was/were* + Present Participle of main verb He <u>was walking</u> to school when it started to rain.
Future Continuous	*will* + *be* + Present Participle of main verb He <u>will be walking</u> to school tomorrow morning at 7:30.

Present Perfect	*have/has* + Past Participle of main verb
	He <u>has walked</u> to school every day this year.
Past Perfect	*had* + Past Participle of main verb
	He <u>had walked</u> to school for six months when his parents bought him a car.
Future Perfect	*will* + *have* + Past Participle of main verb
	He <u>will have walked</u> to school for six months by the time his parents buy him a car.
Pres. Perf. Cont.	*have/has* + *been* + Present Participle of main verb
	He <u>has been walking</u> to school for six months.
Past Perf. Cont.	*had* + *been* + Present Participle of main verb
	He <u>had been walking</u> to school for six months when his parents bought him a car.
Future Perf. Cont	*will* + *have* + *been* + Present Participle of main verb
	He <u>will have been walking</u> to school for six months by the time his parents buy him a car.

NOTE: As you can see in the chart above, when the verb BE is used in any of its forms to create an active* verb tense, it is followed by a PRESENT PARTICIPLE (as, for example, in the continuous tenses).

When the verb HAVE is used in any of its forms, it is followed by a PAST PARTICIPLE (as, for example, in the perfect tenses).

* Sometimes the verb BE is used to form passive sentences. When this happens it is followed by a PAST PARTICIPLE. See #21, below, for more information on passive sentences.

16. **Linking Verb (LV):** a verb which connects the subject of a sentence to a complement. This complement is a noun structure which renames or an adjective which describes the subject it refers to.

> John <u>is</u> <u>a doctor</u>.
>   *LV*   *Comp (noun)*

> John <u>is</u>   <u>happy</u>.
>   *LV*   *Comp (adjective)*

    Common linking verbs are: *appear, be, become* (and *get, turn,* and *grow* when they mean "become"), *feel, look, seem, smell, sound,* and *taste.*
    Some linking verbs have corresponding active meanings. When used in their active meanings, these verbs are followed by adverbs and are no longer linking verbs.

> He <u>appears</u> <u>tired</u>.
>   *LV*   *Comp*

> He <u>appears</u> <u>nightly</u> at the Rathskellar lounge.
>   *V*   *Adverb*

Linking verbs often take on active meanings when the verbs are followed by prepositions.

He <u>looked</u> <u>happy</u>.
    LV   *Adj*

He <u>looked</u> <u>happily</u> at the piece of chocolate cake on his desk.
   V   *Adv*

17. **Transitive Verb:** a verb that is followed by a direct object (DO). Some transitive verbs are also followed by indirect objects (IO).

Leona <u>gave</u>   <u>Rich</u>   <u>a hug</u>.
Transitive verb   *IO*   *DO*

In this sentence, *a hug* is what is given. It is the direct receiver of the verb *gave*. *Rich* is the indirect receiver of *gave*. *Rich* is the recipient of *a hug*.

18. **Intransitive Verb:** a verb that is not followed by a direct or indirect object.

I <u>ran</u>   to the store.
Intransitive verb

Some intransitive verbs have corresponding transitive equivalents.

I <u>ran</u>   <u>the store</u> for my parents.
Transitive verb   *DO*

19. **Helping Verb:** a verb which helps the main verb of a sentence but does not carry the core verb meaning of the sentence. The helping verbs in English are: HAVE, BE, DO and the modals *shall, will, can, must, may, should, would, could,* and *might.* HAVE, BE, and DO can also stand alone as main verbs. The modals cannot stand alone as main verbs.

I <u>have</u>   eaten.
Helping verb

I <u>have</u>   a new car.
Main verb

20. **Agreement:** a correct match between two sentence parts.

Expression of Quantity + Noun: expressions of quantity must agree in number with the nouns they modify.

Article + Noun: articles must agree in number and type (definite or indefinite) with the nouns they come before.

Pronoun + Noun: pronouns must agree in number, form, and gender with the nouns they replace or refer to.

Subject + verb: subjects and verbs in the same sentence must agree in number and person.

Although this basic subject—verb agreement rule is not complex, there are several special rules.

SPECIAL SUBJECT–VERB AGREEMENT RULES

A. Phrases and clauses which come between the subject and the verb do not change the number of the subject.

> The <u>picture</u> of his classmates <u>pleases</u> him.

B. Some pronouns take singular verbs even though the pronouns may seem plural in meaning. These pronouns include:

anybody	nobody	somebody	everybody	each
anyone	no one	someone	everyone	either
anything	nothing	something	everything	neither

> <u>*Everybody*</u> <u>likes</u> this pie.

C. When subjects are joined by *either/or*, *neither/nor*, or *not only/but also*, the verb agrees with the closer subject.

> *Not only* <u>the teacher</u> *but also* <u>the students are going</u> to the conference.

D. When subjects are joined by *and* or by *both/and*, they take a plural verb.

> *Both* <u>Anne</u> *and* <u>Fred</u> <u>are coming</u> tonight.

E. *None, all, some, any, most, majority,* and other similar expressions can take either a singular or plural verb depending on the noun that comes after them.

> *None* of the <u>sugar</u> <u>was</u> eaten.

> *None* of the <u>students</u> <u>were</u> pleased.

F. *Several, both, many,* and *few* are plural words which need plural verbs.

> <u>*Few*</u> <u>were</u> present at the last meeting.

G. *A number of* requires a plural verb. *The number of* requires a singular verb.

> <u>*A number of*</u> my friends <u>were</u> here last night.

> <u>*The number of*</u> classes <u>has been reduced</u>.

H. In sentences beginning with *it*, the verb should be singular.

> <u>*It*</u> <u>is</u> his problems at work that are bothering him.

I. In sentences beginning with *there* or *here*, the verb agrees with the real subject, which comes after the verb.

> *Here* <u>are</u> <u>the pictures</u> you wanted.

J. *A pair of, a flock of, a herd of,* and other expressions indicating groups of things or animals take singular verbs even though nouns used with them will be plural.

   A pair of swans <u>mates</u> for life.

K. The verbs in relative clauses agree with the nouns that their head relative words replace.

   <u>The professor and the student</u>, who <u>were working</u> together, wrote this article.

L. Some nouns which look plural are really singular and take singular verbs. These words include:

   news, politics, and some other abstract nouns

   mathematics, physics, linguistics, and any other academic subjects that end in ——*s*

   Linguistics <u>is</u> his major.

M. Some nouns which look singular are really plural and take plural verbs. These nouns include those for which the singular and the plural form are the same. Some of these nouns are:

   fish   deer   species   series

   Plural: The magazine *series* <u>are</u> all located in the reference section of the library.

   Singular: This television *series* <u>is</u> a popular one.

N. Expressions showing quantities of time, money, weight, and volume look plural but take singular verbs.

   Three days <u>is</u> enough time to finish this project.

   Five dollars <u>is</u> too much to pay for this notebook.

O. Nouns which refer to a country or a nationality can be singular or plural. When one of these words refers to a language, it is singular. When one of these words refers to the people of a country, it is plural.

   French <u>is</u> a difficult language.

   The French <u>are</u> interesting people.

21. **Active and Passive Sentence Pairs:**   two sentences which are nearly the same in meaning but which are formed differently.

Active: Charles broke the window.

Passive 1:   The window was broken by Charles.

Passive 2:   The window was broken.

In forming the passive:

1. The direct object of the active sentence becomes the subject of the passive sentence.
2. The subject of the passive sentence becomes the object of the preposition *by* (Passive 1) or is deleted (Passive 2).
3. The verb of the passive sentence is formed by:
   a. putting the helping verb BE in the same form as the verb in the active sentence, or
   b. adding the past participle of the main verb.

Active: *broke*—past form of main verb
Passive: *was broken*—past form of the verb BE and Past Participle of main verb

NOTE: Only verbs that have objects (transitive verbs) can become passive.

ACTIVE AND PASSIVE SENTENCES

	ACTIVE	PASSIVE
Simple Pres.	The dog eats the bone.	The bone is eaten by the dog.
Simple Past	The dog ate the bone.	The bone was eaten by the dog.
Simple Future	The dog will eat the bone.	The bone will be eaten by the dog.
Pres. Cont.	The dog is eating the bone.	The bone is being eaten by the dog.
Past Cont.	The dog was eating the bone.	The bone was being eaten by the dog.
Present Perf.	The dog has eaten the bone.	The bone has been eaten by the dog.
Past Perf.	The dog had eaten the bone.	The bone had been eaten by the dog.
Future Perf.	The dog will have eaten the bone	The bone will have been eaten by the dog.

NOTE: The future continuous, present perfect continuous, past perfect continuous, and future perfect continuous are not usually used in the passive.

22. **Modal or Modal-like Verb:**   Modals are helping verbs which often express a speaker's attitude or mood. Modals are also used to express probability. Modals are not followed by ——*s* in the third person singular form. Modals are immediately followed by the base form of a verb.

Incorrect: He <u>cans do</u> it.
              He <u>can to do</u> it.

Correct: He <u>can do</u> it.

Modal-like verbs are two-word or three-word helping verbs which have very similar meanings to modals. However, modal-like verbs are different in form from modals. Below is a chart showing English modals and their modal-like equivalents.

MODALS	MODAL-LIKE VERBS
may	
might	
can	be able to
could	be able to
shall	
should	be to/ought to/had better/be supposed to
would	used to
must	have to/have got to
will	be going to
	would like to
	would rather

He <u>can</u> do it. = He <u>is able to</u> do it.

23. **Phrase:**   a group of related words that do not include both a subject and a verb. Phrases cannot stand alone as sentences.

      Noun phrase: <u>The big beautiful dog</u> is mine.
                 Noun phrase

      Prepositional phrase: The book is <u>on the table</u>.
                             Prep. phrase

24. **Preposition:**   a word that joins with a noun structure object to form a prepositional phrase. Below is a list of common English prepositions.

COMMON PREPOSITIONS

about	between	out
above	beyond	over
across	by	since
after	despite	through
against	down	throughout
along	during	to
among	except (for)	toward(s)
around	for	under
as	from	unlike
at	in	until
before	into	up
behind	(un)like	upon
below	near	with
beneath	of	within
beside	off	without
besides	on	

Some prepositions are composed of two or more words. These prepositions are called multiple word prepositions. Below is a list of common multiple word prepositions.

COMMON MULTIPLE WORD PREPOSITIONS

according to	in contrast to/with
ahead of	in favor of
along with	in front of
as a consequence of	in spite of
as a result of	instead of
aside from	in the event of
away from	next to
because of	on account of
by means of	on behalf of
contrary to	on the top of
due to	owing to
for fear of	prior to
for the benefit of	regardless of
for the purpose of	subsequent to
in addition to	together with
in back of	with the exception of
in case of	with reference to
in comparison with	with regard to
in connection with	with respect to
in contrast to/with	

Some prepositions combine with verbs. There are hundreds of such combinations. These combinations are sometimes called phrasal verbs.

Below is a list of some of the common verb + preposition combinations that exist in English. These combinations have been chosen because they are among the most likely to be found on the TOEFL exam. Some of these combinations have more meanings than those listed here. The meanings given here are those most likely to be tested on the TOEFL.

For more comprehensive lists of verb + preposition combinations and their meanings, see *Handbook of American Idioms and Idiomatic Usage*, Harold C. Whitford and Robert J. Dixson, Regents Publishing Company, 1973. Also see *Longman Dictionary of Phrasal Verbs*, Rosemary Courtney, Longman, 1983, 1989.

COMMON VERB + PREPOSITION COMBINATIONS

Combination	Meaning
agree to	be willing to
agree with	feel the same way as/about
approve of	have a favorable opinion of
bring about	cause
bring on	result in
bring up	raise for discussion
call on	ask (someone) to do
call off	cancel
call up	telephone
come up	arise
come out	be published
consult with	get the opinion of
count on	depend on; rely on
consist of	be made of
depend on	rely on; count on
differ from	be unlike
do without	sacrifice
get up	wake up
get over	recover from
give up	surrender
give out	distribute
hand in	submit
keep on	continue
keep up	continue; maintain
listen to	pay attention to the sound of
look after	take care of
look over	review
look up	search for (in a book)
make out	understand
make up	invent; reconcile with
object to	oppose by arguing against
pass out	distribute
pass up	fail to take advantage of
pick up	gather or collect
prepare for	get ready for; study for
put off	postpone
put out	extinguish
recover from	get well
refer to	call or direct attention to
rely on	count on; depend on
reply to	answer
respond to	answer
succeed in	be successful at
take over	assume control
take up	consider; discuss
think about	consider
think of	have an opinion about
turn down	reject
worry about	have concern or anxiety about

Some prepositions combine with adjectives. There are hundreds of these combinations as well. Those most commonly tested on the TOEFL are listed below.

COMMON ADJECTIVE + PREPOSITION COMBINATIONS

associated with	(un)impressed by
aware of	inferior to
based on	interested in
capable of	(un)known for
committed to	(dis)pleased with
composed of	puzzled at, by
confined to	qualified for
confused at/about	(un)related to
conscious of	(dis)satisfied with
dedicated to	similar to
different from	superior to
equal to	surprised by/at
fond of	

---

25. **Prepositional Phrase:** a phrase consisting of a preposition and an object. The object in a prepositional phrase can be one of the noun structures listed in the chart below.

Noun (phrase):   I sat by <u>my mother</u>.

Pronoun: I sat by <u>her</u>.

Gerund: She entertains herself by <u>reading</u>.

Noun Clause: I could tell from <u>what you said</u> that you are not interested in this book.

NOTE: Infinitives cannot function as objects of prepositions.

Prepositional phrases can act as adjectives in a sentence.

     The book <u>on the table</u> is mine.
In this sentence, the prepositional phrase *on the table* describes the noun, *book*. It is therefore acting as an adjective.

Prepositional phrases can act as adverbs in a sentence.

     I put the book <u>on the table</u>.
In this sentence, the prepositional phrase *on the table* modifies the verb, *put*. It is therefore acting as an adverb.

26. **Clause:** a group of related words containing a subject and a finite verb. There are two types of clauses in English: main clauses and subordinate clauses. A main clause can stand alone as a sentence. A subordinate clause cannot.

     <u>After I finished my homework</u>, <u>I watched television</u>.
     Subordinate clause   *Main clause*

27. **Main Clause:** a clause which can stand alone as a sentence. Main clauses can be joined together by the conjunctions *and, but, or, for, so,* and *yet.* When this happens, a comma is usually placed just before the conjunction.

The livingroom is red, *and* the kitchen is yellow.
     S   V   S   V
  Main clause   *Main clause*

Main clauses can also be joined together by clause markers such as *however, nevertheless, in addition, on the other hand, furthermore,* and *moreover.* When this happens on the questions in the TOEFL test, a semicolon is placed just before the clause marker.

John likes the color of the kitchen; *however,*
S V
    Main clause
he does not like the color of the livingroom.
S   V
    Main clause

Below is a chart of common main clause markers. These clause markers are listed according to their meanings.

COMMON MAIN CLAUSE MARKERS

	Preceded by a Comma (,)	Preceded by a Semicolon (;)
Addition	and	besides, likewise, moreover, in addition, additionally
Contrast	but, yet	however, nevertheless, on the other hand, in contrast, in spite of this
Cause	for	because of this, for this reason
Effect	so	therefore, as a result, accordingly, consequently,
Condition	or	otherwise
Time		then, at that point, meanwhile, thereafter, after that
Comparison		similarly, correspondingly, likewise
Example		for example, for instance

28. **Noun Clause:** a subordinate clause which functions as a subject, object, or complement in a sentence.

Noun clauses begin with the clause marker *that* or with one of the following question-word clause markers: *how, how many, how much, what, when, where, why, who, whom, whose,* or *which.* For stress, the word *ever* is sometimes added to a question word that begins a noun clause.

> *That* he wanted to go didn't surprise me.
> *Noun clause subject*

> I don't know *who* she is.
> *Noun clause object*

> He can become *whatever* he wants to become.
> *Noun clause complement*

In some sentences, the clause marker of a noun clause is also the subject of the noun clause.

> I don't know *who* is coming.
>   S

When a noun clause that begins with *that* is functioning as the object of a sentence, *that* may be deleted.

> I thought *that* he was coming.
> I thought he was coming.

29. **Adverb Clause:** a subordinate clause which functions as an adverb in a sentence. An adverb clause begins with a clause marker. Below is a chart of the most frequently used English clause markers for adverb clauses. These clause markers are listed according to their meanings. Some clause markers have more than one meaning.

COMMON ADVERB CLAUSE MARKERS

Time	Cause/Effect	Comparison	Condition	Contrast	Manner
after	because	than	even if	although	as if
as	in order	as	if	even though	as though
as long as	that		in case	in spite of	
as soon as	since		in the event	the fact that	
before	so that		once	though	
by the time	whereas		only if	whereas	
now that			provided that	while	
once			unless		
since			whether or not		
so long as					
until					
when					
whenever					
while					

> We will go out together *after* he comes.
> *Clause marker of time*

> *Even though* he is tired, he must continue working.
> *Clause marker of contrast*

NOTE: When an adverb clause comes at the beginning of a sentence, it is followed by a comma. You can use the comma to help you know when an adverb clause is needed in a TOEFL question.

30. **Adjective Clause:** a subordinate clause which functions as an adjective in a sentence. Adjective clauses come immediately after the nouns they modify and describe, define, identify, or give further information about these nouns. Adjective clauses are sometimes called relative clauses.

Adjective clauses begin with one of the following clause markers, which are often called relative pronouns: *who, whose, whom, which,* and *that.* Sometimes the question words *when, where,* and *why* are also used to begin relative clauses. For stress, the word *ever* is sometimes added to a relative pronoun or to *when, where,* or *why.*

The different relative pronouns have different meanings. Some are used to refer to people. Others are used to refer to things. Some are used as subjects. Others are used as objects or to show possession. The following chart classifies relative pronouns according to their meaning and function in a sentence.

RELATIVE PRONOUNS

	Referring to People	Referring to Things
Subject	who, that	which, that
Object	who, whom, that	which, that
Possessive	whose	whose (rarely)

The woman *who* lives next door is very friendly.
    Subject

The woman *who* I saw next door is very friendly.
    Object

The woman *whose* picture I saw in the paper is my neighbor.
    Possessive

A preposition is never followed by *who* or *that.*

           whom
The boy *about* ~~who~~ this story is written is my cousin.

When commas are necessary in an adjective clause, the pronoun *that* may not be used.
      which
Carbon, ~~that~~ is an element, is one of the building blocks of life.

Relative pronouns functioning as objects are often deleted.

The woman *that* I met yesterday is very friendly.
The woman I met is very friendly.

31. ——*ING* or ——*ED* **Modifying Phrase:** an adjective phrase formed by deleting certain elements of a full adjective or adverb clause.

There are two ways to create ——*ing* and ——*ed* modifying phrases from adjective and adverb clauses:

A. Delete the subject of the clause and the BE form of the verb:

Adjective clause:
   The man who is playing the piano is my husband.
   The man   playing the piano is my husband.

Adverb clause:
   While he was playing the piano, he sang a song.
   While   playing the piano, he sang a song.

B. If there is no *BE* form of the verb in the clause, you can sometimes delete the subject and change the verb to its ——*ing* form:

Adjective clause:
   The book, which consists of six chapters, is short.
   The book,   consisting of six chapters, is short.

Adverb clause:
   After he read the book, he fell asleep.
   After   reading the book, he fell asleep.

An adverb clause can only be changed to a modifying ——*ing* or ——*ed* phrase when the subject of the adverb clause and the subject of the main clause are the same.
An ——*ing* or ——*ed* modifying phrase made from an adverb clause must modify the subject of the main clause.

Example where no change is possible:
   While John was writing, I was playing the piano.

32. **Gerund:** the ——*ing* form of a verb used as a noun. A gerund can function as the subject, object, or complement in a sentence. A gerund is frequently used as the object of a preposition.

   <u>Swimming</u> is fun.
   Subject

   I like <u>swimming</u>.
      Object

   Unlike <u>swimming</u>, golf is boring.
      O of prep

   My favorite sport is <u>swimming</u>.
      Complement

Some verbs are followed by gerunds, not by infinitives. Below is a list of some of the more common verbs followed by gerunds.

VERBS COMMONLY FOLLOWED BY GERUNDS

admit	finish	resent
anticipate	keep	resist
appreciate	mention	risk
avoid	mind	suggest
complete	miss	tolerate
consider	postpone	understand
delay	practice	
deny	recall	
discuss	recollect	
dislike	recommend	
enjoy		

---

33. **Infinitive:** to + the base form a verb used as a noun, adjective, or adverb. Infinitives and infinitive phrases used as nouns can function as subjects, objects, or complements. HOWEVER, INFINITIVES CANNOT FUNCTION AS OBJECTS OF PREPOSITIONS.

<u>To be here</u> is a pleasure.
  Subject

I like <u>to be here</u>.
  Object

My wish is <u>to be here</u>.
  Complement

He is a good friend <u>to have</u>.
  Adjective

I was sorry <u>to see</u> him leave.
  Adverb

You need flour <u>to make</u> bread.
  Adverb

Infinitives often have the meaning of *in order to*, as in the last sample sentence above. This sentence could be rewritten, *In order to make bread, you need flour.*

Some verbs are followed by infinitives, not by gerunds. Below is a list of some of the more common verbs that are followed by infinitives.

VERBS COMMONLY FOLLOWED BY INFINITIVES

afford	forbid*	remind*
agree	force*	require*
allow*	hesitate	seem
appear	hire*	struggle
arrange	hope	swear
ask	instruct*	teach*
beg	invite*	tell*
care	learn	threaten
cause*	manage	urge*
challenge*	mean	volunteer
claim	need	wait
consent	offer	want
convince*	order*	warn*
dare	permit*	wish
decide	persuade*	
demand	plan	
deserve	prepare	
encourage*	pretend	
expect	promise	
fail	refuse	

*NOTE: These verbs are normally followed by a (pro)noun plus infinitive combination (e.g., She warned us to be careful.)

Some adjectives are commonly followed by infinitives, and not by gerunds. Below is a list of some of the more common adjectives that are followed by infinitives.

ADJECTIVES COMMONLY FOLLOWED BY INFINITIVES

afraid	eager	proud
amazed	fortunate	ready
anxious	glad	relieved
ashamed	happy	reluctant
astonished	hesitant	sad
careful	honored	shocked
content	lucky	sorry
delighted	motivated	stunned
determined	pleased	surprised
disappointed	prepared	upset
		willing

34. **Conditional Sentence:** a sentence which expresses a condition. There are several different types of conditional sentences.

Factual conditionals express events that **do** happen when certain conditions described in the *if* clause are met.

If you heat water, it boils.
Condition   Event

In this type of conditional sentence, *if* can often be replaced by *when* and the meaning of the sentence does not change.

Future conditionals express events that **will** or **may** happen in the future if certain conditions described in the *if* clause are met.

If you eat your peas, I will give you some dessert.
Condition   Future event

Hypothetical conditionals express events that are **unlikely** to occur (but possible) if certain conditions described in the *if* clause are met.

If you ate your peas, I would give you some dessert.
Condition   Possible event
(unlikely to be met)

Counterfactual conditionals express events that are untrue because the condition in the *if* clause cannot be met.

If George Washington had been here, he would have known what to do.
Impossible condition   Impossible event

In hypothetical and counterfactual conditionals, it is sometimes possible to delete the *if* and keep the same conditional meaning. When this happens, the subject and the verb of the sentence are inverted and, in hypothetical conditionals, the verb *were* or *should* is introduced.

If you ate your peas, I would give you some dessert.

Were you to eat your peas, I would give you some dessert.

If George Washington had been here, he would have known what to do.

Had George Washington been here, he would have known what to do.

35. **Confusing Words and Expressions:** words and expressions which sound alike and/or which have similar functions in English sentences, but which are not interchangeable (cannot be substituted for one another).

NOTE: Not all meanings of the confusing words and expressions listed below are given. Only those meanings most frequently tested on the TOEFL are discussed.

ACCEPT (verb) / **EXCEPT** (preposition)   The verb to ACCEPT means *to agree to or to concede to*. The preposition EXCEPT means *besides or but*, and is followed by an object.

> He <u>accepted</u> his defeat with dignity.
> Everything <u>except</u> the salad is ready to eat.

ADVICE (noun) / **ADVISE** (verb)   The noun ADVICE means *counsel or guidance*. The verb to ADVISE means *to give counsel or advice*.

> Her <u>advice</u> was that I find someone else to help me.
> Teachers must <u>advise</u> their students on academic matters.

AFFECT (verb) / **EFFECT** (noun or verb)   The verb to AFFECT means *to influence or to modify*. The verb to EFFECT means *to bring about or to cause*. The noun EFFECT means the result.

> The writing of Ray Bradbury has <u>affected</u> me deeply.
> They <u>effected</u> a change in the government by voting for a new president.
> The <u>effects</u> of sunlight are many and varied.

ALIKE (adjective) / **(UN)LIKE** (preposition)   ALIKE is an adjective used to show similarity between two or more noun structures. It usually follows the noun structures it describes. (UN)LIKE means *not like* and is a preposition which must be followed by an object.

> My brother and my sister are very much <u>alike</u>.
> <u>Like</u> my brother, my sister enjoys playing chess.

ALMOST (adverb) / **MOST** (adjective)   The adverb ALMOST means *approximately or nearly*, and is used to modify verbs, adjectives, and other adverbs. The adjective MOST means *the greatest number or part*, and is used to describe noun structures.

> <u>Almost</u> all of the students will come to class tomorrow.
> <u>Most</u> students like this class.

ALREADY (adverb) / **ALL READY** (adjective)   The adverb ALREADY means *previously or prior to another time*, and is used to describe verbs, adjectives, or other adverbs. The adjective ALL READY means *completely prepared* and is used to describe noun structures.

AMONG (preposition) / **BETWEEN** (preposition)   AMONG shows a relationship between three or more noun structures. BETWEEN shows a relationship between two noun structures.

> We will divide the work evenly <u>among</u> Jack, Jane, and John.
> We will divide the work evenly <u>between</u> Jack and Jane.

AMOUNT (noun) / **NUMBER** (noun) / **QUANTITY** (noun)   AMOUNT and QUANTITY refer to uncountable nouns. NUMBER refers to countable nouns.

> A great <u>amount</u> of work is yet to be done.
> A <u>number</u> of students want to stay here during spring break.
> A great <u>quantity</u> of work is yet to be done.

AND (conjunction) / **ALSO** (adverb)   The conjunction AND is used to connect words, phrases, or clauses. ALSO is an adverb meaning *in addition*.

> John <u>and</u> Sarah will be here tomorrow.
> John will be here tomorrow. Sarah will <u>also</u> be here.

ANOTHER (adjective) / **OTHER** (adjective) / **OTHERS** (pronoun)   The adjective ANOTHER is used with single, countable and indefinite nouns. OTHER is used with singular, plural and uncountable definite nouns. OTHERS is a plural pronoun (not found with a noun).

> I would like <u>another</u> piece of pie.
> Please show me some <u>other</u> shoes.
> Jack and Fred are here. Where are the <u>others</u>?

AS (preposition) / **LIKE** (preposition)   AS means *in the role of or in the capacity of.* LIKE means *similar to.* Both of these words are prepositions and must be followed by objects.

> He was happy <u>as</u> the king of his country. (He was really a king.)
> He ate <u>like</u> a king. (He ate in a fashion similar to that of a king, but he was not actually a king himself.)

BASE (noun) / **BASIS** (noun)   BASE means *footing, foundation,* or *support.* BASIS means *evidence* or *reason.*

> The <u>basis</u> for your argument is faulty.
> The computer sits on a sturdy <u>base</u>.

BESIDE (preposition) / **BESIDES** (adverb/ preposition)   The preposition BESIDE means *next to*. BESIDES means *in addition to or moreover*, and can be an adverb describing verbs, adverbs, adjectives, or sometimes entire sentences. It can also be a preposition followed by an object.

> They have a small cabin <u>beside</u> the lake.
> They have four children here <u>besides</u> the three that are at home.

COSTUME (noun) / **CUSTOM** (noun)   COSTUME means *clothing*. CUSTOM means *traditional practice.*

> Her Halloween <u>costume</u> was very elaborate.
> It is a <u>custom</u> in this country to eat turkey on Thanksgiving Day.

DESCENT (noun) / **DECENT** (adjective)   The noun DESCENT means *downward motion.* The adjective DECENT means *respectable or suitable,* and is used to describe noun structures.

> The <u>descent</u> into the Grand Canyon takes several hours.
> It is difficult to find a <u>decent</u> place to work in this library.

DO (verb) / **MAKE** (verb)   DO often means *to complete or to perform.* MAKE often means *to create, to construct, or to produce.*

> I <u>make</u> all of my own clothes.
> She <u>did</u> her homework at the last minute.

ESPECIALLY (adverb) / **SPECIAL** (adjective):   The adverb ESPECIALLY means *particularly* and is used to describe verbs, adjectives, or other adverbs. The adjective SPECIAL means *distinctive, extraordinary, or unique,* and is used to describe noun structures.

> Today, his birthday, is a very special day.
> She felt especially uncomfortable discussing her salary.

FARTHER (adjective) / **FURTHER** (adjective or adverb):   Both FARTHER and FURTHER can be used to refer to distance. Only FURTHER can be used to refer to time, degree, or quantity.

> Montana is farther/further from Vermont than it seems.
> We will provide you with further instructions later.

FIRST (adjective, noun) / **FORMER** (adjective, noun)   FIRST refers to the initial or beginning noun structure in a group of three or more noun structures. FORMER refers to the initial or first in a set of two noun structures.

> The first of her three children was a boy.
> I have seen both Peter and Paul, but I have only met the former.

FORMALLY (adverb) / **FORMERLY** (adverb)   FORMALLY means in a *formal manner.* FORMERLY means *previously or before (in time).*

> She was formally admitted to the Honor Society last night.
> Formerly we lived in Billings; now, we live in Burlington.

HAD BETTER (verb) / **WOULD RATHER** (verb)   HAD BETTER is used to express obligation or advisability. WOULD RATHER is used to express preference.

> We had better leave now, or we will be late for class.
> We would rather not be late for class.

HARD (adjective, adverb) / **HARDLY** (adverb)   The adjective HARD often means *difficult.* It also often means *rigid, the opposite of soft.* The adverb HARD means *diligently.* It follows the verb it describes. The adverb HARDLY means *barely or scarcely.* It usually comes before the verb is describes.

> This book is too hard for me to understand.
> I hardly saw him at Christmas.
> He tried hard to come home for Christmas.

IMAGINARY (adjective) /**IMAGINATIVE** (adjective)   IMAGINARY means *not real.* IMAGINATIVE means *showing great imagination,* creative.

> Unicorns, leprechauns, and trolls are imaginary creatures.
> This imaginative writer has created a wonderful fantasy story.

IT'S (pronoun + verb) /**ITS** (possessive adjective)   IT'S is the pronoun *it* plus the verb *is* or the verb *has.* ITS is the third person singular possessive adjective, used when the noun it refers to has no female or male gender.

> The dog wagged its tail happily when it saw its master.
> It's time to go now, isn't it?

LATER (adjective, adverb)/ **LATTER** (adjective, pronoun)/ **LAST** (adjective)   LATER is the comparative form of the adjective or adverb late. It refers to a time in the future or following a previous time. LATTER refers to the second of two noun structures and can function as an adjective or as a pronoun. It is usually preceded by *the*. LAST is an adjective referring to the final noun structure in a group.

> He arrived <u>later</u> than I did.
> I like both Nancy and Jack, but I spend more time with the <u>latter</u>.
> The <u>last</u> time I saw her, she was thinking of moving to France.

LAY (verb)/ **LIE** (verb)   To LAY means *to put or to place* and can be followed by a direct object. To LIE often means *to repose*. In this meaning, to LIE cannot be followed by an object. These two verbs are confusing because some of their principal parts are the same form.

Base Form	Past Form	Past Participle	Present Participle
lay	laid	laid	laying
lie	lay	lain	lying

> Yesterday, he <u>laid</u> his hat on the table. (to lay)
> Yesterday, he <u>lay</u> in bed all day. (to lie)

LIE (verb)/ **LIE** (verb)   To LIE can have two meanings. It can mean *to repose* or it can mean *not to tell the truth*. Some of the principal parts for these two meanings are different.

Base Form	Past Form	Past Participle	Present Participle
lie (repose)	lay	lain	lying
lie (not tell truth)	lied	lied	lying

> Yesterday, he <u>lay</u> in bed all day.
> Yesterday, he <u>lied</u> to me about the money.

LOOSE (adjective) / **LOSE** (verb)   The adjective LOOSE means *not tight*. The verb LOSE means to *misplace or to be defeated*.

> His belt was so <u>loose</u> that it fell off.
> I hope I don't <u>lose</u> this money.

MAYBE (adverb) / **MAY BE** (modal + be)   The adverb MAYBE means *possibly or perhaps*. MAY BE functions as the verb in a sentence and expresses what might or will possibly exist.

> <u>Maybe</u> we should put more coal on the fire.
> She <u>may be</u> the only person I know who owns a Ferrari.

NEAR (adverb, preposition) / **NEARLY** (adverb)   NEAR means *not too far, close by*. It most often functions to describe verbs or as a preposition followed by an object. The adverb NEARLY means *almost*. It describes verbs, adverbs, or other adjectives.

> She lives <u>near</u>, and he lives far.
> I <u>nearly</u> missed my meeting today.

NO (adjective) / **NOT** (adverb) / **NONE** (pronoun)   The adjective NO makes a noun structure negative. The adverb NOT makes a verb negative. NONE is a negative pronoun.

> There were <u>no</u> cookies in the jar.
> He is <u>not</u> jogging this week because it is too hot outdoors.
> I wanted a cookie, but there were <u>none</u>.

ON THE CONTRARY / ON THE OTHER (HAND)   ON THE CONTRARY is a clause marker used to contradict something which has been said or thought before. ON THE OTHER (HAND) is the second part of the two part clause marker one the one hand...on the other (hand).

> He is not feeling tired today; <u>on the contrary</u>, he is feeling quite well.
> On the one hand, I feel like going out tonight; <u>on the other</u>, I feel like curling up by the fire.

PASSED (verb) / **PAST** (adjective, noun, preposition)   PASSED is the past tense form of to pass, which means *to elapse or to go by*. When PAST means *a time before the present*, it can describe noun structures or be a noun alone. When PAST means *by or in front of*, it is a preposition followed by an object.

> Time <u>passed</u> slowly.
> In the <u>past</u>, we used to eat dinner early.
>   *(noun)*
> She walked calmly <u>past</u> the barking dog.
>   *(preposition)*

QUIET (adjective) / **QUITE** (adverb)   The adjective QUIET means *not noisy* and is used to describe noun structures. The adverb QUITE means *very or fairly*, and is used to intensify the meaning of an adjective or sometimes of an adverb or verb.

> The <u>quiet</u> little boy sat in the back of the room.
> He is really <u>quite</u> interested in studying engineering.

RAISE (verb) / **RISE** (verb)   To RAISE means t*o lift* and can be followed by a direct object. To RISE means *to go up or to ascend*, and cannot be followed by a direct object.

> If you have a question, please <u>raise</u> your hand.
> Warm air <u>rises</u>.

REMEMBER (verb) / **REMIND** (verb)   To REMEMBER means to recall or to think about again. To REMIND means to cause someone to remember.

> I cannot <u>remember</u> her name.
> Please <u>remind</u> John to call me at 5:00.

SENSIBLE (adjective) / **SENSITIVE** (adjective)   SENSIBLE means *reasonable or wise*. SENSITIVE means *touchy, sympathetic, or easily affected by outside influences*.

> A <u>sensible</u> diet includes lots of fresh fruits and vegetables.
> Plants are very <u>sensitive</u> to light.

SET (verb) / **SIT** (verb)   To SET means *to put or to place,* and can be followed by a direct object. To SIT means *to be seated* and cannot be followed by an object. The principle parts of these two verbs are similar and can be confusing.

Base Form	Past Form	Past Participle	Present Participle
set	set	set	setting
sit	sat	sat	sitting

Please <u>set</u> the books on the table.
I usually <u>sit</u> in the seat next to John's.

SO...THAT / SUCH...THAT   Both of these expressions are used to intensify a cause and effect meaning. However, SO...THAT is used with an adjective or an adverb, while SUCH...THAT is used with a modified noun.

He was <u>so happy that</u> he could hardly contain himself.
This is <u>such a good book</u> that I can't stop reading it.

THAN (conjunction) / **THEN** (adverb)   The conjunction THAN is used in forming comparatives. The adverb THEN expresses a time after another time.

Clara is taller <u>than</u> Wade.
We filled out the proper forms; <u>then</u>, we waited for our refund.

THEIR (adjective) / **THEY'RE** (pronoun + verb) / **THERE** (adverb)   THEIR is the possessive third person plural adjective. THEY'RE is the pronoun *they* plus the verb *are*. THERE is an adverb meaning *in that place*. THERE is also used to begin sentences in which the subject has been moved to the end of the sentence.

They put <u>their</u> minds and muscle into finishing the task.
We will wait and see if <u>they're</u> coming.
I left the oranges on the table over <u>there</u>.

THOROUGH (adjective) / **THROUGH** (preposition)   The adjective THOROUGH means *complete*. The preposition THROUGH often means *from one point or place to another on the other side*, and is followed by an object.

She did a <u>thorough</u> job investigating the issue.
She walked <u>through</u> the house to the garden.

TO (preposition) / **TOO** (adverb) / **TWO** (adjective)   The preposition TO has several meanings. It is followed by an object. The adverb TOO indicates an excessive amount and describes a verb, an adjective, or another adverb. The adjective TWO is a number.

Maria went <u>to</u> the bank.
This book is <u>too</u> difficult for me.
There are <u>two</u> people waiting to see you.

TOO (adverb) / **VERY** (adverb) TOO implies a negative result. VERY does not imply a negative result.

> This door is <u>too</u> heavy to open.
> (It is impossible to open the door.)
>
> This door is <u>very</u> heavy, but we must open it.
> (It is possible to open the door.)

WHO'S (pronoun + verb) / **WHOSE** (relative pronoun)   WHO'S is the pronoun *who* plus the verb *is*. WHOSE is a possessive relative pronoun.

> <u>Who's</u> coming to the picnic on Saturday?
> I am not sure <u>whose</u> coat this is.

YOUR (possessive adjective) / **YOU'RE** (pronoun + verb)   YOUR is the second person singular or plural possessive adjective. YOU'RE is the pronoun *you* plus the verb *are*.

> When you received <u>your</u> award, we were all very proud of you.
> You shouldn't feel bad that <u>you're</u> not able to come.

VOCABULARY APPENDIX

CONTENTS

Word Category and Word Form Charts
A. Word Category Chart One: Business
    Word Form Chart One: Business
B. Word Category Chart Two: Arts and Literature
    Word Form Chart Two: Arts and Literature
C. Word Category Chart Three: Natural Science and Biology
    Word Form Chart Three: Natural Science and Biology
D. Word Category Chart Four: Health and Medicine
    Word Form Chart Four: Health and Medicine
E. Word Category Chart Five: Social Studies and History
    Word Form Chart Five: Social Studies and History
F. Word Category Chart Six: Geography
    Word Form Chart Six: Geography
G. Word Category Chart Seven: Science
    Word Form Chart Seven: Science
H. Word Category Chart Eight: Descriptive Words
    Word Form Chart Eight: Descriptive Words

The Vocabulary Appendix supplements the vocabulary development exercises in *The Heinemann TOEFL Preparation Course*. The word category charts and word form charts in this section will give you more practice working with vocabulary. As you continue your preparation for the TOEFL through study and outside reading, use the charts in the Vocabulary Appendix to record and practice with new words.

1. Word Category Charts

See V ✔10, pages 299–304, for introductory study of word category charts. The following word category charts are found in the Vocabulary Appendix.

Read about ways to work with word category charts before you begin work in the Vocabulary Appendix.

Ways to Work with Word Category Charts

1. Look up words that you don't know or are not sure about in a dictionary. Make vocabulary flash cards for more practice.
2. Look up the words in a thesaurus to find synonyms and related words. Make vocabulary flash cards for more practice.
3. Regularly review the vocabulary flash card sets that you develop from the word category charts. Regular practice will improve your quick recall of words and meanings.
4. Read more in the topic areas of the word category charts. Add new words to the word category charts from your own personal study and reading. Create your own word category charts. Use the sentences and readings in *The Heinemann TOEFL Preparation Course* and *The Heinemann TOEFL Practice Tests* as a source of new words.
5. As you study the word category charts in the Vocabulary Appendix, use the words from the charts in short sentences, paragraphs, and compositions. Become more familiar with the topics.
6. Transfer the new words to the word form charts and add their different forms.

2. Word Form Charts

See V✔9, pages 296-298, for introductory study of word form charts. Read about ways to work with word form charts before you begin work in the Vocabulary Appendix.

Ways to Work with Word Form Charts

1. Some words in the word category charts have an asterisk (*) after them. These words often occur in different forms in reading passages. Place these words in their different forms in the word form charts.
2. As you do outside reading in the topic areas of the word category charts and add new words to these charts, add them to the word form charts.
3. Create your own word form charts for new categories of words.

Word Category Chart One: Business

Words marked with an (*) should be used in the Word Form Chart for Business.

Basic Concepts

buy*	speculation*	dividends	revenue
sell*	profit*	stocks	bonds
supply	demand	collateral	regulation*
manufacturing*		deregulation*	
marketing	trade		
budget	risks	salaries	wages
economics (micro and macro)		benefits, fringe benefits	
		bonus	compensation*
_____		commission	earnings
_____		market price	demand curve
_____		cash flow	capital gain
		loans, short–term and long–term	
_____		credit	assets

Finance and Money

capital	capitalism	liabilities*	debt
income (net and gross)		default	
investment*	interest		
prime rate	principal		

_____

_____

_____

Accounting
receivable   payable
income   balance sheet
leases   mortgage*

_____

_____

_____

Marketing
product*   brand
trademark   advertising*
promotion*   pricing*
media   retail*
publicity*   distribution*
wholesale*   discount stores
supermarkets

_____

_____

_____

Trade
gross national product (GNP)
international trade
tariffs   quotas
trade balance   investment*
flexible exchange

_____

_____

_____

Types of Business Arrangements
partnership*   corporation*

sole proprietorship*
stock   monopoly
merger*   franchise
venture   shareholder
stockholder

_____

_____

_____

Manufacturing
assembly line   mechanization*
production*   mass production
merchandise   inventory

_____

_____

_____

People and Relationships
employer*   employee*
manager*   staff
entrepreneur*   delegation*
shareholder   stockholder
labor   labor unions
strikes   collective bargaining
morale   motivation*
profit sharing

_____

_____

_____

Other Words

_____

_____

_____

Word Form Chart One: Business

NOUN	VERB	ADJECTIVE	ADVERB

Word Category Chart Two: Arts and Literature

Words marked with an (*) should be used in the Word Form Chart for Arts and Literature.

Art

abstract	artist*
design*	drawing*
hue	impressionism*
oil painting	painter*
realistic*	sculpture*
shade	sketch
studio	tone
watercolor*	

_____

_____

_____

Literature

anthology	author
characters*	fiction*
genre	nonfiction
mystery*	novel
plot	poetry*
prose	protagonist
publish*	romance*
saga	science fiction
setting	short story
style*	writer*

_____

_____

_____

_____

Dance

ballerina	ballet
choreography*	company
debut	folk dances
modern dance	movement
stage*	step
technique	troupe

_____

_____

_____

Film

actor*	cameraman*
cinema*	director*
drama*	epic
musical	producer*
set*	stage
script	theater*

_____

_____

_____

_____

NOUN	VERB	ADJECTIVE	ADVERB

Word Category Chart Three: Natural Science and Biology

Words marked with an (*) should be used in the Word Form Chart for Natural Science and Biology.

Basic Concepts

adapt*	analogous*
biome	biosphere
behavior*	calorie*
classify*	data
extinct*	flora
fauna	fossil*
habitat	homologous
oxidation*	pasteurization*
phase	recycle
sensory	species
symbiosis	metamorphosis

_____

_____

_____

Cells

cyclic*	hybrid*
mutation*	neuron
nucleus	virus*

_____

_____

Life Forms

algae	amphibian
larva	mammal
plankton	primate
vertebrate	

_____

_____

_____

Elements

carbon dioxide	carbon
oxygen*	

_____

_____

Substances

mineral	nutrient
protein	trace
vitamin	

_____

_____

_____

_____

Genetics

dominant*	dormant
DNA	evolution*
gene*	generation
inherited*	instinct*
recessive	

_____

_____

Plants

chlorophyll	pigment*
root	seed
spore	stem
absorb*	transport*

_____

_____

_____

Other Words

_____

_____

_____

_____

_____

NOUN	VERB	ADJECTIVE	ADVERB

Word Category Chart Four: Health and Medicine

Words marked with an (*) should be used in the Word Form Chart for Health and Medicine.

Basic Concepts

anatomy*   embryo
metabolism   organ*

_____

_____

_____

Breathing

breathe*   diaphragm
lungs   pulmonary

_____

_____

Eating

alimentary canal
stomach   intestines
digestion*

_____

_____

_____

Stimulation

addiction*   stimulant*
caffeine   narcotic
nicotine   withdraw*

_____

_____

_____

Heart

artery   blood type
blood vessel   capillary
cardiac   circulation*
heart   hemoglobin
pulse   vein

_____

_____

_____

Nutrition

fat*   nutrient

nutrition*   obesity*
roughage

_____

_____

Disease

antibiotic   bacteria*
carcinogen*   disease
epidemic   germ
immunization*   infection*
influenza   vaccinate*
virus*

_____

_____

_____

Glands

hormone*   secrete*

_____

_____

Bones

cartilage   ligament
skeleton*

_____

_____

Nerves

olfactory   optical*
reflex

_____

_____

_____

Other Words

_____

_____

_____

Word Form Chart Four: Heath and Medicine

NOUN	VERB	ADJECTIVE	ADVERB

Word Category Chart Five: Social Studies and History

Words marked with an (*) should be used in the Word Form Chart for Social Studies and History.

Basic Concepts

abolish	acculturate
aborigine	authority*
civilization*	compromise
emigration*	exile
expedition	humanitarian*
immigrate*	invention*
metropolitan*	settlement*
territories*	traditional*
rural	urban*

_____

_____

_____

Government

ally *	administration*
amendment*	bureaucracy*
candidate	debate
delegation*	dictator*
govern*	jury
judicial	legal*
majority	mandate
minority	monarchy*
nationalism*	nomination*
oligarchy	oppression*
petition	politics*
prohibit*	ratify*
reform*	represent*
revolt*	sanction
sovereignty*	treaty
tyranny*	unanimous
rotation*	

_____

_____

_____

Issues

bias	ecology*
environment*	ghetto
illiteracy*	overpopulation*
pollution	population density
prejudice*	propaganda*
slum	smog
tenement	wilderness*

_____

_____

Past

ancestor*	artifact
barbarian	colony*
feudal	frontier
heritage	legend*
medieval	nobility*
pioneer	primitive

_____

_____

Trade

barter	blockade*
boycott	capitalism*
charter	competition*
craftsman*	embargo
export*	import*
mass production	ore
mineral	natural resources
ration	reserves
renewable*	statistics*
textile	petroleum
refinery	

_____

_____

_____

Other Words

_____

_____

_____

_____

_____

_____

_____

_____

_____

_____

_____

NOUN	VERB	ADJECTIVE	ADVERB

Word Category Chart Six: Geography

Words marked with an (*) should be used in the Word Form Chart for Geography.

Basic Concepts

boundary	capital
climate *	culture*
demographer*	equinox
fossil*	globe*
topography	wilderness
country	nation*

_____

_____

_____

Agriculture

crop	harvest
horticulture	irrigation*
plant	terracing*

_____

_____

Conditions

arable	arid
coniferous	deciduous
desert	erosion*
fertile*	jungle
tropics*	

_____

_____

_____

Land and Land Forms

archipelago	canyon
coastal*	delta
elevation	estuary
glacier*	grassland
iceberg	icecap
island	isthmus
landlocked	meadow
mesa	oasis
peninsula	plain
polar region	prairie
plateau	reef
savannah	steppe
tundra	

_____

_____

_____

Water and Bodies of Water

aqueduct	bayou
bay	canal
fiord	geyser
gulf	harbor
hydroelectric	lakefront
marine	maritime
oceanic*	reservoir
strait	tidewater

_____

_____

Natural Disasters

cyclone	drought
earthquake	flood
monsoon	typhoon
volcano	

_____

_____

_____

Weather

blizzard	condensation
convection	evaporation*
front	frontal system
precipitation*	storm

_____

_____

_____

Other Words

_____

_____

_____

_____

Word Form Chart Six: Geography

NOUN	VERB	ADJECTIVE	ADVERB

Word Category Chart Seven: Science

Words marked with an (*) should be used in the Word Form Chart for Science.

Basic Concepts

accelerate*   circumference
data   hypothesis*
liter   oxygen*
vertical   volume
technology*   theory*

_____

_____

_____

Biology

cellular*   enzymes
evolution*   genetics
organism*   proteins

_____

_____

_____

Chemistry

atom*   bonding*
catalyst*   compounds
element*   molecules*
hydrocarbon

_____

_____

Energy

conductor*   inertia
kinetic   solar
voltage*   turbine

_____

_____

Experiments

binocular   microscope*
concave   convex
diffuse   formula
heat   insoluble
reaction*   vapor
vacuum

_____

_____

Geology

geothermal   lava
magnetic field   magma
tectonic plate

_____

_____

Physics

mass   matter
refraction

_____

Processes

desalinization*   fusion
fission   oxidation*
reduction*   ionization*

_____

_____

_____

Space

astronaut   astronomer*
atmosphere   constellation
eclipse   gravity*
galaxy   horizon*
meteor*   orbit
ozone   satellite
telescope*   ultraviolet

_____

_____

_____

Other Words

_____

_____

_____

Word Form Chart Seven: Science

NOUN	VERB	ADJECTIVE	ADVERB

Word Category Chart Eight: Descriptive Words

All words in this chart should be used in Word Form Chart Seven.

Ability

adequate	assured
authoritative	bold
brave	capable
cautious	clever
competent	concerned
courageous	curious
daring	determined
durable	dynamic
eager	effective
energetic	fearless
firm	forceful
gallant	hardy
heavy	influential
innocent	intense
inquisitive	lively
loose	lucky
manly	mighty
outstanding	powerful
robust	secure
sharp	skillful
shy	smooth
spirited	stable
steady	tame
tough	victorious
virile	zealous

_____

_____

_____

_____

_____

Expressions and Gestures

smile	grin
wink	blink
squint	frown
scowl	pout
grimace	smirk

_____

_____

_____

_____

_____

Feelings

happy	sad
proud	humble
trusting	suspicious
surprised	determined
disgusted	confused
afraid	worried
angry	nervous
complacent	bored
excited	smug
coy	grief–stricken

_____

_____

_____

_____

Anger

agitated	cranky
aggressive	agitated
annoyed	belligerent
biting	blunt
bullying	callous
cross	cruel
defiant	enraged
envious	fierce

_____

_____

_____

Hostility

furious	harsh
hostile	impatient
insensitive	intolerant
irritated	mad
mean	obnoxious
obstinate	outraged
perturbed	repulsive
resentful	savage
severe	spiteful
terse	vindictive
wicked	wrathful

_____

_____

_____

_____

Gloom and Sadness

dejected	alienated
abandoned	debased
depressed	desolate
discouraged	dismal
downcast	forlorn
grim	humiliated
moody	obsolete
rejected	worthless
bewildered	constrained
futile	grief
hindered	impatient
offended	perplexed
strained	silly
suspicious	weary

_____

_____

_____

Fear and Anxiety

agitate	alarmed anxious
apprehensive	bashful
desperate	dreading
embarrassed	fearful
frantic	hesitant
intimidated	jealous
nervous	overwhelmed
restless	scared
shy	strained
tense	timid
uneasy	worried

_____

_____

_____

_____

Inability and Inadequacy

ashamed	cowardly
crippled	deficient
demoralized	exhausted
disabled	fragile
frail	impotent
incapable	incompetent

inept	inferior
meek	trivial
unfit	unqualified
vulnerable	

_____

_____

_____

Love, Joy, and Concern

bliss	calm
comical	contented
ecstatic	elated
enthusiastic	exuberant
fit	gratified
inspired	jovial
jubilant	proud
relieved	splendid superb
vivacious	witty
altruistic	benevolent
benign	charming
congenial	considerate
courteous	empathetic
generous	hospitable
just	kindly
lenient	mellow
moral	obliging
patient	optimistic
polite	receptive
reliable	thoughtful
worthy	

_____

_____

_____

_____

Quantity

ample	copious
dearth	lavish
meager	paucity
profuse	scant
scarcity	sparing
sparse	sufficient

_____

_____

_____

Appearance

alert	bright
blushing	contoured
crinkled	crystalline
dim	dull
elegant	fancy
filthy	foggy
gleaming	glistening
grotesque	homely
lithe	misty
murky	obtuse
rotund	poised
quaint	sheer
shallow	smoggy
unsightly	weird
wizened	

_____

_____

_____

_____

Size

ample bulky	diminutive
gigantic	huge
immense	massive
microscopic	miniature
petite	portly
prodigious	vast
voluminous	

_____

_____

_____

_____

_____

Smell

acrid	bitter
delicious	fragrant
putrid	rotten
savory	spicy
tangy	tasty

_____

_____

_____

_____

Sound

deafening	faint
harsh	hoarse
melodic	raspy
resonant	screech
thunderous	whine

_____

_____

_____

_____

Time

ancient	annual
decade	dusk
intermittent	lengthy
periodic	punctual
speedy	sporadic
sunrise	swift
twilight	

_____

_____

_____

_____

Touch

breezy	chilly
creepy	crisp
cuddly	filthy
frosty	greasy
prickly	rough
shaggy	silky
slimy	slippery
slushy	smooth
stinging	waxen
tight	wooden

_____

_____

_____

_____

Word Form Chart Eight: Descriptive Words

NOUN	VERB	ADJECTIVE	ADVERB

READING APPENDIX

CONTENTS

1. A Good Overall Reading Strategy
2. More Information About Reading Checkpoints
3. Vocabulary Word List: Signal Words for Organization and Purpose

The Reading Appendix is meant to supplement the Reading Checkpoints treated in this text. The Reading Appendix includes:

1. A Good Overall Reading Strategy

    This section discusses active reading through the procedure of Survey, Question, Read, Review, Recall (SQ3R). Active reading and SQ3R practice good reading skills and strategies that should be used in the Reading Comprehension Section of the TOEFL.
2. More Information About Topic, Main Idea, Title, Purpose and Organization, Reference Words, Details and Factual Information, Making Inferences, and the Attitude of the Author and the Tone of the Passage

    This section provides useful tips on question types on the TOEFL and on aspects of the reading passage that will be asked about on the TOEFL.
3. Vocabulary Words that Express Organizational Patterns and the Author's Purpose.

    This list of vocabulary words is introduced in practice exercises in R✔3. These words are important for good writing and should be studied as you prepare for the TOEFL Test of Written English.

1. A Good Overall Reading Strategy

Active reading is a good overall strategy that will help you be successful on the Reading Comprehension Section of the TOEFL. Active reading means that you, as a reader, interact with the text, a procedure referred to as "SQ3R." SQ3R stands for survey, question, read, review, and recall. In the TOEFL test, the steps survey, question, and read will help you answer the questions that follow the short reading passages. During the TOEFL test itself, you will not have time to use the steps of review and recall; however, these two steps are very valuable as background skills for taking the TOEFL and for future academic success.

☛ BEFORE THE TOEFL TEST

- Survey, Question, Read, Review, and Recall are the steps of the active reading strategy that will help you when you are reading for information.

Learning to use SQ3R for active reading will help you to make the most efficient use of your time as you prepare for the Reading Comprehension Section of the TOEFL. The exercises below will help you to understand the SQ3R procedure.

NOTE: Check your answers for each exercise with the SQ3R Answer Key on page 495 of the Reading Appendix before you do the next exercise. In this way you will use correct information for all the exercises.

EXERCISE 1A: Learning to Survey a Passage

Surveying a reading passage means that you skim the passage quickly and pay attention to the first sentences, the last sentences, and the key words. If the information is important for you, you will read the passage again more carefully. Surveying gives the reader an initial understanding of the topic, main ideas, and organization of the passage. R✔1, page 308, gives you practice using surveying for TOEFL question types about the topic, main idea, and title of a passage.

☞ ON THE TOEFL TEST

- Survey the passages in the TOEFL to find the topic, main idea, or title of the passage.

To Survey:
1. Read the first several sentences of the passage to find out the topic and the main idea of the passage.
2. Read the last sentences for the conclusion.
3. Skim the rest of the passage for key words (important information words) that will give the main points, relationships, and organization of the passage.

EXERCISE 1B: Practice Surveying a Passage

Read the questions that you will answer as you survey Passage One.
Read Passage One to answer the survey questions.
Write your answers in the space provided.

(A) What is the topic of the passage? _____

(B) What is the main idea of the passage? _____

(C) What are the key words and phrases in the passage? Underline these key words and phrases.

(D) What are the relational words in the passage? Circle these relational words.

Passage One:

1. Much communication of ideas, information, and attitudes among American people is carried on through magazines. Thousands of periodicals fall within this category. They range from the slick-paper, four-color monthly with circulation in the millions to the small, special interest quarterly that, though virtually unknown to the general public, may have very strong influence within its field.

2. The magazine exists to inform, entertain, and influence its readers editorially and put before them advertising messages of national or regional scope. Magazines never appear more frequently than once a week; thus their writers and editors have more time to dig into issues and situations than do those on daily newspapers, and consequently they have a better opportunity to bring events into focus and interpret their meaning.

EXERCISE 1C: Learning to Question when Reading a Passage

As you read the passage for the first time using the survey procedure, think about the information. You should be asking yourself questions about the information. These questions should be about the main points of the passage, about relationships between points the author has made, and about the author's point of view in the passage. Logical reasoning and predicting what information might follow a point the author makes will help readers question effectively and read with a purpose. Good readers question automatically as they read and are often not conscious that it is a separate step in active reading.

On the TOEFL test, the questions that you must answer are already prepared for you, and your purpose is to read to answer them.

In order to practice questioning, think about Paragraph One in Exercise 1B above, and decide what questions the author of the passage is answering with the information given.

Your questions for Paragraph One might ask about:
1.   the function of magazines (their purpose),
2.   the number of magazines in circulation,
3.   the types of magazines, what they look like and, how often they are published?;
4.   the range of circulation of magazines,
5.   the people who read magazines, and
6.   the reasons people read magazines.

EXERCISE 1D: Practice with Questions when Reading a Passage

Write questions about the information in Paragraph Two, Exercise 1B.

_____

_____

_____

_____

_____

_____

_____

_____

_____

_____

_____

_____

_____

_____

_____

_____

_____

EXERCISE 1E: Reading Carefully for Information in a Passage

Careful reading means reading to find information. This information could be factual, implied, or about the relationship between different pieces of information. You use careful reading when you need to remember information and answer questions.

After you have completed surveying a passage and formulating questions about the key points, you should go back to the passage and read it again. Careful reading involves finding answers to your questions about the passage. When you read carefully, you will use the skills of skimming and scanning. You should read carefully for factual information, implied information, and information about the author's purpose, attitude, and point of view about the topic. Specifically, you should read to confirm the major points made in the passage and look for the author's support for these points. Read to establish relationships between points of information. Use logical reasoning and your knowledge of vocabulary to understand the meaning of the passage.

Practice careful reading in the TOEFL to answer the questions about the reading passages.

> **NOTE:** Because of the time factor in a TOEFL examination, you must read carefully but quickly. You will not have time for thoughtful reflection about the information as you would in normal reading situations. Therefore, as you prepare for the Reading Comprehension Section of the TOEFL, you must learn to read not only carefully, but quickly in order to finish the test.

After reading Paragraph One carefully, your answers to the questions you made might look like this:
1.   communicate ideas, information, and attitudes
2.   thousands of magazines
3.   elaborate and in color, small, published monthly and quarterly
4.   circulation in the millions to a small circulation
5.   the general public and special interest groups
6.   inform, entertain, advertize and influence

EXERCISE 1F: Practice Reading Carefully for Information in a Passage

Read Paragraph Two, Exercise 1B, carefully and answer your questions from Exercise 1D

_____

_____

_____

_____

_____

_____

_____

_____

_____

_____

_____

_____

EXERCISE 1G: Learning About Review in Active Reading of a Passage

The review stage of active reading is meant to help the reader remember and apply the information found in the reading passage. When you review your understanding of the information of the passage, you paraphrase the information. Paraphrasing means to restate the information in your own words. You use this skill when you write about information you have read, as in essay answers to course examinations. Another way to review information is to apply it to solving a problem or answering a related question. Reviewing reading material will be very important as a procedure for future academic work you might do.

In the Reading Comprehension Section of the TOEFL there is no time for review. You must move immediately to the next reading passage in the test. However, in the TOEFL Test of Written English, the strategies of paraphrase and restatement of information will be very helpful to you in answering the essay question.

To understand how you might review the information in Paragraph One, Exercise 1B, read the paraphrase below.

Magazines help Americans share ideas, information and attitudes. There are thousands of magazines. Some are elaborately printed in color and published every month and are bought by millions of people. Others are published every four months and reach only a small number of interested readers. However, the smaller special interest magazine may also have a big influence within its field.

EXERCISE 1H: Practice Reviewing a Reading Passage through Paraphrasing

Write a paraphrase restating the main points of Paragraph Two, Exercise 1B.

_____

_____

_____

_____

_____

_____

_____

_____

_____

_____

_____

_____

_____

The last step of active reading, which is called recall, usually takes place in the form of a test on the information in the passage or an essay about the passage that is completed without having the passage in front of you. The TOEFL does not require this step of active reading.

Use the strategy SQ3R to read actively.

Use the steps SQR in the Reading Comprehension Section of the TOEFL.

EXERCISE 1I: Practice Using the SQR Strategy

Allow yourself six minutes to read the passage. Circle each correct answer.

> Much communication of ideas, information, and attitudes among
> American people is carried on through magazines. Thousands of
> periodicals fall within this category. They range from the slick-paper, four-
>
> *line*   color monthly with circulation in the millions down to the small, special
> (5)   interest quarterly that, though virtually unknown to the general public,
> may have very strong influence within its field.
>
> The magazine exists to inform, entertain, and influence its readers
> editorially and put before them advertising messages of national or
> (10)   regional scope. Magazines never appear more frequently than once a
> week; thus their writers and editors have more time to dig into issues and
> situations than do those on daily newspapers, and consequently they have
> a better opportunity to bring events into focus and interpret their meaning.

1. What is the main idea of this passage?
    (A) Magazines are more expensive than newspapers.
    (B) Magazines have a special role in communication.
    (C) Magazines carry advertisements.
    (D) Magazines give us information.

2. According to the passage, a small, special interest quarterly
    (A) is usually well known to many people
    (B) can't compete with larger well-circulated magazines
    (C) may exert great influence on those who read it
    (D) is produced in color

3. The word 'periodicals' in line 3 means
    (A) communication
    (B) magazines
    (C) information
    (D) newspapers

4. The passage lists all of the following as functions of magazines EXCEPT
    (A) shape our attitudes
    (B) interpret events and issues
    (C) bring us information
    (D) provide daily news

5. The author states in the passage that magazines are published
    (A) at the most once a week
    (B) every month
    (C) every four months
    (D) whenever writers have enough information

6. We can infer all of the following from the passage about newspapers EXCEPT that
    (A) newspapers are published more often than magazines
    (B) newspaper writers don't have time to do in depth stories
    (C) newspaper articles and magazine stories would be different
    (D) newspapers don't usually carry advertisements

Answer Key for SQ3R Exercises

Exercise 1B
A. magazines
B. Magazines have a special role in communication.
C. inform, entertain, influence editorially, advertising, appear, dig into issues, daily newspapers, bring events into focus, interpret meaning
D. though virtually unknown, thus, more—than do, consequently

Exercise 1D
1. What is the purpose of magazines?
2. What is the scope of magazine advertisements?
3. How often do magazines appear?
4. What advantage over newspaper writers and editors to magazine writers and editors have?
5. How do magazine writers and editors use this advantage?

Exercise 1F
1. to inform, entertain, influence its readers and present advertisements
2. from regional to national
3. never more than once a week
4. more time to dig into issues
5. they bring events into focus and interpret their meaning

Exercise 1H
  Magazines inform and entertain us; they also influence us and bring us advertisements. Magazines are never published more than once a week, and this allows magazine writers and editors the time to go into depth on issues and situations. They can clarify these issues for us and offer an interpretation of their meaning. Newspapers can't do this indepth coverage.

Exercise 1I
1. B
2. C
3. B
4. D
5. A
6. D

2. More Information About: Topic, Main Idea, Title, Purpose and Organization, Reference Words, Details and Factual Information, Making Inferences, and the Attitude of the Author and the Tone of the Passage

More about the **Topic**:
Answer choices to TOEFL topic questions often require students to:
1. distinguish between general and specific concepts and determine which are necessary to correctly state the topic of the passage;
2. identify a paraphrase of the key words and concepts;
3. identify a term which correctly serves as a category word for certain concepts in the passage; and,
4. understand the organization of the passage to determine if the passage is a description, a process, a comparison, etc. and identify the correct organizational word in the answer.

More about the **Main Idea**:
Answer choices for main idea questions often require students to:
1. distinguish between supporting details and main points in a passage;
2. distinguish between true and untrue statements about the passage; and,
3. identify the statement that contains the key words of the controlling idea of the passage.

More about the **Title**:
Answer choices for questions about the best title often require students to:
1. identify the key words in the title which refer to the topic of the passage;
2. distinguish between key words for the main idea and key words for supporting ideas that appear in the title;
3. recognize a paraphrase of the topic or main idea as it is restated in the title; and,
4. recognize the key word which correctly represents the purpose of the passage as it is stated in the title.

More about **Purpose and Organization**:
Answer choices for questions about purpose and organizational patterns often require students to:
1. distinguish between the overall purpose of a passage and the purpose of specific parts of a passage;
2. identify statements that are not true about the passage or are too general for the purpose of a passage;
3. identify category words that restate the purpose of a passage;
4. identify the organizational pattern of the passage by recognizing relationships between points made in the passage; and,
5. recognize signal words in the passage and identify the organizational patterns they represent.

More about **Reference Words**:
Answer choices to TOEFL questions about reference words often require students to:
1. read carefully to find the word or words that match the reference words; and,
2. be sure that the referent chosen is logically correct for the meaning of the passage when substituted for the reference words.

More about **Details and Factual Information**:
Answer choices to TOEFL questions about facts and details require students to:
1. recognize restatements of the factual information in the passage; and,
2. determine what is true and not true in the answer choices.

More about **Making Inferences**:
Answer choices to TOEFL questions about implied information and prediction require students to:
1. understand what the question is asking and know where to find the answer in the passage;
2. relate the information in the answer choice to a synonym or paraphrase of information in the passage; and,
3. determine what is true and not true in the answer choices.

More about the **Attitude of the Author and the Tone of the Passage**:
Answer choices about the attitude of the author and the tone of the passage require students to:
1. understand the meaning of the words used to describe the attitude of the author and the tone of the passage; and,
2. recognize the key vocabulary that reflects attitude or tone.

3. Vocabulary Expressing Patterns of Organization and the Author's Purpose

To express opinions

...thinks
It seems that
In...opinion
To...
...consider
...claims that

seem (seemed) to be
appear (appeared) to be
seemingly
In...view
From...point of views
According to...

To express chronological order

now, today, nowadays
when
before, after, while, during
between...and...
in (date)
later, earlier, formerly
at the turn of the century
prior to, previous to, previously
simultaneously, simultaneous with, at the same time as in the (1900s)
next, then, subsequently
afterwards
derive from, originate
source of, beginning of, origin of

To express a generalization

generally, generally speaking, in general
on the whole
all, every, never, always

To express support for a generalization

for example, for instance, in this instance
to illustrate, let me illustrate, as an illustration
as follows
as proof, let me cite as proof
in substantiation, to substantiate
in practice
according to statistics, according to statistical
from the data, based on the data

To classify

main kinds of, major kinds of, basic kinds of
fundamental, important, significant
minor, unimportant, insignificant
dissimilar, contradictory, opposing, contrasting
clearly distinguishable, easily distinguished
uncontestable differences/ similarities
divide, classify
kinds, methods, parts, divisions
categories, classes, classifications
types, sources, origins, bases
qualities, aspects, attributes, characteristics, factors

To compare
similar to, similarly,
like, alike, likewise
correspond to, correspondingly
resemble, resemblance
almost the same as, at the same rate as
as, just as, in like manner
to have…in common
to be parallel in…

To contrast
differ from
however, otherwise
still
nevertheless
even so
dissimilarly, different from
less than, more than, faster than
in contrast, unlike, in opposition
on the contrary, on the other hand
although, while
the reverse of, mutually exclusive
less vital than, less crucial for

To express cause and effect
so, thus, consequently
therefore, accordingly, as a result
for this reason
hence, because, thus
because of, owing to, due to, since
have an effect on
…results in…
…is the cause of…
…follows from…
as a consequence
such a…that, so…that
…makes…possible by…
reversible, irreversible

To predict
probable result(s)
project (v), projected, projection
It is likely that
foresee, foretell, forecast, foreseeable
most likely consequences
inevitable outcome
the next step
the future implications of…
presume, presumption

To define
in definition
in other words,
to clarify, in clarification

to explain, in explanation
by…is meant
to paraphrase

To refute
untrue, false, falsity, fallacious
in error, erroneous
oppose, in opposition
partially true
inconsistent, lacks consistency
bias, prejudice

WRITING APPENDIX

The Writing Appendix supplements the Writing Checkpoints treated in this text. The Writing Appendix consists of a Handwriting Guide

NOTE: See the Reading Appendix, #3, page 497, for vocabulary words and phrases necessary for success on the Test of Written English.

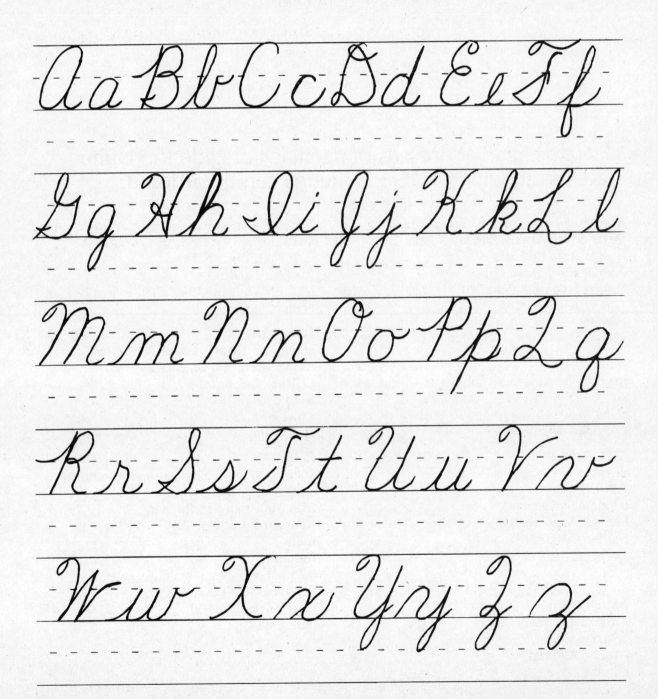

GENERAL APPENDIX

CONTENTS

1. Names and Addresses of Agencies Outside the United States from which TOEFL Bulletins Can Be Ordered
2. Diagnostic Test Scoring Instructions
3. TOEFL Score Conversion Tables
4. Answer Sheets
   A. Diagnostic Test Answer Sheet
   B. Section Tests Answer Sheet
   C. Test of Written English Practice Test Answer Sheets
   D. Complete Practice TOEFL Test Answer Sheet

1. Names and addresses of agencies outside the United States from which TOEFL Bulletins can be ordered.

Algeria, Bahrain, Iraq, Kuwait, Oman, Qatar, Saudi Arabia, Sudan, United Arab Emirates:
AMIDEAST
Testing Programs, Suite 300
1100 17th Street, NW
Washington, DC 20036-4601
USA

Brazil
Instituto Brasil-Estados Unidos
Av. Nossa Senhora de Copacabana
690-8° Andar
22050 Rio de Janeiro, RJ
Brasil

Egypt
AMIDEAST
6 Kamel El Shennawy Street
Second Floor, Apartment 5
Garden City, Cairo
Egypt

    or

AMIDEAST
American Cultural Center
3 Pharaana Street
Azarita, Alexandria
Egypt

Europe—All countries, including Cyprus, Great Britain, Iceland, and Turkey:
CITO-TOEFL
P.O. Box 1203
6801 BE Arnhem
Netherlands

Hong Kong
Hong Kong Examinations Authority
San Po Kong Sub–office
17 Tseuk Luk Street
San Po Kong
Kowloon
Hong Kong

India
Institute of Psychological and Educational
   Measurement
25-A Mahatma Gandhi Marg
Allahabad, U.P. 211 001
India

Indonesia
Institute of International Education
P.O. Box 18 KBYCO
Jakarta Selatan 12950
Indonesia

Japan
Council on International Educational Exchange
Hirakawa-cho Kaisaka Bldg. 1F
1-6-8 Hirakawa-cho, Chiyoda-ku
Tokyo
102 Japan

Jordan
AMIDEAST
P.O. Box 1249
Amman, Jordan

Korea
Korean-American Educational Commission
K.P.O. Box 643
Seoul 110-606
Korea

Lebanon
AMIDEAST
P.O. Box 135–155
Ras Beirut
Lebanon

or

AMIDEAST
P.O. Box 70–744
Antelias, Beirut
Lebanon

Malaysia
MACEE
TOEFL/TSE Services
355, Jalan Ampang
50450 Kuala Lumpur
Malaysia

Mexico
Institute of International Education
Londres 16, 2nd Floor
Apartado Postal 61–115
Mexico 06600 D.F.
Mexico

Morocco
AMIDEAST
25 bis, Patrice Lumumba
Apt. No. 8
Rabat
Morocco

People's Republic of China
China International Examinations
    Coordination Bureau
#30 Yuquan Road, 100039
Beijing

People's Republic of China

Singapore
MACEE
TOEFL/TSE Services
355, Jalan Ampang
50450 Kuala Lumpur
Malaysia

Syria
AMIDEAST
P.O. Box 2313
Damascus, Syria

Taiwan
The Language Training and Testing Center
P.O. Box 23–41
Taipei 10098
Taiwan

Thailand
Institute of International Education
Room 219
A.U.A. Language Center
179 Rajadamri Road
G.P.O. Box 2050
Bangkok 10501
Thailand

Tunisia
AMIDEAST
BP 1134
Tunis, Tunisia

U.S.S.R.
American Council of Teachers of Russian
117049 Moskva
V-49 a/ya No. 1
ASPRIAL/AKCELS
U.S.S.R.

Yemen
AMIDEAST
P.O. Box 22347
Sana'a
Yemen

All other countries and areas:
TOEFL/TSE Publications
P.O. Box 6154
Princeton, NJ 08541–6154
USA

2. Diagnostic Test Scoring Instructions

Follow the steps below to score your Diagnostic Test.

- A. Use the Diagnostic Test Answer Key of *The Heinemann TOEFL Preparation Course Tapescripts and Answers* to check your answers.
- B. Mark a C next to each answer that you get correct.
- C. Add up the number of Cs for each section.
- D. Divide the number of Cs for each section by the total number of questions in that section to get your section percentage score.

$$\frac{\text{Cs in Section One}}{50} = \text{Section One Score}$$

$$\frac{\text{Cs in Section Two}}{40} = \text{Section Two Score}$$

$$\frac{\text{Cs in Section Three}}{60} = \text{Section Three Score}$$

The section which receives the lowest percentage score is your weakest area. You should give special attention to this area as you work through the text.

- E. For more specific information about which parts of Section One are your weakest, you can calculate the percentage score for each part of this section. To do this, you must first count the number of correct answers (Cs) for each part.

$$\frac{\text{Cs in Section One Part A}}{20} = \text{Section One Part A Score}$$

$$\frac{\text{Cs in Section One Part B}}{15} = \text{Section One Part B Score}$$

$$\frac{\text{Cs in Section One Part C}}{15} = \text{Section One Part C Score}$$

The part which receives the lowest score is your weakest part of Section One. You should give special attention to this part as you work through the Section One checkpoint studies.

- F. For more specific information about which structures in Section Two are your weakest, you can refer to the answer key. The answer for each Section Two Diagnostic Test question is coded to a specific Grammar Checkpoint covered in the Grammar Checkpoint Study which begins on page 133. As you work through the Grammar Checkpoint Study, you should give special attention to the checkpoints you missed on the Diagnostic Test.

- G. For more specific information about which subsection of Section Three is your weaker area, you can calculate the percentage score for each subsection of this section. To do this, you must first count the number of correct answers (Cs) for each subsection.

$$\frac{\text{Cs in Vocabulary Subsection}}{30} = \text{Section Three Reading Score}$$

$$\frac{\text{Cs in Reading Comprehension Subsection}}{30} = \text{Section Three Reading Score}$$

The subsection which receives the lower score is your weaker area. You should give special attention to this area as you work through the Section Three Checkpoint Study.

Sample Diagnostic Test Scoring

A student named Mika has just finished taking the Diagnostic Test. She has counted her number correct (Cs) in each section. These are her results:

Section One = 27Cs
Section Two = 29Cs
Section Three = 40Cs

To determine her percentage scores, Mika divides each of these scores by the number of questions in each section.

Section One $\quad \dfrac{27}{50} = 54\%$

Section Two $\quad \dfrac{29}{40} = 75\%$

Section Three $\quad \dfrac{40}{60} = 67\%$

From these percentage scores, Mika can see that Listening Comprehension is her weakest area of TOEFL language proficiency. She will therefore give special attention to study of the Listening Comprehension Section of this book.

However, Mika can also see that she has some weakness in Vocabulary and Reading Comprehension as well. In addition, although grammar is her strongest area, she missed several questions on this section as well.

Mika decides to find out more detailed information about her weak and strong areas of TOEFL proficiency.

For more specific information about which parts of Section One are her weakest, she calculates the percentage score for each part of this section. To do this, she first counts the number of correct answers (Cs) for each part. These are her results:

Part A = 10Cs
Part B = 10Cs
Part C = 7Cs

To determine her percentage score, Mika divides each of these scores by the number of questions in each part.

$$\text{Part A} \qquad \frac{10}{20} = 50\%$$

$$\text{Part B} \qquad \frac{10}{15} = 67\%$$

$$\text{Part C} \qquad \frac{7}{15} = 47\%$$

From these percentage scores, Mika can see that Part C was her weakest part in Section One. However, Part A was also difficult for her. She will give special attention to these parts when she completes the Section One Checkpoint Study.

Mika also decides to find out more specific information about the questions she missed on Section Two of the Diagnostic Test. To do this, she checks the answer key. There she finds the numbers of the questions she missed, and, next to each number, a reference to the checkpoint that was tested with that question. She will give special attention to these checkpoints when she completes the Grammar Checkpoint Study in the course book.

Finally, Mika decides to determine which of the subsections of Section Three was her weaker area of that section of the test.

Again, she counts up the number of correct answers (Cs) in each subsection. These are her results:

Vocabulary = 20
Reading = 20

To determine her percentage scores, Mika divides each of these scores by the number of questions in each subsection.

$$\text{Vocabulary} \qquad \frac{20}{30} = 67\%$$

$$\text{Reading} \qquad \frac{20}{30} = 67\%$$

Mika will give equal attention to both subsections of Section Three when she completes the Vocabulary Checkpoint Study and the Reading Checkpoint Study.

She also decides to find out more specific information about the questions she missed on the Reading Comprehension part of the Diagnostic Test. To do this, she checks the answer key. There she finds the numbers of the questions she missed, and, next to each number, a reference to the Reading Checkpoint that was tested with that question. She will give special attention to these checkpoints when she completes the Reading Checkpoint Study in the course book.

On the basis of the information she has found out, Mika decides to begin her TOEFL study with Section One, Listening Comprehension. She will then complete Section Three, Vocabulary and Reading Comprehension, followed by Section Two, Structure and Written Expression.

3. TOEFL Score Conversion Tables

Use TOEFL Score Conversion Table 1 below to estimate your TOEFL scores for each section on the Diagnostic, Section, and Complete Practice Tests in this book.

SCORE CONVERSION TABLE 1

Number Correct (Cs)	Converted Score Section 1	Converted Score Section 2	Converted Score Section 3
60	——	——	67
59	——	——	67
58	——	——	66
57	——	——	66
56	——	——	65
55	——	——	64
54	——	——	63
53	——	——	62
52	——	——	61
51	——	——	61
50	68	——	60
49	66	——	59
48	64	——	58
47	63	——	58
46	61	——	57
45	61	——	56
44	60	——	56
43	59	——	55
42	58	——	54
41	57	——	54
40	56	68	53
39	55	67	53
38	55	66	52
37	54	64	51
36	53	62	51
35	52	60	50
34	51	59	50
33	51	58	49
32	50	56	49
31	49	55	48
30	49	54	47
29	48	54	46
28	48	52	45
27	47	51	45
26	47	50	44
25	46	49	43
24	46	48	42
23	45	47	41
22	44	46	41
21	44	45	40
20	43	44	39
19	43	43	38
18	42	42	37
17	41	41	36
16	40	40	35
15	40	39	34
14	39	38	33
13	37	37	32
12	36	36	31
11	35	34	30
10	34	34	29
9	33	32	28
8	32	30	27
7	31	29	26
6	30	28	25
5	29	26	24
4	28	25	24
3	27	24	23
2	25	22	22
1	24	21	21
0	20	20	20

Use TOEFL Score Conversion Table 2 below to estimate your Total TOEFL score for the tests in this book.

SCORE CONVERSION TABLE 2

Your total TOEFL score is equal to:

Section One Converted Score	+	Section Two Converted Score	+	Section Three Converted Score

$$\frac{\text{Section One Converted Score} + \text{Section Two Converted Score} + \text{Section Three Converted Score}}{3} \times 10 = \text{Your Score}$$

Sample Score Conversion

Mika, the student discussed above, had the following section scores:

Section One
Number Correct = 27   Converted Score = 47

Using Score Conversion Table 1, she finds that her converted Section One score is 47.

Section Two
Number Correct = 29   Converted Score = 54

Using Score Conversion Table 1, she finds that her converted Section Two score is 54.

Section Three
Number Correct = 40   Converted Score = 53

Using Score Conversion Table 1, she finds that her converted Section Three score is 53.

Using Score Conversion Table 2, she can estimate her total TOEFL score for the Diagnostic Test.

$$\frac{47 + 54 + 53}{3} = 51.3 \times 10 = 513$$

Mika's estimated TOEFL score for the Diagnostic Test is 513.

4. Answer Sheets

On the following pages, you will find:

Diagnostic Test Answer Sheet
Section Tests Answer Sheet
Complete Practice TOEFL Test Answer Sheet
Test of Written English Practice Tests Answer Sheets

Remove these answer sheets from this section of the book and use them when taking the tests for which they are designed.

When marking the Diagnostic, Section, and Complete Practice TOEFL Answer Sheets, make sure that you use a pencil to completely fill in the answer circle that corresponds to the answer you choose. On the actual TOEFL test, you must use a No. 2 pencil.

Example 1:   Ⓐ Ⓑ Ⓒ Ⓓ

Example 2:   Ⓐ
                Ⓑ
                Ⓒ
                Ⓓ

If you need to change an answer, make sure you completely erase the answer you do not want before you fill in the circle that corresponds to the answer that you do want.

Diagnostic Test Answer Sheet

SECTION 1

1. Ⓐ Ⓑ Ⓒ Ⓓ
2. Ⓐ Ⓑ Ⓒ Ⓓ
3. Ⓐ Ⓑ Ⓒ Ⓓ
4. Ⓐ Ⓑ Ⓒ Ⓓ
5. Ⓐ Ⓑ Ⓒ Ⓓ
6. Ⓐ Ⓑ Ⓒ Ⓓ
7. Ⓐ Ⓑ Ⓒ Ⓓ
8. Ⓐ Ⓑ Ⓒ Ⓓ
9. Ⓐ Ⓑ Ⓒ Ⓓ
10. Ⓐ Ⓑ Ⓒ Ⓓ
11. Ⓐ Ⓑ Ⓒ Ⓓ
12. Ⓐ Ⓑ Ⓒ Ⓓ
13. Ⓐ Ⓑ Ⓒ Ⓓ
14. Ⓐ Ⓑ Ⓒ Ⓓ
15. Ⓐ Ⓑ Ⓒ Ⓓ
16. Ⓐ Ⓑ Ⓒ Ⓓ
17. Ⓐ Ⓑ Ⓒ Ⓓ
18. Ⓐ Ⓑ Ⓒ Ⓓ
19. Ⓐ Ⓑ Ⓒ Ⓓ
20. Ⓐ Ⓑ Ⓒ Ⓓ
21. Ⓐ Ⓑ Ⓒ Ⓓ
22. Ⓐ Ⓑ Ⓒ Ⓓ
23. Ⓐ Ⓑ Ⓒ Ⓓ
24. Ⓐ Ⓑ Ⓒ Ⓓ
25. Ⓐ Ⓑ Ⓒ Ⓓ
26. Ⓐ Ⓑ Ⓒ Ⓓ
27. Ⓐ Ⓑ Ⓒ Ⓓ
28. Ⓐ Ⓑ Ⓒ Ⓓ
29. Ⓐ Ⓑ Ⓒ Ⓓ
30. Ⓐ Ⓑ Ⓒ Ⓓ
31. Ⓐ Ⓑ Ⓒ Ⓓ
32. Ⓐ Ⓑ Ⓒ Ⓓ
33. Ⓐ Ⓑ Ⓒ Ⓓ
34. Ⓐ Ⓑ Ⓒ Ⓓ
35. Ⓐ Ⓑ Ⓒ Ⓓ
36. Ⓐ Ⓑ Ⓒ Ⓓ
37. Ⓐ Ⓑ Ⓒ Ⓓ
38. Ⓐ Ⓑ Ⓒ Ⓓ
39. Ⓐ Ⓑ Ⓒ Ⓓ
40. Ⓐ Ⓑ Ⓒ Ⓓ
41. Ⓐ Ⓑ Ⓒ Ⓓ
42. Ⓐ Ⓑ Ⓒ Ⓓ
43. Ⓐ Ⓑ Ⓒ Ⓓ
44. Ⓐ Ⓑ Ⓒ Ⓓ
45. Ⓐ Ⓑ Ⓒ Ⓓ
46. Ⓐ Ⓑ Ⓒ Ⓓ
47. Ⓐ Ⓑ Ⓒ Ⓓ
48. Ⓐ Ⓑ Ⓒ Ⓓ
49. Ⓐ Ⓑ Ⓒ Ⓓ
50. Ⓐ Ⓑ Ⓒ Ⓓ

SECTION 2

1. Ⓐ Ⓑ Ⓒ Ⓓ
2. Ⓐ Ⓑ Ⓒ Ⓓ
3. Ⓐ Ⓑ Ⓒ Ⓓ
4. Ⓐ Ⓑ Ⓒ Ⓓ
5. Ⓐ Ⓑ Ⓒ Ⓓ
6. Ⓐ Ⓑ Ⓒ Ⓓ
7. Ⓐ Ⓑ Ⓒ Ⓓ
8. Ⓐ Ⓑ Ⓒ Ⓓ
9. Ⓐ Ⓑ Ⓒ Ⓓ
10. Ⓐ Ⓑ Ⓒ Ⓓ
11. Ⓐ Ⓑ Ⓒ Ⓓ
12. Ⓐ Ⓑ Ⓒ Ⓓ
13. Ⓐ Ⓑ Ⓒ Ⓓ
14. Ⓐ Ⓑ Ⓒ Ⓓ
15. Ⓐ Ⓑ Ⓒ Ⓓ
16. Ⓐ Ⓑ Ⓒ Ⓓ
17. Ⓐ Ⓑ Ⓒ Ⓓ
18. Ⓐ Ⓑ Ⓒ Ⓓ
19. Ⓐ Ⓑ Ⓒ Ⓓ
20. Ⓐ Ⓑ Ⓒ Ⓓ
21. Ⓐ Ⓑ Ⓒ Ⓓ
22. Ⓐ Ⓑ Ⓒ Ⓓ
23. Ⓐ Ⓑ Ⓒ Ⓓ
24. Ⓐ Ⓑ Ⓒ Ⓓ
25. Ⓐ Ⓑ Ⓒ Ⓓ
26. Ⓐ Ⓑ Ⓒ Ⓓ
27. Ⓐ Ⓑ Ⓒ Ⓓ
28. Ⓐ Ⓑ Ⓒ Ⓓ
29. Ⓐ Ⓑ Ⓒ Ⓓ
30. Ⓐ Ⓑ Ⓒ Ⓓ
31. Ⓐ Ⓑ Ⓒ Ⓓ
32. Ⓐ Ⓑ Ⓒ Ⓓ
33. Ⓐ Ⓑ Ⓒ Ⓓ
34. Ⓐ Ⓑ Ⓒ Ⓓ
35. Ⓐ Ⓑ Ⓒ Ⓓ
36. Ⓐ Ⓑ Ⓒ Ⓓ
37. Ⓐ Ⓑ Ⓒ Ⓓ
38. Ⓐ Ⓑ Ⓒ Ⓓ
39. Ⓐ Ⓑ Ⓒ Ⓓ
40. Ⓐ Ⓑ Ⓒ Ⓓ

SECTION 3

1. Ⓐ Ⓑ Ⓒ Ⓓ
2. Ⓐ Ⓑ Ⓒ Ⓓ
3. Ⓐ Ⓑ Ⓒ Ⓓ
4. Ⓐ Ⓑ Ⓒ Ⓓ
5. Ⓐ Ⓑ Ⓒ Ⓓ
6. Ⓐ Ⓑ Ⓒ Ⓓ
7. Ⓐ Ⓑ Ⓒ Ⓓ
8. Ⓐ Ⓑ Ⓒ Ⓓ
9. Ⓐ Ⓑ Ⓒ Ⓓ
10. Ⓐ Ⓑ Ⓒ Ⓓ
11. Ⓐ Ⓑ Ⓒ Ⓓ
12. Ⓐ Ⓑ Ⓒ Ⓓ
13. Ⓐ Ⓑ Ⓒ Ⓓ
14. Ⓐ Ⓑ Ⓒ Ⓓ
15. Ⓐ Ⓑ Ⓒ Ⓓ
16. Ⓐ Ⓑ Ⓒ Ⓓ
17. Ⓐ Ⓑ Ⓒ Ⓓ
18. Ⓐ Ⓑ Ⓒ Ⓓ
19. Ⓐ Ⓑ Ⓒ Ⓓ
20. Ⓐ Ⓑ Ⓒ Ⓓ
21. Ⓐ Ⓑ Ⓒ Ⓓ
22. Ⓐ Ⓑ Ⓒ Ⓓ
23. Ⓐ Ⓑ Ⓒ Ⓓ
24. Ⓐ Ⓑ Ⓒ Ⓓ
25. Ⓐ Ⓑ Ⓒ Ⓓ
26. Ⓐ Ⓑ Ⓒ Ⓓ
27. Ⓐ Ⓑ Ⓒ Ⓓ
28. Ⓐ Ⓑ Ⓒ Ⓓ
29. Ⓐ Ⓑ Ⓒ Ⓓ
30. Ⓐ Ⓑ Ⓒ Ⓓ
31. Ⓐ Ⓑ Ⓒ Ⓓ
32. Ⓐ Ⓑ Ⓒ Ⓓ
33. Ⓐ Ⓑ Ⓒ Ⓓ
34. Ⓐ Ⓑ Ⓒ Ⓓ
35. Ⓐ Ⓑ Ⓒ Ⓓ
36. Ⓐ Ⓑ Ⓒ Ⓓ
37. Ⓐ Ⓑ Ⓒ Ⓓ
38. Ⓐ Ⓑ Ⓒ Ⓓ
39. Ⓐ Ⓑ Ⓒ Ⓓ
40. Ⓐ Ⓑ Ⓒ Ⓓ
41. Ⓐ Ⓑ Ⓒ Ⓓ
42. Ⓐ Ⓑ Ⓒ Ⓓ
43. Ⓐ Ⓑ Ⓒ Ⓓ
44. Ⓐ Ⓑ Ⓒ Ⓓ
45. Ⓐ Ⓑ Ⓒ Ⓓ
46. Ⓐ Ⓑ Ⓒ Ⓓ
47. Ⓐ Ⓑ Ⓒ Ⓓ
48. Ⓐ Ⓑ Ⓒ Ⓓ
49. Ⓐ Ⓑ Ⓒ Ⓓ
50. Ⓐ Ⓑ Ⓒ Ⓓ
51. Ⓐ Ⓑ Ⓒ Ⓓ
52. Ⓐ Ⓑ Ⓒ Ⓓ
53. Ⓐ Ⓑ Ⓒ Ⓓ
54. Ⓐ Ⓑ Ⓒ Ⓓ
55. Ⓐ Ⓑ Ⓒ Ⓓ
56. Ⓐ Ⓑ Ⓒ Ⓓ
57. Ⓐ Ⓑ Ⓒ Ⓓ
58. Ⓐ Ⓑ Ⓒ Ⓓ
59. Ⓐ Ⓑ Ⓒ Ⓓ
60. Ⓐ Ⓑ Ⓒ Ⓓ

Section Tests Answer Sheet

Choose only one answer for each question. Carefully and completely fill in the oval corresponding to the answer you choose so that the letter inside the oval cannot be seen. Completely erase any other marks you may have made. Choose only one answer for each question.

CORRECT	WRONG	WRONG	WRONG	WRONG
Ⓐ ● Ⓒ Ⓓ	Ⓐ Ⓑ ⊗ Ⓓ	Ⓐ Ⓑ ⊜ Ⓓ	Ⓐ Ⓑ ◉ Ⓓ	Ⓐ Ⓑ ✓ Ⓓ

SECTION 1

1 Ⓐ Ⓑ Ⓒ Ⓓ
2 Ⓐ Ⓑ Ⓒ Ⓓ
3 Ⓐ Ⓑ Ⓒ Ⓓ
4 Ⓐ Ⓑ Ⓒ Ⓓ
5 Ⓐ Ⓑ Ⓒ Ⓓ
6 Ⓐ Ⓑ Ⓒ Ⓓ
7 Ⓐ Ⓑ Ⓒ Ⓓ
8 Ⓐ Ⓑ Ⓒ Ⓓ
9 Ⓐ Ⓑ Ⓒ Ⓓ
10 Ⓐ Ⓑ Ⓒ Ⓓ
11 Ⓐ Ⓑ Ⓒ Ⓓ
12 Ⓐ Ⓑ Ⓒ Ⓓ
13 Ⓐ Ⓑ Ⓒ Ⓓ
14 Ⓐ Ⓑ Ⓒ Ⓓ
15 Ⓐ Ⓑ Ⓒ Ⓓ
16 Ⓐ Ⓑ Ⓒ Ⓓ
17 Ⓐ Ⓑ Ⓒ Ⓓ
18 Ⓐ Ⓑ Ⓒ Ⓓ
19 Ⓐ Ⓑ Ⓒ Ⓓ
20 Ⓐ Ⓑ Ⓒ Ⓓ
21 Ⓐ Ⓑ Ⓒ Ⓓ
22 Ⓐ Ⓑ Ⓒ Ⓓ
23 Ⓐ Ⓑ Ⓒ Ⓓ
24 Ⓐ Ⓑ Ⓒ Ⓓ
25 Ⓐ Ⓑ Ⓒ Ⓓ
26 Ⓐ Ⓑ Ⓒ Ⓓ
27 Ⓐ Ⓑ Ⓒ Ⓓ
28 Ⓐ Ⓑ Ⓒ Ⓓ
29 Ⓐ Ⓑ Ⓒ Ⓓ
30 Ⓐ Ⓑ Ⓒ Ⓓ
31 Ⓐ Ⓑ Ⓒ Ⓓ
32 Ⓐ Ⓑ Ⓒ Ⓓ
33 Ⓐ Ⓑ Ⓒ Ⓓ
34 Ⓐ Ⓑ Ⓒ Ⓓ
35 Ⓐ Ⓑ Ⓒ Ⓓ
36 Ⓐ Ⓑ Ⓒ Ⓓ
37 Ⓐ Ⓑ Ⓒ Ⓓ
38 Ⓐ Ⓑ Ⓒ Ⓓ
39 Ⓐ Ⓑ Ⓒ Ⓓ
40 Ⓐ Ⓑ Ⓒ Ⓓ
41 Ⓐ Ⓑ Ⓒ Ⓓ
42 Ⓐ Ⓑ Ⓒ Ⓓ
43 Ⓐ Ⓑ Ⓒ Ⓓ
44 Ⓐ Ⓑ Ⓒ Ⓓ
45 Ⓐ Ⓑ Ⓒ Ⓓ
46 Ⓐ Ⓑ Ⓒ Ⓓ
47 Ⓐ Ⓑ Ⓒ Ⓓ
48 Ⓐ Ⓑ Ⓒ Ⓓ
49 Ⓐ Ⓑ Ⓒ Ⓓ
50 Ⓐ Ⓑ Ⓒ Ⓓ

SECTION 2

1 Ⓐ Ⓑ Ⓒ Ⓓ
2 Ⓐ Ⓑ Ⓒ Ⓓ
3 Ⓐ Ⓑ Ⓒ Ⓓ
4 Ⓐ Ⓑ Ⓒ Ⓓ
5 Ⓐ Ⓑ Ⓒ Ⓓ
6 Ⓐ Ⓑ Ⓒ Ⓓ
7 Ⓐ Ⓑ Ⓒ Ⓓ
8 Ⓐ Ⓑ Ⓒ Ⓓ
9 Ⓐ Ⓑ Ⓒ Ⓓ
10 Ⓐ Ⓑ Ⓒ Ⓓ
11 Ⓐ Ⓑ Ⓒ Ⓓ
12 Ⓐ Ⓑ Ⓒ Ⓓ
13 Ⓐ Ⓑ Ⓒ Ⓓ
14 Ⓐ Ⓑ Ⓒ Ⓓ
15 Ⓐ Ⓑ Ⓒ Ⓓ
16 Ⓐ Ⓑ Ⓒ Ⓓ
17 Ⓐ Ⓑ Ⓒ Ⓓ
18 Ⓐ Ⓑ Ⓒ Ⓓ
19 Ⓐ Ⓑ Ⓒ Ⓓ
20 Ⓐ Ⓑ Ⓒ Ⓓ
21 Ⓐ Ⓑ Ⓒ Ⓓ
22 Ⓐ Ⓑ Ⓒ Ⓓ
23 Ⓐ Ⓑ Ⓒ Ⓓ
24 Ⓐ Ⓑ Ⓒ Ⓓ
25 Ⓐ Ⓑ Ⓒ Ⓓ
26 Ⓐ Ⓑ Ⓒ Ⓓ
27 Ⓐ Ⓑ Ⓒ Ⓓ
28 Ⓐ Ⓑ Ⓒ Ⓓ
29 Ⓐ Ⓑ Ⓒ Ⓓ
30 Ⓐ Ⓑ Ⓒ Ⓓ
31 Ⓐ Ⓑ Ⓒ Ⓓ
32 Ⓐ Ⓑ Ⓒ Ⓓ
33 Ⓐ Ⓑ Ⓒ Ⓓ
34 Ⓐ Ⓑ Ⓒ Ⓓ
35 Ⓐ Ⓑ Ⓒ Ⓓ
36 Ⓐ Ⓑ Ⓒ Ⓓ
37 Ⓐ Ⓑ Ⓒ Ⓓ
38 Ⓐ Ⓑ Ⓒ Ⓓ
39 Ⓐ Ⓑ Ⓒ Ⓓ
40 Ⓐ Ⓑ Ⓒ Ⓓ

SECTION 3

1 Ⓐ Ⓑ Ⓒ Ⓓ   31 Ⓐ Ⓑ Ⓒ Ⓓ
2 Ⓐ Ⓑ Ⓒ Ⓓ   32 Ⓐ Ⓑ Ⓒ Ⓓ
3 Ⓐ Ⓑ Ⓒ Ⓓ   33 Ⓐ Ⓑ Ⓒ Ⓓ
4 Ⓐ Ⓑ Ⓒ Ⓓ   34 Ⓐ Ⓑ Ⓒ Ⓓ
5 Ⓐ Ⓑ Ⓒ Ⓓ   35 Ⓐ Ⓑ Ⓒ Ⓓ
6 Ⓐ Ⓑ Ⓒ Ⓓ   36 Ⓐ Ⓑ Ⓒ Ⓓ
7 Ⓐ Ⓑ Ⓒ Ⓓ   37 Ⓐ Ⓑ Ⓒ Ⓓ
8 Ⓐ Ⓑ Ⓒ Ⓓ   38 Ⓐ Ⓑ Ⓒ Ⓓ
9 Ⓐ Ⓑ Ⓒ Ⓓ   39 Ⓐ Ⓑ Ⓒ Ⓓ
10 Ⓐ Ⓑ Ⓒ Ⓓ   40 Ⓐ Ⓑ Ⓒ Ⓓ
11 Ⓐ Ⓑ Ⓒ Ⓓ   41 Ⓐ Ⓑ Ⓒ Ⓓ
12 Ⓐ Ⓑ Ⓒ Ⓓ   42 Ⓐ Ⓑ Ⓒ Ⓓ
13 Ⓐ Ⓑ Ⓒ Ⓓ   43 Ⓐ Ⓑ Ⓒ Ⓓ
14 Ⓐ Ⓑ Ⓒ Ⓓ   44 Ⓐ Ⓑ Ⓒ Ⓓ
15 Ⓐ Ⓑ Ⓒ Ⓓ   45 Ⓐ Ⓑ Ⓒ Ⓓ
16 Ⓐ Ⓑ Ⓒ Ⓓ   46 Ⓐ Ⓑ Ⓒ Ⓓ
17 Ⓐ Ⓑ Ⓒ Ⓓ   47 Ⓐ Ⓑ Ⓒ Ⓓ
18 Ⓐ Ⓑ Ⓒ Ⓓ   48 Ⓐ Ⓑ Ⓒ Ⓓ
19 Ⓐ Ⓑ Ⓒ Ⓓ   49 Ⓐ Ⓑ Ⓒ Ⓓ
20 Ⓐ Ⓑ Ⓒ Ⓓ   50 Ⓐ Ⓑ Ⓒ Ⓓ
21 Ⓐ Ⓑ Ⓒ Ⓓ   51 Ⓐ Ⓑ Ⓒ Ⓓ
22 Ⓐ Ⓑ Ⓒ Ⓓ   52 Ⓐ Ⓑ Ⓒ Ⓓ
23 Ⓐ Ⓑ Ⓒ Ⓓ   53 Ⓐ Ⓑ Ⓒ Ⓓ
24 Ⓐ Ⓑ Ⓒ Ⓓ   54 Ⓐ Ⓑ Ⓒ Ⓓ
25 Ⓐ Ⓑ Ⓒ Ⓓ   55 Ⓐ Ⓑ Ⓒ Ⓓ
26 Ⓐ Ⓑ Ⓒ Ⓓ   56 Ⓐ Ⓑ Ⓒ Ⓓ
27 Ⓐ Ⓑ Ⓒ Ⓓ   57 Ⓐ Ⓑ Ⓒ Ⓓ
28 Ⓐ Ⓑ Ⓒ Ⓓ   58 Ⓐ Ⓑ Ⓒ Ⓓ
29 Ⓐ Ⓑ Ⓒ Ⓓ   59 Ⓐ Ⓑ Ⓒ Ⓓ
30 Ⓐ Ⓑ Ⓒ Ⓓ   60 Ⓐ Ⓑ Ⓒ Ⓓ

Save these pages until you have completed all of the Section Tests
AND
the Complete Practice TOEFL Test

Complete Practice TOEFL Test Answer Sheet

NAME (print):

Choose only one answer for each question. Carefully and completely fill in the oval corresponding to the answer you choose so that the letter inside the oval cannot be seen. Completely erase any other marks you may have made. Choose only one answer for each question.

CORRECT	WRONG	WRONG	WRONG	WRONG
Ⓐ ● Ⓒ Ⓓ	Ⓐ Ⓑ ⊗ Ⓓ	Ⓐ Ⓑ ⊙ Ⓓ	Ⓐ Ⓑ ◑ Ⓓ	Ⓐ Ⓑ ✓ Ⓓ

SECTION 1

1 Ⓐ Ⓑ Ⓒ Ⓓ
2 Ⓐ Ⓑ Ⓒ Ⓓ
3 Ⓐ Ⓑ Ⓒ Ⓓ
4 Ⓐ Ⓑ Ⓒ Ⓓ
5 Ⓐ Ⓑ Ⓒ Ⓓ
6 Ⓐ Ⓑ Ⓒ Ⓓ
7 Ⓐ Ⓑ Ⓒ Ⓓ
8 Ⓐ Ⓑ Ⓒ Ⓓ
9 Ⓐ Ⓑ Ⓒ Ⓓ
10 Ⓐ Ⓑ Ⓒ Ⓓ
11 Ⓐ Ⓑ Ⓒ Ⓓ
12 Ⓐ Ⓑ Ⓒ Ⓓ
13 Ⓐ Ⓑ Ⓒ Ⓓ
14 Ⓐ Ⓑ Ⓒ Ⓓ
15 Ⓐ Ⓑ Ⓒ Ⓓ
16 Ⓐ Ⓑ Ⓒ Ⓓ
17 Ⓐ Ⓑ Ⓒ Ⓓ
18 Ⓐ Ⓑ Ⓒ Ⓓ
19 Ⓐ Ⓑ Ⓒ Ⓓ
20 Ⓐ Ⓑ Ⓒ Ⓓ
21 Ⓐ Ⓑ Ⓒ Ⓓ
22 Ⓐ Ⓑ Ⓒ Ⓓ
23 Ⓐ Ⓑ Ⓒ Ⓓ
24 Ⓐ Ⓑ Ⓒ Ⓓ
25 Ⓐ Ⓑ Ⓒ Ⓓ
26 Ⓐ Ⓑ Ⓒ Ⓓ
27 Ⓐ Ⓑ Ⓒ Ⓓ
28 Ⓐ Ⓑ Ⓒ Ⓓ
29 Ⓐ Ⓑ Ⓒ Ⓓ
30 Ⓐ Ⓑ Ⓒ Ⓓ
31 Ⓐ Ⓑ Ⓒ Ⓓ
32 Ⓐ Ⓑ Ⓒ Ⓓ
33 Ⓐ Ⓑ Ⓒ Ⓓ
34 Ⓐ Ⓑ Ⓒ Ⓓ
35 Ⓐ Ⓑ Ⓒ Ⓓ
36 Ⓐ Ⓑ Ⓒ Ⓓ
37 Ⓐ Ⓑ Ⓒ Ⓓ
38 Ⓐ Ⓑ Ⓒ Ⓓ
39 Ⓐ Ⓑ Ⓒ Ⓓ
40 Ⓐ Ⓑ Ⓒ Ⓓ
41 Ⓐ Ⓑ Ⓒ Ⓓ
42 Ⓐ Ⓑ Ⓒ Ⓓ
43 Ⓐ Ⓑ Ⓒ Ⓓ
44 Ⓐ Ⓑ Ⓒ Ⓓ
45 Ⓐ Ⓑ Ⓒ Ⓓ
46 Ⓐ Ⓑ Ⓒ Ⓓ
47 Ⓐ Ⓑ Ⓒ Ⓓ
48 Ⓐ Ⓑ Ⓒ Ⓓ
49 Ⓐ Ⓑ Ⓒ Ⓓ
50 Ⓐ Ⓑ Ⓒ Ⓓ

SECTION 2

1 Ⓐ Ⓑ Ⓒ Ⓓ
2 Ⓐ Ⓑ Ⓒ Ⓓ
3 Ⓐ Ⓑ Ⓒ Ⓓ
4 Ⓐ Ⓑ Ⓒ Ⓓ
5 Ⓐ Ⓑ Ⓒ Ⓓ
6 Ⓐ Ⓑ Ⓒ Ⓓ
7 Ⓐ Ⓑ Ⓒ Ⓓ
8 Ⓐ Ⓑ Ⓒ Ⓓ
9 Ⓐ Ⓑ Ⓒ Ⓓ
10 Ⓐ Ⓑ Ⓒ Ⓓ
11 Ⓐ Ⓑ Ⓒ Ⓓ
12 Ⓐ Ⓑ Ⓒ Ⓓ
13 Ⓐ Ⓑ Ⓒ Ⓓ
14 Ⓐ Ⓑ Ⓒ Ⓓ
15 Ⓐ Ⓑ Ⓒ Ⓓ
16 Ⓐ Ⓑ Ⓒ Ⓓ
17 Ⓐ Ⓑ Ⓒ Ⓓ
18 Ⓐ Ⓑ Ⓒ Ⓓ
19 Ⓐ Ⓑ Ⓒ Ⓓ
20 Ⓐ Ⓑ Ⓒ Ⓓ
21 Ⓐ Ⓑ Ⓒ Ⓓ
22 Ⓐ Ⓑ Ⓒ Ⓓ
23 Ⓐ Ⓑ Ⓒ Ⓓ
24 Ⓐ Ⓑ Ⓒ Ⓓ
25 Ⓐ Ⓑ Ⓒ Ⓓ
26 Ⓐ Ⓑ Ⓒ Ⓓ
27 Ⓐ Ⓑ Ⓒ Ⓓ
28 Ⓐ Ⓑ Ⓒ Ⓓ
29 Ⓐ Ⓑ Ⓒ Ⓓ
30 Ⓐ Ⓑ Ⓒ Ⓓ
31 Ⓐ Ⓑ Ⓒ Ⓓ
32 Ⓐ Ⓑ Ⓒ Ⓓ
33 Ⓐ Ⓑ Ⓒ Ⓓ
34 Ⓐ Ⓑ Ⓒ Ⓓ
35 Ⓐ Ⓑ Ⓒ Ⓓ
36 Ⓐ Ⓑ Ⓒ Ⓓ
37 Ⓐ Ⓑ Ⓒ Ⓓ
38 Ⓐ Ⓑ Ⓒ Ⓓ
39 Ⓐ Ⓑ Ⓒ Ⓓ
40 Ⓐ Ⓑ Ⓒ Ⓓ

SECTION 3

1 Ⓐ Ⓑ Ⓒ Ⓓ   31 Ⓐ Ⓑ Ⓒ Ⓓ
2 Ⓐ Ⓑ Ⓒ Ⓓ   32 Ⓐ Ⓑ Ⓒ Ⓓ
3 Ⓐ Ⓑ Ⓒ Ⓓ   33 Ⓐ Ⓑ Ⓒ Ⓓ
4 Ⓐ Ⓑ Ⓒ Ⓓ   34 Ⓐ Ⓑ Ⓒ Ⓓ
5 Ⓐ Ⓑ Ⓒ Ⓓ   35 Ⓐ Ⓑ Ⓒ Ⓓ
6 Ⓐ Ⓑ Ⓒ Ⓓ   36 Ⓐ Ⓑ Ⓒ Ⓓ
7 Ⓐ Ⓑ Ⓒ Ⓓ   37 Ⓐ Ⓑ Ⓒ Ⓓ
8 Ⓐ Ⓑ Ⓒ Ⓓ   38 Ⓐ Ⓑ Ⓒ Ⓓ
9 Ⓐ Ⓑ Ⓒ Ⓓ   39 Ⓐ Ⓑ Ⓒ Ⓓ
10 Ⓐ Ⓑ Ⓒ Ⓓ   40 Ⓐ Ⓑ Ⓒ Ⓓ
11 Ⓐ Ⓑ Ⓒ Ⓓ   41 Ⓐ Ⓑ Ⓒ Ⓓ
12 Ⓐ Ⓑ Ⓒ Ⓓ   42 Ⓐ Ⓑ Ⓒ Ⓓ
13 Ⓐ Ⓑ Ⓒ Ⓓ   43 Ⓐ Ⓑ Ⓒ Ⓓ
14 Ⓐ Ⓑ Ⓒ Ⓓ   44 Ⓐ Ⓑ Ⓒ Ⓓ
15 Ⓐ Ⓑ Ⓒ Ⓓ   45 Ⓐ Ⓑ Ⓒ Ⓓ
16 Ⓐ Ⓑ Ⓒ Ⓓ   46 Ⓐ Ⓑ Ⓒ Ⓓ
17 Ⓐ Ⓑ Ⓒ Ⓓ   47 Ⓐ Ⓑ Ⓒ Ⓓ
18 Ⓐ Ⓑ Ⓒ Ⓓ   48 Ⓐ Ⓑ Ⓒ Ⓓ
19 Ⓐ Ⓑ Ⓒ Ⓓ   49 Ⓐ Ⓑ Ⓒ Ⓓ
20 Ⓐ Ⓑ Ⓒ Ⓓ   50 Ⓐ Ⓑ Ⓒ Ⓓ
21 Ⓐ Ⓑ Ⓒ Ⓓ   51 Ⓐ Ⓑ Ⓒ Ⓓ
22 Ⓐ Ⓑ Ⓒ Ⓓ   52 Ⓐ Ⓑ Ⓒ Ⓓ
23 Ⓐ Ⓑ Ⓒ Ⓓ   53 Ⓐ Ⓑ Ⓒ Ⓓ
24 Ⓐ Ⓑ Ⓒ Ⓓ   54 Ⓐ Ⓑ Ⓒ Ⓓ
25 Ⓐ Ⓑ Ⓒ Ⓓ   55 Ⓐ Ⓑ Ⓒ Ⓓ
26 Ⓐ Ⓑ Ⓒ Ⓓ   56 Ⓐ Ⓑ Ⓒ Ⓓ
27 Ⓐ Ⓑ Ⓒ Ⓓ   57 Ⓐ Ⓑ Ⓒ Ⓓ
28 Ⓐ Ⓑ Ⓒ Ⓓ   58 Ⓐ Ⓑ Ⓒ Ⓓ
29 Ⓐ Ⓑ Ⓒ Ⓓ   59 Ⓐ Ⓑ Ⓒ Ⓓ
30 Ⓐ Ⓑ Ⓒ Ⓓ   60 Ⓐ Ⓑ Ⓒ Ⓓ

TWE Answer Sheet (front)

Note: Photocopy 7 times

Name_____ **Topic**_____

Begin your essay here. If you need more space, use the other side

_____

_____

_____

_____

_____

_____

_____

_____

_____

_____

_____

_____

_____

_____

_____

_____

_____

_____

_____

_____

_____

_____

_____

_____

_____

_____

_____

TWE Answer Sheet (back)

Note: Photocopy 7 times

Continuation of essay

_____

_____

_____

_____

_____

_____

_____

_____

_____

_____

_____

_____

_____

_____

_____

_____

_____

_____

_____